RETURNING TO OURSELVES

RETURNING TO OURSELVES

*Second Volume of Papers
from the
John Hewitt International Summer School*

edited by
Eve Patten

LAGAN PRESS
BELFAST
1995

Published by
Lagan Press
PO Box 110 BT12 4AB, Belfast

The publishers wish to acknowledge the financial assistance
of the Arts Council of Northern Ireland and the Cultural Traditions Group
in the production of this book.

© Individual contributors, 1995
Introduction © Eve Patten

The moral right of the contributors has been asserted.

A catalogue record of this book is available from the British Library.

ISBN: 1 873687 56 7
Editor: Patten, Eve
Title: Returning to Ourselves
Subtitle: Second Volume of Papers
from the John Hewitt International Summer School
1995

Front Cover Photograph: John Hewitt (1978)
Cover Design: December Publications
Set in New Baskerville
Printed by Noel Murphy Printing, Belfast

in memoriam
Jack McCann
1917-1993

CONTENTS

Introduction   *xi*

Neal Ascherson
The Left and Eastern Europe   1

Jerzy Jarniewicz
Words and Utopias   8

Edna Longley
Progressive Bookmen: Left-wing Politics and Ulster Protestant Writers   16

Peter McDonald
The Fate of 'Identity': John Hewitt, W.R. Rodgers and Louis MacNeice   41

Patrick Crotty
'That Combat on the Shabby Patch':
Hugh MacDiarmid, Edwin Muir and the Matter of Scotland   61

Mary Thompson
The Round Tower and the Black Church:
Aspects of Austin Clarke's Cultural/Religious Identity   86

Fergus O'Ferrall
The Mart of Ideas: Seán Ó Faoláin 1900-1991   99

Richard English
'Scenes that surround certain conflicts':
The literature of Peadar O'Donnell reconsidered   112

C.L. Dallat
A Single Flame   120

Patricia Craig
The Liberal Imagination in Northern Irish Prose   130

Tom Clyde
Uladh, Lagan *and* Rann: *The 'Little Magazine' comes to Ulster*   145

Henry Patterson
Socialism in Ulster   154

James D. Young
A Very English Socialism and the Celtic Fringe 1880-1911   168

Bob Purdie
Internationalism & the Civil Rights Movement: An Epitaph   187

Derek Franklin
Eiresponsibilities:
Rhythm and Revolution in 'The Rime of the Ancient Mariner' — 209

George O'Brien
The Big Elsewhere & the Wayward Hyphen:
Further Gleanings from the Clarity Archive — 217

Michael Allen
The Parish and The Dream: Heaney and America 1969-1987 — 227

Colin Graham
Derek Mahon's Cultural Marginalia — 240

Kathleen McCracken
Shaping Special Worlds: Louis MacNeice's Anti-Parable — 249

Eamonn Hughes
Sent to Coventry: Emigration and Autobiography — 261

Karlin J. Lillington
Woman as 'Elsewhere' — 276

Patricia Horton
'Time that was extra, unforeseen and free':
Representations of childhood in the poetry of Seamus Heaney — 287

Norman Vance
Pictures, Singing and the Temple:
Some Contexts for John Hewitt's Images — 297

Martin McLoone
The Primitive Image:
Tradition, Modernity and Cinematic Ireland — 310

John Wilson Foster
Imagining the Titanic — 325

Alvin Jackson
Irish Unionist Imagery 1850-1920 — 344

Aodán Mac Póilin
'Spiritual Beyond the Ways of Men': Images of the Gael — 360

Frank Ormsby
Tomorrow with His Notes:
Editing the Collected Poems of John Hewitt — 384

Notes on Contributors — 397

Introduction

"History is selective", John Hewitt wrote in 'Mosaic', the title poem of his 1981 collection. Seeking out the objective role, history obscures the fragmentary, the marginal, accidental and peripheralised:

> ... Give us instead
> the whole mosaic, the tesserae,
> that we may judge if a period indeed
> has a pattern and is not merely
> a handful of coloured stones in the dust.

Until recently, the same plea for inclusiveness was applicable to the work of the poet himself, which remained at the mercy of selections and anthologies. One of the most welcome literary events to have taken place, therefore, since the first volume of essays in honour of John Hewitt, *The Poet's Place: Essays on Ulster Literature and Society* (1991), has been the publication by Blackstaff Press of the *Collected Poems of John Hewitt*, edited by the poet Frank Ormsby. Ormsby's modest self-projection as a literary hack of Hewitt's description ("Tomorrow with his notes a man will come ..."), does nothing to disguise the value of this scrupulously annotated volume, both to those already familiar with the poetry and to the newcomer. The book has made Hewitt accessible to more holistic readings than were previously possible, illuminating not only his creative processes and incentives, but also his misjudgements and failures, obsessions and anxieties, his intellectual touchstones and political deliberations.

On reading the essays which follow, it is easy to see how the expansion of the poet in terms of textual availability has helped to sustain and develop the Summer School which has taken place annually in the Glens of Antrim since his death in 1987. Clearly, the School is not 'about' one individual. While remaining central to the event, Hewitt has become simultaneously the filter through which a variety of issues and interests are given prominence. The range of his commitments—literary, political, artistic, social—has facilitated an academic diversity and a conscientiousness essential to the "council of sunburnt comrades" which swells and modifies itself each year. As such, the John Hewitt International Summer School has been able to register in some way the varied forces and currents within which the north of Ireland has been implicated, historically, domestically and internationally, in the transitions of the early 90s, a representative impulse which this collection of essays seeks to reflect.

Hewitt's essentially *social* persona, and the extent to which his writing is—like that of Yeats—heavily populated, has continued to provide an incentive to look at the work of his enlisted "visitants": the protestors, dissenters and non-conformists for whom C.L. Dallat stakes a claim here, the Victorian social philosophers who provided what Edna Longley terms "the smack of the 19th century" in his thinking, and, not least, the society of his contemporaries—the poet, playwrights, novelists and socialists with whom he shared common ground. Peter McDonald assesses an Ulster triumvirate of Hewitt, Rodgers and MacNeice, Richard English considers the literary politics of Peadar O'Donnell, and Mary Thompson develops the complex religious inheritance of Austin Clarke, to whom Hewitt dedicated the mythological poem 'Those Swans Remember'. Patrick Crotty's detailed study of the fraught relationship between Edwin Muir and Hugh MacDiarmid exposes something of the political and linguistic pressures being brought to bear, meanwhile, on the lives of writers across the Irish Sea.

Beyond individuals, a sense of the communities of cultural discourse is foregrounded in these essays. Patricia Craig reconstructs the environs of 30s Belfast, with Campbell's Café, the informal and now legendary meeting place for the voices of liberalism in an increasingly sectarian city. With the same attention to the background dynamics of Irish writing, Tom Clyde scrutinises the difficulties of literary production in his history of the 'Little Magazine' in the north, and the conditions which determined the emergence, policies and style of *Uladh, Lagan* and *Rann*.

In terms of overarching political philosophies, Hewitt's socialism remains fundamental to an understanding of his work and his milieu. It was perhaps typical of the independence of the School in general that, while media pundits everywhere announced the collapse of the left, several of the lecturers who spoke at Garron Point were seeking to establish—in some respects for the first time—what exactly the 'left' comprised in Ireland, past and present. In an essay which re-establishes Hewitt's proximity to James Connolly as much as William Morris, Edna Longley explodes the Anglo-centrist conceptualisation of the '30s generation' by turning to the respective leftism of the poet, examined in the supportive context of Belfast writers John Boyd and Sam Thompson, and in comparison to MacNeice. Her efforts to delineate the particularities of an Irish, and indeed a *northern* Irish socialism are reinforced by James Young who distinguishes the 'peripheralised' social and political philosophy of Scottish socialism, and by Henry Patterson who, tracing the provenance and progress of the labourist tradition in Ireland, succeeds in outlining the intricate history of Ulster socialism.

The focus for a second set of lectures over the three years was the movement beyond (and through) the impasse of the Northern Irish crisis to variations of 'elsewhere', conceived in a range of terms from the geographical and the historical to the gendered. As Michael Allen states in his discussion of Heaney and America, the commitment to a local culture "does not preclude a culture-flow from elsewhere". More than this, the tension engendered by the matrix of departure, exile and return—played out in Hewitt's 'exile' to Coventry in 1957—has been a consistent stimulant to the creative imagination in Ireland. For Eamonn Hughes and Colin Graham, in their respective essays on Northern Irish fiction and the poetry of Derek Mahon, it is the horizon, and indeed the coastal or seaward journey which can define, reflexively, the texture of home. Meanwhile, beyond Paul Muldoon's enigmatic "open sea", the USA is held up as the distorting mirror of these islands by George O'Brien, whose epistolary essay on "the Wayward Hyphen" caricatures with some savagery the excesses of the Irish-American academic circuit.

If the look westward has been humorous, the look eastward has been powerfully illuminating and ironically familiar. Again the precedent can be found in Hewitt's own concerns, as his political convictions were tried by the reality of the Soviet imperialist exercise. His intimation of the insecurity in central and eastern Europe are marked in poems such as 'Lake Bled: Slovenia' (1965) and later in the ironic 'Conversations in Hungary'—a poem which closes on the subterranean fractures of eastern Europe, as paralleled by the beginning of the Northern Irish troubles in 1969. The legacy of ill-drawn borders, of long-term colonial consequences in countries other than Ireland, and most tragically in view of recent years, of ethnic diversity straining at the seams of 'national' definition, was brought into focus as the Summer School responded to the events of 1989 and their still unsettled dust. Neil Ascherson's lecture on the fate and viability of the left in the social and institutional transitions of eastern Europe was both timely and prophetic. Similarly, Jerzy Jarniewicz, who visited the Summer School from Poland with his colleague and fellow writer Piotr Sommer, illustrates here the linguistic vulnerability—familiar already in Northern Ireland—which resulted from the vast cultural and political dystopia of which his country was part. That the School has maintained its commitment to interaction with Poland, Hungary, former Yugoslavia and Romania is a reflection of its ability to fuse local concerns with international as the paradigms of nation, identity and culture undergo radical shifts. The events of these years, moreover, far from undercutting Hewitt's regionalism—much discussed in the early years of the Summer School—have given it a recontextualised and urgent place on the agenda.

The Summer School of 1993, entitled 'Substance and Shadow', turned to the image and the image-maker, in Ireland and beyond. Again, the subject derived from Hewitt's own interests, as a gallery man, an enthusiast and critic of both Irish and European art, and a writer whose descriptive powers—in nature poems and others—repeatedly negotiate the effects of light, shade, perspective and reflection. The emphasis on visual imagery at this session further stretched the interdisciplinary capacity of the School as art historians, film-makers and visual artists offered contributions, including Micky Donnelly's slide show on contemporary Ulster painting and Belinda Loftus' deconstruction of Belfast's gable-end iconography. The subject of the image features in this collection in Martin McLoone's analysis of cinematic representations of Ireland, Alvin Jackson's account of the manufacture and dissemination of popular unionist imagery, and Aodán Mac Póilin's sensitive and vivid history of the representation of the Gael. John Wilson Foster reproduces the text of his illustrated lecture on the *Titanic*, a study which combines a defining moment in Belfast's social, cultural and economic history with a visual and theoretical exploration of modernism.

The keynote lecture in 1993 was given by Norman Vance, and its topic raised, finally, the moral sensibility which informs the concept of vision, a theme which might perhaps be understood to pervade the Summer School papers as a whole. Working from Hewitt's pattern of reference to paintings in his poetry, Vance highlights the issues of vision as it emerges in 'The Spectacle of Truth', Hewitt's poem of an Amsterdam lens-grinder caught between "the strict justice of light" enabled by his skills, and the less exacting, but sympathetic, blurring of focus which is the charitable option of the naked, defective, mortal eye. Hewitt was later to retread the territory of this poem with his more whimsical 'Bifocal in Gaza', and both pieces combine to underline his concern with the conditions in which things, quite simply, are brought into view. While the object of the gaze is important, the distance and

Introduction   *xv*

location from which it is envisaged must likewise be subject to interrogation or definition. In an incidental poem, 'By Air to Birmingham on a mid-June Evening', from which the title of the present collection is taken, Hewitt juxtaposes the suddenly dislocated, panoramic view of his city from a plane with the intimate knowledge of walking grounded, through its "fragments of existence". If the options are irreconcilable, it is clear at least which one the poet himself prefers and trusts. It would seem that the contemporary critic or historian must contemplate a similar choice of perspective.

    These papers represent only a portion of the material which the Summer School generated over three years, and such a collection can never, inevitably, attempt to reproduce the interactive work of seminars, debates and discussions, or the contributions of the novelists, poets, musicians, dramatists and raconteurs who have been present, and whose performances or readings have helped to characterise the event. Nonetheless they reflect the way in which the School remains able to absorb a diversity of interests while maintaining focus and direction each year. The John Hewitt International Summer School is not above criticism, nor is it resistant to change. It has pre-empted, to a significant extent, the move of cultural studies into the curriculum and the public imagination, and has remained ahead of the game in constructing a forum appropriate to the level of criticism and engagement demanded by the rapidly shifting circumstances of recent years.

    The School has gained in strength and influence, therefore, since the proceedings of the first three years. It has also suffered losses. Frank Kinahan, whose riotous reminder of the excesses and peversities of over-indulgent historicism is reprinted here, died in 1993. His humour, personality and presence have been deeply missed. Frank Wright, a distinguished contributor to the School and the author of *Northern Ireland: A Comparative Analysis* (1992) died in the same year. Bob Purdie publishes his own essay here, on 'Internationalism & the Civil Rights Movement' as a tribute to him. Finally, Jack McCann, the School's founder, died in 1993. This collection is dedicated to him, in memory of the warm spirit which he represented for so many participants.

Eve Patten
1st June, 1995

The Left and Eastern Europe

Neal Ascherson

They tell us that, after the year of 1989, we should stop using the terms of 'left' and 'right' because they no longer mean anything. Those terms which, as you probably know, started in the French Assemblée Nationale after the Revolution and described the seats on the left of the hemicycle where the wild men of the Mountain sat and the benches over to the right where the liberals and moderates and Girondins sat—all long before there was such a thing as socialism, of course.

They say that 'left' and 'right' ceased to mean anything long ago, when the Marxists became the conservatives in power and in privilege and when the revolutionary radicals, cramming the prisons or duplicating illegal leaflets, espoused the views of John Stuart Mill. They present two scenes separated by 80 years—or rather I present them, for the sake of this argument. Here is a heavily pregnant young woman being taken off the train by frontier guards in 1905. The brutes give her a shaking until there is a loud crash and, instead of pregnancy, there are 20 copies of August Bebel's work on the *Problem of Woman* strewn on the customs-house floor. She is a socialist, they are pious monarchists. Here she comes again in 1985, her blue eyes blazing with outrage as she is dragged off, and this time when the gendarmes shake her what falls to the floor is the philosophy of Roger Scruton, the essays of Irving Kristol and the collected speeches of Margaret Thatcher. She is a neo-conservative, they are Marxist-Leninists.

And let me tell you something else about those two defiant, red-cheeked girls. The first one is the beloved grandmother of the second one. They will both certainly turn out to come from a well-known family who used to be landowners and spoke French before the servants and had holidays at Biarritz or Fiume, a family all of whose members, male and female, have been on the files of secret police forces for a hundred years.

They tell us 'left' and 'right' ceased to have meaning when a Catholic working class took on a state run in the name of the proletariat and won. Or when, after the revolutions of 1989, nationalists and conservatives accused the liberals who had led those revolutions and who had spent many years in prison, of being 'leftists'. During the upheavals in Poland, as the Solidarity movement split painfully into two, the Lech Walesa wing made these kinds of remarks about the Democratic Alliance people around Mazowiecki and Adam Michnik and Jacek Kuron, and challenged them to state where on the political spectrum they stood. I think it was Frasyniuck, one of the heroes of the underground struggle in the 80s, who replied: "We are west of centre."

All these examples really tell me is not that 'left' and 'right' have lost their meaning, but that they have won their freedom—words being almost as imprisonable as people. There has been a long period in which Marxism occupied these terms to exclusion, although Lenin was much keener on them than Karl Marx himself. To be left was to be loyal to communism, while to be right meant that you were an adherent of traditional order and of capitalism. Considering how ill that use of the terms fitted real politics, it is strange how completely many of us absorbed it. National Socialism in Germany, for example, which was far more radical and iconoclastic than the officially-Marxist Social Democracy, had to be called rightist, although in retrospect it made nonsense of the polarity. As for those who, even in the 30s, thought that the communist movement was too cautious and opportunistic, they were supposed to suffer from the infantile disease of ultra-leftism.

Now it is clear that 'left' and 'right' are abiding forms whose content varies through the ages. There is the fight for the exploited and downtrodden, which requires different books as times change but requires always the same generous, angry heart which would rather go to jail than condone injustice. There is the fight to make the world safe for the powerful few and their army of mercenaries, a defence which has also shown that it can adapt almost any ideology—nationalism, Marxism, the free market, protectionism, fascism, and so on—to its own purposes. But we should try to understand who declared the death of left and right, and why they did so.

I have been aware of two very different sources. One was in the west: the conservative part of the intellectuals in 1968 who retorted to the student revolutionaries that their intolerance and their preference for action, rather than persuasion, was indistinguishable from the intolerance of the fascist right. In West Germany, where old academics could remember how Nazi student gangs had terrorised and purged the campus, this spurious identification carried some weight. The other source was eastern Europe during the past decade, where the developing opposition groups tried patiently to dismantle the impacted mass of ideological assumptions which western visitors brought in their suitcases. Many such visitors simply could not grasp that what they identified as left could in fact be some institution of *quasi*-feudal privilege defended by state terror flying a red flag; while industrial workers who hated the word 'socialist' and were ostentatiously Catholic were not therefore in favour of giving the big estates back to the aristocracy and expelling Jews from university departments.

What has ended is the Bolshevik revolution. Not the problems which it caused, not even all the ideas which passed through it, but the momentum of October 1917. It would be a nice question to define when the French Revolution ended. Plainly not with Thermidor or with Napoleon, unless you take a rather purist view that a revolution ceases to exist when it betrays its original principles. Both of these revolutions came to institutionalise themselves territorially, in terms of European zones of control, so perhaps the answer is that the French Revolution ended at Waterloo. The old, beef-eating English thought so and, in a way, they were right. In that sense, the Bolshevik revolution, although not defeated in battle, ended when the Soviet Union lost control of eastern Europe and parts of its own periphery between 1988 and 1990. Obviously, some of the ideas of both the French revolutionaries and the communist movement are such fundamental perceptions that they will live on and be components of the fuel in future explosions and revolutions. But the Russian revolution itself is now dead and extinct.

The consequences in eastern Europe, for socialists, have been curious. In open plural elections, the communists lost power everywhere north-west of a diagonal line running—or wandering—from Lwow in the western Ukraine to Dubrovnik on the Adriatic. South-east of that line, the communists, more or less renamed or deployed or both, survived in government, at least for a time, in Albania, Serbia, Macedonia, Bulgaria, Romania. The fact that this line marks a sort of cultural frontier between the Catholic, Habsburg part of Europe and the Orthodox, Turk-slaying regions should be treated with caution. There are intense, tribally-felt nationalisms here and in several cases—

Romania and Albania perhaps, Serbia most certainly—the communists were able to metamorphose themselves into authoritarian nationalist movements. Nobody can tell where this process will end, but my own forecast is that economic reform—the breaking down of the centrally-planned economy—will come only very slowly to those countries, where the old *nomenklatura* of the Communist Party will gradually convert itself into a property-owning class in possession of the privatised industries and services which used to be state controlled. Something like that may be the future of Russia, in fact, where many people expect an unholy alliance of the Russian mafia with local ex-party bosses to take over the economy: autocracy replaced by kleptocracy.

North-west of the line, communism as a political force has survived far less well, but still rather better than might have been expected. A lot of people—something like 12 per cent—voted for the Communist Party of Czechoslovakia in free elections. Some of the leaders of these new 'social democratic' parties, like Gregor Gysi of the PDS in Germany or Cimoszewicz in Poland, or Pozsgay and Gyula Horn in Hungary, are admitted to be likeable and impressive politicians even by their enemies. But everyone knows what these winning little parties used to be called and how they used to rule, and their chances of staging any sort of comeback are remote.

The uncertainties created by the discredit of anything calling itself 'socialist' are very great. They amount to this: what sort of political movement will represent the losers in the huge transformations of society now under way in eastern Europe? It is not hard to see who the winners and losers are, and anybody who grappled with the problems of introducing market forces into communist economies could see it as far back as the 60s. The losers are, first, anyone on a fixed income or pension who will be hit by inevitable inflation and, secondly, the great majority of the industrial working class. Little state industry will survive exposure to market forces, as we see in Poland now. The workers must pay the main price of this transformation in unemployment, falling living standards and purchasing power and general insecurity. The winners, on the other hand, are the well-educated and well-qualified experts and intellectuals who could not use or benefit from their abilities under a system where party loyalty was the main qualification for responsibility.

The proposition—and it is a bold proposition—is that, when the new capitalist economy is operating, it will make everyone, workers included, better off than before. Meanwhile, the workers are asked to accept compensation in national and personal liberty. On the whole, so far, they have been prepared to do this. The Mazowiecki government of Poland, for example, began in 1990 with one of the most savagely deflationary policies in modern history, but kept public trust for at least most of that year because most of its members had been the persecuted, dauntless leaders of Solidarity under martial law.

But all revolutions, even velvet ones, devour their children. The sort of men and women who made the oppositions and then the revolutions and then the first post-revolutionary governments tended to share some characteristics. They were usually intellectual, took a sophisticated and internationalist view of the world, were friendly to but slightly sceptical of the churches, held social-democratic views about how a free society should work, were often ex-communists or the children of convinced communists from the pre-war generation, and not infrequently were, as they say, 'of Jewish origin'. After the revolutions, however, different political forces came out of the woodwork. These were the remains of the old conservative and nationalist streams of thought which had been brutally stamped out at the beginning of Communist rule. Since then, their underground groups had remained few and very cautious, and had taken little part in active opposition. Now, however, they emerged to challenge these liberal internationalists—the Kurons and the Miklos Harasztis—accusing them of secret 'leftist' leanings and of intellectual élitism. In some such movements, like the Hungarian populists who became the Democratic Forum, a fair claim to have more authentic roots in political tradition went with a sharp whiff of all-too-authentic racism.

The process so far has seen the populists, to give them a general name, replacing the liberals in government. The Democratic Forum governs Hungary, while the victory of Lech Walesa in the Polish presidential elections of 1990 led to the resignation of Mazowiecki and many of his ministers and a more populist tone in public life. As a generalisation, the populist is more disposed to intervene in the economy to control the damage which the free market may do to decent people and sacred cows alike.

Given the weakness of traditional forms of socialism, it seemed possible that the losers' vote would be picked up by rabble-rousing authoritarian nationalist movements. Mass unemployment and inflation would all turn out to be the fault of Jews, Masons, crypto-communists and their agents in the IMF. But this has not really happened. The political balance has swung in the populist direction, but extremism is not on the rampage (with the exception, I suppose, of the terrible Mr. Tyminski and his supernatural know-nothing 'party' in Poland).

What has perished, and this is indeed the end of an old song, is the dream that there could be a third way between capitalism and communism; not the mixed-economy social democracy which is familiar and pedestrian in the west, but a new form of self-managing society based upon enterprises operating in a free market but controlled democratically by their workers—an old song, which the British used to call Guild Socialism and which Stalin used to shoot people for proposing. It appealed to many of those post-Marxian dissidents, clever and idealistic, who already knew something of the west and wanted to avoid its vices while borrowing some of its virtues.

Here East Germany was the battlefield. The New Forum group, proposing that East Germany remain a separate German state but a third-way type of democratic experiment, was obliterated at the 1990 elections by a stampede towards unification. The public mood towards the west was less critical approval than a cargo cult. Nor can they be easily blamed. They said, unanswerably: 'We have escaped from one great social experiment. Why should we instantly sign up for another, when the one thing we know about the western system is that it works?'

Now, of course, the people of what they euphemistically call *die neue Bundesländer* are finding out that the western system can work quite badly. There is little prospect that they will return to Mr. Gregor Gyst and his remodelled communism. But will they drift towards the Social Democrats in favour of a more humane and moderate capitalism? Indeed, after the end of the Bolshevik revolution, is democratic socialism in western Europe relieved of a burden or weakened still further?

This is not really my topic here. But I suspect that socially radical politics will now develop more rapidly. The Trotskyite left will not change at all, because their analysis does not allow them to be surprised or to re-examine their beliefs as the Soviet experiment ends. The reconstructed communists of Spain or Italy will not recover much, I think, because in spite of all their liberalism and openness, the spinal nerve of European communism at the base has always been a romantic, ultramontane loyalty to Moscow. You can remove that nerve by surgery, but then paralysis and death ensue.

But non-dogmatic, active socialism has a clearer run, a more open park now. And here eastern Europe is relevant again. It is becoming clear that there is a huge, widening gap between what western governments say they do and what they really do. They have prescribed for Poland and Hungary and Russia a free market economy of the most ruthless and radical kind. This, they say, is what we practise and what makes us so hardy. What a big lie that is, though! The poor Poles may think that they are practising Thatcherism, but if anything like their economic regimen had been applied to Britain in the 80s, there would have been a revolution. In practice, 'free market capitalism' in Britain and Germany is an intimate partnership between private capital and state spending and guidance, between incentive and welfare provision, whose terms do not vary fundamentally whoever is in power.

I find this hypocrisy cheering because it is becoming obvious. And when it becomes obvious, many inhibitions about voting for social-democratic parties will evaporate too. Certainly the left, in the old sense, was the loser by what happened in 1989; but the right, in the old western sense, has also been deprived of an argument. The left lost its shirt, but the right lost its trousers. And the natural fight between the sense of human justice and the nonsense of privilege is free to go into the next round. I wish I knew what the granddaughter of that blue-eyed, angry young woman will have strapped round her waist when they haul her off an inertial transit in 2065, and we can't even imagine what slogans she will shout in the customs-house. But she will be there, and though she isn't carrying a baby, she will be carrying inside her that small flame we call the left.

Words and Utopias

Jerzy Jarniewicz

I

The Casualties of History

Recent events in eastern Europe have overthrown governments and numerous well-established institutions, destroyed political careers and launched new political careers, redrawn maps and withdrawn foreign troops, repainted urban landscapes and reshaped human expectations. One way of looking at these galloping events is to see what has happened to *words*. As a writer, and not a professional politician, I find it most fascinating and revealing to concentrate on the changes in the usage and meaning of words that occurred in the turbulent years of Polish history.

When, over 40 years ago, as a result of an election fraud, the Communist Party took over political power in Poland, one of the first things the *régime* did was to change the names of several institutions associated with the old, overthrown system. Underlying this decision was clearly a shamanistic belief that in changing the name you change the institution itself. That is what happened with the 'Police', which was hastily re-christened as 'Militia'. The official propaganda presented the newly-formed militia as an organisation which had no resemblance to, and no continuity with, the old mechanisms of repression active in the pre-war, semi-authoritarian state. Needless to say, the militia very quickly started to play the role of a new means of repression, becoming a highly-centralised institution at the disposal of the party, designed to suppress any manifestation of dissent, and to control all possible spheres of social life. It was not a surprise, then, that during street demonstrations against martial law, crowds attacked by the People's Militia shouted back at them *Gestapo!*—thus proving the inefficiency of the magical powers of the communist lexicographers. In 1989, when communism was overthrown, the word 'police' returned triumphantly: all police cars had to be repainted. Words, just like individuals, monuments and institutions, can become victims of history.

For 40 years of practically one-party rule in Poland, the word 'party' has meant the Communist Party (although Polish communists always avoided using the word 'communism', preferring to call their organisation, less riskily, the Workers' Party). 'Are you a party member?' was the question which meant nothing more than 'Are you a communist?' The effect of this illegitimate identification is that today newly-formed political parties do not use this word in their names: they are called unions, alliances, congresses, federations. These political groups, steering away from the dangerous word 'party', launch individual politicians rather than produce political programmes. In popular opinion, it is the individual who is known and respected, and not the party he or she belongs to. Party politics is always suspicious and brings to mind the practices of former years. In the long run, it may prove to be a serious shortcoming of the Polish political scene.

Among the words most affected by historical change in eastern Europe one should first of all mention 'socialism', 'left', 'communism'. When, in 1980, Solidarity was born as a mass movement of workers and intellectuals (or rather the intelligentsia), its slogan was 'Socialism— yes; distortions of socialism—no!' At that time, hardly any leader of the democratic opposition would voice doubts about the need for a social system: the movement of 1980 was to improve the system from within, not to destroy it. Words like 'free-market' or 'unemployment' did not appear in the pronouncements of the opposition leaders. Martial law, introduced 18 months later, was a clear indication that the 'owners' of the Polish People's Republic (as the communists were called then) had no intention to reform, to negotiate, to reach a consensus, to share their power with anyone. It was then that many dissidents realised that the system could not be reformed. Any minute change meant its end. Milosz wrote that, with the introduction of martial law, hope was murdered. Now it was either/or. The divisions were clearer than ever. History demonstrated that by introducing martial law, the communists started the inevitable, suicidal process of the destruction of their system.

Nine years later, in 1989, Polish opposition leaders sat at the round table talks and discussed the possibilities of a peaceful departure from, what they called then, the 'Stalinist model'. For some time, hardly anybody would use other words to describe the system they were fighting against. At that stage, only such a formula was acceptable to the Polish communists and it harmonised well with the changes in the Soviet Union. Thirty-five years after Stalin's death, 30 years after Khrushchev's secret report denouncing Stalinism, leaders of the Polish opposition defined their political goal as the elimination of Stalinist elements! That clearly was a case of what I would call 'tactical semantics' ... Yet this was very a brief period: after the overwhelming victory in the elections of 1989 (99 per cent of senators were Solidarity candidates), nobody felt the need to pretend that the real objective was the destruction of communism and not only of its Stalinist version.

But once the process started, it could not be stopped. The communists in their propaganda have very skilfully and successfully appropriated the notion of socialism—to the point of making socialism and communism indistinguishable terms to the common citizen. Unashamedly, communist organisations call themselves 'socialist'. At the same time, obsequious historians were busy re-writing history in order to eradicate all forms of socialism: all those who cherished different views on what socialism means were either declared renegades and sentenced to non-being, or presented in a way that concealed all crucial differences and problematic issues—after which modifications, these unorthodox socialists could be put in the line of the only true history of socialism running from Marx through Lenin to Brezhnev. In communist Poland, where everyone had to study the history of the working-class movements, just a few realised that there were essential differences between, for example, Rosa Luxembourg and Lenin. That the word 'socialism' has become so vulnerable is also due to the vagueness of its meaning. Is socialism an economic dogma that does not allow for the private ownership of the means of production? Or does it concern only the distribution of goods and accept state intervention in this field? Or does it simply mean that the state should provide social security with free health service, free education, labour legislation? If socialism as an economic theory has failed, does it mean that its other forms are equally abortive? However harmful it may be to the state of Polish political thought, it was not surprising that, when communism collapsed, socialism also fell victim to the dissatisfied, disillusioned and angry people. The odium attached to the word 'socialism' gave birth to an almost unanimous acceptance of the idea of the free market and popular distrust of any political movement that associates itself with socialist tradition. Except for one insignificant group, there is no party of the Polish left that would call itself socialist. The only palatable term akin to socialism is social democracy, and this too has been made suspicious since the former communists, during just one night, underwent mystical transfiguration and called their new party Polish Social Democracy. This miraculous process of change did not take place at Mount Tabor, but in the Warsaw Palace of Culture named after Stalin and known to be the most shocking example of socialist taste in architecture: marbles, spires, chandeliers, colonnades, dozens of figures of idealised, muscular, healthy, optimistic workers—larger than life. The change of the party's name was yet another instance of the perversities of political semantics: only a few years earlier, the list of words that functioned in the communists' lexicon as words of abuse included anarcho-syndicalist, revisionist, reformist, Trotskyist, and social democrat. These were very dangerous words, used to attack and denounce the political opponents of communism.

On the other hand, the unreserved support for the idea of the free market made it the most popular word now in the Polish political dictionary, used as lavishly as the word 'socialism' was formerly—by politicians of various, mutually incongruous political orientation. 'Free market' is a shibboleth, a phrase understood differently by different people, but that is not important: what matters is that today it legitimises one's political sincerity, gives credibility, and functions as a visa to a future political career. It is interesting that, in this turbulent political situation, nearly every concept is questioned, even 'democracy'—one of the leading politicians has recently called for the abandonment of the dogma of democracy, believing that it is not possible to get rid of the totalitarian system by means of pure democratic changes; the situation demands authoritarian, decisive leadership which will be able to create conditions for the later development of the truly democratic system. But even though democracy is questioned, the concept of the 'free market' shares with the Pope the dogma of infallibility.

The spectacular collapse of communism did not only mortally infect the word 'socialism', but also affected the more general term 'the left'. It is a significant fact that many Polish politicians, who apprenticed in the opposition and whose background and political views are clearly leftist, take pains to avoid the use of the word 'left'. The division between left and right is now widely considered anachronistic and inadequate. An *emigré* Polish philosopher, Leszeck Kolakowski, claims that the division lost its meaning after the outbreak of the World War I, when the leftist belief in internationalism proved only wishful thinking as national interests won out over the class issue. The use of the words 'left' and 'right', says Kolakowski, has lost its sense. It is possible now to imagine the following conversation: *A*. 'So you say you're a leftist, but this means you support Stalin, Pol Pot and Ceausescu? And Hodza's regime in Albania?' *B*. 'Oh no, I support Mitterand, not Stalin. But you are right-wing. Does it mean you give support to Pinochet, to apartheid in South Africa, to the anti-Semitic groups in Poland?' *A*. 'Certainly not. I do not support Pinochet, but John Major.' Instead of using these ambiguous and misleading labels, Kolakowski suggests speaking of 'open' and 'closed' mentality. The former adheres to the ideas of tolerance, social equality, rational discussion; the latter characterised by tribal, chauvinistic and xenophobic thinking.

Unfortunately, it has to be made clear that years spent in opposition to a totalitarian *régime* do not necessarily guarantee the open mentality. It is a Romantic myth to believe in the redeeming powers of participating in a just struggle. Fighting with evident injustice, as was the case in Poland, does not always make one more tolerant, understanding and open-minded. Struggling against the common enemy is an abnormal situation which develops its own logic—and, often, it has to be a simplified logic, the main assumption of which is that the world has a manichean character and is divided into black and white, good and evil. Following that logic, one takes for granted that 'the enemy of our enemy is our friend'—Polish trade unions used to treat Margaret Thatcher and Ronald Reagan as cult figures. Following that logic, one is inclined to believe that 'if you are not with us, you are against us', with the consequence that a few public figures, who kept apart from political discussions of the last decade, were ostracised by public opinion. Following that logic, one tended to make political views the main criterion in assessing people, without any real regard for their competence, intelligence, skill, or artistic talents.

Living in a totalitarian state was like living in a permanent state of emergency, where many values and norms have been suspended. It could not be a favourable milieu for developing an open mentality. The present-day political scene in Poland is, in many ways, an aftermath of that state of emergency. The chaos generated by communism and introduced to the world of words and ideas, the real casualties of history, will still haunt not only my part of Europe.

II

The Waning of Utopias

"Heard melodies are sweet, but those unheard are sweeter," writes John Keats in his *Ode on a Grecian Urn*. Confined in the world of space, time and matter, subjected to the irreversible processes of change and decay, unheard melodies of perfect harmony lose much of their potential beauty. Reality tends to dissatisfy by brutally dragging down our most cherished ideals—an open spectrum of unlimited possibilities including everything that might be, from potency to act, to the horizontal world of earthly dimensions. There can be no symmetry between what is and what might be; the latter always possesses the unique and enviable privilege of ignoring the prosaic and unexciting domain of yards, pounds and minutes.

Dissatisfaction with the factual world goes hand in hand with the dream of an ideal and perfect reality. This dream may become a model for the rearrangement of the dissatisfying world, turning into utopias visions of perfect communities living in harmony, free from anxiety, unhappiness, poverty, hunger, frustration, inflation and other possible dangers. In the hands of fervent revolutionaries, utopias work as practical guidebooks: instructions on how to mould the world into a shape resembling the inspired vision.

Dissatisfaction with the actual world may be directed towards the past or to the future. It often happens that people idealise certain periods from history, real or mythological, and perceive them as Arcadias: lands of innocence that remind us of our own childhood when everything was simple and unproblematic. The world used to be better; present ailments may be cured by a return to the ways things were. It is an idealised past: our memory tends to select the most beautiful aspects, shifting into the dark hole of forgetfulness everything that could introduce discord. This is nostalgia.

But there are others who, dissatisfied with present reality, project their visions into the future and see them as realisable potentials, guide-posts even, on the road of their missionary activity. This is utopia.

Utopia is totalising: it is the product of one's inner belief that everybody should live in happiness. It disregards those who would dream of a different kind of happy life, those who understand the meaning of this very vague word in a different way. Utopia is blind to the fact that human beings are often ready to resign from happiness in order to affirm individual sovereignty. Programmed, declared happiness may be oppressive; curtailing one's freedom. In Aldous Huxley's *Brave New World*, one of the chief characters, John, rejects the comfortable, affluent life and retreats to a desert where he wilfully exposes himself to suffering and pain. This may seem the most unreasonable act to perform in the light of what we usually understand by the word happiness. However, what is most important to John is the need to exercise his free will, his freedom, without which human beings cease to be human. And this freedom includes the freedom to be unhappy.

Utopia is reductive: by defining 'happiness', it perverts a meaning which is, in fact, open and indefinable. In the same way, trying to define a 'human being' usually enslaves man in a dead formula, excluding simultaneously all those who do not conform to the definition—they are non-humans, who may be variously called madmen, perverts, dissidents, *untermenschen*, Blacks or Jews; in any case, there is no place for them in the well-programmed machinery of the utopian community. There is no room for them among humankind fixed in a clear-cut formula. If happiness is reduced to purely social, political, or economic terms, then all the anxiety that stems from biological limitations of a human being, or from the existential context, is declared to be mystified, immature consciousness—and to be ignored, neglected and ridiculed.

Utopia is dogmatic; the elementary dogma is that man is essentially good. What makes people behave in an evil way are social conditions which can be altered. If social injustice, social inequality, poverty, hunger, unemployment, exploitation are removed, people will be kind to each other; aggressive and destructive acts will be unheard of, altruism will flourish. This belief in the essential goodness of mankind has been responsible for a long-lasting blackmail. For years, we have been told by the most powerful utopian thinkers of this century that the concept of the evil nature of man has always been used by authoritarian, repressive institutions—the Church, the Family, the State—to legitimise their power and privileges. Whoever spoke of the evil nature of mankind was accused of taking part in a conspiracy with the forces of repression, a conspiracy aimed at keeping people in ignorance and subjugation.

Today, we can observe the spectacular dilapidation of the castles of utopian thinking. Two great totalitarian monstrosities, Nazism and Stalinism, have taught people to be suspicious about any system which tries to define the value of an individual by the degree of his or her participation in a bigger organism—state, nation, class. Together with the unmasking of the true face of states that try to control all aspects of human life, there has come the distrust of any theory that ventures to encompass everything by generating reductive definitions and systematic explanations. Poetry today, responding to this historical experience, looks at the world through a microscope, rather than a telescope: it scans everyday trivia, the low and the insignificant, the ephemeral and the intimate. Leaves of grass, wet pebbles, wooden knockers, black spiders, old shoes, and hot pavements, inhabit much of modern verse. This narrowing of perspective to a small area protects us against totalitarian aspirations, and serves as guarantee of the authenticity of experience, free from mystification and any manipulative intentions.

This turning away from the all-embracing systems is also a manifestation of distrust towards any thinking that reduces the variousness of the world, including the human world, to one aspect only, be it economics, biology, or some other abstract concept. Poets are now "drunk with things being various", sceptical of any organising, autocratic schemes and imposed structures.

Yet possibly the greatest discovery of recent times is the recognition of human limitations, a long forgotten truth and a turning away from the idea of perfection. East European philosophers, such as Leszeck Kolakowski, once a Marxist, speak most sincerely about the crucial significance of the concept of evil to our civilisation. Man is not God, and will never be. This truth, however cruel it may sound, is a safeguard against the temptations of the Promethean pride, arrogance and aspirations which—as recent history demonstrated—often turn against mankind itself. The real lesson that recent history has taught us is to doubt; to accept that human limitations cannot be eradicated and to learn how to live with them. To act as gods and attempt to build Eden here on earth proved to be the most serious danger mankind has ever faced. On their way to the ideal world of Utopia, people forget that, in order to pass the gates of Heaven, one has to die. There is no other way to the heavenly bliss than by death. Meanwhile, those who would rather live listen to the nightingale who sits in the dark tree in the corner of the garden and sings for a few minutes, and then is gone, frightened by the creeping cat who has just woken up from a short slumber.

Progressive Bookmen
Left-wing Politics and Ulster Protestant Writers

Edna Longley

I

Left-wing Ulster Protestants have a distinctive tale to tell. In 1921, they inherited a messy palette of Red, Orange and Green, and faced a unionist *régime* which was quite as anxious about socialism as about nationalism. Then Northern Ireland entered the slump and the 30s:

> Thousands of men whom nobody will employ
>   Standing at corners, coughing.
>
> —Louis MacNeice, *Autumn Journal*

After World War II, the left, though split, won an astonishing 126,000 votes in the 1945 Stormont election. But support collapsed four years later when the Irish Republic had been declared and, as a result, Westminster consolidated unionism with the Ireland Act. In the early 60s, polarisation having eased once more, the Northern Ireland Labour Party began to make modest advances. This provoked a strong unionist counter-attack. When the troubles began, class-politics were sucked into the tribal maw which had always threatened their survival. In his novel *The Hollow Ball* (1961), Sam Hanna Bell, one of the writers whose reminiscences helped me with this essay, satirises a political meeting in 30s Belfast:

> The man behind the table struck a push-bell and stood up.
>   'Comrades and friends, this meeting is called by the Unemployed Workers' Organisation and other progressive bodies to consider the problem of Ulster men and women —'

'Irish men and women,' said a voice from the front ...
The chairman paused and allowed his glance to linger thoughtfully over the audience so that they should be quite clear as to who was wasting whose time. 'Comrade,' he said, 'this problem is above any petty partisanship.'
'That's what I mean,' said the voice, unabashed, 'so call us something we can all accept—Irish.'
The audience watched the man behind the table discarding the rest of his introductory remarks. 'I call on Brother McKelvey to give us the trade union view.'
'On what?' prompted Brother McKelvey without leaving his chair. Reluctantly the chairman straightened up again: '—the trade union point of view on workers being forced across the water to seek employment.' With his backside poised over his chair he added, 'And I hope the meeting's time won't be wasted by comrades dragging in issues dead as Brian Boru.'[1]

Similarly, John Hewitt's short story 'Insurrection' (1930) shows a communist, an anarchist and a trade unionist failing to make common cause with the republican movement.[2]

I want to outline a view of relations between Northern Irish writing and left-wing politics from the late 20s until 1960, the year in which the performance of Sam Thompson's play *Over The Bridge*, an exposé of sectarianism in the shipyards, consummated such relations. Among those who sweated it out in the dark ages before the world media arrived were John Hewitt (1907-87), my principal subject, Sam Hanna Bell (1909-90) and the playwright and autobiographer John Boyd (*b*. 1912). I also want to develop a contrast between Hewitt's politics and those of his expatriate contemporary, Louis MacNeice. Different environments influenced their approach to the issues that obsessed their literary generation. While Hewitt shared W.R. Rodgers' feelings about being "schooled in a backwater of literature out of sight of the running stream of contemporary verse"[3], MacNeice's poetry abounds in images and self-images of water on the move—"river turning tidal"—images that represent the flux of consciousness and of history. Domicile in England placed MacNeice close to certain historical currents: *Autumn Journal* (1939) capitalises on that proximity. On the other hand, although his poetry suffered from aesthetic time-lags, Hewitt was closer than MacNeice to direct political involvement. Neither joined the Communist Party, but the passionately committed Hewitt wavered on the brink, and would never have said with MacNeice: "My sympathies are Left. On paper and in the soul. But not in my heart or my guts."[4]

Even if sponsored by Samuel Hynes' fine book, the term 'Auden

Generation' should be laid to rest. Its Anglo-centric and metropolitan assumptions contradict the pluralistic tumult sketched by Valentine Cunningham in *British Writers of the Thirties*:

> Orthodoxies impose unities. And perhaps the most important cautionary note to sound about the 30s is one against the too ready professions and appearances of unity. If we think of the 30s as a seamless political whole we are grossly distorting them. Even on the Left there was great disunity. The United Front was a seamed patchwork of revolutionaries, old liberals, young liberals, pacifists, Trotskyites, Stalinists, members of the Communist, the Labour, and the Independent Labour Parties, as well as members of no party at all. To call the Front's sympathisers Red would be exaggerating mightily ... And within the literary United Front, if that's how we may think of the sphere commanded by the Left Book Club and other associations for thinking and creative Leftist people, the same mixed shades and ragged divisions obtained ... And politics exacerbated the usual proneness to such differences of opinion and divisive dealings within the cultural world.[5]

Yet, although MacNeice is prominent (Hugh MacDiarmid and Lewis Grassic Gibbon much less so), *British Writers of the Thirties* might as well be called *English Writers of the Thirties*. The dust-jacket photographs are of Auden, Isherwood and Spender, the perspectives English. MacNeice's cultural-political chemistry eludes Cunningham, who notes his interest in 'the divided self' and discusses 'The Hebrides' as an instance of travelogue (to 'Seedy Margins'), without recognising that Ireland might have disposed him both to self-division and to island-fancying.[6] But, on the other island, neither Hewitt nor MacNeice figures in Michael Smith's anthology *Irish Poetry: The Thirties Generation* (1971). And does '30s generation' have the same resonances in the context of the Free State? Seemingly, the literary 30s and the political 30s look different according to the point on the archipelago from which they are surveyed now or were experienced then. Specifically, Belfast complicates the perspectives as it once upset the manifestos. Hewitt's still unpublished autobiography, *A North Light*, contains a chapter about the 30s: 'My Generation.' This memoir both belongs to and deviates from Cunningham's scenario. Indeed, its subtext might be a struggle (within Hewitt himself, too) between local particularism and metropolitan party-lines. In 1942, Hewitt wrote a defiant uncollected poem 'On Reading Auden and Others' (the others possibly include MacNeice), which began: "These men have spoken for a generation/But not for me ..."

II

'Dead as Brian Boru'—an epitaph that the plot of *The Hollow Ball* shows to be premature—parallels a strand in John Hewitt's political formation and vocabulary:

> Then, by the mid-1920s, with the new ministries in gear and the nonentities trooping to the Westminster back benches, it seemed evident that the Unionists were a right-wing offshoot of the British Tory Party, who at home fought every election on the border, and that the Nationalists, the representatives of the Catholic minority, were merely obsolete clansmen with old slogans, moving in an irrelevant dream, utterly without the smallest fig-leaf of a social policy. So my concern went to the Labour Party—I was branch delegate at one annual conference—the party of Sam Kyle and Billy McMullen, who had a policy about 'the ownership of the means of production, distribution and exchange'.[7]

Here Hewitt was building on shaky foundations. Kyle and McMullen had been elected to Stormont in 1925 "after a campaign in which the anti-partitionist positions of prominent members of the Labour Party had been repressed rather than discarded".[8] This, like the republican comrade in *The Hollow Ball*, raises the ghost of James Connolly and his still-contested legacy to the Irish left. In 1912, Connolly clashed with William Walker, anti-home ruler and leading light of the Independent Labour Party, on the grounds that Walker's professed internationalism was really a disguised colonialism. During its prosperous years, bourgeois unionism used a rhetoric of 'progress' to fend off domination by the economically more backward south (compare the tensions between the Northern League and Rome). So when Ulster Protestant socialists invoked 'progress'—as do Hewitt's adjectives "obsolete", "old", "irrelevant"—they might be complicit in unexamined unionism or a sense of superior civilisation.

In 1942, Hewitt called northern nationalists "sectarians, a Redmondite rump stupefying in snugs and clubs".[9] Similarly, his poem 'An Irishman in Coventry' (1958) is based on a clash between progressivist utopianism and the "whiskey-tinctured" behaviour of Irish brickies. (Hewitt's Methodist background explains his attitude to alcohol.) The poem sets up a rather schematic opposition between Coventry's "eager", "tolerant", welfarist spirit—"image of the state hope argued for"—and the dystopian, atavistic fatalism of "my creed-haunted, God-forsaken race". In fact, the brickies were rebuilding Coventry, and Irish immigrant votes, not necessarily motivated by

Marx, helped to keep the local Labour Party in business. For all Hewitt's identification with "my race", 'An Irishman in Coventry' appears blind to its own political unconscious. It also points to contradictions in his view of the relation between ideology (always understood as conscious manifesto) and practical politics. And, just as Ulster unionism historically attached itself to the Tories, so Hewitt tends to idealise Labour England as the locus of political thought and action. Despite some homesickness, Hewitt's years in Coventry (1957-1972), where he became friendly with E.P. Thompson and other left intellectuals, brought him closest to an earthly paradise.

However, Connolly's own contradictions anticipated his advent in the General Post Office. Witness his theoretical evasion of the religious question (relegated to a personal matter), instinct for Irish Catholic cohesion, rejection of 'foreign' i.e. English values, and romance with the Gael as opposed to the "hybrid Irishman".[10] Connolly offers *Labour in Irish History* (1910) as a contribution to "the literature of the Gaelic revival" and locates his proto-socialist utopia in "the Gaelic principle of common ownership".[11] Seán Ó Faoláin was later to hold him chiefly responsible for propagating "the grand delusion" of the "Gaelic mystique"[12], a susceptibility fanned by his upbringing outside Ireland. Altogether, it is not surprising that Connolly had limited sympathy with the skilled Protestant working-class in Belfast. This class (now reduced in numbers and influence) has, indeed, proved unsympathetically prone to put unionism before trade unionism when exhorted to do so. In *Over the Bridge*, violent bigotry defeats the language of brotherhood. Yet traditional Connollyite concepts may over-stress the degree to which Protestant workers have been manipulated or duped, and over-mythologise strategic cross-sectarian solidarity during essentially economic campaigns like the Outdoor Relief strike of 1932. Peadar O'Donnell notes: "it is often in the name of his fierce Orange beliefs that [an Orangeman] enters a progressive fight."[13] Henry Patterson argues that more "serious analysis of Protestant politics ... might have prevented the easy identification of intransigent class opposition to bourgeois Unionism with a nationalist or republican position".[14] (In today's recession, working-class loyalists may criticise middle-class unionist indifference to their needs, but see the Fair Employment Agency as a device for transferring jobs to Catholics.)

What of John Hewitt's attitude to Connolly? In 'No Rootless Colonist', he recalls his youthful "vague sense of a romantic Irish nationalism, with Oisin and Connolly, Maeve and Maud Gonne, bright in the sky"; but also insists: "our politics looked beyond to the world. Sacco and

Vanzetti were, for us, far more significant than any of the celebrated 'felons of our land'."[15] Once again Hewitt questionably severs Ireland's myths and mists from the real or great world. In fact his *juvenilia*, verse written in the late 20s, establish no clear hierarchy of political values. He did indeed write a poem about the controversial death-sentences passed on the American anarchists Sacco and Vanzetti (1927). But he also wrote two elegies for Connolly and 'Song for Mayday' (1928), which ends:

> ... in my dreams I see a host of hero martyrs
>   who are dead:
> John Brown, James Connolly, and Christ, for you
>   I wear my ribbon red.

'Easter Tuesday' and 'To the Memory of James Connolly' also equate Connolly with Christ. However, in Hewitt's early notebooks salutes to the dead of 1916 mingle with laments for World War I victims and veterans, attacks on Ulster unionists and English Tories, and scorn for Ramsay MacDonald's betrayal of the British Labour Party. His radicalism seems at once ardent and promiscuous.

What does begin to emerge is a northern dissidence. 'Dublin: Easter 1928' notices "the barefoot children in the street", and ends: "The only change wrought by new law—the pillarboxes now are green". In 1929 Hewitt wrote 'Two Sonnets on the Free State Censorship Bill' which call up Swift

>   to say the bitter thing
> Or pen the words that hiss and stab and sting
> And flay the foul flesh of the Pope's brigade.

Certainly this puts the issue more bluntly than do Yeats's resorts to Swift's "sibylline frenzy blind". A year later in ''98', Hewitt doubts his credentials, as a non-Dubliner, to write about "MacDonagh, Plunkett, Pearse", whereas: "I know well where William Orr,/McCracken, Dixon, talked before/those brief bright weeks of '98/bore them away to brutal fate."

This is an early sign of the Ulster Protestant writer's tendency to use 1798 rather than 1916 as a radical benchmark—and one which may define difference from, rather than solidarity with, the southern state. (Tom Paulin's excoriations of the Republic are a recent case in point.[16]) Sam Hanna Bell, who described his younger self as "a radical with a faint Nationalist colouration" and "a nostalgic hankering for

1798", found the Presbyterian radicals attractive partly as an alternative to most versions of nationalism then on offer.[17] His novel *A Man Flourishing* measures the moral decline of a former '98 Volunteer by the fact that he becomes a capitalist and strike-breaker, rather than by any culpable indifference to the rest of the island. Bell at one time helped to edit *Labour Progress*. Similarly, Hewitt's favourite United Irishman was James Hope, the weaver of Templepatrick, whom he salutes along with William Thompson as "the brave old pre-Marx Marxists of Ireland".[18] He also reveres Mary Ann McCracken. These emphases contrast with those of an older writer, the Protestant republican Denis Ireland (1894-1974). Whereas Hewitt and Bell dwell on the northern and proto-socialist '98, Ireland wrote a book on Wolfe Tone called *Patriot Adventurer* (1936) and turned out courageous but repetitious polemics with titles like *Six Counties in Search of a Nation* (1947). He carried consistency so far as to abstain from a *Bell* symposium nominating 'The Best Books on Ulster', because "the books that have enlightened me about Ulster have always been books about Ireland as a whole".[19] No socialist (as well as no regionalist), Ireland rejected 'Connolly the economic thinker', while declaring: "Connolly the patriot will live for ever."[20] Thus Connolly's choice of 1798 (let alone a conjectural Gaelic collective) as the cornerstone for an all-Ireland socialist edifice, does not understand the potential fissures within the tradition he claims.

One obvious fissure is religion: presumably Hewitt was an atheist by 1930 when he castigated the Pope's resolve to "pray for Russia", doubting his moral authority to "point/a jewelled finger at the Slav's disgrace". Like later references to Catholicism in Hewitt's poetry— "the lifted hand between the mind and truth"[21]—this shows how hard it is for an Ulster Protestant radical to tread the line between atheism or secularism and anti-Catholicism. Any 'superstition' destined to wither away is bound to have a popish aura. (This was true in 1798— and 1789.) However, the campaigns of "the Pope's brigade" were then alienating socialists and writers throughout Ireland. This is why MacNeice's 'Eclogue from Iceland' (1936) celebrates Connolly in a roll-call of "Soldiers of fortune, renegade artists, rebels and sharpers" who have kept the faith but lost the battle: "There was Connolly/ Vilified now by the gangs of Catholic Action." Catholic Action was an umbrella for para-religious groups, flourishing in the 20s and 30s, and part of Rome's wider anti-communist front, whose propaganda helped to ensure that Catholic doctrine would prevail in the institutions of the Free State.

A North Light spells out Hewitt's distaste for the republican-socialist axis. Looking back from the early 60s, he tells how he met fellow radicals in a Belfast pub, The Brown Horse, in 1937, and agreed to become literary editor of a new journal, the *Irish Democrat*. (He had long been contributing poems to leftist periodicals such as the *Irishman* and *Worker's Voice*.) His inaugural manifesto urged: "Proletarian writers of Ireland Unite! We must mobilise against War and fascism." Yet the unity of the *Democrat* itself fell apart after it began to be edited from London. Hewitt says:

> By means I have never been able to understand, *The Democrat* became the monthly organ of the Connolly Club, a Communist-inspired Irish Association in London, and continues to this day. It seems to me now an altogether deplorable production, its pages well padded with the words of sentimental Irish songs ... Wildly wrong in its interpretation of Irish affairs, foolishly supporting the reactionary IRA, lacking in frankness, blatantly opportunist, it has nothing to do with what we intended.

But he adds, movingly:

> Yet when, on the fringes of an open-air meeting in an English city, a young man with a thick brogue invites me to buy a copy, I always experience a momentary thrill of emotion for those far away days of the Left Book Club, The Popular Front, Aid for Spain, the snug in the Brown Horse, and take my copy and, turning its pages, rage at the betrayal of our dream.

The poetic corollary to all this can be traced in Hewitt's and MacNeice's similar reactions to *Goodbye, Twilight* (1936), an anthology edited by Leslie Daiken. Daiken's introduction attacks "the capitalist Free State", "Ireland's unregenerate manhood", "the *betrayal of the national aspirations by the Treaty of 1921*" (his italics), Joyce's "thorough-going isolation" and Yeats's "Twilight renaissance".[22] One of Hewitt's two reviews, while hankering after "a real sharp and singing contribution ... from the workers and peasants", runs into a conflict between Marxism and aesthetics:

> We recognise that no art can ... be entirely independent of its economic background ... But we will not submit to the crying down of Browning, say, as a middle-class tourist, or the crying up of 36 of these 40 poets as poets ... this book is ... final. Rockbottom.[23]

His review in the *Irish Democrat* queries the anthology's unitary subtitle—

Songs of the Struggle in Ireland. Because of "Too much weight on the Southern contributions", "the Irish Struggle becomes the Free State or Republican Struggle"; whereas "the Irish Struggle has many variations and is being fought out in Derry and Strabane, in Sandy Row and Short Strand."[24] Hewitt's keenest thrusts conflate stylistics and politics: "The old counters are proffered again and again ... Ireland's Dead, The People, The Name of Tone ... Dark Rosaleen." He remarks that the "majority of these poets, if they write from experience, must have spent the greater part of their lives at republican conventions".[25] Thus, despite his hostility to Yeats's politics, Hewitt accepts Yeats as the public voice to beat, rather than to be dispatched into the twilight zone: "If anyone can make poetry of the stuff of politics he can ... Stand on his shoulders, and there get your wider vision."[26]

MacNeice discusses *Goodbye, Twilight* in the chapter of *The Poetry of W.B. Yeats* (1941) which compares Yeats to contemporaries and successors, both Irish and English. From his own double vantage-point, and perhaps staking his own double claim, MacNeice too finds literary cliché and political contradiction:

> ... proletarian poetry will have to become a great deal less bourgeois; at the moment it relies upon clichés, and is trying to fight the bourgeois with his own discarded weapons ... Some of the poems ... are marked by a deliberate irreverence towards the Celtic renaissance ... such poems, being conditioned by Irish dislikes, are still specifically Irish. Other poems ... are the conventional utterance of the international working class ... Many, however, are still blatantly nationalistic and some are even devoutly Roman Catholic.[27]

Goodbye, Twilight irritates MacNeice and Hewitt into taking particularly fierce issue with the Marxist axiom that propaganda and literature are indistinguishable. Perhaps Irish factors, including the influence of Yeats, made it unlikely that either could ever endorse a wholly materialist account of poetry. Here and elsewhere MacNeice argues that poetry is conditioned, but not determined, by its socio-economic context: "The Marxist historian is ... employing bad logic if, having proved that poetry in any period is *conditioned* by the social and economic background, he goes on to assume that either the *cause* or the function or the end of poetry can be assessed in sociological or economic terms."[28] Today, *Goodbye, Twilight* seems 'dead as Brian Boru'.

III

Hewitt's nostalgia over the *Irish Democrat* proves that it can be difficult to draw clear boundaries between the pan-Irish, British, and Northern Irish 30s. Nevertheless, by the end of the 20s, a left-wing literary conscience was struggling to be born in the Ulster environment that MacNeice characterises in *Autumn Journal* XVI as "A culture built upon profit;/Free speech nipped in the bud". The mystical point of origin, the Helicon of protest, is usually identified as David (Davy) McLean's Progressive Bookshop, which opened in 1928. In 1929, Hewitt wrote a touchingly naive 'Sonnet for the Progressive Bookshop, 17 Union Street':

> This is the Mermaid Tavern of Belfast.
> The young men come to talk, argue and show
> brave lyrics to their friends. They seek to know
> how long the dark conspiracy will last
> that holds men chained to wheels embedded fast
> in old Tradition's bog.

Sam Hanna Bell recalled the unionist ethos at the time as "so cloying that almost anything came as a relief".[29] John Boyd writes that "we despised Belfast for its political and religious obscurantism", and that John Hewitt "was the centre of a small circle of left-wingers who thought the intellectual life of the city stagnant and who, by political action and thought, were trying to stir things up".[30] Boyd was a working-class scholarship boy from Ballymacarrett with trade union activists in his family. Hewitt had absorbed socialism from his father, a Methodist schoolteacher who admired James Larkin and Keir Hardie, and introduced his son to the English radical tradition. If Yeats owed his soul to William Morris, Hewitt owed to Morris the soul of his politics.

In his *juvenilia*, some of which can be found in Frank Ormsby's excellent edition of the *Collected Poems* (1991), Hewitt speaks as a revolutionary, rebel, Jacobin, anarchist, man with a secret mission, 'The Agitator in the Dock'. He discovered barricades before the 30s had got underway, and set out to champion the poor and unemployed. These verses scourge complacent unionists/Tories, such as the Duke of Abercorn opening the Stormont parliament in 1927, or the residents of 'Malone Park' (re-titled 'Aristocratic Area'): "There is one thing I mean to do:/When spring runs down this leafy length:/I'll gather in this avenue/The slum folk in their ragged strength." Even if he never kept this promise, Hewitt was not all talk. During the 30s, despite the energy that he put into his work at the Municipal Museum and Art Gallery (now the Ulster Museum and Art Gallery), he became an activist—indeed, hyper-activist: public speaker, committee-founder, manifesto-addict. By the end of the decade, he was lamenting that politics "devour the time/that I could better spend at rime": a couplet that makes its own point. For instance, Hewitt and his wife Roberta assisted the National Council for Civil Liberties with their investigation into the B-Specials. He says in *A North Light*: "Although we had no sort of sympathy with the gunmen, some of us considered that there were provisions in [the Special Powers Act] which diverged a long way from sound democratic practice, as, for instance, the authority to dispense with inquests in any given area." During the investigation, he became "acquainted with the nature of state authority and its techniques of the opened letter and the tapped telephone".[31]

Another cause was the Belfast Peace League, which the Hewitts helped to found, and of which Roberta became secretary. Hewitt's manifesto for the League includes a 30s waiting-for-the-end scenario: "Air raid on London and the Home Counties. Whitehall in ruins ... Gas fog stretches from Victoria to Piccadilly."[32] At the same time, he understood the "paradox" of "working for international peace [while] in my native city, Catholics were burnt out of the York Street area".[33] Hence *The Bloody Brae* (1936), his dramatised apology for planter blood-guilt. Besides doing his bit for civil rights and following global issues, he attended to the nitty-gritty of political action—watching out for anti-Catholic discrimination in the Gallery, befriending the manual workers there. He also had to defend art: against a curator who pandered to Unionist aldermen; and against a notorious Lord Mayor, Sir Crawford McCullagh, who ordered him to remove "disgusting" prints of Van Gogh and Monet from the walls of Belfast Castle.

If Hewitt might have shared such problems with aesthetes in Dublin, he shared others with comrades in Britain. Today when the British left has virtually cut its Ulster links, with the Labour Party nominating the nationalist SDLP (whose 'L' has been a dead letter since the departure of Paddy Devlin and Gerry Fitt) as its 'sister party', we forget the interpenetration that once existed. The Progressive Bookshop mustered 350 members of the Left Book Club: names reputed to be on RUC lists. The common interests of Lagan and Clyde generated much political traffic. When Hewitt met and liked James Maxton, leader of Red Clyde, at an Independent Labour Party Summer

School in Welwyn Garden City (1933), he had already heard Maxton speak several times at the Ulster Hall. Yet, crossing the water, Hewitt was apt to be disillusioned by more theoretical and literary socialists such as those who frequented a summer school run by John Middleton Murry. MacNeice, longer acclimatised, writes sardonically about "militant socialist" neighbours ("The word proletariat hung in festoons from the ceiling"), preferring his Birmingham students because, "coming from the proletariat themselves, they were conscious of the weaknesses of the Prolet-Cult".[34] Similarly, Hewitt preferred "the warmth and affection of fellowship and neighbourliness with the ILP at Welwyn" to Murry's "steaming fish tank of supercharged egos".[35]

The dream betrayed is a 30s narrative to which Hewitt's disappointments bring a Northern Irish accent. For MacNeice, resistant to 'slogans' and totalising claims, the poets' "great flirtation ... with the Third International"[36] had always harboured a suspect Romanticism. His poem 'To a Communist' (1933), possibly addressed to Anthony Blunt, warns:

> Your thoughts make shape like snow; in one night only
> The gawky earth grows breasts,
> Snow's unity engrosses
> Particular pettiness of stones and grasses.
> But before you proclaim the millenium, my dear,
> Consult the barometer—
> This poise is perfect but maintained
> For one day only.

But if MacNeice's eye for "Particular pettiness" now makes him look more politically intelligent than many of his contemporaries, it does not make him look conservative. He could be ironical about Blunt's switch of creeds from aestheticism to Marxism, yet respond to John Cornford as "the first inspiring communist I had met".[37] Years later Cornford's lover, Margot Heinemann, returned the compliment, when she urged that "though [MacNeice] is usually presented in surveys of the period as a 'sceptical liberal' in contra-distinction to the more radical and Marxist Auden, Spender and Day Lewis ... his work of the late thirties is if anything more 'political' than theirs".[38] In the later 30s, Hewitt was still radical, Marxist and activist, as international politics penetrated Belfast in the shape of Basque and Jewish refugees, and the imperatives of republican Spain. He wrote finely in *Irish Jewry*: "the Jew, who made German science distinguished, German music significant, German painting discussed, and German literature admired, is in exile, his books burnt, his apparatus smashed, his fiddle shattered in a thousand fragments."[39]

Hewitt's anti-fascism was more clear-sighted than his devotion to the Soviet Union—a dream that endured into the post-war period. MacNeice resembled George Orwell in being undeceived by "the Soviet myth" and in criticising its totalitarian and millenarian effects on English intellectuals. In *The Strings are False*, he attacks the Marxist who "finds it such fun practising strategy—i.e. hypocrisy, lying, graft, political pimping, tergiversation, allegedly necessary murder—that he forgets the end in the means ... Siberia fills with ghosts".[40] It can be no coincidence that he proceeds to an ironic précis of Anthony Blunt's political and artistic opinions. Judging by his ingenuous rebuke to the Pope, Hewitt began a romance with Russia in his early 20s. He also wrote 'A Chant for the Workers of the World on the 13th Anniversary of the Revolution', which has the regrettable chorus: "Shoulder to shoulder, woman and man,/Another heave for the five-year plan." In 1937 he praised the social-realist Soviet contributions to a touring exhibition of children's art, while condemning Finnish works as "escape into romance, adventure, or the supernatural". (The Winter War fills with ghosts.) "What troll," Hewitt asks, "is so grotesque and interesting as a blast furnace?" He tolerates "not particularly good" drawings (of the "Red Army ... children helping at socially necessary tasks ... collective"), because "one can't help feeling behind them the growing up of a new kind of man".[41] He should have trusted the political acuteness of his aesthetic sense. Hewitt was later to charge his friend John Luke, the Ulster painter, with too much emphasis on technique and a disappointing "lack of any comment, direct or indirect, on social relationships".[42] One might compare MacNeice's argument with Blunt over Diego Rivera.

Hewitt had already met (in 1936) George Orwell whom he calls, in *A North Light*, "the first man of the Left in my acquaintance who could have fairly been called Anti-Soviet". He continues with an apologia for himself and others: "while, from time to time, we learned things about the Russian régime which disturbed us, in so much as it seemed on the right side, that we felt public criticism was letting the side down, playing into the capitalists' hands". He then says that reports from Spain, about the behaviour of the communists to the anarchists, later made him and Roberta "more objective". Yet on 11th April, 1945, in a letter to Patrick Maybin, he condoned Soviet treatment of the Poles on the grounds that they were rooting out wartime corruption: "And so the Reds have had to clean up and so the Poles have yelled murder." More forgivably, he complained that, when Belfast was celebrating the European armistice, "somebody deliberately kept the supply of Red flags short—at most they flew on a few public buildings".

IV

If some dreams failed, the dynamics of the 30s produced the Welfare State. This dragged Stormont in its wake: both towards reform and towards new kinds of abuse. The literary energies of the decade also had consequences for Northern Ireland, influencing poetics and cultural ideology. If the utopianism of Hewitt and MacNeice can ultimately be seen as a displaced form of Protestant nationalism, it also stems from the intersection between the British 30s and the flawed political entities in Ireland. This intersection, which cuts two ways and may have implications for culture and poetry in the other island too, was itself subject to change during the years 1939-45.

World War II, spent by MacNeice (mainly) in London and by Hewitt in Belfast, redefined their concepts of the relation between poetry and society. In blitzed London, in "the bandaging dark which bound/This town together" ('Aftermath'), MacNeice found true community for the first (and last) time: a classless warmth that temporarily healed his deepest wounds. Before the war, *Autumn Journal* had raised—if only to dash—the Irish literary intellectual's perennial hope of doing "local work which is not at the world's mercy". During the war, MacNeice praised Orwell's meditation on Englishness, *The Lion and the Unicorn*, for its "insistence on *local* factors" as opposed to "the dogma of the pedants and the jargon of the arm-chair reformists"; and, in 1952, he criticised 30s "social consciousness" for promoting a "narrow and inhuman conception of society—a 'society' in which neither personal relationships (or at any rate the sense of family) nor regional loyalties nor religious ties should count".[43] Perhaps, in the 30s, the social thrust of his poetry had been really about reconceiving, in more collective terms, the local ties which centralised urban England was allowing to lapse—Raymond Williams' "knowable community". (This concern has been put to new tests in contemporary Northern Irish poetry.) MacNeice differs from Patrick Kavanagh as a democratiser of the Yeatsian sublime because he stresses 'community', rather than 'parish'—perceiving words themselves as a community-product. Despite its particularist virtues, the parish constitutes a nuclear model for poetry and society: one that assumes homogeneity and pre-modern forms of contract. 'Community', with its 30s nuance, is MacNeice's humanising of 'communism'. He agreed with the Marxist poet-critic Christopher Caudwell that "the instinctive ego of art is the common man into which we retire to establish communion with our fellows"[44]—the socialism of the poem, perhaps.

John Hewitt's war work was indeed local work. He tried, not very enthusiastically, to join up, but being in a reserved occupation found himself (like MacNeice in the BBC) aiding civil defence and the cultural wing of the war effort. Confinement to Northern Ireland incubated the philosophy of 'regionalism' which was to keep Hewitt—and others—going for 15 years and beyond. Yet Hewitt's writing had always contained a potentially regionalist substratum. It first came to the surface when, in the mid-30s, he gathered into one notebook all his verse featuring Ulster people, places, placenames and dialect. He called the sequence 'The Red Hand: a poemosaic' and gave it the epigraph: "How can I write of Ulster? Every word/I ever wrote has Ulster back of it." Patriotic emotion had been crystallised by an experience that Hewitt recounts in his poem 'The Return' (1935). A professional visit to Bristol, during which he was stirred by English local heritage, "a microcosm of England", had sensitised him to Ulster's own distinctiveness. 'The Return' links this revelation with a holiday spent on Rathlin Island at a time of international and local violence: Mussolini's invasion of Abyssinia, sectarian riots in Belfast. Here Hewitt records the kind of epiphany which Irish Protestant poets more often attach to a western island than one off the north coast: "islands are well-heads of the world's salvation". Like MacNeice's 'Western Landscape' (1945), the poem briefly grasps transcendence in "the lair of light", but moves back into history:

> Not once a social conscience troubled us.
> Leaning on rocks, or perched precarious
> on the stone walls between bare field and field,
> we let the free heart flutter ...
>
> But in the city of our dreadful night
> men fought with men because of a threadbare flag ...

Hewitt's knowledge of Ulster became deeper, more locally particular, as a result not only of renting a cottage in the Glens of Antrim, but of lecturing to troops stationed all over Northern Ireland. When Hitler attacked the Soviet Union, he was even conscripted to interpret the new ally: "And so the Marxist Dialectic was wafted from Ballymoney to Newry."[45] John Wilson Foster has argued that Hewitt's later position was "at best a radicalism stiffened by tradition and nostalgia into conservatism" and that his "30s socialism ... rings truer".[46] Hewitt's socialism did not end with the 30s, although his Marxism weakened. I would suggest that in the 40s he and others converted, rather than diverted, political aims and energies into cultural channels which might accelerate a progressive flow. Peadar O'Donnell said in 1942: "It is not really very important whether Belfast writers speak from the Stormont camp or from the Customs House steps: a Balzac would perhaps be more destructive than a Zola. What is vitally important is that Belfast writers should write. But they need more than a magazine. They need a full size literary movement."[47]

They were, at least, to get a magazine—*Lagan*, founded in 1943 by John Boyd, Sam Hanna Bell and Bob Davidson. *Lagan*, which lasted three years, always disclaimed other than modest beginnings. But its impulse if not its achievement was Balzacian, complementing Seán Ó Faoláin's ambition as founding editor of *The Bell* (in 1940) to "blueprint the society" rather than theorise about Irishness.[48] A prominent mode, as in *The Bell* and in 30s Britain, was the social-realist short story. John Boyd's editorials, while pleading against "'reportage' that tries too obviously to align us with a political group", keep social ends in view: "the struggle for a way of writing is part of the struggle for a way of life".[49] Besides impeding other traffic between north and south, the war made Dublin more distant as a literary capital. Meanwhile *literati* in the forces, such as Rayner Heppenstall and the Australian poet John Manifold, enlivened Belfast. But neither *Lagan* nor Hewitt's regionalism—the magazine's ideological engine—involved a declaration of literary separatism. *Lagan* was modelled on, not oppositional to, *The Bell*. One of the few Dublin-based organs to take an empirical interest in Ulster life, *The Bell* published Hewitt, MacNeice, Sam Hanna Bell, Thomas Carnduff (the shipyards poet and playwright) and other northern writers alongside Ó Faoláin and Hubert Butler. It sponsored debates about Protestantism and about the north. Peadar O'Donnell, Donegal man and socialist (also a somewhat erratic republican), was an important bridge. O'Donnell, who later became editor, understood the north better than Ó Faoláin, generous but sometimes inaccurate. Hewitt pays tribute to his friend O'Donnell in a poem which originally appeared in *The Bell* (July 1942): 'Calling on Peadar O'Donnell at Dungloe.'

Yet Ó Faoláin did stimulate Hewitt's regionalism on a partly oppositional basis—just as England had triggered his sense of Ulster. He was annoyed by Ó Faoláin's response to the north, and to the Museum and Art Gallery, in his book *An Irish Journey* (1940). In *A North Light*, Hewitt criticises Ó Faoláin's interesting assumption that exhibits such as "Viking ornaments, the inauguration chair of the O'Neill's ... a skeleton of the extinct Irish elk" must somehow be "foreign" to "the Six Counties". He remarks, for instance:

> Mr. O'Faolain could hardly be expected to know that in the entrance hall of almost every big house in the North the antlers of a great Irish deer dug out of an adjacent bog will hang opposite the half-length portrait of King William from the Kneller factory: by the first totem the family is making its assertion of Irishry, by the second of its membership of the Protestant Ascendancy.

But, on the other hand, Ó Faoláin's strictures provoked Hewitt into examining the deficiencies of cultural policy and cultural self-understanding in the north: "I was compelled to meditate more deeply and analytically on what the purpose and scope of our museum and art gallery should be, in the context of a split nation and divided allegiance." One of his first moves in the museum after the war was to "add a meagre halfcase illustrating the Social Life of the Handloom Weaver [and including] the tattered remnants of one old weaver's book of verse". The 'rhyming weavers', poets of the pre-industrial rural working class who wrote in the Ulster Scots vernacular, were to remain a touchstone for Hewitt. That he began his important work on them at this period suggests how socialism and regionalism were fusing in his imagination.

Hewitt's radical pantheon was augmented, rather than deposed, by new influences like Lewis Mumford, who warned of "apoplexy at the centre and paralysis at the extremities", or the geographer Estyn Evans who showed that "Ulster, even the Irish-Ulster, has its legacy of difference and individuality since the horned cairns were built".[50] However, writing to Patrick Maybin in 1945, he was unsure whether the Northern Ireland Labour Party had the capacity "to be the instrument for effecting my regionalist conception". Thus Hewitt set about effecting it himself, with all the energy he had formerly brought to socialist activism. In *A North Light*, he has the grace to quote the satire on his zeal in F.L. Green's Belfast novel *Odd Man Out*:

There was hardly a platform which [Griffin] could prevent himself from taking, and from which he theorised in a robust, crisp fashion. There was scarcely a stranger to the city who, coming to the North for information regarding its history, literature, drama, painting, politics, commerce, hopes, was not swiftly and adroitly contacted by Griffin and as swiftly loaded with facts. And, similarly, when a new artist or novelist, poet, politician, playwright, appeared from amongst the population, Griffin was there to study him from some vantage point and thereafter applaud him or dismiss him in a few theorising remarks.[51]

'Freehold', Hewitt's verse-manifesto for regionalism (written in 1944-46), presses several vocabularies into its utopian prospectus:

Mine is historic Ulster, battlefield
of Gael and Planter, certified and sealed
by blood, and what is stronger than blood,
by images and folkways understood
but dimly by the wits, yet valid still
in word and gesture, name of house or hill ...
But there is much to do before our pride
can move with mercy in its equal stride;
wet fields to drain, bare hills to plant with trees,
and power to gather from the plunging seas
and sprawling rivers, sagging walls to shore,
lost acres to resume, and skills restore,
and towns to trim to decency—and more,
bright halls for art and music, rambling parks
not fenced or gravelled by some board of works,
and simple trades to nurture, till again
potter and miller are familiar men ...

The trace elements here include Estyn Evans, the Protestant work ethic, the rationales of planter and commissar, progressivist machine-socialism, nostalgic craft-socialist, post-war reconstruction, Thomas Davis and Young Ireland, even blood and soil. But for all its contradictions, for all its primary focus on cultural definitions that night serve the Ulster Protestant, Hewitt's new way of thinking about the north rephrases the political impasse which had blocked socialist advance: "Wales and Scotland are, after all, well-defined geographical and national entities ... Where then does Ulster stand? After all, we have a frontier. What then of Donegal?"[52] The cultural-political vista that opens up at the end of 'Regionalism: The Last Chance' (1947) is being revisited and revised 40 years on:

> Ulster, considered as a region and not as the symbol of any particular creed, can, I believe, command the loyalty of every one of its inhabitants. For regional identity does not preclude, rather it requires, membership of a larger association. And, whether the association be, as I hope, of a federated British Isles, or a Federal Ireland, out of that loyalty to our own place, rooted in honest history, in familiar folkways and knowledge, phrased in our own dialect, there should emerge a culture and an attitude individual and distinctive, a fine contribution to the European inheritance and no mere echo of the thought and imagination of another people and another land.[53]

But, in 1953, Hewitt missed an important chance to implement his vision when unionist intrigue denied him the directorship of the museum. This was largely due to his 'communist' opinions. In the same year, he published 'The Colony', which translates his cultural meditations into his most sophisticated poetic model of Ulster politics. The poem permits itself one utopian simile: "as goat and ox may graze the same field/and each gain something from proximity".

Regionalism, the quest for "a native mode", certainly improved on textbook socialism as a stimulus to Hewitt's poetry. But he had never been *only* a man of the left—hence, perhaps, John Wilson Foster's remark about conservatism—always evincing the holistic ambition of Belfast's Victorian polymaths. Hewitt refers to "my thought" as to something more organic and moral than theoretical. His copiousness and didacticism smack of the 19th century as well as the 30s. To the detriment of art, he generally had something to say. As Foster shows[54], another ancestral prompter must be Methodism. Vivian Mercier has analysed the evangelical origins of the Irish Literary Revival, and a similar missionary spirit links the Hewitt who urged proletarian writers to mobilise, with the Hewitt who tried to enthuse Ulster Young Farmers about their poetic heritage in a journal otherwise devoted to flax policy. Behind both incarnations lurks Alexander Irvine, the Antrim-born preacher, social-reformer and writer. Irvine, in Hewitt's words, "had exposed the outrages of the chain-gangs in the Southern States [and] ... stood shoulder to shoulder with Jack London"[55]—an unusually attractive 'Scotch Irish' exemplar. Hewitt, in the early 30s, was inspired first by a sermon of Irvine's, then by a controversial speech at the Labour Hall celebrating "the agitator Christ, and the communism of the early disciples".[56] Then there was a private occasion when Irvine told him that in Ulster "Someone was needed to say unpopular things, to maintain the imperilled values". Hewitt turned this episode into a short story called 'The Laying on of Hands'.[57]

From the mid 40s, a small number of cultural missionaries were at work in various savage quarters—for instance, Sam Hanna Bell and John Boyd in the BBC. Although Hewitt later abandoned regionalism as a coherent theory, it served or caught its time. There are some artistic and intellectual continuities, including Seamus Heaney's attention to the regionalist era. When Hewitt reviewed Heaney's *Death of a Naturalist* in 1966, he employed the value-terms of his regionalist aesthetic: "actual ... grounded ... concrete ... firm ... spare", and related Heaney to Ulster writers like Michael MacLaverty and Peadar O'Donnell who "inhabit the same region of our national feeling".[58] Hewitt has been castigated for (in 'The Bitter Gourd') nominating Protestant New England as a regional role-model. Yet, he possibly guided Heaney towards Robert Frost.

At this point, MacNeice may seem to have fallen out of the frame. Indeed, his flat *Autumn Sequel* (1954) contrasts with the evangelical conviction of 'Freehold'. Both these long poems celebrate friends and creative spirits, but the former fails to locate any larger "knowable community". What Hewitt criticised as MacNeice's lack of 'roots' may finally show in his inability to reanimate the unifying communitarian impulse of *Autumn Journal* or his wartime poetry. Yet MacNeice's legacy to his Northern Irish successors had not become wholly aesthetic, in that the Kafkaesque world of his last dark parables reflects the politics of the BBC in London and Belfast. MacNeice took a hand in the three-year fight to get Sam Thompson's *Over the Bridge* on to the stage: a juncture where culture and politics effectively reunited and won a famous victory over the unionist establishment which had attempted to suppress the play. Thompson, the working-class socialist who shattered unionist censorship in a way from which it never quite recovered, was encouraged (to write for the BBC) by Sam Hanna Bell. He was also guided by Bell's friend the literary lawyer and socialist, Martin McBirney, later assassinated by the IRA. John Hewitt had taught Thompson in a WEA Class. It was MacNeice who had recruited Bell for the BBC. MacNeice consistently used his own clout in the London Features Department to fortify Bell and Boyd in their constructive subversion of the unionist grip on BBC Northern Ireland. Douglas Carson has said of these two producers: "together they democratised local radio."[59] *Over the Bridge*, which could not have existed without this left-wing literary milieu, without the Progressive Bookshop and all that, was used by unionists opposed to Lord Brookeborough (whom the scandal weakened) in their campaign to replace him with Terence O'Neill. And we know to what that led.

Douglas Carson, in a lecture partly based on conversations with Sam Hanna Bell, has shown how MacNeice's support for *Over the Bridge* preceded the review in which he greeted it as a revival of the 30s spirit: "a play *about* something. Social consciousness seems to have become, among the younger generation, a dirty phrase [so] it is very refreshing to encounter a work such as this which reaffirms the eternal commonplaces of the misery—and the dignity—of man."[60] *Over the Bridge*, originally scheduled for production at the Belfast Group Theatre in 1957, was dropped when a member of the theatre's board of management set the alarm bells ringing at Stormont. The same man was Head of Programmes at BBC Northern Ireland. In Carson's words:

> The result was the famous battle which lasted three years. Most of the Group company resigned. Thompson sued the management. They settled out of court, but controversy raged in the press and at Stormont.
> Behind the scenes Sam Hanna Bell was working for Thompson. MacNeice was less inhibited and took Thompson's side openly.
> The BBC was not well pleased ... [61]

Unlike MacNeice, Hewitt lived to rethink his politics and cultural politics in the context of Northern Ireland after October 1968. 'The Coasters', written in 1969 and published in *An Ulster Reckoning* (1971), has unique authority to tell the unionist middle class 'I told you so':

> Now the fever is high and raging;
> who would have guessed it, coasting along?
> The ignorant-sick thresh about in delirium
> and tear at the scabs with dirty fingernails.
> The cloud of infection hangs over the city,
> a quick change of wind and it
> might spill over the leafy suburbs.
> You coasted too long.

This eerily echoes Hewitt's 'Malone Park' of 40 years before. Here, too, a characteristic trope of the 30s—metaphors of physical and psychic illness—finds a belated occasion. Hewitt's coasters have also ignored his early warning of Protestant crisis in 'The Colony'. "Sure that Caesar's word/is Caesar's bond", most 'colonists' do not see the need to "convince/my people and this land we are changed/from the raw levies which usurped the land ..." In 1986, Hewitt published *Freehold and Other Poems*. This collection reprinted (for the first time in book-form) both 'The Bloody Brae', product of the pessimistically political

30s, and the title poem, product of the optimistically cultural 40s. In his preface to *An Ulster Reckoning*, Hewitt ruefully recalls "an apparent softening of the hard lines and a growing tolerance between the two historic communities". *Freehold* also juxtaposes two poems which suggest how cultural visions must accept the reality and challenge of political forces. 'Ulster Names', written in 1950, proclaims the regionalist spirit: "I take my stand by the Ulster names,/each clean hard name like a weathered stone." Its dark twin, 'Postscript, 1984', lists:

> Banbridge, Ballykelly, Darkley, Crossmaglen,
> summoning pity, anger and despair,
> by grief of kin, by hate of murderous men
> till the whole tarnished map is stained and torn,
> not to be read as pastoral again.

Two complementary poems by Hewitt and MacNeice can be interpreted as epitaphs or elegies for their own literary-political endeavours, and for the utopianism of a generation. Hewitt's 'A Local Poet' (1975), which again revises and darkens an earlier text, measures the distance between ambition and achievement:

> He followed their lilting stanzas
> through a thousand columns or more,
> and scratched for the splintered couplets
> in the cracks on the cottage floor,
> for his Rhyming Weavers fell silent
> when they flocked through the factory door.

Besides regretting the failure of literature to unite weavers, factory-workers and the 'mannerly' middle-class poet, the poem—perhaps Hewitt's best—registers the obduracy of the political "problems and cleavages"[62] that had been his starting point:

> He'd imagined a highway of heroes
> and stepped aside on the grass
> to let Cuchullain's chariot through,
> and the Starry Ploughmen pass;
> but he met the Travelling Gunman
> instead of the Galloglass.

MacNeice's 'Epitaph for Liberal Poets' (1942) foresees the obsolescence of free thought, the death of the individual and the poet, the triumph of "Those who shall supersede us and cannot need us—/The tight-lipped technocratic Conquistadores". Yet, MacNeice did not cease to question and resist the Conquistadores, any more than Hewitt ever relinquished his local burdens.

Notes

[1] Sam Hanna Bell, *The Hollow Ball* (London, 1961; Belfast 1990), pp. 143–4.
[2] Published in the *Northman* 2, p. 6 (June 1930).
[3] Note to *Awake! and other Poems* (London, 1941); quoted by John Hewitt in 'The Bitter Gourd: Some Problems of the Irish Writer' (1945), reprinted in *Ancestral Voices: The Selected Prose of John Hewitt*, edited by Tom Clyde (Belfast, 1987), p. 119.
[4] Louis MacNeice, *I Crossed the Minch* (London, 1938), p. 125.
[5] Valentine Cunningham, *British Writers of the Thirties* (Oxford, New York, 1988), p. 33.
[6] *British Writers of the Thirties*, p. 218; pp. 358–9.
[7] John Hewitt, 'No Rootless Colonist' (1972), *Ancestral Voices*, p. 149.
[8] Henry Patterson, *Class Conflict and Sectarianism* (Belfast, 1980), p. 149.
[9] Letter to Patrick Maybin, 11th February, 1942.
[10] See Foreword to *Labour in Irish History* (Dublin, 1910), p. xxx.
[11] *Labour in Irish History*, pp. xxx–xxxi.
[12] Seán Ó Faoláin, *The Bell* 9, 3 (December 1944), p. 190.
[13] *The Bell* 4, 6 (September 1942), p. 392.
[14] Patterson, *Class Conflict and Sectarianism*, p. 148.
[15] Hewitt, *Ancestral Voices*, p. 150.
[16] On a TV discussion, chaired by Tariq Ali, in which he defended the *Field Day Anthology* against Irish feminists, July 1992. Paulin's collection *Liberty Tree* (1983) celebrates the 'dissenting green' and 'rebel minds' of the Presbyterian United Irishmen.
[17] In conversation with the author.
[18] 'James Hope, Weaver, of Templepatrick' Hewitt, *Ancestral Voices*, p. 137. Originally published in *Northern Star* 2, 2 (April 1941).
[19] *The Bell* 4, 4 (July 1942), p. 251.
[20] Denis Ireland, *Six Counties in Search of a Nation: Essays and Letters on Partition* (Belfast, 1947), p. 68. For a portrait of Denis Ireland see John Boyd, *The Middle of My Journey* (Belfast, 1990), pp. 20–2.
[21] The original text of a line from 'The Glens' (1942), which now reads "the lifted hand against unfettered thought". Hewitt changed the line after realising that it was "arrogant" and "gave offence to kindly and gentle Catholics". See Frank Ormsby, *The Collected Poems of John Hewitt* (Belfast, 1992), p. 626.

[22] *Goodbye, Twilight*, edited by Leslie Daiken (London, 1936), Introduction, pp. xii–xvi.
[23] *Forum*, supplement to *Irish Jewry* (January 1937).
[24] Another review of *Goodbye, Twilight*, *Irish Democrat* (? 1937).
[25] *Forum*, supplement to *Irish Jewry* (January 1937).
[26] *Forum*, supplement to *Irish Jewry* (January 1937).
[27] Louis MacNeice: *The Poetry of W.B. Yeats* (London, 1941, 1967), p. 186.
[28] *The Poetry of W.B. Yeats* (London, 1941, 1967), p. 184.
[29] In conversation with the author.
[30] John Boyd, *Out of My Class* (Belfast, 1985), p. 147, p. 177.
[31] *North Light* MS; 'No Rootless Colonist', *Ancestral Voices*, p. 151.
[32] 'The Peace League', *Northman* 2, 3 (Autumn 1934), p. 20.
[33] 'No Rootless Colonist', *Ancestral Voices*, p.151.
[34] Louis MacNeice, *The Strings are False* (London, 1965), p. 134, p. 154.
[35] 'Adelphi Centre', *North Light* MS.
[36] MacNeice, *The Strings are False*, p.146.
[37] *The Strings are False*, p. 157.
[38] Margot Heinemann, 'Louis MacNeice, John Cornford and Clive Branson: Three Left-Wing Poets', in *Culture and Crisis in Britain*, edited by Jon Clark *et al* (London, 1979), p 110.
[39] *Forum*, supplement to *Irish Jewry* (January 1937).
[40] MacNeice, *The Strings are False*, p.161.
[41] *Forum*, supplement to *Irish Jewry* (January 1937).
[42] 'The War Years II', *North Light* MS.
[43] 'London Letter 4', in *Selected Prose of Louis MacNeice* Edited by Alan Heuser (Oxford, 1990), p. 127; 'Notes on the Way' *Selected Prose*, p. 180.
[44] Christopher Caudwell, *Illusion and Reality: A Study in the Sources of Poetry* (London, 1991), p. 155.
[45] 'The War Years', *North Light* MS.
[46] John Wilson Foster, 'The Dissidence of Dissent', in *Colonial Consequences* (Dublin, 1991), p. 120.
[47] *The Bell* 4, 6 (September 1942), p. 392.
[48] Editorial: *The Bell* 4, 6 p. 381.
[49] Editorials: *Lagan* 3 (1945), p. 11; *Lagan* 1 (1943), p. 6.
[50] Quoted in 'Regionalism: The Last Chance', *Ancestral Voices*, p. 123; 'The Bitter Gourd', *Ancestral Voices*, p. 120. Hewitt was profoundly influenced by E. Estyn Evans's *Irish Heritage* (Dundalk, 1942).
[51] F.L. Green, *Odd Man Out* (London, 1945), pp. 187–8
[52] 'The Bitter Gourd', *Ancestral Voices*, p. 108.
[53] 'Regionalism: The Last Chance', *Ancestral Voices*, p. 125. For one update of Hewitt's ideas, see John Wilson Foster, 'Radical Regionalism', *Colonial Consequences*, pp. 278–95.
[54] In '"The Dissidence of Dissent": John Hewitt and W. R. Rodgers', *Colonial Consequences*, pp. 114–132.

[55]See 'Alec of the Chimney Corner', *Honest Ulsterman* 4 (August 1968), pp. 5–12 (p. 7): an extract from *A North Light*.
[56]*Honest Ulsterman* 4 (1968), p. 7.
[57]*Honest Ulsterman* 4 (August 1968), p. 9; and see *The Bell* 16, 1 (April 1948), pp. 27–36.
[58]*Belfast Telegraph*, 19th May, 1966.
[59]In a lecture 'Caliban and Ariel: Louis MacNeice and the BBC', John Hewitt International Summer School, July 1991.
[60]Louis MacNeice, review of *Over the Bridge, Observer*, 31st January, 1960, p. 23.
[61]Douglas Carson, lecture at John Hewitt International Summer School, July 1991.
[62]"Ulster's position in this island involves us in problems and cleavages for which we can find no counterpart elsewhere in the British archipelago", 'The Bitter Gourd', *Ancestral Voices*, p. 109.

The Fate of 'Identity'
John Hewitt, W.R. Rodgers and Louis MacNeice

Peter McDonald

The brief Foreword to John Hewitt's *Collected Poems 1932-1967* (1968) covers more ground than is usual for such preliminaries: along with the customary obligations of acknowledgement, its four short paragraphs map out in miniature a journey that the book itself will go on to describe. There is, centrally in the Foreword, the modest adequacy of Hewitt's self-description—"by birth, an Irishman of Planter stock, by profession an art gallery man, politically a man of the Left"[1]— which properly owns up to, and helps to account for, the first-person voice prominent in so many of the poems. But the identity given this shorthand delineation is not fixed in one place: some of the poems, Hewitt informs the reader, "originated in frequent sojourns in the Glens of north-east Antrim". Finally, the journeying goes beyond "sojourns" to residence in "the English Midlands" where, the poet tells us, he "settled" in "the spring of 1957". The trajectory thus plotted from one settlement to another is strangely mirrored by Hewitt's account of the movements of the poems themselves: "a number figure in about two dozen anthologies, British and American", "some have found place in textbooks", "Half a dozen ... have travelled farthest and have been used most often". What might appear at first no more than meticulous book-keeping seems eventually to record a long journey away from points of origin.

Hewitt's Foreword, with its careful indications of ground travelled, prepares the way for the *Collected Poems* itself, with its journey from 'Ireland', the first piece in the book, towards the last, 'To Piraeus', its title both directional and foreign. Between these two points, there is the poetry of sojourn, of exploration, of ideological engagement; and that of departure, exile, disengagement and disillusion. The poetic voice, with the stated instincts and beliefs that seem to give it an identity, is remarkably constant throughout, testing its changing surroundings against measured and steady convictions. 'Ireland' (dated, by Hewitt, 1932) begins by speaking, with forced confidence, as "We Irish", but the poem's voice soon discovers that "We are not native here or anywhere", finishing with intimations of departure[2]:

> So we are bitter, and are dying out
> in terrible harshness in this lonely place,
> and what we think is love for usual rock,
> or old affection for our customary ledge,
> is but forgotten longing for the sea
> that cries far out and calls us to partake
> in his great tidal movements round the earth.

It is appropriate, then, that the *Collected Poems* should end at sea—another sea, the Aegean—this time in the company of "a strong small barrel-built man" who takes out "his tasselled string of beads" to pray after lunch. So Hewitt ends the poem, and the book, by escaping from solitude, mobile, and ready to move on further still: "I would feel safe/ travelling to the moon with him."[3]

The parabola described in *Collected Poems 1932-1967* is scarcely in line with the better-known formulations of Hewitt's regionalism: if its travels are those of "a *rooted* man"[4], then he is rooted in something other than place. Hewitt's embarkation upon a second phase of his poetic career after the publication of this book can obscure the fact that the 1968 *Collected Poems* is organised so as to display a process of engagement and disengagement, placing and displacement which, in its way, entombs the regionalist enterprise with which the poet's name is so commonly associated. It is clear that Hewitt's later poetry often revisits the grave of regionalism, but only to replay obsequies, not to witness or wait for some authentic resurrection. It should be added, however, that the failure of this particular complex of ideas does not vitiate such success as Hewitt's poetry achieves; in fact, it forms a necessary component of that success, and is even perhaps its inevitable condition.

The connotations of 'failure' in political discourse, or that of ideas in general, are harsh ones; but in poetry the 'failure' of an idea, project, or group of beliefs, can lay bare unexpected and imaginatively fertile areas. This article will address some aspects of the works of three poets—Hewitt himself, W.R. Rodgers, and Louis MacNeice, all of them born in the north of Ireland and all members of the generation which came to maturity in the 30s—with an eye to the possibilities of 'failure'. It is necessary to take particular account of the formation, in the post-war years, of a literary idea of 'identity' in Ulster, the different kinds of testing this idea undergoes in the work of the three poets, and the implications of certain failures that result from such engagements. The journey represented in—and by—Hewitt's 1968 *Collected Poems* shows how poetry survives the failure of ideas; the ideas are, in any case, not destinations, but staging-posts in the kinds of journey good poetry has to make. Rodgers and MacNeice also, in their different ways, engage and disengage from notions of allegiance, place, and identity. Moreover, all three poets are of a generation for whom ideas of solidarity, often expressed in political terms, were significant pressures. If MacNeice encountered such pressures early, in the various imperatives of the British intellectual left of the 30s, the experiences of Hewitt, himself "a man of the Left", later form, in the mixed fortunes of regionalism, a suggestive parallel. Both traditions, that of the intellectual left and that of Ulster regionalism, are tenacious of influence; but it could be argued that both are now imaginatively sterile, subjects of primarily historical interest. I want to examine here the question of how far, or how effectively, the poetry of Hewitt, Rodgers, and MacNeice contrives to outlive certain ideas surrounding it, and to ask how usefully this process of survival can inform an understanding of Northern Irish culture in the future.

Writing under the double cover of anonymity and the dialogue form, W.R. Rodgers contributed a 'Conversation Piece' to *The Bell* in 1942, in which the identity of the Ulster Protestant was up for discussion. When he uses the term "racial difference" to describe the situation, one of the dialogue's two voices is pulled up and made to explain the phrase[5]:

> It is a convenient term by which I refer to that backward pull of custom and forward pluck of morality, that common fund and accumulation of interest which makes the character of a group of people distinctive. The racial difference is, I think, fundamental to an understanding of Ulster.

W.J. McCormack has cited this as one of the "disturbing invocations of 'race' and 'rootedness' even among writers who were otherwise notably and courageously liberal"[6] that occur tellingly in the work of Irish Protestants; yet Rodgers' statement (or, more properly, his representation of a possible statement) is part of a 'liberalism' with a poetic rather than a political agenda. The existence of a validating source of a regional ('radical') identity is precisely in the nature of a 'common fund' for Rodgers, enabling him to subsidise his own creative bargaining between 'pull' and 'pluck', melodic comfort and staccato urgency, romantic reassurance and individual unease. For Rodgers, a common 'character' has to exist in order to give meaning to the poet's departures from, or heightenings of, its available orthodoxies and distinguishing traits. Even so, the division between 'pull' and 'pluck' in Rodgers' poetry is a severe one, often expressed violently, and is an internal rift which he cannot finally close. When, later in the 'Conversation Piece', the proposition is made that "We are really a 'split' people, we Protestant Ulstermen", Rodgers' simplistic division of allegiances ("Our eyes and thoughts are turned towards England, but our hearts and feet are in Ulster") relies upon oppositions his own poetry embodies.[7] Identity (or 'character') for Ulster is therefore poetically necessary for Rodgers; in its implications it is also, we should remember, necessarily poetical.

"Oh this division of allegiance!"[8], Louis MacNeice's more than half ironic exclamation, roughly contemporaneous with Rodgers' 'Conversation Piece', seems to sum up a perceived problem which the ideas of Ulster regionalism also tried to address. In his 1947 article, 'Regionalism: The Last Chance', John Hewitt emphasises the subsidy offered to the individual artist by this common fund of regional identity, a solution which, although it begins with the individual, must immediately pass beyond the individual and react upon the community".[9] Again, there is some ambiguity involved in the argument: does regionalism give birth to the individual artist, or does the artist create for his community the viable concept of regionalism? Hewitt's definition of 'the region' does not greatly help in this respect:

> ... an area which possesses geographical and economic coherence, which has had some sort of traditional and historical identity and which still, in some measure, demonstrates cultural and linguistic individuality.[10]

As a practical, or broadly speaking a political definition, this is fatally flawed: Hewitt smooths over some very rough patches of analysis with his "some sort of" and "some measure".[11] As would become apparent, the gap between artist and community, so quickly bridged in Hewitt's definitions, was more difficult to close than the post-war enthusiasm would admit. Like Rodgers, Hewitt engages himself in creating a 'common fund' to back his own poetic enterprises, a source of deep unity that will give coherence and significance to the departures and innovations of the artist. As in his poetry, so in his arguments for regionalism, Hewitt returns again and again to the tropes of stability, rootedness, and community; but again, as in the poetry, his arguments for these things, and his habitual attraction towards them, serve also to intimate how far they are from successful realisation. Like the smoothness of his favoured pentameters, Hewitt's regionalist analysis tends often to reach its conclusions by loading certain points with more stress than they will easily bear.

It is true, however, that Hewitt's poetry cultivates from the start a certain feeling for distances. Sometimes, the poet chooses to present these as gaps between urban and rural identities, as in 'O Country People'[12]:

> I recognise the limits I can stretch;
> even a lifetime among you should leave me strange,
> for I could not change enough, and you will not change;
> there'd still be levels neither'd ever reach.

This recognition of limits, an intuition of levels of community out of reach of the individual speaking voice, comes later to condition Hewitt's judgement of the regionalist project as a whole. In a sense, the poetry's feeling for 'limits' operated substantially in advance of Hewitt's prose arguments that tried to 'stretch' over too great a gap between self and region, the individual and a 'common fund' of identity. Late interviews offer the poet's final perspectives on such questions, treating them, with the benefit of hindsight, as in some ways historically conditioned:

> I became a regionalist in my thinking during the war years. That was important because the North of Ireland was cut off from England ... So we were different and I thought this emphasised our difference and identity ... but I was wrong. Ulster is not one region, it's several regions ... My concept of regionalism was trying to bring together incompatible pieces.[13]
>
> I thought that if we could establish a regional consciousness for the north of Ireland it would give us something to cling to, a kind of key to our identity ... I did a lot of agitation with no result whatsoever.[14]

If this sounds like a meditation on failure, we should bear in mind that the artistically fruitful meditations had taken place much earlier, in the fabric and design of Hewitt's own poetry—notably in the very shape made by the 1968 *Collected Poems*, its brooding on the significance of place counterpointed by the explicit mobility and constant displacement of the poetic voice. Late in that volume, in one of his sequence of poems set in Greece, Hewitt waits in the ancient theatre at Epidauros[15]:

> But only near the dark green grove
> with the pine-scent and the light airs
> among the fronded fans,
> was I somehow strangely at home,
> receiving, open, myself;

Here, "the limits I can stretch" have become unexpectedly and rewardingly wide; the poet can be "strangely at home" while simply "myself", unrooted, without region or community. Stretched open like this, Hewitt's poetic identity can travel away from its geographical starting-points for a fresh "sojourn". But this freedom, with which the poet brings his *Collected Poems* to a close, is something quite distinct from "some sort of traditional and historical identity which still, in some measure, demonstrates cultural and linguistic individuality"; here, it has no agenda, and it "demonstrates" nothing, but what it achieves is a kind of autonomy, freeing the self to become "receiving, open" rather than constant and confined.

This is not to imply that Hewitt's poetic successes should make us treat lightly his later expressions of disappointment and disillusion: the failures of regionalism are real, and they matter—especially so at a time when some of the terminology of the ideas, notably the recourse to 'identity', is still kept in circulation. Hewitt's struggle with the "incompatible pieces", carried out "with no result whatsoever", exercises a persistent fascination in the context of contemporary Northern Ireland: the stubborn materials to which the poet applied himself are still present, still problematic, and still susceptible of regionalist analysis. John Wilson Foster's proposals for 'Radical Regionalism', almost half a century on from the beginnings of Hewitt's ideas, announce their programme clearly enough and acknowledge freely their affinities with earlier schemes.[16] And yet, whatever their merits or demerits, such cultural agendas hope for much more in the way of definable 'identity' in Ulster than Hewitt, for one, was able ever to smooth out from that rough, uneven, and recalcitrant matter. For the purposes of neo-regionalist arguments, John Hewitt is a poet of a certain breed, who performs an identifiable function. In John Wilson Foster's reading, for example, "it is precisely because his Irishness is problematical that Hewitt's worrying of the matter for decades has enabled him to forge the conscience of the Scots-Irish in Ireland, and that may be his chief significance".[17] Similarly, for Roy Foster, it is Hewitt "who articulated that quintessential combination of Protestant scepticism and commitment, linked with a sense of place that was absolutely Irish."[18] The language of formulations like these—"the conscience of the Scots-Irish", "that quintessential combination", "absolutely Irish"—relies upon an underlying acceptance of the possibility, and the desirability, of working concepts of 'identity' (OED: "absolute or essential sameness; oneness", "The sameness of a person or thing at all times or in all circumstances"). However, such judgements approach the poetry with too little caution: as literary criticism, they offer too easy an assessment, importing the categories of broad description into a body of work which finds such categories ultimately unworkable. The question is not whether neo-regionalist appropriations of Hewitt are part of an otherwise unjustifiable cultural agenda, but whether their discourse of 'identity' can survive its being set in context by literary history and criticism.

It may be useful to compare this situation with another context that runs parallel to Ulster regionalism, that of the British poets of the 30s generation. Hewitt and Rodgers, no less than MacNeice, could be said to belong here: it was W.H. Auden's poetry, for example, which both influenced the apprentice Hewitt in the 30s and inspired much of Rodgers' earlier work, as well as setting the terms and challenges for a good deal of MacNeice's writing of the period. The apparent flirtation of a number of poets at the time with left-wing politics has always tempted critics into political rather than literary judgements, regardless of the resistance to such analysis put up by much of the poetry under discussion. Here, again, there is the importation of fundamentally inappropriate categories: notwithstanding several excellent works of literary history which have begun to clear away the rubble of dogma and myth from the poetry of Auden and others, it was still possible in 1991 for a critic to remark ruefully that "In the political and aesthetic ideologies of the poets ... nowhere have we encountered any sustained attempt to develop a Marxist poetic or a Marxist poetry"[19]. The critic goes on to find what he is looking for in some obscure corners which have been neglected, of course, through the literary bias of literary criticism. Yet the critic's own bias prevents him from considering the fact that developing a 'Marxist poetry' might be rather like cultivating Marxist flower-arranging or golf—a purely speculative theoretical perversity, with no real bearing on the activity in question. The manifest inadequacy of this kind of critical approach (which must label MacNeice, regretfully, as "a conservative, liberal, individualist"[20] and, therefore, much over-rated by the bourgeois literary establishment) seems anachronistic; it is speaking the language of the *Left Review* 50 years too late. But there is a very similar inadequacy in attempts at critical neo-regionalism, a parallel importation of unsuitable criteria and categories. The fact that abstract constructions like "the conscience of the Scots-Irish" or the "quintessential combination of Protestant scepticism and commitment" are commonly granted plausibility, whereas 'a Marxist poetry' can no longer claim any real currency, tends to obscure what is a fundamental affinity. And yet, if we are to reject the confusion of ideology and value in left-wing critical attempts to re-read the British 30s, we should be equally wary of the blurring of the line between value and 'identity' which is prevalent in neo-regionalist approaches to Hewitt and his generation in Ulster.

Despite all this, it is extremely difficult to avoid discussion of 'identity' when dealing with Hewitt's poetry, or indeed with that of Rodgers or MacNeice; very often, the poets implicitly acknowledge the presence of the concept in their work. It is possible, however, to trace the fortunes and influence of the idea in their poetry without conferring on notions of 'identity' any literary or cultural value. It is worth noting, firstly, that MacNeice was often found wanting in identity by regionalists themselves[21]: the article of faith that, in John Boyd's formulation of 1943, "no writer, however talented, should uproot himself in spirit from his native place"[22], made unlikely MacNeice's acceptance as anything other than a sapless hybrid by the Hewitt circle. "There is little in either his work or his outlook to identify him as an Ulsterman," wrote J.N. Browne in the 1951 *The Arts in Ulster: A Symposium*, "and the influences which have moulded him have not been the regional ones."[23] The same critic suffered no such difficulties when he went on to contemplate in Hewitt's verse "the wholesome, nourishing grain that makes us think, somehow, of wheaten bread."[24] By the same token, the fluffy *patisserie* of Rodgers' poetry was insufficiently substantial for regionalist appetites, though not so indigestible as MacNeice's 'English' ingredients. If, then, both MacNeice and Rodgers engage with notions of 'identity' in their writing, it does not follow that this 'identity' is necessarily the same concern as that central to regionalist analysis (one might also, though with more caution, make this same point in relation to some of the poetry of Hewitt himself). A second consideration should be that, although all three poets find uses for 'identity', their poetry also tests the concept, turning it sometimes in unexpected directions and, on occasion, fracturing it altogether: it is neither an unquestioned good, nor an end in itself.

When he fell back on the *cliché* of "a 'split' people" to describe 'Protestant Ulstermen', W.R. Rodgers had in mind an 'identity' clearly distinct from "sameness ... at all times or in all circumstances". In negotiating his own 'identity' in poetry, Rodgers is similarly divided between 'pull' and 'pluck', as for example in the first lines of 'Ireland'[25]:

> O these lakes and all gills that live in them,
> These acres and all legs that walk on them,
> The tall winds and the wings that cling to them,
> Are part and parcel of me, bit and bundle,
> Thumb and thimble. Them I am ...

There is something outlandish about this putting-on of a composite identity, or at least a degree of licence which the poetry, with (as so often in Rodgers) its slightly irritating verbal play, simply has not earned. Rodgers' feeling that his poetry comes from "a clash between two opposites" is relevant here; but one notices that, as all too often, words, imagery, and ideas do not 'clash', but stage a mild disagreement, reconciled both by the poet's musical command and his first-person authority—"Them I am." The overly-controlled conflict of his habits of perception and composition never really threatens Rodgers' authorial identity, and his attitudes towards, or his memories of, Ulster tend on the whole to serve a similar purpose, corroborative rather than unsettling[26]:

> Maybe it is the liking for strong black and white contrast that makes me partial to the Belfast I knew, with its long files of women and girls in black shawls, streaming out of the linen mills; or the dark city at dusk with the rain stippling the puddles and silvering the pavements, and the 'Islandmen' thronging the red tramcars and filling the red-blinded pubs.

This is just as vivid, and in its way just as detached, as MacNeice's reminiscences of the north of his childhood. But where MacNeice allows such potent memories their inherent resonances of the inconclusive and the ambiguous, Rodgers makes them underwrite his own poetic authority. Essentially, Rodgers encounters in memory the "strong black and white contrast" of his poetic imagination; in remembering Belfast, he constitutes a literary identity.

The habit of linking a sense of identity with authority is evident in

Rodgers' short poem 'Words', where the speaking poet and the island of Ireland merge into each other:[27]

> Always the arriving winds of words
> Pour like Atlantic gales over these ears,
> These reefs, these foils and fenders, these shrinking
> And sea-scalded edges of the brain-land.

This conceit is no more convincing when Rodgers ends the poem by anticipating how words, "Arrowed and narrowed into my tongue's tip", will finally "speak for me—their most astonished host". Here again, the assertion of identity between the personally-underwritten poetic voice and the words it employs is either a disingenuous statement of a fallacy, or an indication that the poetry is not fully engaged with its own language, forgetting that words are more than the vessels of images and sounds. As with the perception of "a 'split' people", there is an insufficient regard here for the need for language to be answerable to something other than the private requirements of the self.

Although he has remarked acutely on Rodgers' belief that "he could fashion oneness merely out of his love for Ireland and in the finitude of his poems", John Wilson Foster follows the poet's logic too faithfully when he explains the constant duality embedded in the poetry by noting that "life in Ulster has always been at one crucial level twofold, Protestant and Catholic".[28] To posit this as the cause of Rodgers' stylistic habits seems perverse; to suggest it as an analogue to them, though a more plausible proposition, is to fail to take account of the deficiencies and problems involved in the poetry's "finitudes". Perhaps this is a critical difficulty similar to that presented by Hewitt's work: where Hewitt presents us with an unwarranted smoothness, Rodgers offers an artificially-achieved system of division. The techniques of both poets claim to answer to something in the 'identity' of Ulster, but neither does so with the subtlety or circumspection proper to such an attempt. I have suggested already that some of Hewitt's poetry takes account of the problems inherent in this kind of enterprise, and relocates its senses of 'identity' as a result. In the case of Rodgers, also, the best poems outgrow the complacencies of his slacker work, opening ideas of 'identity' to the challenges of artistic exposure.

In 'Summer Holidays', a long and in certain respects derivative poem, heavily influenced by such 30s panoramas of urban life as MacNeice's 'Birmingham', Rodgers ends with an evocation of the human condition which goes beyond the simplicities of 'split' identity to reveal a friction at the core of his own work[29]:

> The spin of flesh on the spindle of bone
> Concentring all, with its brute ambitions,
> Its acute and terrible attritions.

The very familiar verbal tricks are operating here as usual, but to greater than usual effect: the idea of an individual identity as something *concentred*, put together from the delicate and the durable, the blunt and the sharp, finds its best expression in the poem's final phrase. Already, in this relatively early piece, Rodgers has found the proper description for his imaginative process of self-identification: not conflict, or the clear, decisive "clash of opposites", but the "acute and terrible attritions" of, among other things, sound against sound. At the centre, the point where the poet's memories, skills, beliefs and ideas consort, there is not an 'identity', a coherence and sameness sharpened through division, but a changing self, alive to and worn down by the processes of attrition. One sense of this term (though Rodgers' use of the plural is unusual) in the OED is "The action or process of rubbing one thing against another; mutual friction". Perhaps, also, the word carries here overtones of its specifically theological meaning, "An imperfect sorrow for sin, as if a bruising which does not amount to an utter crushing". The "spin of flesh", and its development into the more solid "spindle", hovers close to the "spine" which Rodgers imagines his 'Ulster Protestant' possessing in the 'Conversation Piece'—in this situation, words are altogether more substantial things than "arriving gales"[30]:

> He would *like* to have eloquence. But he suspects and hates eloquence that has no bone of logic in it. It seems to him glib, spineless, and insincere. It freezes him into silence.

It is as though Rodgers is imagining a negative pressure that could be brought to bear on his own writing, with its relentless 'gift of the gab'; as against his poetic preference for verbal harmony, he presents the Protestant voice as "sharp, expulsive, jerky", the noise of a resistance that rubs away at the more luxuriant mouth-music of Rodgers' lines.

Although Rodgers learns how to turn this process of 'attrition' to poetic advantage in his best work, it is possible still to see, in a fragmentary poem late in his career, the instinct to back up the poetic voice by projecting an 'identity' for Ulster. In this case, the poem is

Rodgers' unfinished 'Epilogue' to his never-completed project *The Character of Ireland*, a book of essays to be co-edited with Louis MacNeice. Here, the poet returns to the "sharp, expulsive, jerky" Ulster accent and, as in his earlier poem 'Words', serves self-consciously as the 'host' of their antagonistic sounds[31]:

> I am Ulster, my people an abrupt people
> Who like the spiky consonants in the speech
> And think the soft ones cissy; who dig
> The *k* and *t* in orchestra, detect sin
> In sinfonia, get a kick out of
> Tin cans, fricatives, fornication, staccato talk,
> Anything that gives or takes attack,
> Like Mick, Tagues, tinkers' gets, Vatican.

This *tour-de-force* of mimicry crosses the line into caricature: the dramatic identity which Rodgers assumes is a limiting one, heightened and distorted into poetic melodrama. The hailstorm of fricatives develops into a line of sectarian abuse, angry and offensive noise. There is a degree of effective ironic detachment in this; at the same time, however, the verbal excess betrays a certain complacency, a willingness to schematise, generalise, and divide:

> An angular people, brusque and Protestant,
> For whom the word is still a fighting word,
> Who bristle into reticence at the sound
> Of the round gift of the gab in southern mouths.

The angular and the round, like Rodgers' other paired opposites, answer to forces operating within his poetry more fully than to his ostensible subject-matter. The division between distrust of language and linguistic rapture is Rodgers' distinctive concern, a fundamental instability which makes poems like 'The Swan' and 'The Net' so remarkable. But the Rodgers who can announce that "I am Ulster" has lost his balance, falling into a simple identity from that of the riskier, more precarious openness in which words are the agents of freedom rather than fixity. Unfinished as it is, the 'Epilogue' is a significant failure of Rodgers' powers, exposing a shortcoming in his grasp of the Ulster that he takes as his subject. Terence Brown has noted how the poem tries to approach "the cultural neuroses and psychoses in the collective mind of Ireland", an abstract construction made up of "the sum of her inhabitants' warring myths and identity problems", but has also remarked on how Rodgers falls short of any "simple therapeutic solution" to the problem he confronts.[32] Perhaps this line of investigation can be pursued further: is Rodgers' failure the result of a deficiency in imaginative and intellectual resources, or might it be the outcome of applying such resources to a phantom subject, what he calls, in a letter accompanying the unfinished 'Epilogue', "my favourite theme, the characteristics of Irishmen"?[33]

Rodgers would not be the first or the last Irish writer to pursue this particular chimera, and certainly both Hewitt and MacNeice are on occasion hot on its trail. Writing (it would seem) for an overseas audience during World War II, Louis MacNeice approached the subject of "Northern Ireland and her people", paying attention to stereotypes. MacNeice examines, for example, the "one word that at once jumps to the Englishman's lips: the word 'dour'".[34] The poet meets this half-way, admitting that it "is certainly appropriate to the typical Belfastman", and picturing "tough figures in cloth caps whose first glance at you seems to imply antipathy and whose mouths are shut tight like a money-box". After more of such description, he admits that "in general the Northern character ... can be described as dour". However, MacNeice will not leave the matter there, showing how the outsider's perspective turns out to be doubly misleading. On the one hand, the 'dourness' is, "in nine cases out of ten", "very deceptive", concealing what MacNeice calls "hospitality", a willingness to "go out of their way to help you and refuse to take any reward for it". But, on the other hand, there is something behind 'dourness' which does not accord quite so well with the tourist-brochure tones:

> What, however, disturbs the Englishman more than the Ulsterman's dourness is what is often called his bigotry. Party feeling takes a more savage form here than in any other part of the British Isles ... Some of this political vehemence can be taken with a grain of salt; it is a standing joke that the Irish, whether south or north, love an argument—or a fight—for its own sake. The root of the matter, however, lies in history—and a very tangled history it is.

The manifest deficiencies of this, and of the potted history of Ulster which follows it, are too great to be excused on the grounds that MacNeice is addressing here an international (and possibly largely ignorant) audience. The poet is too ready to dismiss politics and history as elements to be taken *cum grano*, and his provision of an Irish stereotype to help explain this hardly helps matters. Is it, then, MacNeice playing exactly that role which many of his contemporaries in Ireland (and many Irish critics since) assigned to him—that of the outsider, cut off from an understanding of Ireland by his English education and manners? And yet, the blindspots here—most notably the blanket description of the Ulster character, the lack of attention to the realities of sectarian division or the machinery of Protestant power (we are assured that the Orange Order's "bark is worse than its bite"[35])—along with the focus on local colour and provincial oddities, are surprising to find in MacNeice. Indeed, in his own poetry on Irish topics in the 30s and after, these are the blindspots that are opened up to become focal points. However, they seem very close to the deficiencies of Rodgers on the Ulster 'character', or even to Hewitt's choice of themes at the same time. Trying to serve up an easily-comprehensible identity for Ulster, MacNeice turns to the techniques of the regionalist analysis, the combination of simplification with generalisation, ignoring as far as possible areas that prove recalcitrant to such an approach.

It would be wrong, of course, to dismiss either MacNeice's wartime article on Ulster, or the arguments of regionalists at the time, on the grounds that they do not accommodate the problems of political violence in more recent experience. Yet there is a reticence, perhaps a principled shyness, in the approach to the issues of allegiance and nationality among those writers who were raised, after all, in a decidedly 'political' generation in the 30s. It seems that the very process of addressing Ulster, and Ireland, leads the writers to exclude, or postpone, a problem central to any consideration of 'identity', that of a national definition of the subject. The discourse of 'identity' is employed in such a way as to put problems of definition, and division, on the back burner. Hewitt's well-known sliding definition, which elides the Ulsterman of Planter stock with Irish, British, and European identities, might be seen as passing off *personal* self-definition as something more widely significant or exemplary. The same elision of awkward problems of group-definition could be found in John Boyd's announcement of 1951, that "Ulster is part of Ireland, which is part of the British Isles, which is part of Europe", so that "Our literature should belong to our own country, to the British Isles, to Europe."[36] But "our own country" remains without definition in this, as in other such archipelagic formulas. With the arrogance of hindsight, it is all too easy to observe that, with so much on the back burner, the pots are bound eventually to boil over.

However, it would be perverse to use later knowledge of the weaknesses or inadequacies of the ideas behind some regionalist and associated writing in order to judge the literary value of its products.

The harsh term 'failure' is sometimes necessary, but needs to be balanced by a feeling for the kinds of success that were also involved. As far as Rodgers and MacNeice are concerned, one 'failure' in particular is relevant to the question of creative writing and the agendas of 'identity'. This is the project, which was carried on for at least 15 years before its complete abandonment, of co-editing a collection of essays to be entitled, with grand ambition, *The Character of Ireland*. Rodgers' unfinished 'Epilogue' was just one crumbling component of this unstable, and, in the end, unviable book. Although the project's scope was obviously more wide-ranging than that of regionalism, its beginnings are closely associated with the period of greatest effort by Hewitt and others. The idea for a volume of this nature seems to have occurred to Rodgers in the late 40s, and, by 1952, he and MacNeice were in a position to put together a list of contributors, both possible and already signed-up. At this stage, these contributors included Estyn Evans on 'The Irish Countryman', Elizabeth Bowen on 'The Big House', Frank O'Connor on 'English Literature', Sam Hanna Bell on 'The Six Counties', and John Hewitt on 'The Visual Arts'. Other names included Theodore Moody, J.C. Beckett, Geoffrey Taylor, Seán Ó Faoláin, and Conor Cruise O'Brien. As the project began to take shape under the aegis of the Clarendon Press in 1952, it seemed promising—a gathering of material on Ireland north and south by a literary generation who had for the most part come to maturity in the post-independence, or post-partition years. Rodgers, whose field researches on Irish 'character' of many varieties had been successful in his radio portraits of Irish writers, was a natural choice as editor[37]; MacNeice, with his stricter, and more detached interests in Ireland seemed an excellent complement. And yet, as the project's long-suffering publisher, Dan Davin, recalls in his memoirs of the two poets, *The Character of Ireland* floundered for many exasperating years before finally coming to grief with the deaths of its editors.[38] Conceived at a high-point of enthusiasm for the possibilities of putting on paper some broad, many-faceted approach to, or even definition of, the modern Irish 'character', the project dragged on through the 50s and half of the 60s: contributors defaulted or withdrew; completed articles went out of date; ideas of balanced coverage proved hard to sustain. Above all, as Davin's memoirs make clear, the editors themselves could hardly finish their own contributions: MacNeice's verse 'Prologue' did finally arrive in 1959, seven years after it was first promised, but Rodgers never brought his 'Epilogue' close to completion. It is difficult to tell, so great is the catalogue of set-backs, mistakes, and delays, whether *The Character of Ireland* was a failure in collaboration or a collaboration in failure.

The whole story of delay and vacillation is related effectively by Davin, who sees a near-tragic significance of the failing project for Rodgers in his last exhausted years. The role of *The Character of Ireland* in MacNeice's late career is less sombre, crossing, as it does, into his late period of imaginative renewal and poetic strength rather than, as in the case of Rodgers, coinciding with the progressive failing of poetic powers. Indeed, it would appear that MacNeice's interest in the project was at its strongest in the early 50s—for him poetically a strained and difficult time—but tailed off as he found his own poetic resources renewing themselves in the late 50s and early 60s. In the cases of both poets, the need to invest in 'identity' may be linked to the necessity of drawing upon a 'common fund' that might help to 'float' their own work. By the time he had completed his 'Prologue' to the volume, MacNeice was already past this need, and the poem indicates this in its lengthy meditation on Ireland in terms of the imagery habitual to many of his other poems—the prismatic colours of light on landscape, and, above all, the fluidity and clarity of water. What MacNeice specifically excludes from the 'Prologue' is any settled notion of 'identity', going so far as to question the assumptions of the project itself:[39]

> 'The Character of Ireland'? Character?
> A stage convention? A historical trap?
> A geographical freak? Let us dump the rubbish
> Of race and talk to the point: what is a nation?

The recognition of 'identity' for a country, or indeed for a self-constituting 'race' within a country, as "a historical trap", makes good the kind of poetic intuition which MacNeice's 'Prologue' explores. Ireland's status as a 'nation' soon dissolves to become "this land of words and water", something unfixed and many-sided. Along with the imagery of flowing water (which always carries overtones of Heraclitean flux for MacNeice), the figure of the prism helps make solid the many paradoxes which the poet observes in Ireland[40]:

> The water
> Flows, the words bubble, the eyes flash,
> The prism retains identity, that squalor,
> Those bickerings, disappointments, self-deceptions,
> Still dare not prove that what was love was not;

The Irish become here the "Inheritors of paradox and prism", putting them in possession of an 'identity', far removed from the constructions of writers like Rodgers or Hewitt, removed, indeed, from the ideas behind a project like *The Character of Ireland*. MacNeice's wartime 'Northern Ireland and her People' had remarked how "sunlight in Ireland has the effect of a prism; nowhere else in the British Isles can you find this liquid rainbow quality which at once diffuses and clarifies".[41] The poet had used the same image in his book on W.B. Yeats of 1941, noting the "pantomimic transformation scenes" of the Irish landscape: "one moment it will be desolate, dead, unrelieved monotone, the next it will be an indescribably shifting pattern of prismatic light."[42] The prism that "retains identity" is associated with the dual process of clarification and diffusion, bringing about both concentration and separation. It is in this sense that MacNeice uses the prism to figure identity. If one aspect of this is the brilliant colour and light celebrated in flux in the 'Prologue', another is the "dead", unrelieved monotone of completely united, identified colours. This is the aspect of Ireland which enters MacNeice's earlier poem, 'Valediction', as "inbred soul and climatic maleficence", where the Irish must "pay for the trick beauty of a prism/In drug-dull fatalism".[43]

Fatalism may be one corollary of a sense of 'identity', an unforeseen one perhaps, as in the case of regionalism, but something sensed in poetry by MacNeice and others. To discover and define 'identity' for the self, and beyond that for a broader community, is also to flirt with what are ultimately determinist conceptions of character. One question which has to be asked about 'identity' is how far the term encodes a purpose, forcing discussion and thought in a pre-determined direction. When, for example, a Northern Irish Protestant 'identity' (however that might be defined) is accepted as a usable concept, the term itself is dictating a certain line of reasoning, and aligning the perspective in vital ways with broadly determinist ideas common in nationalism. Solidarity, community, place: all of these values, which strengthened and helped mark out a literary generation on both sides of the Irish Sea, proved in the end less flexible or liberating than the creative work they helped bring to birth; 'identity', as part of the same complex of ideas, though it may lay claim to plurality, cannot accommodate the fluidity into which 'character', in all good poetry, necessarily dissolves.

Perhaps *The Character of Ireland* fell into "a historical trap" of its own construction; certainly, the passing of time turned the project's initial bright ideas into ever darker and more involved problems. In particular, the required coverage of Northern Ireland proved difficult: despite

John Hewitt's efficiency on 'The Visual Arts' ("one of the earliest and most promptly delivered articles", according to Rodgers in 1955, and dutifully revised in 1957[44]), important dimensions were missing. Again, the reticence of regionalism with regard to 'politics' seems to play a part: where southern contributors were on the whole willing to give outspoken views (if sometimes under cover of a pseudonym, as in the case of Conor Cruise O'Brien on 'The Catholic Church'), the northern writers were more guarded. Writing to Dan Davin in 1957, Rodgers touches on the area of difficulty[45]:

> You'll recall that initially we asked Sam Hanna Bell to contribute a piece on the Six Counties: he refused, partly, I think, because he thought it would involve dealing with political issues. I still think, and Louis agrees, that a general article on Ulster by Bell would balance the book better. Otherwise we won't get the feeling or flavour of that determined place.

Here the frustration of the editor rubs against the poet's instinct for the mot juste: "that determined place" combines exasperation and felicity in its registering of the double pressures exerted by 'identity'. "Determined" stretches both to "self-willed" or "independent" and to "fore-ordained", "fated". In witnessing the slow failure of *The Character of Ireland*, as well as participating in and contributing to it, Rodgers re-encounters the desperate gaps his own poetry continually sets out to bridge, between "pull" and "pluck", "spin" and "spindle". Like that of Hewitt and MacNeice, Rodgers' best poetry understands that ambitions for 'identity' in Ulster are inevitably worn down by what they hope to transcend, the "acute and terrible attritions" of "that determined place".

Notes

1 John Hewitt, *Collected Poems 1932-1967* (1968), p. 5.
2 Ibid., pp. 11–12.
3 Ibid., p. 144.
4 John Hewitt, 'The Bitter Gourd: Some Problems of the Ulster Writer' (1945), in Tom Clyde (ed.) *Ancestral Voices: The Selected Prose of John Hewitt* (Belfast, 1987), p. 115.
5 *The Bell*, Vol. 4 No. 5 (August 1942), p. 307.
6 W.J. McCormack, "'The Protestant Strain' Or, A Short History of Anglo-Irish Literature from S.T. Coleridge to Thomas Mann', Gerald Dawe and Edna Longley (eds.) *Across A Roaring Hill: The Protestant Imagination in Modern Ireland*

(Belfast, 1985), p. 62.
7 *The Bell*, Vol. 4 No. 5 (August 1942), p. 307.
8 Louis MacNeice, *The Strings Are False: An Unfinished Autobiography* (1965), p. 78.
9 John Hewitt, *Ancestral Voices*, p. 122.
10 Ibid.
11 See Barra O Seaghda, 'Ulster Regionalism: The Unpleasant Facts', *The Irish Review* 8 (Spring 1990), pp. 54-61 on 'geographical coherence'.
12 John Hewitt, *Collected Poems 1932-1967*, p. 70.
13 John Hewitt, Interview with Ketzel Levine, *Fortnight*, No. 213 (4th-17th February, 1985), p. 17.
14 John Hewitt, interview with Damian Smyth, *North*, No. 4 (Winter 1985), p. 14.
15 John Hewitt, *Collected Poems 1932-1967*, p. 136.
16 See John Wilson Foster, 'Radical Regionalism', *The Irish Review* 7 (Autumn 1989), pp. 1-15.
17 John Wilson Foster, "'The dissidence of Dissent': John Hewitt and W.R. Rodgers', Dawe and Longley (eds.) *Across a Roaring Hill*, p. 144.
18 Roy Foster, 'Varieties of Irishness', Maura Crozier (ed.) *Cultural Traditions in Northern Ireland* (Belfast, 1989), p. 22.
19 Adrian Caesar, *Diving Lines: Poetry, Class and Ideology in the 1930s* (Manchester, 1991), p. 203.
20 Ibid., p. 104.
21 See Peter McDonald, 'Ireland's MacNeice: A *caveat*', *The Irish Review* 2 (2 (1987), pp. 64-69.
22 John Boyd, *Lagan* No. 1 n.d. [1943], p. 5.
23 J.N. Browne, 'Poetry in Ulster', Sam Hanna Bell, Nesca A. Robb and John Hewitt (eds.), *The Arts in Ulster: A Symposium* (1951) p. 142.
24 Ibid., p. 145.
25 W.R. Rodgers, *Collected Poems* (1971), p. 42.
26 W.R. Rodgers, script for *The Return Room* (1945), quoted in Darcy O'Brien, *W.R. Rodgers (1909–1969)* (Lewisburg, 1970), pp. 23-4.
27 W.R. Rodgers, *Collected Poems*, p. 2.
28 John Wilson Foster, " 'The Dissidence of Dissent': John Hewitt and W.R. Rodgers", p. 153.
29 W.R. Rodgers, *Collected Poems*, p. 26.
30 *The Bell* Vol. 4 No. 5 (August 1942), p. 309.
31 W.R. Rodgers, *Collected Poems*, 147.
32 Terence Brown, *Northern Voices: Poets from Ulster* (Dublin, 1975), p. 88.
33 W.R. Rodgers, *Collected Poems*, p. 144.
34 Louis MacNeice, 'Northern Ireland and Her People' (? c. 1941-44), in Alan Heuser (ed.), *Selected Prose of Louis MacNeice* (Oxford, 1990), pp. 144–5.
35 Ibid., p. 149.
36 John Boyd, 'Ulster Prose', *The Arts in Ulster*, p. 99.

37 A collection of Rodgers' radio programmes, *Irish Literary Portraits* was published in 1972.
38 See Dan Davin, *Closing Times* (1975).
39 Louis MacNeice, 'Prologue', Terence Brown and Alec Reid (eds.), *Time Was Away: The World of Louis MacNeice* (Dublin, 1974), p. 2.
40 Ibid., p. 3.
41 Louis MacNeice, 'Northern Ireland and Her People', *Selected Prose*, p. 151.
42 Louis MacNeice, *The Poetry of W.B. Yeats* (1941 repr. 1967), p. 50.
43 Louis MacNeice, *Collected Poems* (1966), p. 53.
44 W.R. Rodgers, letter to Dan Davin, 21st March, 1953.
45 W.R. Rodgers, letter to Dan Davin, 7th March, 1957.

'That Combat on the Shabby Patch'
Hugh MacDiarmid, Edwin Muir and the Matter of Scotland

PATRICK CROTTY

Hugh MacDiarmid and Edwin Muir are conventionally seen as the polar twins of modern Scottish poetry, eternal antagonists as predestined for conflict as the heraldic beasts of Muir's poem 'The Combat'[1], which supplies the title of this essay. The contrasts between the two scarcely require rehearsal: MacDiarmid volcanic, Stalinist, nationalist and confrontational; Muir formal to the point of gentility, mystical, pessimistic about politics, and distasteful of controversy. These oppositions are only part of the truth, however, perhaps the least interesting part. Behind them lies a tale of parallel lives—of two writers coming to maturity in adverse circumstances and with a shared sense of cultural deprivation; of a remarkable measure of agreement in diagnosing the causes of that deprivation; and of mutual admiration and friendship. In 1936, the friendship ended, spectacularly, when Muir published *Scott and Scotland: The Predicament of the Scottish Writer*—a predicament which might be said to have been illuminated more bleakly by the row it caused than by Muir's book itself. My concern here is to sketch the relationship between the two poets, with particular reference to the cultural and linguistic issues raised by their unprepossessing and yet not unedifying quarrel.

I

Commentators have made much of the fact that MacDiarmid and Muir came from opposite ends of Scotland. Langholm in the Border country, where MacDiarmid was born Christopher Grieve in 1892, and Wyre in Orkney, where Muir first saw the light of day five years earlier, are clearly very different places both topographically and culturally.

The roles they play in the two bodies of writing under discussion are not, however, so dissimilar. As most readers of modern poetry know, Wyre represents for Muir an Edenic state which he had already lost before his descent into the hell of Glasgow on his family's move to the mainland when he was 14. Though the island has a concrete presence in only a handful of his poems, it everywhere serves to authorise what he called the Fable behind the Story, offering a first-hand revelation of part of the timeless pattern underlying the disorder of experience.

The deaths in rapid succession of his father, mother and two brothers lent a catastrophic dimension to Muir's loss of his first world which has no counterpart in Grieve's biography. Yet the latter, too, saw adulthood in terms of exclusion from a numinous rural locale. His characteristic attitude is more complex than Muir's, in that he regards exclusion as part of the price of awareness. Thus, in the *Clann Albann* poems of the early 30s, he uses "the Muckle Toon o' the Langholm" as a metaphor for regression even in the act of celebrating its many felicities. If MacDiarmid's apprehension of reality, like Muir's, involves a sense of Paradise Lost, it conspicuously lacks a Fall: innocence for him is ultimately poverty of consciousness rather than freedom from evil, intellectual deficiency rather than moral good. That is why he can evoke Langholm only to dismiss it:

> Extinction? What's that but to return
> To juist anither Muckle Toon again?
> — A salutary process bringin' values oot
>   Ocht else 'ud leave in doot.[2]

Passionate for the particular, MacDiarmid's work pays considerably more detailed attention to Dumfriesshire than Muir's does to Orkney. Even when not its explicit focus, the Muckle Toon pervades the poetry and features centrally in the Scots fiction. MacDiarmid himself referred to the place as his "secret reservoir"[3], and he drew upon memories of it again and again during the 11 hectic years of his career as a lyric poet in Scots. The plant at which the protagonist of his most famous book gazes so furiously offers one of the most significant, if least obvious, examples of the power of the "hame-scenes"[4] to inform his verse: the Drunk Man's thistle is the Scottish national emblem, but it is also, crucially, a fantastic projection of the huge composite thistle carried through the streets of Langholm at the climax of the town's great summer festival, the Common Riding.[5]

It is tempting to see the influence of geography in the mentalities of Muir and MacDiarmid. Muir's rather colourless poetry, with its yearning for deliverance from temporal process, shares something of the character of the remote, treeless, self-contained world disclosed to the tenant-farmer's boy in Orkney, a world which *An Autobiography* presents as essentially static and timeless. Similarly, MacDiarmid's sense not only of physical but of human nature—and, indeed, of language too—as teeming resource would seem to be rooted in his earliest impressions of his environment, a Dumfriesshire countryside all "columbe and colour-de-roy"[6], abundant plant life and ever-changing weather.

In one respect, the political, Langholm and Wyre left almost identical legacies. While MacDiarmid was always more vehement in his politics than Muir, it is not until the 30s that he took up the hard-line communist stance with which he is usually identified. When they first met, both poets were socialists of the Independent Labour Party variety, and Muir had not yet abandoned a quietist Scottish nationalism. Indeed, after their opinions diverged on these matters, both writers continued to give vocal support to the Social Credit proposals of their compatriot, Major C.H. Douglas. My point is not so much that the political differences between them have been exaggerated, but that their ameliorist views in social and economic matters were alike founded—to a degree, at least—upon a fractured rural idyll.

Published a few weeks after his arrival in Edinburgh at the age of 16 to train as a teacher, 'Memories of Langholm', Grieve's earliest extant poem, finds the stony grandeur of the capital "hopeless and dead" after Dumfriesshire's "gorgeous rioting"[7] of colour; in doing so, it expresses an attitude towards urban life which would be one of his poetry's few consistencies. Though *Lucky Poet* proclaims his faith in "the growth of the third factor between Man and Nature—the Machine"[8], in his instinctive preferences MacDiarmid always remained a countryman: his detestation of capitalism was at root an aversion from what industrialisation did to the earth and to the lives of the poor. He would have vigorously denied such a claim, of course, but the poetry supports it. Very rarely after 1933 do we get verse of any rhythmic life whatever from MacDiarmid, and when we do its informing emotion is almost always revulsion from the squalor of Glasgow. A vision of Glasgow as Hell, of its denizens as the damned or, at least, the comprehensively dehumanised, provides the common ground between Muir's *Autobiography* and the most animated passages of MacDiarmid after his creative collapse of 1933:

> Where have I seen a human being looking
> As Glasgow looks this gin-clear evening—with face and fingers
> A cadaverous blue, hand-clasp slimy and cold
> As that of a corpse, finger-nails grown immeasurably long
> As they do in a grave, little white eyes, and hardly
> Any face at all? Cold, lightning-like, unpleasant, light, and blue
> Like having one's cold spots intoxicated with mescal.
> Looking down a street the houses seem
> Long pointed teeth like a ferret's over the slit
> Of a crooked unspeakable smile, like the Thracian woman's
> When Thales fell in the well, a hag
> Whose soul-gelding ugliness would chill
> To eternal chastity a cantharidized satyr ...[9]

II

Their construction of childhood as a radiant state in a place apart is not the only parallel between Muir and MacDiarmid. Also significant is the fact that both poets were self-educated. We learn in *An Autobiography* that there were few books in Muir's home other than pious texts like *The Pilgrim's Progress* and *The Scots Worthies*.[10] Grieve was more fortunate. Though his parents were stricter Calvinists than Muir's, perhaps no poet since Browning grew up in so physically bookish an environment. His father, James Grieve, was postman for the Ewes Valley, and so the family was housed in Langholm's Post Office and Library Building— on the ground floor, directly underneath the town library to which Christopher had access through his mother's stewardship of the keys. "I ... used to fill a big washing-basket with books and bring it downstairs as often as I wanted to," he recalls with characteristic self-satisfaction in *Lucky Poet*.[11]

MacDiarmid was a luckier poet than Muir in his formal schooling as well. The note on the author in a number of his books tells us that he was "educated at Edinburgh University"[12], a claim based, if we are to believe his friend Norman MacCaig, upon the fact that he ran an errand to that institution while a cub reporter with the *Edinburgh Evening Dispatch*.[13] Yet he did attend the Broughton Junior Student Centre in the city, and had almost completed his three-year teacher-training course there when asked to leave over a misdemeanour. To have remained under instruction until 18 and won the admiration of one's mentors was, by Muir's standards, achievement indeed. The Orkney poet had no schooling beyond primary level, his attendance being intermittent and undistinguished. "This must be a particularly stupid boy," opined a member of Her Majesty's perspicacious Inspectorate in 1894.[14]

There may be in the self-conscious intellectualism of both poets a measure of over-compensation for the uncertainty of their educational setting forth. Critics have been quicker to detect the uneasy intensity of the autodidact in Grieve's writing than in Muir's, which might seem odd in view of their respective academic histories. Muir, though, made up much of the leeway in an energetic and disciplined programme of reading during his years as a clerk in Glasgow and Fairport; whereas MacDiarmid always remained the boy with the laundry-basketful of books, oddly, even hugely, learned, but frequently undiscriminating and at times superficial in his enthusiasms. G.S. Fraser's judgement that "Muir represented the civilised mind, MacDiarmid the passion of the fanatic" greatly overstates the differences between them, however, misled by the surface characteristics of their critical prose.[15] If the Orcadian was the acuter critic, he felt scarcely more constrained than MacDiarmid to limit his comments to matters in which he had genuine expertise: we shall see, when we come to comment on *Scott and Scotland*, that the polished reasonableness of Muir's style can conceal a good deal of bluster and overstatement.

III

Grieve's and Muir's encounter with the intellectual life of their time furth of Scotland—their education in contemporaneity—came *via* the same route, A.R. Orage's *The New Age*. Both were eventually to contribute reviews to the paper and Muir was to work as editorial assistant on it after his marriage and move to London in 1919. *The New Age* introduced a generation to the ideas of Nietzsche, Dostoievski, Solovyov, Ouspensky and Freud, ideas whose impact on the intellectual development of MacDiarmid and Muir can hardly be overestimated. But the periodical's content was perhaps of less importance to them than its tone, recalled in *An Autobiography* as "crushingly superior and exclusive"[16]. Such a tone had an obvious appeal for two young writers struggling towards self-definition in an environment they saw as peculiarly antipathetic to the arts and to the life of the mind generally. The rather showy intellectuality of *We Moderns* (1918) and *Annals of the Five Senses* (1923), the first books of Muir and Grieve respectively, owes more than a little to it—indeed, the texts collected in *We Moderns* had originally been written for Orage's periodical.

Neither writer seems to have thought of himself primarily as a poet when these early works were composed, a consequence perhaps of the slow ripening MacDiarmid held to be symptomatic of the decrepitude of Scottish culture. Muir, in fact, did not bring out his first volume of verse for another seven years after 1918, and his best poetry was decades away. The prose sketches which make up the main bulk of *Annals of the Five Senses* had been completed in 1920 but, by the time Grieve managed to have the book published three years later, he had already been transformed into the Scots lyricist MacDiarmid.

We Moderns—issued under the pseudonym Edward Moore—is a collection of *pseudo*-Nietzschean aphorisms and short philosophical essays. Its content and style were to embarrass Muir in equal measure in later years and need not detain us here. One feature of the book, however, represents a lasting preoccupation: the title's gauche assertion of the author's membership of a modern *élite*. Anxiety about modernity, fear of failing to be fully European, fully alive in one's own time, would be a motivating force in Muir's development and the key artistic decisions of his career are only to be understood in the light of it. It was an anxiety Grieve shared to the full. The differences between the two careers can in fact be plotted in terms of divergent strategies of response to the challenge of modernity. Longing for contemporary relevance runs much deeper in both poets than nervousness about educational credentials, as it springs from a fearful apprehension of Scottish national identity as an obstacle to the realisation of an adequate humanity.

Scottishness was problematic for Muir and MacDiarmid and, to begin with at least, problematic in the same way. The Matter of Scotland, Sir Walter Scott's great theme, had become for his successors in the early 20th century a question of the matter *with* Scotland. A unitary critique of the cultural plight of the country emerges from Grieve's furious castigations of Kailyardism in the periodicals he launched after his return from World War I, and from the essays and reviews on Scottish subjects contributed by Muir to English and American periodicals in the 20s. This critique involves a view of the Reformation as a disaster which brought Scotland's intellectual traditions to an abrupt end and robbed her of a fertilising contact with Europe; and a view of the union as no less a catastrophe, which deprived the nation of a focus for its political life and ultimately even a language—Scots—in which it might render its experience to itself.

Not surprisingly, since they were verbal artists, it was to the question of language that Muir and MacDiarmid devoted most attention. Both tended to formulate in terms of politics and nationality a predicament which, while undoubtedly the product of historical forces, was essentially psychological in its practical manifestations. Muir wrote in 1923:

> No writer can write great English who is not born an English writer and in England; and born moreover in some class in which the tradition of English is pure, and it seems to me, therefore, in some other age than this. English as it was written by Bunyan or by Fielding can not be written now except by some one who like them has passed his days in a tradition of living English speech. A whole life went into that prose; and all that Stevenson could give to his was a few decades of application. And because the current of English is even at this day so much younger, poorer and more artificial in Scotland than it is in England, it is improbable that Scotland will produce any writer of English of the first rank, or at least that she will do so until her tradition of English is as common, as unforced and unschooled as if it were her native tongue.[17]

Melville, James, Conrad, Yeats, Joyce—it hardly takes five words to demolish Muir's opening argument. The tradition of English is younger in Ireland, or among a majority in Ireland, than it is in Scotland and yet that has been no inhibition to literary achievement in the language—on the contrary. American literature in the 75 years before Muir made these remarks, like Commonwealth literature in the subsequent 75, further exposes their curiously Anglo-centric myopia. There is a sort of desperate wishful thinking in Muir's bid to foist on the whole Anglophone world beyond England a disability which is perhaps peculiarly the preserve of the Scottish writer brought up in a strong dialect tradition. If Muir's own very considerable difficulties with English style derived from his cultural circumstances, it was less his lack of English nationality as such that was to blame than the fact that his native tongue was a sharply differentiated—and self-consciously unEnglish—variant of English.

The language problem in Muir and MacDiarmid goes back, like so much else, to Wyre and Langholm. As a child, Muir spoke the Orkney dialect of Scots, while the first speech Grieve heard was Southern Scots. *Facts are chiels that winna ding*, said Burns, and any worthwhile discussion of the language of the poetries of Muir and MacDiarmid must take cognisance of the realities of their earliest linguistic experience. MacDiarmid's mother, Elizabeth Graham, a barely literate woman from Westerkirk, could not have spoken the Queen's English even if she had wanted to do so. Her son's recourse to the Scots lexicon in 1922 was artistically rewarding insofar as it was a return to source, a tapping into the energies of his first linguistic world. True, MacDiarmid did not go on to write in Langholm Scots, but his Lallans usage is characteristically held together by a sense of rhythm rooted in his childhood speech, a sense of rhythm of a subtlety to be found nowhere in his English verses. It is, therefore, arguable that in key respects, for all its self-consciously modernist eclecticism, MacDiarmid's Scots is no more 'artificial' than Muir's English.

Even in its simplest form, the exclusion of the native Scots speaker from English involves a far more poignant and intimate dilemma than that of Joyce's Catholic Irishman fretting in the shadow of the English Dean of Studies' language. Outside a few rapidly dying Gaeltacht areas, the Irish, of whatever political or religious affiliation, speak English from infancy and English is consequently in a simple and profound sense *their* language. Writers may capitalise on the distinctive features of Hiberno-English, but speakers of the Irish dialect do not consider it to have an *either/or* relationship with the standard. The communities in which Grieve and Muir learned to speak, however, identified southern English with privilege, hypocrisy and an over-refinement of feeling. The process of mastering literary English entailed for them, as for Hume and Stevenson before them, a deliberate unlearning of Scots—or, at the very least, a shedding of Scotticisms which inevitably led to an internalisation—both of the historical retreat of the language, and of the subsumption of Scottish in English national power which helped bring it about. The inhibitions to a native Scots speaker's development of a full-blooded English style need be laboured no more than the psychologically explosive possibilities of a genuinely recuperative employment of a colloquially-based literary Scots.

To say this, of course, is to diagnose rather than to prescribe. Muir was the first of many Scottish writers who would seek with indifferent success to follow Grieve's lead in opening up an affective domain by turning to the lexicographical and formal resources of the Scots canon:

> I wandered in the woods my lane
> I heard a wind did sob and mane.
>
> A dowie wind passed me by
> Yet there was nae wind in earth or sky ...[18]

Grieve saw fit to publish 'Ballad of the Monk' and other Scots pieces by Muir in his *Scottish Chapbook*, but their risible pastiche of the old ballads could hardly be further from the spirit of that periodical's slogan, 'Not Tradition, Precedents!'. It seems clear on the basis of these that there was, for Muir, no practical alternative to writing in English.

IV

A reviewer in *The New Age* wrote of *Annals of the Five Senses*:

> (I)n its approach to ideas and to life in general it has an originality so arresting that one feels it as somehow unusual, almost foreign. It is as if an alien were writing in English without attempting to be English in anything but his language ... (I)n a something exotic and almost excessively accomplished in his style, Mr. Grieve is not unlike Mr. Joyce; and I should say that, except Mr. Joyce, nobody at present is writing more resourceful English prose.[19]

This is high praise indeed for a book which consistently fails to find an idiom adequate to its subject—the mercurial shifts in the consciousness of the alienated, self-absorbed protagonists of its six prose sketches. Yet that observation about the foreignness of Grieve's approach is acute. The reviewer, one Edwin Muir, was well qualified to recognise the author's relative lack of ease in English, as he had been sufficiently impressed by MacDiarmid's first Scots poems to have written to him a short time previously urging him to attempt a longer work "in the language you are evolving".[20]

The story of Hugh MacDiarmid's astonished conversion to Scots as a result of an encounter with Jamieson's *Etymological Dictionary of the Scottish Language* (1818) is a familiar, if slightly inaccurate one. The switch from the southern to the northern dialect did not, in fact, entail a clean break with what had gone before, for in essence what Scots offered him was a means of realising the modernity to which the turgid modishness of his English prose had vainly aspired. Indeed, in his supporting propaganda for his early Scots work, MacDiarmid made the point that the old tongue's merit lay precisely in its capacity to express with economy and force just such states of mind as he had struggled to convey in English in *Annals of the Five Senses*:

> The Scottish vernacular is the only language in Western Europe instinct with those uncanny spiritual and pathological perceptions alike which constitute the uniqueness of Dostoevski's work, and word after word of Doric establishes a blood-bond in a fashion at once infinitely more thrilling

and vital and less explicable than those deliberately sought after by writers such as D.H. Lawrence in the medium of English which is inferior for such purposes because it has an entirely different natural bias which has been so confirmed down the centuries as to be insusceptible of correction. The Scots Vernacular is a vast storehouse of just the very peculiar and subtle effects which modern European literature in general is assiduously seeking...[21]

MacDiarmid's Scots poetry of the 20s is pre-eminently an art in which "peculiar and subtle effects" serve "uncanny spiritual and pathological perceptions". While the interstellar perspectives of the lyrics collected in *Sangschaw* (1925) and *Penny Wheep* (1926) seem to have derived from a creative interrogation of the folk idioms the poet found in *Jamieson*, his forging of a style adequate to the dislocations of the modern was not a narrowly linguistic matter. The liberating insight behind *A Drunk Man Looks at the Thistle* (1926) involved a recognition of a potential connection between the hallucinatory inwardness of *Annals*, on the one hand, and Scottish literature's traditional appetite for the eldritch, the macabre and the unearthly, on the other.

It involved, that is to say, a cultivation of Scottishness rather than simply of Scots idioms. In the following lines, for example, a note of weirdness familiar from the ballads is sounded to communicate a manifestly post-Freudian sexual unease:

> It's a queer thing to tryst wi' a wumman
> When the boss o' her body's gane,
> And her banes in the wund as she comes
> Dirl like a raff o' rain ...[22]

(*boss*: rounded mass   *dirl*: rattle   *raff*: gusty shower)

A bawdry worthy of Dunbar's 'Tretis of the Tua Mariit Wemen and the Wedo' facilitates the poems's most surreal moment, the Drunk Man's metamorphosis into a beer-barrel:

> My belly on the gantrees there,
> The spigot frae my cullage,
> And wow but how the fizzin' yill
> In spilth increased the ullage!
>
> I was an anxious barrel, lad,
> When first they tapped my bung,
> They whistled me up, yet thro' the lift
> My freaths like rainbows swung.

> Waesucks, a pride for ony bar,
> The boast o' barleyhood,
> Like Noah's Ark abune the faem
> Maun float, a gantin' cude,
>
> For I was thrawn fu' cock owre sune,
> And wi' a single jaw
> I made the pub a blindin' swelth,
> And how'd the warld awa'! ...²³
>
> (*gantrees*: bottle stand *cullage*: scrotum *yill*: ale *spilth*: overflow *ullage*: deficiency in a vessel's contents *lift*: sky *freaths*: froths *Waesucks*: alas *barleyhood*: drunkenness or fit of temper *faem*: foam *Maun*: must *gantin'*: yawning, gaping *cude*: tub *fu'*: full *owre*: too *sune*: soon *jaw*: spurt *swelth*: whirlpool *how'd*: washed)

As in the 'Tretis' and 'Tam o' Shanter', the device of drunkenness lends a natural social context to visionary experience. In particular, it enables MacDiarmid to render convincingly for the first time the fevered subjectivity which had been one of his major concerns from the beginning and which, he believed, assured his solidarity with an international post-war *avant garde*:

> Is it the munelicht or a leprosy
> That spreids aboot me; and a thistle
> Or my ain skeleton through wha's bare banes
> A fiendish wund's begood to whistle?
>
> The devil's lauchter has a *hwyl* like this.
> My face has flown open like a lid
> —And gibberin' on the hillside there
> Is a' humanity sae lang has hid! ...²⁴
>
> I tae ha'e heard Eternity drip water
> (Aye water, water!), drap by drap
> On the a'e nerve, like lichtnin', I've become,
> And heard God passin' wi' a bobby's feet
> Ootby in the lang coffin o' the street ...²⁵

The continuity of the purpose between *Annals* and *A Drunk Man* is perhaps at it most obvious in an extended passage²⁶ in the second half of the poem where, by way of an associative, phantasmagoric meditation on the meanings of the thistle, MacDiarmid succeeds in evoking the fluidities of consciousness so cumbersomely and ineffectually imitated in the prose sketches. Nowhere does the poem's modernity emerge more clearly as a function of its deliberate Scottishness, for this expressionist *tour-de-force* was composed in an attempt to illustrate "the Caledonian Antisyzygy", the theory of the duality of the Scottish imagination proposed in G. Gregory Smith's *Scottish Literature: Character and Influence* (1919) and promoted—in a highly partisan version—in MacDiarmid's propaganda on behalf of his 'Scottish Renaissance'.

V

MacDiarmid's period of highest achievement coincided with his friendship with Edwin Muir. In a country as small as Scotland, it was no doubt inevitable that the two should meet, but coincidence played its part in bringing them together. Muir's wife, the novelist and critic Willa Anderson, though a Shetlander by birth, had grown up in the eastern town of Montrose, where her parents still in the 20s kept a draper's shop, and where for most of that decade Grieve was employed as a correspondent on the local newspaper. The Muirs returned to Scotland after a five year absence in 1924, spending the second half of the year and shorter periods of 1925 and 1926 at Willa's parents' in the High Street. Christopher and Peggy Grieve lived in a council house at the edge of the town and the two couples saw much of each other. Willa Muir's rather caustic reminiscences of their acquaintance in her autobiography *Belonging*, like Grieve's disclosure to Peter Butter that Edwin wanted to talk only about his dreams while *he* wished to discuss ideas, are not perhaps entirely reliable, given that they postdate the bitter split of 1936.[27]

Even without the Montrose connection, the two poets would have met through their friendship with the composer Francis George Scott. Scott, born in 1880 in Hawick—20 miles from Langholm—had befriended Muir in Glasgow, where he worked as teacher and later as a lecturer. In 1905 and 1906, he had been Grieve's class teacher in the sixth form at Langholm Academy. On composing a setting for a MacDiarmid lyric in 1923, he discovered the true identity of its author and thereafter became—and remained for more than two decades— his former pupil's chief artistic advisor. Scott may well have written to Muir about his fellow-Borderer, as in a letter of December 1923 the Orcadian cited Grieve's "stirring up" of the Scottish scene as a reason for his own desire to return home from the continent.[28] The composer used to make day-trips from Glasgow to be in the company of the two poets and, in 1928, both the Scotts and the Muirs took their summer holidays in Montrose.

Clearly then, MacDiarmid and Muir figured largely in each other's lives in the 1920s. There is some confusion as to the degree of their intimacy: temperamental differences were evident from the beginning, as when Muir confided to his brother-in-law that "Grieve is ... everything that is out-and-out".[29] The depth of their mutual esteem, however, cannot be doubted. Muir wrote highly favourable reviews of MacDiarmid's early books and dedicated his study of John Knox (1929) to him. MacDiarmid published an early version of Muir's 'Chorus of the Newly Dead' in *The Scottish Chapbook*, both published and wrote in praise of his ballads—particularly, if not surprisingly, of his Scots ballads—and hailed him in the *Scottish Educational Journal* as "incomparably the finest critic Scotland has ever produced".[30] He also dedicated his first longer poem in Scots to him.[31] Yet there is not a single reference to Grieve in *An Autobiography*, and no indication amid the invective of *Lucky Poet* that the two writers were ever close (unless one is to identify Muir as the subject of the following:

> [I] have never lost a friend once made—except once; and in that case, as I shall show, the one I happened to value most and for whom I would if need be have sacrificed all the others.[32]

It is typical of the chaotic organisation of *Lucky Poet* that nothing further is heard of this invaluable friend).

VI

In his essay 'The Place of Edwin Muir', Seamus Heaney observes:

> Muir's Scottishness, once assailable for not displaying a sufficiently nationalist fervour or not sporting the correct ethnic regalia, now appears pristine in the light of an older alliance between Scotland and Europe.[33]

But does it? How Scottish was Muir's Europeanism? More to the point, how genuine was it in creative terms? Heaney's judgement implies that Muir's career, rather than MacDiarmid's, recalls pre-Reformation Scotland's free intercourse with the whole world of Christendom, that his achievement is somehow of less restricted, less merely local significance than his younger contemporary's.

Certainly, Muir had a detailed and profound knowledge of European literature and he engaged far more thoroughly with the moral issues in European politics at mid-century than MacDiarmid did. His work as a translator is of no little importance: to have introduced the English-speaking world to the fiction of Kafka is to have made a signal contribution to the imaginative life of one's time. He was acquainted at first hand with the agonies of central Europe under tyrannies of both right and left—indeed there could hardly be a more devastating measure of the inanity of MacDiarmid's Stalinist posturing than the *Autobiography's* account of the communist coup in Prague in 1948.

But none of this has much relevance artistically. Muir never succeeded in evolving poetic forms in which to accommodate his widened horizons—as MacDiarmid did again and again in *A Drunk Man* and in his poetry of the early 30s, striking strange and unpredictable harmonies from his collisions with the ideas of Bergson, Shestov, Dostoevski, Solovyov, Rilke and a dozen other European thinkers and poets. One has to look only a little further than *The New Age* and Prince D.S. Mirsky's two histories of Russian literature to find where MacDiarmid came upon these ideas, but their source is not important. The poetry is in what he made of them.

Faced with a national culture they both saw as debilitatingly provincial, the two poets reacted in opposite ways. MacDiarmid created an enabling fiction of a Scottishness radically at variance with any that could be extrapolated from the conditions all round him, consecrating his literary and political energies to a sort of Yeatsian opposite of the actual Scotland. But it was in the actual Scotland that he needed his books bought or at least read, and after his last Scots volume, *Scots Unbound and Other Poems* (1932), failed to sell more than 50 of its 350 copies (and the impoverished poet was called on to pay the £25 he had promised against any loss sustained by the publisher), the fiction lost its power to sustain him.[34] And yet, chaotic and foreshortened though his career as a lyric poet may have been, it seems unlikely that it would have taken off at all without his high Romantic faith in his role as prophet of a regenerated Scotland.

Muir's reaction to the prevailing cultural conditions was more reasonable, certainly, but also more timid. He attempted to put Scotland behind him, retreating further and further from imaginative confrontation with the country, until he concluded, in *Scott and Scotland* that the people who lived there would only be whole when it had become indistinguishable from England in all things except its weather. Avoidance of cultural marginalisation was the object alike of MacDiarmid's attempt to remake himself in the image of the Uncanny

Scot and of Muir's to shuffle off the coil of national identity. (Muir's attitude is anticipated and rejected in *A Drunk Man*, when the protagonist rebukes himself for striving to shirk the ghastly weed which is simultaneously his crucifix and skeleton:

> Thistleless fule
> Ye'll ha'e nocht left
> But the hole frae which
> Life's struggle is reft ...[35])

Though creatively less rewarding, Muir's course of action was, in one respect at least, healthier than MacDiarmid's. Both poets rejected their Calvinistic upbringing, but only the former took serious steps towards emancipating himself from its influence. There is no biographical contrast more suggestive than that between Muir's liberation of his creativity under psychoanalysis in London and Grieve's destruction of his in the massive act of repression he undertook in Shetland in the summer of 1933, that shutting of the theatre of his sensibility recorded in the appropriately nerveless English of 'On a Raised Beach'.

In a letter of 1931, Muir commented, "(O)ne wants to be there. And there is no there for Scotsmen".[36] Neither, alas, is there any 'there' for readers of the poetry of Edwin Muir. In essays written 35 years apart, he identified a "something materialistic in the imagination", "a particularised rendering of the factual" as "one of the greatest qualities" of the literature of the Scots.[37] As these are precisely the qualities in which his own work is most damagingly deficient, one might be tempted to link the poetry's failure to register the sensuous world with a mental disengagement from Scotland on the part of the author. A profound, perhaps even pathological, distrust of the empirical arising from his traumatic early life provides a more likely explanation, however. It is as if Muir could never again depend on the evidence of his senses after losing his family to the struggle to adapt to the inchoate rigours of life in Glasgow. In the stench of the Greenock boneyard where he worked for two years—after seven in a bottle-factory—he endured a present so terrible that he refused to accept it had as much reality as his past. His alienation transformed Orkney into a timeless, symbolic landscape, an actually-encountered Eden to set against the terrors of Clydeside and the modern world generally.

In the shambles of his own history, Muir saw a paradigm of all histories: events are meaningless if measured on their intrinsic terms.

Only by divining the archetypal pattern behind the chaos of living—the Fable behind the Story—can significance be attributed to experience. Muir comes dangerously close in all of this to reinstating the Calvinist dualism he attacks in his Scottish criticism, to according life meaning by draining it of substance. It would be unfair, however, to say that the featurelessness of his verse is an inescapable consequence of his philosophy: poets as diverse as Vaughan, Blake and Yeats, after all, have created poetry out of a temporal/eternal opposition. The problem is less the Fable/Story dichotomy in itself than Muir's identification of poetry with the timelessness of Fable, and prose with the temporality of Story. This seems to have been what led him to expunge from his verse the concrete particulars upon which he might have built an effective symbolism. The poetry could have survived planting "one foot in Eden", that is to say, if only its other foot had remained on more familiar terrain.

It is astonishing to come from the pallor and timidity of the poetry to the colour and vivacity of Muir's recreation of his Orkney years in the opening chapter of *An Autobiography*. Incidents recalled in rich detail there cry out for the sort of treatment Seamus Heaney was to give to strikingly similar material in *Death of a Naturalist*. Yet they are either passed over in the verse or else mythologised out of existence (as happens, for example, to the memory of a terrified escape from a proffered school-boy fight in 'Ballad of Hector in Hades'[38]).

The reader is haunted by a similar sense of lost opportunities when faced with the poetry based on Muir's experience as director of the British Council's Institute in Prague over a three-year period from the autumn of 1945. The physical devastation of central Europe, the plight of the refugees, the first-person accounts of atrocity, and then, following the communist *putsch* in 1948, the direct experience of political terror in (appropriately) the city of Kafka—all moved him deeply, corroborating his sense of history as chaos. 'The Border', 'The Good Town', 'The Usurpers' and a number of other poems were drafted in response, but Muir's weeding out of specificities in the hope of making these pieces more 'symbolical'[39], ensures that they are no stronger in their impact than earlier, merely scholastic allegories of totalitarianism like 'The Ring'. No English-speaking poet was better placed to register the trauma of post-war Europe: once again, however, Muir's aesthetic let him down.

His lack of clear-sightedness about poetic procedure turns almost every connection between Muir and other 20th-century poets to his disadvantage. A comparable sense of the Fall is adumbrated in the more autobiographical among Louis MacNeice's lyrics, where it is rendered at once sadder and less sentimental by subtle attention to the "incorrigible" pluralities of the phenomenal world. The sceptic MacDiarmid illuminates the implications of the incarnation far more vividly in 'Harry Semen' than the believer Muir in the inert 'The Annunciation' ("The angel and the girl are met"). Heaney's parables in *The Haw Lantern* probably owe something to such late Muir pieces as 'The Difficult Land'—has any other contemporary poet read him half so closely?—but they only serve to demonstrate how an allegorical approach can be vindicated by wit (in both senses) and a severe formal self-consciousness.

Muir's elaborate figurative strategies issue in emblems rather than symbols—in two-dimensional correlatives for what the *Autobiography* and letters insist were three-dimensional apprehensions. Syntax increases in muscularity as the career unfolds, the rhythmical constrictions of the early work are gradually shed, and yet the poems never quite lose their thin-blooded, enervated character. Even those among them for which the highest claims have been made—'The Combat', 'The Journey Back' and 'The Labyrinth'—set their action at too great a remove from the quotidian to implicate the reader in the outcome. The customary description of the last of these as 'Kafkaesque' typifies the indulgent nature of most commentary on Muir: comparison with Kafka can only highlight the stubbornly literary quality of the nightmare of recurrence in 'The Labyrinth', its lack of the ordinariness, the horrible plausibility, of *The Castle* and *The Trial*.

It is curious, given its lack of a spatial dimension to complicate and complement its obsessive temporality, that Muir's work so centrally employs the word 'place'—'The Narrow Place', 'The Original Place', 'The Unattained Place', "the longed for place" and so on. Most of the poet's places, however, remain airy nothings rather than local habitations. When he writes of specific locations—of Orkney in the very early 'Childhood', the late 'The Brothers' and the two 'Horses' poems, or even of Salem Massachusetts, in the slight though telling late lyric of that name—his verse suddenly comes to life. On those very rare occasions when he dwells on the actuality of a contemplated scene, Muir's symbolism takes on an uncharacteristic resonance. There is, perhaps, an ultimate propriety about the fact that his truest poetry arises in response to a direct descriptive approach to the visible realities of Scotland, the place he assiduously avoids confronting through the generality of his career:

Scotland's Winter

Now the ice lay its smooth claws on the sill,
The sun looks from the hill
Helmed in his winter casket,
And sweeps his arctic sword across the sky.
The water at the mill
Sounds more hoarse and dull.
The miller's daughter walking by
With frozen fingers soldered to her basket
Seems to be knocking
Upon a hundred leagues of floor
With her light heels, and mocking
Percy and Douglas dead,
And Bruce on his burial bed,
Where he lies white as may
With wars and leprosy,
And all the kings before
This land was kingless,
And all the singers before
This land was songless,
This land that with its dead and living waits the Judgement Day.
But they, the powerless dead,
Listening can hear no more
Than a hard tapping on the sounding floor
A little overhead
Of common heels that they do not know
Whence they come or where they go
And are content
With their poor frozen life and shallow banishment.[40]

VII

The ironies surrounding *Scott and Scotland* are multiple. The book is famous for its strictures against the use of Scots for serious literary purposes, yet it was commissioned by the two most eminent practitioners of Scots and Scottish English since Burns and Stevenson (in their respective domains of verse and prose)—MacDiarmid, and the novelist Lewis Grassic Gibbon—for their Routledge series, *The Voice of Scotland*. By the time it was published in 1936, Gibbon was dead and MacDiarmid had ceased to write in Scots, though he had not acknowledged the fact, and the enormous gap between the composition and the collection of his poems would occlude it for many years. In a further irony, *Red*

Scotland, MacDiarmid's own contribution to the series of which he was now sole surviving founder, had been blocked by the publishers and its manuscript lost.

Much of the controversy aroused by *Scott and Scotland* in the 30s and 40s seems from the vantage point of the 90s to have been misplaced, as the book is less a work of empirical criticism than the projection of a mood. Even Willa Muir, Edwin's most redoubtable and indeed intimidating defender, admitted as much in *Belonging* when she related its bitter tone to her husband's despondency in the wake of his tour of the country at the height of the unemployment crisis of 1935 to research his book *Scottish Journey*.[41] Other, less flattering, reasons might be adduced to account for the splenetic character of the study, Muir's frustrating struggles with English poetic idiom among them.

Even if we take *Scott and Scotland* on its own terms, it soon becomes clear that it is, in essence, an attempt to flesh out a subjective, poetic apprehension of Scotland as a negative entity. The second paragraph states that Sir Walter Scott

> spent most of his days in a hiatus, in a country, that is to say, which was neither a nation nor a province, and had, instead of a centre, a blank, an Edinburgh, in the middle of it.[42]

In order to support the claim that the novelist operated in a cultural vacuum, Muir is forced to ignore an array of biographical facts, and to misread the extracts from the *Journal* he consulted at second hand in John Buchan's *Life*. The inadequacies of Muir's critique of Scott have been put beyond dispute by a number of recent commentators[43], so there is no need to linger over them.

MacDiarmid, in any case, was upset less by the reflections on Scott which make up the second half of the book than by the opening chapter on 'Scottish Literature'. Muir's main argument here is that Scottish culture after the Reformation underwent a "disassociation of sensibility" (he uses a variation of Eliot's phrase), and that Scottish life has ever since been characterised by internal division. He finds this division in literature in the tendency of writers to feel in one language— Scots—and to think in another—English. Muir makes some passing references to MacDiarmid, but never admits him to his argument. The absence of *A Drunk Man Looks at the Thistle* from his deliberations is as startling as the absence of serious reference to Yeats' poetry would be from an account of Anglo-Irish literature in 1936—or perhaps rather more startling, given that the project of MacDiarmid's art had from the outset been the reintegration of Scottish literary sensibility, the healing of the very divisions which provide Muir's main subject.

Muir's failure to acknowledge the nature and scope of MacDiarmid's poetry is most damaging to his thesis when he turns his attention to G. Gregory Smith's 'Caledonian Antisyzygy'. He argues—convincingly— that the texts chosen by Smith to illustrate the antisyzygy in his *Scottish Literature: Character and Influence* (1919) are typified by static division rather than dialectical energy. MacDiarmid, however, had not stopped to consider whether this was so when he read Smith in the 20s: it is hardly too much to say that, fired by what he construed as a corroborative description of his own imaginative processes, and supplied with a theoretical framework which allowed him to see those processes as continuous with a centuries-old national tradition, he went on to create in *A Drunk Man Looks at the Thistle* a text richly illustrative of the qualities Smith had strained his ingenuity to ascribe to an array of less dynamic writings in 1919.

Muir's persistent slighting of his achievement does not fully account for the younger poet's histrionic response to *Scott and Scotland*. Tiresomely prone to *braggadocio*, Grieve was not really capable of *hubris*. The rage of impotence rather than of wounded pride is suggested by the ferocious and frequently irrational campaign he launched against Muir in 1936 and sustained up to and beyond the latter's death 23 years later. As our knowledge of the chronology and biographical context of MacDiarmid's work grows, it looks increasingly obvious that he was, by 1936, no longer capable of producing the Scots poetry which might have allowed him refute Muir's arguments by example rather than invective. His last rhythmically-adept Scots poems were written in May and June 1933, in the first weeks of his eight-year sojourn in Shetland. 'Harry Semen', 'Ex-Parte Statement on the Project of Cancer' and the stronger passages of 'Ode to All Rebels', along with a number of other pieces, rival the fluency and associative power of *A Drunk Man*. A descent into visionary madness provides the common theme of these poems, which implicitly identify the Scots language with a dangerous primal domain of instinct and emotion. Exactly contemporary with these Scots works are such English poems as 'Vestigia Nulla Retrorsum', 'Stony Limits' and 'On a Raised Beach'— cold, anti-lyrical celebrations of the subjection of instinctual and affective life to the controlling power of intellect. In their linguistic medium and *quasi*-scientific 'objectivity', these latter pieces point towards the subsequent development of MacDiarmid's writing, perhaps the only development open to him if he was to avoid the lair of unreason and deranged emotion that Scots had come to represent:

> Particle frae particle'll brak asunder,
> Ilk ane o' them mair livid than the neist.
> A separate life?—incredible war o' equal lichts,
> Nane o' them wi' ocht in common in the least.
> Nae threid o' a' the fabric o' my thocht
> Is left alangside anither; a pack
> O' leprous scuts o' weasels riddlin' a plaid
>   Sic thrums could never mak.[44]

The psychological turmoil of this period of the poet's life—the long, complex aftermath of the break-up of his first marriage—issued eventually in a complete mental and physical breakdown and a six-week hospitalisation in Perth in 1935. The poet was still in convalescence in June of the following year when extracts from Muir's book appeared in *Outlook*.

Given these conditions, and the fact that the Grieves considered the Muirs to have been unhelpful to the point of callousness during the poet's illness on the mainland, it is not surprising that MacDiarmid should have seen *Scott and Scotland* as a betrayal. (Between leaving Whalsay and registering at the Gilgal Nursing Home in Perth's Murray Royal Hospital, Grieve and his wife, Valda, stayed for a few days at F.G. Scott's rented summer house in St. Andrews. The Muirs had settled in the town earlier in 1935. Valda saw much of them after her husband's removal to Perth. Scott, who insisted on Grieve's hospitalisation and paid his bills, presumably left Edwin and Willa in no doubt as to the dire state of their one-time friend's personal and economic circumstances.[45])

MacDiarmid's vituperative response to what Alan Bold[46] not unreasonably depicts as Muir's attack on him centres on *Scott and Scotland*'s challenge to the cultural and linguistic programme of the Scottish Renaissance Movement. Muir's deterministic, selective arguments about the use of Scots and the impossibility of a modern Scottish literature might easily enough have been rebutted, as, indeed, they subsequently have been by a series of Scottish critics. But it was on MacDiarmid's individual artistic predicament rather than his ideological position that Muir landed his most telling blows. Hence the fury and intermittent incoherence of the Borderer's response. The following, crucial comments seem as precisely applicable to MacDiarmid's case as they are problematically appropriate to Scottish literary culture generally:

> [If a Scottish writer] wishes to add to an indigenous Scottish literature, and roots himself deliberately in Scotland, he will find there, no matter how long he may search, neither an organic community to round off his conceptions, nor a major literary tradition to support him, nor even a faith among the people themselves that a Scottish literature is possible or desirable, nor any opportunity, finally, of making a livelihood by his work. All these things are part of a single problem which can only be understood by considering Scottish literature historically, and the qualities in the Scottish people which have made them what they are; it cannot be solved by writing poems in Scots, or by looking forward to some hypothetical Scotland in the future.[47]

Whether or not these words were intentionally descriptive of Grieve, they fit his plight in the climacteric of the mid-30s with a devastating exactness. He had significantly—and, as posterity seems in the process of agreeing, permanently—added to an indigenous Scottish literature with his lyrics, *A Drunk Man Looks at the Thistle* and various short and middle-length poems of the early 30s. An artist is usually in his own judgement only as good as his next work, however, and the sacrifices incurred by MacDiarmid in creating his poetry up to 1933 made further such achievement impossible. The month before the first extracts of *Scott and Scotland* were published, he despondently confided to a friend his fear that his lyrical capacity had become impaired.[48] He blamed the break-up of his first marriage and his consequent loss of his children for this, but the lack of an audience to remunerate him for his work or even to receive it with a minimal degree of interest—the contextual problems outlined in the passage by Muir—surely played their part as well.

From being a man after Edwin Muir's heart, MacDiarmid became, in a by now proverbial variation on one of his own phrases[49], a man after Edwin Muir's blood. His reckless, relentless pursuit succeeded only in casting the older poet in the role of victim. Muir was dubbed "a leader of the white-mouse faction of the Anglo-Scottish *literati* and a paladin in mental fight with the presence of a Larry the Lamb".[50] MacDiarmid excluded him from *The Golden Treasury of Scottish Poetry* (1940), apparently on the grounds that he was an Orcadian rather than a Scot.[51] The most ill-advised of the Borderer's attacks was published in the second issue of his periodical *The Voice of Scotland* (September-November 1938) in the form of a cartoon by Barbara Niven of an enormous, bathing-costumed Willa Muir with her arm round a tiny lamb wearing Edwin's face. The cartoon conflated MacDiarmid's Larry the Lamb jibe with Valda's reminiscence of Willa on the beach at St. Andrews in the fateful summer of 1935: "sprawling ... in one of those modern bathing costumes—four sizes too small—just oozing with grossness & holding forth unnecessarily on her favourite topic—phallic symbolism."[52]

Muir never responded to MacDiarmid's onslaughts, though some passages of his poetry can be read as evidence that he was deeply troubled by them. His most nearly explicit treatment of the quarrel, 'The Letter', published before the appearance of the Niven cartoon[53], takes no responsibility for inaugurating the breach and offers reconciliation in terms of 'chivalry' and a Platonic view of the relation of time to eternity—terms which could be expected to make little appeal to the dialectical materialist in MacDiarmid:

> But should this seem a niggardly
> And ominous reconciliation,
> Look again until you see,
> Fixed in the body's final station,
> The features of immortality.
> Try to pursue this quarrel then.
> You cannot. This is less than man
> And more. That more is our salvation.
> Now let us seize it. Now we can.[54]

Now they cannot. Twenty years later Norman MacCaig, MacDiarmid's closest friend in the post-war period, tried to mediate between them. Muir was willing to forget two decades of insult and denunciation, though whether he was prepared to admit to any culpability in offending his friend at the lowest and most vulnerable point in his life is not clear. MacDiarmid, however, was immovable: he would have nothing to do with him.[55] And so their disagreement, as Muir feared, has taken on "the features of immortality".

Notes

[1] Peter Butler (ed.), *The Complete Poems of Edwin Muir*, (Aberdeen: The Association for Scottish Literary Studies, 1991), p. 170. Hereafter CPEM.
[2] 'Water of Life', Michael Grieve and W.R. Aitken (eds.), *The Complete Poems of Hugh MacDiarmid*, (London: Martin Brian & O'Keefe, 1978), 2 vols. Vol. 1, p. 317. Hereafter CPHM.
[3] Hugh MacDiarmid, *Lucky Poet: A Self-Study in Literature and Political Ideas, being the Autobiography of Hugh MacDiarmid (Christopher Murray Grieve)*. 2nd edition. (London: Jonathan Cape, 1972), p. 20. Hereafter LP.

[4]'Kinsfolk', CPHM 2, p. 1147.

[5]See Ruth McQuillan, 'A Look at the Langholm Thistle', *Calgacus*, Vol. 1, No. 3 (Spring 1976), pp.14-17.

[6]Dedicatory poem to *Stony Limits and other poems*, CPHM 1, p384. First published in *The Scottish Educational Journal*, 9th June, 1933, as 'A Dumfriesshire Boy'. See LP, pp. 219–22, for an account of the "inexhaustible ... bountifulness" of Langholm's environs.

[7]'Memories of Langholm' by Alister K. Laidlaw (one of the more persistent of Grieve's many pseudonyms). Published in *The Eskdale and Liddlesdale Advertiser*, 25th November, 1908. Recovered by Ruth McQuillan and reprinted in *Lines Review*, No. 69 (December 1978).

[8]LP, p. 3.

[9]'Glasgow', CPHM 2, pp. 1049-50.

[10]Edwin Muir, *An Autobiography*, (London: The Hogarth Press 1954. Reissued 1980), p. 28. Hereafter AA.

[11]LP, p. 8.

[12]This claim was most recently repeated on the cover of T.S. Law and Thurso Berwick (eds), *The Socialist Poems of Hugh MacDiarmid*, (London: Routledge and Kegan Paul, 1978).

[13]Norman MacCaig, in conversation with the present writer, March 1977.

[14]AA, p. 41.

[15]G.S. Fraser, *A Short History of English Poetry*, (Shepton Mallet: Open Books, 1981), p. 313.

[16]AA, p. 123.

[17]Edwin Muir, *Uncollected Scottish Criticism*, edited and introduced by Andrew Noble. London and Totowa: Vision and Barn & Noble, 1982. p. 156-57. Hereafter USC.

[18]CPEM, p. 28.

[19]USC, p. 255. Muir's review originally appeared in *The New Age*, XXXIV (15th November, 1923) pp. 32-33.

[20]'Braid Scots: An Inventory and Appraisement', CPHM 2, p. 1234. This earlier, longer version of 'Gairmscoile' (CPHM 1, p. 72) appeared in *The Scottish Chapbook* of November–December 1923 under a dedication to Muir. A note (p. 63) explained that the poem had been, "Written extempore on receipt of a letter from Mr. Muir suggesting that 'a long poem in the language you are evolving would go tremendously'". 'Gairmscoile' appeared in *Penny Wheep* in 1926 without a dedication.

[21]Hugh MacDiarmid, *Selected Prose*, Alan Riach (ed.), (Manchester: Carcanet, 1992), pp. 22-23. This passage introduced the editorial of the Scottish Chapbook, No. 8 (March, 1923).

[22]CPHM 1, p. 112.

[23]CPHM 1, p. 110.

[24]CPHM 1, pp. 94-95.

[25]CPHM 1, p. 147.

[26]From "The language that but sparely floo'ers" (CPHM 1, p122) to "—Water again! ..." (p. 150).

[27] See Willa Muir, *Belonging: A Memoir*, (London: The Hogarth Press, 1968), pp. 115-118. Hereafter B. See also Peter Butter, *Edwin Muir: Man and Poet*, (Edinburgh and London: Oliver & Boyd, 1966), p. 111.
[28] Letter to the Thorburns, 20th December, 1923, in P.H. Butter (ed), *Selected Letters of Edwin Muir*, (London: Hogarth Press, 1974), pp. 29-30. Hereafter L.
[29] Letter to George Thorburn, 14th May, 1927, L, p. 64.
[30] Hugh MacDiarmid, *Contemporary Scottish Studies*. Edinburgh: The Scottish Educational Journal, 1976. p. 30. Grieve's essay 'Edwin Muir' originally appeared in *The Scottish Educational Journal*, 4th September, 1925.
[31] 'Braid Scots: An Inventory and Appraisement'. See note 20 above.
[32] LP, p. 47.
[33] *Verse*, Vol. 1, No. 6 (March 1989), p. 33.
[34] Grieve's correspondence with Eneas Mackay of Stirling, publisher of *Scots Unbound and other poems*, is preserved in the National Library of Scotland, Acc 7913. See letter from Mackay to Grieve, 9th December, 1932.
[35] CPHM 1, p. 100.
[36] Letter to J.H. Whyte, 10th September, 1931, L, p. 71.
[37] USC, pp. 143, 162.
[38] CPEM, p. 19. See AA, pp. 42-44.
[39] See Muir's comment in BBC broadcast of 3rd September, 1952 quoted by Butter, CPEM pp. 343-44.
[40] CPEM, p. 214.
[41] B, p. 194.
[42] Edwin Muir, *Scott and Scotland: The Predicament of the Scottish Writer*. London: Routledge, 1936. pp. 11-12. Hereafter SS.
[43] See, for example, P.H. Scott, 'Muir and Scotland', in C.J.M. MacLachlan and D.S. Robb (eds.), *Edwin Muir: Centenary Assessments*, (Aberdeen: Association for Scottish Literary Studies, 1990), pp. 87–94. See also Thomas Crawford, 'Scott's Mind and Art', (Edinburgh: Oliver & Boyd, 1969), pp. 1-20, particularly 14-15. Also P.H. Scott, *Walter Scott and Scotland* (Edinburgh: William Blackwood, 1981), pp. 44, 90-91 and *passim*.
[44] 'Harry Semen', CPHM 1, p. 484.
[45] See Alan Bold, *MacDiarmid: A Critical Biography*, (London: John Murray, 1988), pp. 332–34. Hereafter ACB.
[46] ACB, p. 341.
[47] SS, pp.15-16.
[48] ACB, p. 340.
[49] See LP, pp. 28-29 for source of this near legendary misquotation.
[50] LP, p. 21.
[51] Hugh MacDiarmid (ed.), *The Golden Treasury of Scottish Poetry*, (London: Macmillan, 1940, 2nd edition, 1946). See Introduction, p. xxx.
[52] ACB, p. 333.
[53] Muir's poem was published in *London Mercury* XXXVII in November 1937, six years before being collected in *The Narrow Place*.
[54] CPEM, p. 101.
[55] Norman MacCaig, in conversation with the present writer, March 1977.

The Round Tower and the Black Church
Aspects of Austin Clarke's Cultural/Religious Identity

Mary Thompson

Integral to the fabric of Austin Clarke's writing are the rituals and traditions of the Catholic Church—its dogma, its spirituality or lack of it, its essential transcendentalism. His memoirs highlight how his upbringing revolved around religious practice, as was the convention at the turn of the century. His early experience of Catholic education was so similar to Joyce's that *A Portrait of the Artist as a Young Man* "became confused with his own memories or completed them".[1] Whatever the nature of his belief in the Christian god, Catholicism was a vital force in his work, at once life-giving and life-denying. Like Joyce, he retained the form of his Catholicism and the reservoir of imagery it provided.

However, the magisterium of official teaching provoked his resistance; he was not prepared to accept the authoritarianism of the hierarchy. Furthermore, like many of his literary contemporaries and recent predecessors, he was carried on the tide of the increasing secularisation of the imagination. He discovered, as Yeats had done, that, by enacting opposing states of consciousness, he could generate change and release a poetic energy at odds with the denial of life he perceived about him. Within the confines of the page, he could impose an order not always attainable in life. So in his work is posited a self that denies the constraint of fact, that releases a poetic energy at odds with the denial of life around it. This anti-self identifies, not with Joyce's priest of the imagination, but variously with Luther, Swift, Eriugena and even Milton's Lucifer.

Clarke's resistance to the perceived monolith of institutionalised Catholicism takes a specific form, that of a dissenter or protester, although not a specifically denominational protester. His adoption of this persona does not imply the rejection of what Joyce called the logical and coherent in favour of the illogical and incoherent absurdity.[2] It does not imply that Catholicism is entirely abandoned. Rather this persona interrogates and rebukes the follies and limitations of his childhood faith. It suggests that, within the confines of the page, if not in mundane reality, its creator could be, like John Hewitt, imaginatively his own man.[3] It serves also to suggest the complexity of literary continuity, the problems of defining selfhood and the strategies of deliberate crossing of boundaries.

This resisting persona might be broadly described as Protestant, in the sense in which Edmund Burke uses the term:

> All Protestantism, even the most cold and passive, is a sort of dissent. But the religion most prevalent in our northern colonies is a refinement on the principle of resistance: it is the dissidence of dissent and the Protestantism of the Protestant religion.[4]

Wearing the mask of the protester enables Clarke to draw a rich and varied cluster of attitudes and associations which rebuke the operations of institutionalised Catholicism and its pervasive influence on Irish cultural and political life. In the early poetry (up to 1936), this fluid protean persona can facilitate the expression of a cultural identity reminiscent of that of earlier cultural revivalists, thus affirming the young poet's right to an *entrée* into literary life; later, it foregrounds the right of private judgement and elevates individual and closely-observed experience over the *a priori* pronouncements of tradition. It defines or implies certain concepts of a civil state and secularises mystical experience. This persona's remorseless scrutiny and questioning of authority can be discerned in the radical scepticism which underlies the Clarke's mature poetics, which can serve to undermine apparent certainties.

Twice Round the Black Church articulates the *modus operandi* by which Clarke can defy the fact of his inherited Catholicism and become imaginatively his own man. This is highlighted, on the one hand, by foregrounding his Protestant ancestry and, on the other, denying the more dominant Catholic inheritance. He eschews kinship with his beloved, easy-going father ("Of the Clarkes I know nothing," he writes [p. 14]. However, their rural Catholicism is attested in the records of the Wicklow diocese). He chooses, by an act of will, as it were, to inherit "the rich red blood of the Brownes" (p. 7), together with their obstinacy and pride. From Clarke's point of view, the Brownes' great claim to fame was their readiness to protest against the superstition which he perceives associated with Catholicism. Chief among these is Archbishop Browne, who renounced papal authority and, in an iconclastic act, burnt the national relic, the *Bachall Iosa*, thus, "putting the unchristian pooka to flight". The archbishop's suppression of devotional practices strove to dispense "with the apes and toys of the antichrist, the bowing and beckings, kneeling and knocking" (p. 21).

Clarke notes that little is known about Browne's early life except that he was an Austin clerk (p. 12), that is, a priest in the Order of St. Augustine. A characteristic of Clarke's work is his delight in homonymic possibility. Here the close nominal association of writer and bishop suggests that the latter-day Austin Clarke aspires to or possesses something of his chosen forbear's singleness of mind, his desire to rid the country of superstition. This is further reflected in his approval of the "plain and temperate daylight" (p. 24) that bathed the interior of the so-called Black Church, St. Mary's Church of Ireland. Catholic churches, he notes, were "shadowy and mysterious" (p. 23) and nurtured superstition.

Apart from the Protestants in the matriarchal line, one other unidentified ancestor attracts Clarke's attention. This is the unknown Browne who, Clarke claims, was the last to exercise private judgement, on the occasion when he reverted back to the old faith. "I envy those who can trust in private judgement", he writes (p. 13), as he emulates them by choosing to create an enabling lineage.

Clarke knows that this eclectic reappropriation of his ancestry is no more than an act of the imagination. Genealogy, he admits, is a bastard science (p. 14), and will not withstand rigorous examination. But there is a precedent for such deliberately fanciful assertion, for such mythologising of history. It is to be found in Yeats' summoning of an Anglo-Irish Protestant ascendancy to which he could be heir. For Clarke, as for Yeats, tradition became an instrument of the present, affirming cultural and literary status. In an act as bold as Yeats', he articulates his alignment with the very group which Yeats considered the indomitable Irishry, the predominantly Protestant *literati* of the Literary Revival, a self-styled *élite* to which he aspired to belong as early as 1914.

Among those whom Clarke names as seminal influences are Standish James O'Grady, an arch-conservative who excoriated the rising middle classes. His buoyant rhetoric imparted a rapturous zeal for the ancient myths and sagas. There was Douglas Hyde, who, as lecturer at the National University, had already awoken Clarke's interest in the lost centuries. George Sigerson is credited with raising Clarke's consciousness to the contributions of antiquarians who saved the literary tradition from extinction (pp. 166-167). Yeats' influence was sustained, all-pervasive, often disabling, yet an influence Clarke regretted came so late to him.[5] Yeats' poetic quarrel with the self, his *fin de siècle* obsession with imminent death and gloom, the mordant twilight atmosphere of his early poems, reflected Clarke's own deepening despair and suggested that poetic capital might be made of it. More importantly, Yeats' and AE's mysticism suggested that a spiritual dimension was still attainable, albeit on the margins of orthodox religion.

Clarke's early prose and epics like the *Vengeance of Fionn* and *The Sword of the West*, echo Yeats' articles of faith as outlined in his essay 'Magic'—that many minds can flow into one another and that our memories are part of one great memory.[6] Clarke posits an unbroken continuity of racial memory, evident in the "elemental" storehouse that is the physical landscape of Ireland. He declares that poetry is not to be found in the folkmind, but in heroising the race. The epic is now his favoured form of poetic expression, as it was for Ferguson; lyricism, he claims, is to be avoided.[7] Clarke had discovered the mystical, transcendent dimension for which he yearned, and which was stifled under the weight of cloying Italianate devotionalism in his mother church, among a handful of admittedly atypical middle-class Protestants. Like them, he replaced the matter of God with the matter of Ireland, empathising with their post-Protestantism.

By the end of the 19th century, the Anglo-Irish were no longer confidently 'of' Ireland; two decades later, they were further marginalised and the adoption of their seemingly timeless ethnic identity distanced Clarke from the devotional pieties of his inherited religion, and from his unfashionable (in terms of current templates of cultural identity) urban, middle-class roots. The Anglo-Irish exemplified the heroic antithesis of the mundane existence that stifled his imagination. By identifying with them, he could disown the vulgar puritanism, the sexual oppression, the crass *petite-bourgeois* nationalism and theological casuistry which he would later denounce with considerable invective.

Moreover, there was a literary advantage to Clarke's alignment with this self-proclaimed Ascendancy. As W.J. McCormack has pointed out, their antique dignities and guilts rendered the Celtic revivalist invocation of medieval and feudal sources all the more plausible. To Clarke, a latecomer to the revivalist movement from which Yeats had already moved on, the need for such affirmation was all the greater.

Pilgrimage (1929) reflects to some degree a measure of Clarke's desire to distance himself from Yeats' ubiquitous shadow. Many of the poems are set in the historically verifiable, late medieval, Celtic-Romanesque period. This was territory to which neither Yeats nor any other contemporary poet had laid claim. The anxiety of influence could be stilled, it seemed. However, this is the pre-Reformation Celtic church with which certain members of the Church of Ireland—notably the 17th-century Archbishop Ussher—claimed continuity. This choice of site, charged as it was with ancient spirituality, suggests that, following Ferguson's dictum, Clarke still continued to live back in the country he lived in. The strategy that served to signify his independence of Yeats and his mythologising aligned him further with Anglo-Irish antiquarians, by extending their project of investing the past with the spiritual charge of the sacred. Moreover, as Robert Garrett has observed, Clarke interpreted Yeats' movement away from the literary tradition with which he was so strongly associated as a defection, and

> ... Identified himself as the inheritor of a tradition which he felt compelled to extend and develop ... By setting his work into a historical framework, he would fulfil another important aim of the Revival, informing the present age of its rich past.[8]

The fact that he continued to use the medieval setting for his prose romances and dramas right through to mid-century affirms the extent of the shaping influence of revivalism. As was the case with the epics, his writing continued to be a bulwark against an unstable modern world.

A recurring theme of *Pilgrimage* is what Clarke calls "the drama of racial conscience"[9]—the conflict between sexual desire and clerical teaching. This was the topic ignored by the revivalists. To an extent, it prefigures Clarke's later sustained and often vitriolic attacks on clerical interference in sexual matters. Women like the Young Woman of Beare and Gormlai[10], caught in a circle of desire and condemnation, are defiant. They are ambivalent about their sinfulness, yet they retain a sense of moral responsibility. Implicit in these poems is the suggestion that matters relating to sexuality should be governed by private judgement and are not the province of the clergy.

While the poems of *Pilgrimage* signify that Clarke continues to identify with the genteel Protestant *literati* of the previous century,

Night and Morning (1938) traces the evolution of an austere, uncompromising individualism. It enacts Clarke's anguished struggle to reconcile faith and reason, faith and church, authority and conscience, and it places a high value on private judgement. While the conflict may have Joycean overtones, and while a familiarity with the rituals and liturgy of the Catholic Church may facilitate an understanding of these poems, Clarke's self-conscious Protestant anti-self expresses itself in specifically religious terms, with the anguished speaker re-enacting Luther's protest:

> I hammer on that common door,
> Too frantic in my superstition,
> Transfix with nails that I have broken
> The angry notice of the mind.[11]

Here, intellectual freedom is privileged over the Catholic Church's demand of orthodoxy and the superstitions it tolerates; human godliness is perceived in the intellectual capacity. Robert Farren has noted that "of the words which recur in Clarke, thought is most frequent; most of his 'matter' is treated at the level of thought (though thought experienced, of course)". He goes on: "the sensuous words with their load of smouldering intellect make strongly individual work."[12] Within this paradigm lies the danger—and the attraction—of the sin of intellectual pride, of which the speaker is fully cognisant. As a schoolboy, the speeches of revolt of Milton's "majestic fallen angels stirred my mind so that I forgot the grovelling and insincerity of our medieval training [at Belvedere College]." (p. 72-74)

Having denied itself the consolations of filiation, the intellect strives in mental isolation against fear and superstition in a mood of deep rebellion and dissent. However, whether it is ever possible for faith and reason peacefully to coexist remains uncertain:

> O when all Europe was astir
> With echo of learned controversy,
> The voice of logic led the choir.
> Such quality was in all being,
> The forks of heaven and this earth
> Had met, town-walled, in mortal view
> And in the pride that we ignore,
> In the holy rage of argument,
> God was made man once more.[13]

This stanza may be read to suggest that ratiocination reduces God's omnipotence to human proportions; thus interpreted, reason and faith are mutually exclusive categories. Conversely, the lines may suggest that only in impassioned dialogue which distances itself from magical reverence is the fullness of the Trinity revealed. It can be interpreted as a response in keeping with the Protestant principle of prophetic protest, which calls upon believers to question all structures and institutions, especially their own church. Within so honest and sceptical a mind, there are, however, no certainties; thought lives in pain, in sharp contrast to the delusory consolations of Martha Blake's anti-intellectual, saccharine faith.[14] The logical result of the speaker's high value on reason may be the death of God; if the individual is the prior system, then all forms of authority—even the Supreme—are to be distrusted.

The lonely, impassioned struggle fought in the poems 'Tenebrae' and 'Night and Morning' continues in the period beginning with *Ancient Lights* (1955). Now, however, it rages on in other battlefields, namely, in the acute consciousness of the difficulty inherent in truth-telling, and in the allied, radical scepticism that underlies Clarke's poetic technique. Within the spirit of his evolving Protestant individualism, he is impelled to document and record scrupulously the true history of what he observes. According to McKeon, Protestantism

> ... elevates individual and closely observed experience over the *a priori* pronouncement of tradition. But Protestantism is also the religion of the book, of the documentary object, and as such it tends to elevate the truth of scripture as the truth of 'true history'.[15]

Clarke's documentary and empirical emphasis is evident not just in his autobiographical memoirs, *Twice Round the Black Church* and *A Penny in the Clouds,* but also throughout his poetry. An aura of scrupulous historicity is maintained; this is prose and poetry that documents the lives of people who have lived and loved and died.

Clarke read of the fate of Rosanna Ford in the *Irish Press* and kept the cutting in one of his poetry notebooks. The experiences of Martha Blake are based on those of a close relative.[16] A footnote is added to the poem 'Miss Marnell', to the effect that "the actual facts [of Miss Marnell's case] were even more distressing", drawing the reader's attention to the authenticity of the poor woman's plight.[17] Tirades against the church and state are so localised and specific that their author earned the title of "local complainer".[18] Factual errors are few, although they did occasionally occur; for instance, in his outrage at the death of innocent children in an orphanage fire and the insensitive response of the Catholic hierarchy, he gives an incorrect number of fatalities.[19] Such an error serves more to underline the authenticity of the bulk of information supplied, as do the glossaries which he added to editions of poems he edited himself. Insofar as they can be ascertained, the facts of *Twice Round the Black Church* and *A Penny in the Clouds* are reliable. Clarke the chronicler is apparently trustworthy.

However, as the genealogical high jinks quoted earlier suggest, he is no naïve empiricist. He is conscious that the authority and evidence required of narrative, which might permit it to signify truth to readers, is other than that of mere verifiable fact or transparent realism. That fact would suggest a dependence on received authority and *a priori* tradition past whose nets he is trying to fly. So he gropes towards a mode of narrative truth-telling which, through its consciousness of its own literariness rather than literalness, through its defensive strategy, can attain a higher level of truth. It can, however, also result in the clotted texture, the ruptured diction, the obscurantism, the congestion which is characteristic of much of the poetry of the late mid-century.

The precision of the framing of the two books of personal memoirs highlights this quest after a sophisticated, stratified mode of discourse: *Twice Round the Black Church* opens with the young Clarke terrified of a portrait of a watching Shakespeare. "I was certain, because of his name, that the stranger was treacherous" (p. 12), Clarke writes. His observation gives rise to at least two comments: first, that beyond the very real terror of a small boy with a powerful imagination lies the equally enervating anxiety of the young writer faced with the authority and tradition of the literary canon, which Shakespeare exemplifies; secondly, it raises the issue of naming—its power, its reliability, its potential for exploding certainties—which is central to his poetic being. The book ends with Clarke in his final year at Belvedere College, signifying his *non serviam* by delighting in the opening lines of *Paradise Lost* (p. 172). The movement is from the absolute authority of the inherited literary canon to the definitive authorisation of dissent. The writer's intention may resemble that of Stephen Dedalus in *A Portrait*, but the specific reference to Milton implies an identification with the latter's plea for "the trial and exercise of truth", for "the liberty to know, to utter and to argue freely according to conscience, above all liberties"[20], which was to be the guiding principle of Clarke's mature writing.

On the first pages of *A Penny in the Clouds*, we are introduced to young Clarke, now a university student, contrasting the symbols of the 'Protestant Nation' (the quotation marks are the author's, and direct the reader's attention to the fictionalising that he indulged in) with the apparently graceless and lowly National University, of which he is a student (pp. 1-3). His destiny is set to be the antithesis of the aristocratic, elegant and heroic, which was the right of the begowned students of Trinity College. However, by the end of the book he has become a citizen of that now tattered 'Protestant Nation', and is confidently engaged in a robust defence of his poetic technique against the attacks of an elder, George Moore (pp. 209-211). Without losing the historicity that is crucial to his principled integrity, he suggests that behind empirical evidence accrete layers of often contradictory truths, relating to identity and narrative truth-telling which can only be broached with reticence and obliquity.

At other times, the scepticism and self-reliance that led him to dissent in the first place displace even the most fundamental closure. Antinomial categories collapse into each other in, for example, a poem such as 'Ancient Lights'. The first three stanzas describe the disabling, guilt-laden legacy of formative religious practice and the final two the speaker's baptism of self within the parameters of the Protestant, so-called Black Church. The liberation of this self-naming, self-appointing ceremony is conducted within the "spun loneliness" that is characteristic of the individualism it implies. Hereafter, filiation is replaced by affiliation. Clarke will go on, rationally and humanely, to interpret doctrines of sin and law, to promote justice and to live in heightened dialogue with authority, however manifested. However, the binary categories, Catholic oppression and Protestant individualism, unravel. The speaker "walled by heresy ... absolved" himself. This absolution blurs the lay/clerical distinction characteristic of Catholicism; only the ordained priest is invested with the power to absolve sin, yet here is the speaker empowering himself and exulting in the new dispensation. Yet his retention of the concept and language of the sacrament of penance indicates that his new-found self coexists with the old. The "effelgence" he experiences is reminiscent of the celebrations of a saint's feast day, or as he put it, "as though I gained/ For life a plenary indulgence". In the context of his identification with Luther, this comparison of his new-found joy in life with that very abuse against which Luther had nailed his opposition at Wittenburg—the plenary indulgence—shakes our certainties.

Earlier, in stanza six, regretting his inheritance of guilt, he admonished himself:

> ... So think, man, as Augustine
> Did, dread the ink-splattered ex-monk,
> And keep your name.[21]

Ostensibly, the speaker here urges himself to keep to the path of rectitude trodden by his namesake, St. Augustine, and to stay clear of heresy, Lutheran or otherwise. When it is remembered that Luther, too, was a priest of the Order of St. Augustine, an Austin clerk, the oppositions are seen to be less clear cut. When the reader is aware that St. Augustine is associated with the heresy of Manicheism, which sees a tension in the world between good and evil, with the balance weighing in the favour of evil, the orthodoxy implied by reference to an ecclesiastical father is shaken by that very reference. Contested categories contest each other. Semantic possibilities abound.

Much further evidence exists of Clarke's attempts to document the complex truth of individual experience with an honesty and self-consciousness that takes account of the language's inherent capacity to mislead. A reading of 'Sermon on Swift'[22] releases a multiplicity of meanings, but few certainties. The poem documents an actual event, Clarke's 'sermon' on Swift, on the occasion of the tri-centenary of Swift's birth. The focus of the introduction is on factual details—a precise place, date, even time of delivery are given—and this privileges the historicity of the occasion. "In this first lay sermon, must I/Not speak the truth?", the speaker, who is closely identifiable with Clarke, enquires. The rhetoric implies a positive response, while the interrogative form suggests at least a hesitation; a tacit admission of the difficulty of truth-telling, reminiscent of the work of his admired subject, Swift.

The speaker then sketches the life of Swift as described by "known scholars" and "specialists" as a knowable, local eccentric churchman, a "chuckling rhymster" framed in the Deanery window or sharing quips with friends. Into the night this dean goes "when modesty wantoned/With beau and bell". 'Wantoned': an adjective made verb, alienated from its normative function, it goes on to make strange the cosy dean, implying a dark underside to a revered local personage. 'Wantoned' means undisciplined, dissolute, lustful, recklessly disregarding consequences, free play without constraint. The complexity of Swift's character is further implied and expanded upon in the following lines:

> ... A pox on
> Nighthours when wainscot, walls, were dizziness,
> Tympana, maddened by inner terror, celled
> A man who did not know himself from Cain.

Here the language enacts Swift's dis-ease. This is the man in whose imagination the decaying Struldbrugs, Corinna the diseased prostitute, the Yahoos and the ordured city vie for grotesque supremacy.

Clarke immediately establishes a personal intimacy with this complex Swift—he stands in the "pure clear ray" that once touched the dean. With his aforementioned ancestor, Archbishop Browne, this trio share a desire to dispel fear and superstition. Another writer, Rabelais, is introduced, a man whose work appears to rest on modern, progressive Protestantism, opposed to tyranny and dogmatism. Through their comic, inexhaustible inventiveness, through their obscenity, invective and plenitude, Swift and Rabelais refuse to reify truth. Linguistic transgression as a mode of bearing honest witness, the correlative of Browne's iconoclasm, is foregrounded. Clarke has left behind consolatory fictions and is now involved in a radical and sceptical apprehension of reality.

I have already referred to the common ground that exists between Clarke and his friend and contemporary, John Hewitt, who was, in his own eyes, "the ultimate Protestant", since he had never been baptised or vaccinated against contagious diseases. He chose as a symbol "of the strange textures of my response to this island of which I am a native" the stump of a round tower within a planter's Gothic tower.[23] Clarke's singular engagement with this island might similarly be symbolised by a round tower within the Black Church of his prose and poetry. His resistance to the perceived restrictions and superstitions of Irish Catholicism can be seen in the guise of its anti-self, a protesting, dissenting persona. In the first place, it took the shape of a cultural identification which enabled Clarke imaginatively to find common ground with the established cultural revivalists, themselves accomplished shapechangers—the round tower of the antiquarians. The empowerment of self through the recognition of individual responsibility for destiny is symbolised in the act of self-baptism performed within the forbidden confines of the Black Church. The evolving persona privileges a sophisticated mode of truth-telling that acts as a counter-critique to, rather than a denial of, the dogmatic certainties which shaped his childhood and which debilitated his capacity for personal judgement.

Notes

[1] Austin Clarke, *Twice Round the Black Church* (Dublin: Moytura Press, first published by Routledge Kegan Paul, 1962), p. 26.

[2] James Joyce, *A Portrait of the Artist as a Young Man* (London: Jonathan Cape, 1968), p. 248.

[3] John Hewitt, *Ancestral Voices: The Selected Prose of John Hewitt*, Tom Clyde (ed.) (Belfast: Blackstaff Press,1987), p. 28.

[4] Edmund Burke, Speech on Conciliation with America, 1775, *The Works of Edmund Burke* (London: Bohn, 1855).

[5] Austin Clarke, *A Penny in the Clouds: More Memories of Ireland and England* (Dublin: Moytura Press, 1987, first published by Routledge Kegan Paul, 1968), p. 201.

[6] W.B. Yeats, *Essays and Introductions*, (London: Macmillan, 1974), p. 28.

[7] I am grateful to Mr. Dardis Clarke for allowing me access to unpublished drafts of an essay, probably written during or earlier than the 20s, variously entitled 'Materials of the Irish Epic' and 'Aspects of Modern Irish Poetry' which significantly enhanced my understanding of Clarke's identification with the literary revivalists.

[8] Robert Garrett, *Modern Irish Poetry*, (Berkeley: University of California Press, 1978), pp. 106-107.

[9] Austin Clarke, *The Collected Poems of Austin Clarke*, (London: George Allen and Unwin, 1936), p. 313.

[10] 'The Young Woman of Beare' and 'The Confession of Queen Gormai', *Collected Poems*, pp. 99-105 and 89-96 respectively.

[11] Austin Clarke, 'Tenebrae', *Poems 1917-1938*, Liam Miller (ed.) (Dublin: Dolmen Press, in association with Oxford: Oxford University Press, 1974), p. 183.

[12] Robert Farren, *The Course of Irish Verse*, (London: Sheed and Ward, 1948), p. 158-159. The italics are Farren's.

[13] 'Night and Morning', *Poems 1917-1938*, p. 181.

[14] 'Martha Blake', *Poems 1917-1938*, pp. 184–185.

[15] Michael McKeon, 'Generic Transformation and Social Change: Rethinking the Rise of the Novel', *Modern Essay in Eighteenth Century Literature*, Leopold Damrosch (ed.) (Oxford: Oxford University Press, Oxford, 1988), p. 165.

[16] I am grateful to Mr. Dardis Clarke for these two items of information.

[17] Austin Clarke, *Poems 1955-1966*, Liam Miller (ed.) (Dublin: Dolmen Press in association with Oxford: Oxford University Press), p. 354.

[18] 'Local Complainer' is the title of a poem in *Poems 1955-1966*, p. 211. In 'Austin Clarke', *We Irish: Essays on Irish Literature and Society* (Berkeley: University of California Press), p. 245, Denis Donoghue writes: "As a local complainer he was tireless and therefore tiresome. Thank God he was a poet too".

[19] In his note to 'Three Poems About Children', *Poems 1955-1966*, p. 353, Clarke writes that 60 children died. In fact there were 36 victims, of whom 35

were children.
[20] John Milton, *Prose Writings* (London: Dent Everyman, 1958), p. 220.
[21] *Poems 1955-1966*, pp. 199-201.
[22] Austin Clarke, *Poems 1967-1974*, Liam Miller (ed.) (Dublin: Dolmen Press, Dublin in association with Oxford: Oxford University Press, Oxford, 1974), pp. 457-460.
[23] John Hewitt, *Ancestral Voices*, pp. 28 and 29.

The Mart of Ideas
Seán Ó Faoláin 1900-1991

Fergus O'Ferrall

I

There were three fundamental transitions in the long literary life of Seán Ó Faoláin. Given that Ó Faoláin's career is central to an interpretation of 20th-century Irish society, it is important to explore such changes in Ó Faoláin's outlook and to indicate his contribution in the light of them. This is the purpose of this essay.

Preliminary to such shifts in Ó Faoláin's world-view a long period of gestation occurred in his intellectual life—"brimmings" he called them in *Vive Moi!*:

> All my moments of understanding have been like that—accumulations of minute experience, drop after drop, each unobserved at the time, brimming over at last as a little or a great fountain of light.[1]

His early childhood in Half Moon Street, Cork, with his fascination for the theatre and the Catholic Church—the two filters through which he imagined life—"brimmed over" when John Whelan made the transition to Seán Ó Faoláin. This fundamental shift from the loyal little empire boy, the son of an admired RIC man, to the romantic nationalist rebel, occurred after he was "dazed" by Lennox Robinson's play, 'The Patriot', in 1915. By 1918, he had assumed the name Seán Ó Faoláin; he had learned Irish and had enthusiastically invested his whole life in the new nationalist identity so easily available after 1916.

The second fundamental transition resulted from his total disenchantment with 'the romantic dream' of Irish nationalism and it coincides with his growing commitment to becoming a full-time writer in Ireland. The central text of this transformation is his great biography of Daniel O'Connell, *King of the Beggars* (1938). Long before the historiographical revolution, launched by T.W. Moody and R. Dudley Edwards in the late 30s, had achieved any public effect, Ó Faoláin single-handedly re-interpreted Irish history. Now a radical liberal democrat, he portrayed modern Ireland in *King of the Beggars* as the creation of Daniel O'Connell, the founder of Irish democracy. He argued that Gaelic Ireland—aristocratic, hierarchic and anti-democratic—had died in the 18th century. The fantasy of a Gaelic state should be abandoned and he urged that an honest and realistic acceptance of a modern, democratic English-speaking, Irish society should lead to a positive recognition of the constructive nation-building that remained to be done. Ó Faoláin's 'O'Connellism' pervades his editorship of *The Bell* (1940-46) and his approach to Irish affairs from the late 30s.

The third transition, and the one which requires perhaps most attention in understanding Ó Faoláin's later commitments in literature and politics, extends over the period 1946 to 1954. He emerges as a convinced Christian, a radical and liberal Catholic and the cosmopolitan Man of Letters. The key texts in this transition are *A Summer in Italy* (1949) and *Newman's Way* (1952).

II

What is revealed in Ó Faoláin's biography is "the history of an imagination" fired by ideas: "my lust is for thinking", he once confessed.[2] His own mind was always a veritable "mart of ideas"—the title of an important editorial he wrote for *The Bell* (June 1942). His non-fiction work is characterised by intellectual discussion and by the refinement of ideas which are then absorbed imaginatively and emotionally in his fiction. Literary critics should not ignore Ó Faoláin's own account of his mental and intellectual development, which he has provided in the non-fiction works when seeking to understand his fiction. Conor Cruise O'Brien was guilty of this in his seminal critical essay 'The Parnellism of Seán Ó Faoláin', published in *Maria Cross* (1953), when he ignored *A Summer in Italy* and *Newman's Way*.[3] When we look at these works, we see that Ó Faoláin is not simply to be understood through his anti-clerical nationalism (or 'parnellism' [with a small 'p'] as defined by O'Brien—i.e. young people seeking national, spiritual and sexual emancipation through anti-clerical nationalism). Ó Faoláin moved rapidly to dismiss romantic nationalism and is best understood through what might be termed his 'O'Connellism' until the late 40s. His later career is best approached through his religious sensibility and his deep commitment to the use of both imagination and intelligence as vital to a life-enhancing religious faith.

I propose, then, to treat at some length Ó Faoláin's relationship to Catholicism, as it is crucial to our appreciation of his work and of his prophetic contribution to modern Ireland.

III

The Catholicism John Whelan experienced as a boy in Cork certainly did not prepare or equip him for "a complex and challenging world". It was a childhood of pretence and over-protection:

> ... a pretence that we were not what we were, a bobby, a bobby's wife, and a bobby's kids. We were shabby-genteels at the lowest possible social level, always living on the edge of false shames and stupid affections, caught between honourable ambitions and pathetic fears, between painful strugglings and gallant strivings, never either where we were or where we hoped to be, janus-faced, throwing glances of desire and admiration upwards and ahead, glances of hatred or contempt downwards and behind.

His Catholic mentors behaved

> ... as if they believed that if nobody mentioned sex organs we would not notice we had them, or as if they had decided that in all such matters as the flesh, familiarity breeds desire, or as if they considered that God, in creating desire for woman in man, had been guilty of a lapse of taste about which the least said the better.[4]

As a republican in the civil war, he suffered the condemnation of the Catholic Church. He was a double loser: he lost his political cause and he lost the solace of his church. He had gambled his soul on a purely human victory and he had lost. From the trauma of the civil war, he was forced to think through fundamental theological questions, in particular the existence of evil, and also to reflect on the inadequacy of Irish Catholicism. This process, indeed—this internal crisis—preoccupied his inner mental life from the 20s to the early 50s.

He reflected upon the inability of the Catholic Church in Ireland to cope with doubt, ideas or criticism:

> ... so while our priests always treated sin with infinite kindness and pity,

doubt was much more likely to be considered as a manifestation of intellectual vanity, or traced to the reading of 'bad books' or the keeping of 'bad company'. Religion in Ireland has always tended thereby to flower as a mystical experience and to wilt as an intellectual possession. Buttressed by emotional appeal and social habit rather than by thought or reason it has even tended to disappear completely when transferred to other climates ...[5]

So behind his fundamental motivation to write were the "mental shocks" which he suffered and which shattered those

... three refracting lenses: Family, Fatherland, and Faith ... Those three lenses had to be shattered because they amounted to other people's clotted thought-filters, composed of received opinions, social convention, political ideas, inherited prejudices.

It took him, he reckons, about 40 years to get free, for he "clung too long to too many loyalties".[6]

His liberation finally came when he experienced European Catholicism, specifically though his encounters with Italian Catholics. He recounts, in *A Summer in Italy*, his chance meeting with "my friend Cipolla" in the great piazza of St. Peter's in Rome. Here was the sort of Catholic who could help him resolve an issue which "had troubled him all his life"; the discovery of non-sectarian Catholicism was "to alter my whole life" quite decisively.

Cipolla was a man whose intellect "had sold itself neither to his race nor to his religion". Ó Faoláin loved the expression of Christian freedom he experienced in Italian Catholicism—a religion "so limber and so light-hearted"—"I had never conceived that it could be so. I fell in love with it on the spot." How different, it seemed to him, from "the defensive sectarian mind" in Irish Catholicism:

> All the Catholics I had hitherto known or known of in Ireland or England had either a chip on the shoulder (Mr. Evelyn Waugh), developed complexes (Mr. Graham Greene), been controversialist (Mr. Arnold Lunn), been terrified rigorists (the type illustrated by our Irish Censorship), or lived in a hallucinatory blue funk (anti-Communists in Connemara) ... Dear Signor Cipolla, I salute you. You are as legion as your race. And, yet, I had never known you existed until we sat in that pub under the Vatican walls, which you both defended and assailed with so much gusto, and with your finger wandering in the beer-stains all unknowingly drew my line of fate.

Ó Faoláin's immediate and passionate wish was "to become one with him in Christ"; in a fever of haste, he rushed to confession and, in St.

Peter's, "was caught, and caught for ever" as he experienced a vivid sense of the Incarnation in the people at prayer: "The Light of the World became flesh of their flesh." Buying a rosary from a pedlar, he set out for the Janiculum to reflect on his conversion experience:

> To myself I said: 'I have left a nation and joined an empire.' As to what kind of empire ... I thought of John Henry Newman's—'a vast and ever-growing imperial Church great enough to make flaws and imperfections of no account'. A bit strong, that, a bit too of-the-earth; a little bit too philosophical ... Yet, Newman was essentially right. Imperfect in an imperfect world. Should it not be said honestly, though, when the imperfections showed? ...

Ó Faoláin concluded that nobody can be "a sound Catholic who cannot be, if he wants to be, an anti-clerical. It is his self-assurance of an inmost and unassailable core of Faith".[7]

Later, he reflected on conversion experience:

> ... in religion, as in love, we can have no certain premonitions of our fate; the *coup de foudre* that strikes us in an instant generates a storm that may have to cross seven oceans for its delicate appointment with our hearts.[8]

IV

Ó Faoláin commenced a deep and sensitive study of the way to Rome of John Henry Newman which issued in *Newman's Way*. He was exploring here a possible model for his own liberal Christian awareness and his freedom as a believer to use his mind fully, as he later remarked in *Vive Moi!*: "Maruriac was right—the Christian sensibility needs the Christian intelligence."[9] Newman's life exemplified the unity of those two qualities:

> One of the greatest attractions—perhaps the great attraction of the adult Newman—is this blending of intellect and poetry, of brains and imagination.[10]

Ó Faoláin was preoccupied by the unitary functions of religious feeling and thought—or, in other words, by the interdependent processes of imagination and reason. In a key passage in *Newman's Way*, he reflects on this:

> All his life he oscillates between the intellectual expressible thing, which emerges from man as law or morality, and the irrational, inexpressible

thing, which enters into men as faith or mysticism. The one is known; the other is experienced. The one is generic, the other is personal. One might call the one classical, the other romantic: that is to say, morality is homocentric and generalised, whereas the mystical experience is deocentric and uniquely experienced. Furthermore, in classical minds the object has priority and is finite: in romantic minds the subject has priority and reaches to infinity. It is never possible to say of John Newman that he gives primacy to one rather than the other.[11]

In this "courtship between the Imagination and Reason", Ó Faoláin saw Newman primarily as the artist rather than the theologian or philosopher.[12] Imagination is crucial in apprehending the mystery of religious faith and for the employment of symbols to mediate between the spiritual and the sensual, the temporal and the eternal, the finite and the infinite, and to emphasise the interconnections between them.

He was acutely aware of the difficulty of expressing religious ideas:

> For what have we, in the end, to express any ineffable idea but images from mortality applied to immortality, and what can these temporal images do, no matter how finely we draw them out, but approximate to the reality of things that are of their nature incapable of expression. Instead of enlightening our affections we may in practice deprave them.

The best we can do is to realise, as Ó Faoláin did, that the "intellect and the imagination are a single co-penetrative force", and we do not have "to choose between two forms of creative freedom".[13] Describing Newman's experience at Segesta in Sicily, Ó Faoláin comments:

> Everyman has his symbol. We must feel that this solitary temple was in some way the image of his heart's desire ... a form of classic grace.[14]

V

From quite early in his life, Ó Faoláin was troubled by very basic theological questions which oppressed him and which became, he says, often "unbearably insistent". Questions like 'why must life be like this?' arose, as he pondered his mother's sufferings and worries: "my mother thus became for me Ivan Karamazov's one innocent child whom God allowed to be assaulted, a prime instance of the seeming monstrous and cruel world He created."[15] When he was 54, he had a momentous meeting with Ivan Ilyich, the priest-philosopher, to discuss the question of evil in the world and why God allowed it—his mother's pathetic life, executions in the civil war, De Valera's execution of former comrades, atrocities elsewhere in the world—the sorts of painful experiences which seared his soul and which left "a blue bruise on the skin of my heart". Ilyich discussed how God, as creator and bestower of human free will, could accept whatever happened, "once it had happened", and can continue always

> ... to whisper to us, plead with us, encourage us, so that we go on trying to make our will coincide with His, feebly or irresolutely, that is to say humanly, to the end. It was when he said that sentence containing the four wonderful words 'once it had happened' that my barricades revealed themselves, and crashed.

Ó Faoláin's insight here was to see that God's action in history is through human activity and responses: if God willingly accepted whatever happened, why should he not also accept it? He did not presume God always approved of that which "had happened" and neither need he:

> For what I finally accepted, that day, was that microscopic portion of the universe called me. I fell in love with me ... And in loving me I suddenly felt expanding in me a great love for everybody else ... life-acceptance involves not only immense joy but immense risks, of complacency, smugness and self-deception. So I was filled with both happiness and terror to know that, inside the shape of this world, without the fallible human will there could be no divine will, that our weakness is part of His strength, that without evil there could be no life, that without the humanity of sinful man the whole of God's creation would fall into as fine a dust as a meringue crushed in a cook's fist.[16]

VI

The encounter with Ilyich so impressed Ó Faoláin because it was the culmination of "several other things that had, over the years, impressed me, faint preliminary brimmings or wellings".[17] For, in truth, his intellect and imagination were always focused upon such religious issues and questions; throughout all his writings, one finds this interest in universal realities, the truths of the Christian tradition and how these are experienced in everyday common experiences. It was precisely "the mystical contempt for common actuality" that he condemned in the Catholic Church in Ireland which revelled

... in the liquefaction of common life, the vapourisation of the mortal into the mystical, the veiling of the natural in the fumes of the supernatural, always at the expense of failing to develop the character of men as social animals.[18]

Ó Faoláin's great slogan in his watershed period as editor of *The Bell* was 'Life Before Abstraction'; "in general," he stated in his first editorial, "*The Bell* stands ... for life before any abstraction, in whatever magnificent words it may clothe itself."[19]

He took pride, in the second issue, that every writer wrote from actual experience, declaring in the third: "a perfect furrow at a ploughing match is as artistic an achievement as a perfect poem." This was not just rhetoric: he wrote an illustrated article, 'Fine Cottage Furniture' in the same issue of *The Bell*. He was seeking to root ideas in the firm ground of actual facts and experiences: he rejected as 'Blatherskite' the typical Irish pub-talk which never gets anywhere:

> *The Bell* believes that the first thing we must do in Ireland is to see clearly— *voir clair*—to have the facts and understand the picture. This has never been attempted before. When Ireland reveals herself truthfully, and fearlessly, she will be in possession of a solid basis on which to build a superstructure of thought, but not until then.[20]

One key "brimming", he remembers, occurred when he was 25. A young professor turned to him and, to his astonishment, said: "You know I think you have made a very useful point there in our discussion." Ó Faoláin noted the Irish enjoyment of "the hot and vivid pleasures of aimless disputation"

> ... for it is of the essence of the Irish love of argument that the destination of a discussion shall never be considered as interesting as the journey. Indeed it is considered rather bad taste to arrive at any destination at all, since this at once ends the pleasure of the dispute.

After the young professor's remark, Ó Faoláin "beheld for the first time ... the calm and elegant satisfactions of constructive discussion as against the heady joys of purely contentious shindyism".[21] Disillusioned with "the mesmerism of the romantic dream" and what passed for political or intellectual discourse in Ireland, he set out to provide in *The Bell* a "mart of ideas", rooted in the actual experiment of daily life. He detested the mental climate of the middle class in Ireland—"full of pietism, profits and ignorant bumptiousness". He saw them as "ossified by an innate dread of insecurity":

> They breed defeatism in politics, laissez-faire in social reform, a hypocritical pietism in religion.[22]

His analysis, in November 1941, sums up his position:

> ... We now find ourselves caught in an enormous, ravelled, simple-minded web—which nobody knows how to disentangle—of Gaelic Revivalism, stark Isolationism, timid and therefore savage Puritanism, crazy Censorship, all originally adumbrated on the highest moral motives, but also on the lowest intellectual level. We do not need to look far for the revenge of life. We find it in the people driven headlong from the loneliness of the land, driven from the barrenness of country life, driven even out of the country itself to a bombed world. Which is, surely, the ultimate commentary on this thing's disconnection with all practical history, all practical life.[23]

Political nationalism served to absolve people "from the need for intelligent, constructive thought".[24] People had retired "to a funk-hole from the traffic of ideas".[25] He sensed "the contraction in Irish life ... the shrinkage one feels most ... and ... the problems that go with these things—men fumbling for power; men fumbling for place; men fumbling for standards, moral, social, cultural; men fumbling on all sides to find out what it is all about, and what it is all leading to ..."

This "intellectual shrinkage" had only one antidote:

> One must only insist that we must have the guts to see ourselves with an absolute honesty, to speak and think without a trace of bunk. For that the requisite is the old one—complete freedom of speech, and a readiness to believe that when a man utters opinions he does so with as much regard for his country and for truth as the man who violently disagrees with him.

He condemned leaders who have "got the squint from looking over their shoulders before they speak or act".[26] Later, he condemned the "complete intellectual vacancy as far as the realities of political ideas are concerned". The example shown by politicians was critical:

> In the largest ways public men serve as models for the whole nation. They can disseminate a general philosophy of living, popularise certain attitudes of mind, set standards and create values, apart altogether from what they can do for the lesser graces of living.[27]

VII

Seán Ó Faoláin was 46 when he "finally abandoned the faith of my fathers, and, under the life-loving example of Italy became converted to Roman Catholicism".[28] In assessing Ó Faoláin's contribution, it is appropriate to recall his own words:

> So every man, certainly every artist, before passing into death, leaves behind him his testament, his witness, his book, his poem, his picture, his music, or his play which we take up with more or less reverence, delight and understanding according as *our* life seems to resemble his. We cherish only what we recognise.[29]

What do we recognise in Ó Faoláin's work to cherish with reverence, delight and understanding?

I suggest that, for the foreseeable future of this island, what we might cherish most in Ó Faoláin's witness and in his art is how he linked his intelligent openness to ideas with his profoundly Christian sensibility. As a *Roman* Catholic, he felt free to resist institutional pressures which forced men and women to put, as he says, "the old wine into new bottles"; without losing touch with "the old Roman vineyard" he did his "own bottling".[30]

In the course of a long life, his anger abated but his passionate reflection on the entire human condition remained. His work imperceptibly provokes his readers to ponder his concern for 'wholeness'. He remained

> ... fascinated to understand, in sympathy, what flaws in the intricate machinery of human nature keep it from fulfilling itself wholly, from achieving complete integrity other than in moments as brief, if one compares them with the whole span of a human life, as a lighthouse blink. I would, then, in my late life-acceptance, embracing as much as I had the courage to embrace of all of life's inherent evil and weakness, try to write, however tangentially, about those moments of awareness when we know three truths at one and the same moment: that life requires of each of us that we should grow up and out whole and entire, that human life of its nature intricately foils exactly this, and that the possibility of wholeness is nevertheless as constant and enormous a reality as the manifold actuality of frustrating compromise, getting caught in some labyrinth, getting cut short by death.[31]

It is this passion for 'wholeness', that makes Ó Faoláin's religious sensibility so central to his whole life's work. In *Newman's Way*, he quotes approvingly Berdyaev's apothegm: "The idea of God is the greatest human idea, and the *idea of man is the greatest divine idea*."[32] "I have come that you might have life and have it in its fullness" is Jesus of Nazareth's own summary of his mission. To have this authentic and full human life, truth and freedom are bound together: "You will know the truth, and the truth will set you free."[33] Ó Faoláin fought against the chopping up of people's lives as moralists so often try to do: "Cannot the flesh and the spirit, the pity and the sorrow of love, nature and the supernatural lie together in one passionate bodily embrace?" he asks.[34] Life should be lived "to the full, brimming it over"; our lives are "an indivisible oneness". So let us not, he pleads, "tuck God away in the church and Venus away in the bed, and miserably and foolishly drain each part of life of the richness of the other".[35]

When we understand Ó Faoláin's fundamental motivation and orientation, we can appreciate better why he was so revolted by Irish censorship.[36] He was angry because censorship banned reflections on questions "about God and Love and Sin and the Devil, and it is these that they like most of all to ban".[37] He confronted distorted religiosity—distorting forces which he felt affected the possibilities of genuine self-understanding and authentic affirmation of religious truth. His example to his generation of writers—the first generation of Irish writers who have had to *think* themselves into personal release, as he described them—was given on "the real battle-ground of contemporary Irish writing".[38] Seeing Ireland as only at the beginning of a "long search for intellectual and imaginative freedom", he felt that writers had a particular responsibility.[39] In *The Bell* in 1945, he wrote:

> It is the nature of writers to have a passionate love of life and a profound desire that it should be lived in the greatest possible fullness and richness by all men.[40]

He wanted to nurture a literature that would nourish Life, that portrayed Life with a Pattern and a Destination. He felt Irish writers should "put theology to the test of experience, either to uphold it or not as their experiences prompt".[41] He regretted, as he put in a title, *The Vanishing Hero* in modern literature:

> Nobody can affirm out of personal integrity alone. Only when certainty returns to men at large, that is, to what we call the world, can affirmation return to literature, and with it the representative Hero. And that, surely

depends on the re-emergence for the purposes of the arts of a general body of human faith.[42]

Why is it so significant that Ó Faoláin made his decisive contribution to the creation of a modern liberal culture in Ireland from a Christian perspective? The question is answered in Professor Patrick Corish's conclusion to his historical survey of Irish Catholic experience:

> The Irish have only slender traditions of a philosophical humanism, much less of a secularist humanism. What humanism they are capable of is rather rooted in religion. It is in some ways a daunting thought that the real elements of pluralism in Ireland may well be the confessional churches; but if this is so, there is nothing to be gained by a refusal to face it.[43]

Ó Faoláin operated within his confession—and applied his radical spirit to his own confession—in order to bring it to a new consciousness of the gospel of Christian liberty. It will be found, as Ó Faoláin says that the priest and the writer, in the end, "ought to be fighting side by side"; there will not be, however,

> ... such common ground as long as the Church follows the easy way of authority instead of discussion or takes the easy way out by applying to all intellectual ideas the test of their effect on the poor and the ignorant.[44]

Ó Faoláin's testament and witness, therefore, contains a continuing central challenge: can we develop a Christian theology for a free and plural society in Ireland—a society that will be infused by Gospel values from a range of different churches? As the *Irish Times* editorial on Seán Ó Faoláin on 22nd April, 1991, put it: "If as a nation we have made any progress towards freeing ourselves spiritually, it was Ó Faoláin and a few like him who urged us on our way."

Notes

[1] Seán Ó Faoláin *Vive Moi!* (Boston, 1964), p. 95.
[2] *Vive Moi!* p. 24 and S. Ó Faoláin *A Summer in Italy* (London, 1949), p. 33.
[3] Daniel Murphy 'Religion and Realism in Seán Ó Faoláin's Prose' in *Imagination and Religion in Anglo-Irish Literature 1930-1980* (Dublin, 1987) for excellent corrective in understanding Ó Faoláin's religious imagination.
[4] *Vive Moi!*, p. 72, p. 21.
[5] Ibid., p. 102.
[6] S. Ó Faoláin 'A Portrait of the Artist as an Old Man', *Irish University Review*, Vol.

6, No. 1, Spring 1976, pp. 14-17.
[7] *A Summer in Italy*, pp. 157-167 for Ó Faoláin's account of his conversion.
[8] S. Ó Faoláin *Newman's Way* (London, 1952), p. 38.
[9] *Vive Moi!*, p. 24.
[10] *Newman's Way*, p. 96.
[11] Ibid., p. 189.
[12] Ibid., pp. 227-228.
[13] Ibid., p. 191 and *Vive Moi!*, p. 258.
[14] *Newman's Way*, p. 183.
[15] *Vive Moi!*, p. 230.
[16] *Vive Moi!*, pp. 227-232 and M. Harmon 'The Making of Seán Ó Faoláin, *Studies*, Vol. 79. No. 316, Winter 1990, p. 394.
[17] *Vive Moi!*, p. 230.
[18] S. Ó Faoláin 'A Portrait of the Artist As An Old Man', *op. cit.*, p. 13.
[19] 'This is Your Magazine', *The Bell*, Vol. 1, No. 1, October 1940, p. 8.
[20] 'Answer to a Criticism', *The Bell*, Vol.1, No.3, December 1940.
[21] *Vive Moi!*, pp. 95-96.
[22] *The Bell*, Vol. 2, No. 6, September 1941, p. 9 and *The Bell*, Vol. 3, No. 1, October 1941, p. 3.
[23] 'The Gaelic and the Good', *The Bell*, Vol. 3, No. 1, November 1941.
[24] 'The Gaelic League', *The Bell*, Vol. 4, No. 2, May 1942.
[25] 'Ireland and the Modern World', *The Bell*, Vol. 5, No. 6, March 1943.
[26] 'Silent Ireland', *The Bell*, Vol. 6, No. 6, September 1943.
[27] 'Eamon De Valera', *The Bell*, Vol. 10, No. 1, April 1945.
[28] 'A Portrait of the Artist as an Old Man', *op. cit.*, p. 13.
[29] *Vive Moi!*, p. 27.
[30] 'A Portrait of the Artist as an Old Man', *op. cit.*, p. 13.
[31] *Vive Moi!*, p. 226
[32] *Newman's Way*, p. 212.
[33] The Gospel of John 10:10; 8:31.
[34] *A Summer in Italy*, p. 21.
[35] Ibid., p. 22
[36] see account of Ó Faoláin and censorship in Michael Adams *Censorship: The Irish Experience* (Dublin, 1968), pp. 81-84 and see also J. Carlson (ed.), *Banned in Ireland: Censorship and the Irish Writer* (London, 1990).
[37] *A Summer in Italy*, p. 33.
[38] S. Ó Faoláin 'Fifty Years of Irish Writing', *Studies*, Vol. 51, 1962, p. 100.
[39] S. Ó Faoláin, *The Irish* (Harmondsworth, 1980 edition), p. 131.
[40] 'Principles and Propaganda', *The Bell*, Vol. 10, No. 3, June 1945, pp. 204-5.
[41] 'Fifty Years of Irish Writing', *op. cit.*, p. 102.
[42] S. Ó Faoláin *The Vanishing Hero: Studies in Novelists of the 20s* (Boston, 1957, reprinted New York, 1971), p. pxlii.
[43] P. Corish, *The Irish Catholic Experience: A Historical Survey* (Dublin, 1985), p. 258.
[44] *The Irish*, p. 119.

'Scenes that surround certain conflicts'
The literature of Peadar O'Donnell reconsidered

Richard English

Scholars have tended either to study Peadar O'Donnell's politics without considering his creative literature, or to discuss his literature without seriously scrutinising his politics. This paper argues that neither aspect of O'Donnell's career—his literature or his politics—can properly be understood unless the other aspect is thoroughly explored and appreciated. The paper is divided into three sections: first, an examination of O'Donnell's literary purposes; secondly, a discussion of his sources and the influences acting upon his work; thirdly, an exploration of some of the problems contained within his central argument.

I

"My pen is just a weapon and I use it now and again to gather into words scenes that surround certain conflicts." So wrote Peadar O'Donnell to his publisher, Jonathan Cape, in February 1933. In the same year, he described his play *Wrack* (1933) as a reply to the 1931 Irish bishops' pastoral, which had attacked O'Donnellite republican radicalism. The bishops, he continued, had blamed the contemporary social unrest on 'Russian gold'; O'Donnell held that the cause lay with "such things as the slapping of wet skirts against people's legs. Therefore *Wrack*". Indeed, the play itself sees a central character declare, "I hate the slapping of wet skirts on my legs", and (like much of O'Donnell's writing) the work emphasises poverty and hardship among the author's Donegal communities.

As these examples demonstrate, O'Donnell's creative writing was engaged writing, emphatically part of a political conflict. It is only possible fully to understand his work if this engaged quality is appreciated. His attitudes towards other writers clearly reflected his own approach. Of Sean O'Casey:

> A great dramatist he was, and his plays are very good theatrically, yet his plays do not excite or stimulate me. His *Plough and the Stars* I find nauseating. There is no character in that play from whom any revolutionary action could proceed.

Arguably, it weakened O'Donnell's own work that he held to such a binding formula. Like John Steinbeck, who also wrote of migrant labourers with a sense of didactic mission, O'Donnell is most convincing when he ceases to preach. But such a suggestion would have earned gruff rejection from the author. In his view, there was an ongoing political conflict, in which his literature played some part. O'Donnell believed the mass of the Irish people was instinctively on his side. In 1932, he confidently declared:

> I know that I know the insides of the minds of the mass of the folk in rural Ireland: my thoughts are distilled out of their lives.

And not only did he know their minds, but he also found the contents agreeable. The mass of the people was, in his view, naturally on an O'Donnellite path. His task was merely to make them aware of themselves and thus to nudge them in the direction in which it was entirely natural for them to proceed. In contrast, when his opponents (bishops, governments, press) tried to draw people in other directions, they were engaged in unnatural pursuits. Of the 1931 red scare episode, for example, he wrote that

> ... the Irish bishops were playing havoc with the rural minds which would naturally, if left free to themselves, sympathise with those they were being incited to destroy.

So O'Donnell's novels and play had only to offer a plausible picture of how things actually were, of life's actual conflicts, and the people would be pushed along the good and natural road. Writing in 1933, again to his publisher, O'Donnell remarked on the one thing needful: "I think that writers today should floodlight the facts of life around them." Again, he described one of his own novels from the 30s as "more like evidence of the way folk live in a townland than a novel".

O'Donnell's thinking here evinced his profound optimism.

O'Donnell and Liam O'Flaherty are sometimes coupled in scholarly discussions, and they indeed manifested some similarities. Virtual contemporaries (O'Donnell 1893-1986, O'Flaherty 1896-1984), both had humble social origins in the west of Ireland and both were writers who displayed left-wing and republican sympathies. But the melancholy, gloomy mood of O'Flaherty's novels, such as *Mr. Gilhooley* (1926), is starkly different from that brighter atmosphere which pervades O'Donnell's fiction. O'Donnell's comparatively jolly treatment of the Irish civil war in *The Knife* (1930) can, for example, be compared with the much darker tone used by O'Flaherty in 'The Mountain Tavern' (1929). It is interesting that Ernie O'Malley—civil war republican and friend both of O'Donnell and O'Flaherty—greatly admired 'The Mountain Tavern' and O'Malley's account of the civil war (*The Singing Flame* [1978]) was nearer to O'Flaherty's melancholy reading than to the merry mood of O'Donnell's civil war autobiography (*The Gates Flew Open* [1932]). Indeed, O'Donnell declared in this latter work his great liking for P.G. Wodehouse and the O'Donnellite presentation of civil war prison is not entirely dissimilar to Wodehouse's version of British public school: japery, jollity, naive optimism, and boyish good humour pervade the wings, the sport, the educational classes.

II

The influences acting upon O'Donnell's political development were many. The social radicalism of his mother and uncle, the encounter with Scottish socialism while investigating migrant experiences, the crucial and massive intellectual impact which Karl Marx had upon his thinking, the arguments and careers of nationalist heroes (including Tone, Lalor, and the Fenians)—all of these played their part. But it is vital to stress that the particular social and regional background of O'Donnell's small farm in Donegal was crucial in moulding his political outlook. That this was so becomes clear on close inspection of his creative writing, and it does so in two main senses.

First, O'Donnell's novels and play identify the problems which, in the view of the socialist republican O'Donnell, needed to be addressed. His books portray life as he felt it actually to be, and in doing so they depict poverty, hunger, starvation, (e)migration, inequality. The Doogan family in *Islanders* (1927) and the Dalachs in *Adrigoole* (1929) epitomise the suffering central to O'Donnell's vision of existing political realities. His experience of these communities had instilled in him the need for social revolution. Secondly, his literature demonstrates that O'Donnell's belief in the possibility of, and route towards, social redemption also had its roots in his social and regional background. His books describe communities characterised by a self-regulatory, communal toughness, by an inherent neighbourliness, by a self-reliance strengthened and defined by a culture of mutual help. O'Donnell argued that "the small farm countryside" had a tradition of "rural socialism in its most militant sense", and from his novels it is clear that his Donegal experiences filled him with the belief that socialism was somehow plausible—even natural—as a way of revolutionising and emancipating those suffering and exploited in capitalist Ireland.

Thus, if one interrogates O'Donnell's literary work, it becomes clear that his Donegal background framed both his sense of the gravity of the problem to be addressed and also his notion that neighbourly self-reliance offered the means of social salvation. Scholars have sometimes misinterpreted this connection between the socialist author and the Donegal subject matter. Terence Brown has suggested that into the social world of O'Donnell there obtruded epic, mythic readings of the west. Certainly, sentimentalised and Romanticised mythic depictions do appear in O'Donnell. But it is less the case that Romantic myth obtrudes into the socialist's realistic setting than that the socialist's socialism was substantially derived in the first place from Romantic conceptions of the strength, neighbourliness, and redemptive resilience of his western folk. Myth was at the heart of the socialist's supposed realism.

III

The logic of much of O'Donnell's political argument evaporates on serious scholarly inspection. Five points need to be made. First, the central thesis running through O'Donnell's socialist republican career was deeply flawed. Those who have sought to explain the failure of the republican left in modern Ireland in terms of factors external to the movement have missed this crucial point: Irish republican socialism has failed primarily because of the weakness and incoherence of its central argument. Just as the collapse of the post-second world war French revolutionary left has to be understood in terms of internal intellectual developments, so too the failure of the inter-war Irish republican left has to be understood in terms of its ultimate intellectual feebleness. O'Donnell held that the struggle between the oppressed nation (Ireland) and the oppressor nation (England) was mirrored by and interwoven with the struggle within Ireland between the oppressor classes and the oppressed working classes. According to this argument, English involvement in Ireland grew out of the desire for economic exploitation *via* capitalist structures. England's influence over Ireland would, therefore, sustain capitalism, and those with a social imperative to uproot capitalism (the working classes) had a social imperative to support Irish republicanism. Similarly, those with a vested social interest in maintaining capitalism would lean towards some form of imperial link with England. Thus, in O'Donnell's view, cross-class republicanism was a contradiction in terms. In December 1927, he declared: "It is about time we heard the last of the childish talk of uniting all classes to free the country. Such balderdash is ages out of date." Social and national struggles were held to be symbiotically related. As the Republican Congress movement (of which O'Donnell was a leading member) declared in the 30s: "We believe that a Republic of an united Ireland will never be achieved except through a struggle which uproots capitalism on its way."

The problem with his argument is that the relation between, on the one hand, economic interest or background and, on the other, attitudes towards nationalism was in fact far more complicated than O'Donnell would have us believe. There were a variety of social classes whose economic interests led them towards sympathy with Irish republican separatism, and very few of these groups desired the sort of anti-capitalist class struggle envisaged by O'Donnell. Moreover, substantial sections of the working class—most spectacularly in Ulster—defied republican socialist logic. Nationalist workers tended to prefer the socially conservative projects of, for example, the capitalist Fianna Fáil party to the more radical ambitions of the republican left; while Ulster Protestant workers identified their economic best interests as lying within, rather than outside, a United Kingdom framework.

Secondly, republican socialists of O'Donnell's hue lacked an adequate theory of power. Where Fianna Fáil scooped up authority by means of pragmatic endorsement of majoritarian practice, the O'Donnellites preferred to remain in the extra-constitutional and purist margins. Reserves of strength were built up by those willing to build on the actual power of independent Ireland's state structures. Those who howled angrily at the illegitimacy of this mean compromise of a state were increasingly drowned in the noise of electoral activity and by the enormous practical power which participative political action enabled constitutional nationalists to wield.

Thirdly, the early 20th-century republican left, in which O'Donnell was so energetically active, lacked an effective politics of the land. In the inter-war Irish political climate, this was a crushing weakness. When the left endorsed policies of land nationalisation, they were greeted with a deafening thud of disapproval—just as similar endeavours on the part of Michael Davitt and James Connolly had previously met with similar rejection. Having fought to acquire peasant proprietorship, O'Donnell's sought-after constituency was simply unprepared to tread the path to his preferred state farming policy. Yet if republican socialists compromised and suggested that those who wanted to hold their land would be able to do so, then farmers understandably looked on with some caution and opted to hear the same promise from people who had greater power and greater credibility (most particularly, again, Fianna Fáil). O'Donnell did indeed equivocate. His own preference was for state farming, but he at times endorsed the right of farmers to hold their own land. Such equivocation bore meagre fruit.

Fourthly, O'Donnell and his comrades failed to offer any plausible reading of the one part of the island which actually possessed a sizeable urban proletariat. O'Donnell argued, rightly, that different forms of economic development were significant in determining the existence of Irish partition. But he failed to take the next intellectual step forward and recognise that, precisely because of the industrial context of Ulster's economic development, Protestant workers in particular would identify their economic interests as being best served by the continuation, rather than the breaking, of the British link. The republican left continually proclaimed that the workers of north and south shared a common interest in fighting against the oppression of capitalist bosses. But they were unable to persuade Ulster Protestants that this was in fact the case, and made virtually no impression on unionist politics in the inter-war period.

Fifthly, O'Donnell was incoherent in his approach to political violence. He was critical of those who centralised the "cult of armed men" and stressed, instead, that force should be used only as an adjunct to a mass social struggle built on economic foundations. He was respectfully critical of the people who provided the main focus of opposition to the 1921 Anglo-Irish treaty, suggesting that they were soldiers/martyrs rather than true revolutionaries: "They were the stuff that martyrs are made of, but not revolutionaries, and martyrdom should be avoided." And he was disrespectfully critical of the purest of physical force IRA men, Sean Russell, when he described him as having "no brains". But while O'Donnell's theory stressed the need to move away from the "cult of armed men" version of Irish republicanism, in practice he worked at the heart of that quintessential republican armed cult, the IRA. He was in the army's inner circle during the 1924-34 decade, despite the fact that, at no point during that period, did the organisation endorse O'Donnell's view that social struggle, rather than physical force, should be the central dynamic of republican advance.

O'Donnell attempted to square the circle by claiming that the IRA had been born out of popular class-struggling intentions:

> The execution of James Connolly [in 1916] was the awakening of the Irish workers. The driving force of plain humanity in Irish unrest was explained to the Irish workers by the teaching, life and death of one man ... It was as Connolly's Union that the Irish Transport and General Workers' Union gripped the country. The Irish political struggle came under a new light. Out of the ranks of the workers and peasants the Irish Republican Army grew. The imperialism of the gombeen man was plain to the workers from their new class-viewpoint, and the national inspiration merged into the social longings and hopes of the workers. The workers became the insurrectionary nation.

In fact, the IRA in the post-1916 period is not capable of being explained in terms of these class-struggling dynamics; the cross-class nature of the republican struggle and ideology of these years is one of their most striking characteristics. But the tension between assumed popular social radicalism and actual conservative impulse was sufficiently great to push O'Donnell into, first, working impotently against the physical force grain in the IRA until 1934 and, secondly, leaving the IRA when he finally realised that the organisation was not in fact an appropriate vehicle for the expression of socialist republican ideas. The army's concentration on the centrality of force predictably and unavoidably marginalised O'Donnellism.

Thus, in conclusion, it is vital to any full appreciation of Peadar O'Donnell's literature to grasp the nature of his political purposes and it is equally crucial to our understanding of his political project to scrutinise his creative literature. Moreover, the political argument pervading his literary and other activities emerges as a distinctly unconvincing one. The central economic-nationalist argument is confused; there is no adequate theory of political power; the question of land is unsatisfactorily answered; Ulster is poorly understood; and the attempt to work through the medium of the physical force tradition was doomed to dismal failure. In later life, O'Donnell declared: "I never was on the winning side in any damn thing I ever did." After serious consideration of his politics, this should not perhaps come as much of a surprise.

For fuller treatment of O'Donnell and his political career see R. English, *Radicals and the Republic: Socialist Republicanism in the Irish Free State 1925–1937* (Oxford: Oxford University Press, 1994). This book argues that the crucial reason behind socialist republicans' failure lay in the intellectual weakness of their argument. In this it resembles Sunil Khilnani's treatment of the post-war revolutionary left in France (*Arguing Revolution: The Intellectual Left in Postwar France* [New Haven: Yale University Press, 1993]) and differs from the most recent treatment of the Connollyite left in Ireland, W.K. Anderson's *James Connolly and the Irish Left* (Blackrock: Irish Academic Press, 1994). The latter book leaves unscathed Connolly's supposed "recognition that the struggle for national independence was an inseparable part of the struggle for socialism, and that by combining the forces of socialism and nationalism both would be strengthened". Anderson offers little discussion of Peadar O'Donnell and does not seriously address the problems with the socialist republican argument which have been outlined in this paper.

A Single Flame

C.L. Dallat

I begin with an apology to those attracted to this talk who assume the eponymous flame owes something to the Confucian maxim, "It is better to light a single candle than to sit and curse the darkness". As this aphorism has become an epigram for the co-operative movement and its heirs, the Workers' Educational Association, Credit Unions *et al*, it might have been reasonable to assume that a seminar under this *aegis*, within a school under the crimson banner 'Comrades and Contemporaries', would explore the concepts of self-help and self-improvement as John Hewitt's inheritance from the free-thinking tradition. This talk is, on the contrary, about religion rather than politics and its intention is, albeit unfashionably, to emphasise rather than bury religious differences. In this context, the single flame which I maintain is part of Hewitt's legacy may be seen, as we proceed, to owe more to as unlikely a source as John Henry Newman's hymn 'Lead Kindly Light'.

This perverse line of thought began in Guernsey last summer just after the third John Hewitt International Summer School, as I listened to a Salvation Army band play 'Crimond' outside a Methodist chapel surrounded by traffic signs in Norman French *patois*, looking out to Castle Cornet, the last bastion of royalism in the English civil war. These conjunctions spoke confusedly of the relation of religion to place, the Channel Islands being notionally Protestant as part of the Anglican See of Winchester—yet maintaining a Mediterranean *ambience* and finding themselves politically, at least in Cromwell's day, on the Catholic—or rather Arminian—royalist, episcopal side.

The following day saw me back in my office in Coventry, the city where Hewitt spent his years of exile in "an alien place/among bland strangers". Eating my sandwiches in the bombed-out shell of the cathedral, as I imagine Hewitt to have done under the baleful Polynesian stare of the Epstein sculptures, I was moved—as I unfailingly am in that place—by the way in which the ruins have evolved as a centre for reconciliation rather than as a monument to wartime antipathies. This observation leading rather obviously to a reflection on whether Garron Tower, in its Summer School clothing, is capable of having the same effect. Is it, in fact, Hewitt's "council of sunburnt comrades" or merely, like the Ulster Folk Museum, "a field for the faction fights" (or rather 'fiction fights', since the paving stones are, in this case, predominantly literary rather than literal)? Thus one moves from thinking about John Hewitt the man, to thinking about 'the Hewitt', the institution.

Interestingly, at the end of the third Summer School, I overheard the chance remark that "the Catholics are getting it this year": this clearly in response to certain talks which attempted—in perhaps too sophisticated a fashion—to probe the inadequacy of existing Protestant and Catholic binary polarities. It is not surprising that such divisions, created through struggles which demanded the amalgamation of ever larger groupings on either side to the detriment of the varieties of belief and opinion assimilated to them, find ready acceptance in news media, where the space to explore subtle gradations is largely unavailable. In such a context, all attempts to work towards mutual understanding (even in a more sophisticated context) are viewed as either horse-whipping or self-flagellation; alternate bouts of criticism and—in the best Maoist style—enforced self-criticism.

The problem is not, clearly, a local one; anyone who has witnessed the conception and limited impact of Greens, Lib-Dems and others in the Westminster power-game will know that such un-Occamian schisms are largely incomprehensible to the public at large, the question 'Are you a Tory Green or a Labour Green?' being universally acknowledged as the direct descendant of a well-known Belfast Jewish joke. What is important to recognise is not that such reductions exist, but that all means towards the understanding and resolution of conflict must first recognise difference and diversity and then pointedly refuse to deal on them-and-us terms, and reject the megaphone diplomacy which is, sadly, as popular with progressives as with reactionaries.

Typically, liberal opinion has seen 'balance' as being the operative method. Thus, when an opposition spokesman has unearthed a *scandalum magnatum* about the incumbent party and exposed it, chapter and verse on, say, the BBC's *Today* programme, a government spokesman is naturally allowed airtime to deny totally all that has been said and, normally, to question the accuser's lineage. One of the problems with such liberal balancing acts is the assumption that all opinions are equal or equally valid; this is predicated on the presumption that all are simply different versions of each other. Thus it is assumed that Northern Ireland and the Republic have simply arrived at two equitable, but different, post-colonial settlements (one of which is believed by some—and feared by others—to be merely an interim stage in some pattern of 'true' post-colonial development). In the same way, it is assumed that all talk of 'freedom' refers to the same abstract notion, even when one group aspires to 'freedom from' a particular form of government, while others cherish their perceived 'freedom to' worship as they please.

What is perplexing is the status and assurance of the many who do not seem to have grasped that Catholicism and Protestantism, at least in the dominant strains in Ireland, are not simply two different versions of the same thing. Exhibit A: a recent Graham Reid television play in which a girl returns from England to her dying father in the Falls. When she comes downstairs, the 'priest' kneels (Catholic-style) with her and extemporises a prayer (Presbyterian-style) rather than saying a decade of the rosary. Even post-Vatican II, this is scarcely credible and is worrying precisely because the writer has felt able to tackle the issues without a grasp of the practicalities. Exhibit B: Jennifer Johnston, in her novel *The Railway Station Man*, has Father Quinlan say of his housekeeper, "I'm sure I can find some soothing *text* to soothe her." (emphasis mine) Text? What do they teach about the Reformation in Protestant schools, for goodness' sake?

There is, obviously, a similar vagueness in Catholic perceptions of Protestantism: Denis Donoghue's line, "A Protestant was as alien to me as a Muslim", in *Warrenpoint*, depends on a very literalist interpretation of alienhood; he did, after all, live in the local barracks and must have seen the odd one or two, in uniform, if not in the cells. Seamus Heaney's 'Docker' is a particularly troubling example, quite apart from the obvious gaffe that it is not, as he appears to assume, Catholic priests who wear Roman collars. It is the poet, rather than his fictional docker, who displays prejudice in assuming "That fist *would* drop a hammer on a Catholic" (my emphasis); of course, this was all a long time ago ... when Heaney was an 'aggrieved young Catholic'.

What we need to recognise, then, is twofold: first, that the two dominant religious groupings are not simply two sides of a coin, two options from which one selects as arbitrarily as, say, deciding between pizza and a fish supper; and, secondly, that the 'non-Catholic' grouping is much more diverse historically and in its present-day manifestations than many inside and outside the region would prefer to believe. The classic assumption in Ireland that Protestant equals Ascendancy, reactionary, imperialist, is vastly at variance with the history of Protestantism in the north. And the knee-jerk leftist identification of 'Catholic' or 'native Irish' (the term is used to harness some empathy from 'native American') with 'working-class', is equally misleading. While it is true that the populating of the north owed something to the English religious wars of the 17th century, it should be borne in mind that the vast majority of settlers were not establishment Anglicans with grants of land, but were the same "masterless men" (in Christopher Hill's phrase) who were, in England, driven off the land by enclosure and improvement and who arrived in the cities, having lost their sense of belonging to place and parish, their sense of trust in the land and seasons and logically therefore, their feudal sense of loyalty to church and monarchy.

It is tempting to see the Puritans as the first 'working-class' movement, yet the Puritan split took place within the Established Church; Cromwell had previously worn ermine in the House of Lords and, on his death, his followers attempted to set up his son and heir, Richard, as Protector, hence (absurdly) establishing a new hereditary succession. The English civil war was, in fact, like most 'first' revolutions, essentially a conflict between the new bourgeois, oppidan class and the former dominance of the Norman aristocracy. Hewitt, however, was not fooled: he identified only the abstentionists, the Diggers and the Levellers, and the preacher Gerard Winstanley as his political precursors. These were genuinely the first major groups to set a socialist agenda, and to divorce themselves both from bourgeois liberals (if one may call Puritans liberal) and from the conservative or royalist party. In retrospect, it is an agenda of which the "sunburnt comrades" of the 30s or any group of 60s radicals could have been proud: reclaiming expropriated land; campaigning for free education and health; establishing rights for women (which were at an all-time low in some of the new sects which were springing up); and proposing a militantly pacifist agenda.

On the way home from Coventry, I made a stop in the village of Burford to read the inscription in the churchyard of St. John the Baptist, a favourite haunt of Hewitt's and a scene of pilgrimage for today's socialists:

To the Memory of Three Levellers

CORNET THOMPSON
CORPORAL PERKINS
PRIVATE CHURCH

Executed and Buried in this Churchyard
17th May 1649

Looking at the names, it was impossible to avoid reflecting (quite apart from the significance of 'Private Church' and the use of the rank 'cornet', which has always seemed much more civilised and understated than the 'buglers' so beloved of Kipling and Hopkins) that these individuals, who had rejected both the Stuart monarchy and Cromwell's New Model Army in favour of a communist alternative, are nonetheless buried in the Established Church and buried under the military titles they rejected; as if, say, Luther had been remembered as Brother Martin, Talleyrand as the Bishop of Autun and James Connolly as a British soldier.

What Hewitt's espousal of such minor 'eccentrics' or 'drop outs' indicates is that he allied himself notionally, not with muscular Protestantism, but with the smaller, free-thinking, leaderless, disputatious and occasionally pacifist sects whose legacy disappears from official histories (at least until its resurrection by Hewitt's contemporaries in the 30s). Thus, the 'protestantism' he espouses is continually protesting and is as critical of leaderships, hierarchies, corruption and venality as of any political or religious colouring.

It is also worth noting that the legacy of the religious turmoil of the 17th century is to be found not only in the north of Ireland, but in the United States of America, in that nation's constitutional separation of the functions of church and state. In the north of Ireland, it survives both in memories of '98, where it 'protested' at the yoke of the Established Church, and in the variety of religious sects which are determined by belief or support for a particular pastor rather than by affiliation to parish or diocese. Even the terms—'Mission', 'Tent', 'Tabernacle', 'Gospel Hall'—imply a rejection of religion as a system for dividing and ruling by geographical area.

A powerful illustration of over-simplification by would-be intellectuals is the frequent misconstruing of Hewitt's 'anti-Catholic' position. Since the world insists that one is either for or against a particular ideology, the line "the lifted hand between the mind and truth", from the poem 'The Glens' (1942), is seen as implying that Hewitt has swallowed whole the Reformation assertion that Catholicism is the enemy of intellectual progress. The fact that the line was later changed to "the lifted hand against unfettered thought", in *The Selected John Hewitt* (1981), seemed to be a modification which recognised that the church's prohibition was on excess of free thought rather than on access to some arbitrary (or Protestant) 'truth'. What observers frequently fail to recognise is that although both these strictures come from a writer with a Protestant background, they actually represent the opposition between secularism and 'received truth', that is, between the atheist and Catholic, rather than between Protestant and Catholic.

Indeed, Hewitt undermines any easy Protestant assumption of 'free-thinking' superiority in 'The Coasters' (1969):

And you who never had an adventurous thought
were positive that the church of the other sort
vetoes thought.

Who, then, is being attacked here? Protestants in general? Or Hewitt's own earlier assumptions? It would be attractive to make a case for a growth of tolerance in Hewitt's own supposedly 'Protestant' ideas with the onset of age, but the facts do not substantiate this. Take, for instance, 'Freehold' (1946), where he describes the "faith protestant" (the lower case is Hewitt's) of his father's people, "that denied/the hope of mercy to the papist side", but goes on to note that, although his people despised "rites of Rome", they had replaced them, outside their spartan churches, with ritual "sashes, banners, fife and drum". (He might have extended this discourse to include the secular left which, in its trade union guise, developed its own tradition of banners, bands, 'chapels' and fraternal forms of address.)

Hewitt was not one to blur distinctions and so the references to a "vainer faith" abound in his work — "edict of the Vatican" ... "the spells and fears their celibates surround them with" ... "feared all priests" ... "to curse the Pope of Rome" ... although the phrase "more violent lineage" in 'The Glens' (1942) would be hard to substantiate and the epithets "creed-haunted, Godforsaken" in 'An Irishman in Coventry' (1958) could well be applied to the whole soggy mess. One might then be tempted to identify the limits on Hewitt's liberalism with those of John Locke who believed that religious toleration should be extended to all except "Roman Catholics". But note that Locke does not make it in to 'Roseblade's Visitants', the poem in which Hewitt canonises (in the sense of elevating to a list rather than sainthood) his particular non-conformist forefathers, Morris, Toland, Winstanley and Cobbett. There is still clearer evidence of Hewitt's genuinely complex response to Catholicism in Ireland than this simple omission of Locke. It is worth reading closely, for example, his account in 'The Lonely Heart' of a visit to a church where, after describing the plaster saints and candles which conformed exactly to his Protestant expectations, he notices "a shabby woman in a faded shawl" praying. Here Hewitt's work has more than a little in common with Heaney's 'Poor Women in a City Church', a questionably devout exercise placed immediately after 'Docker' in *Death of a Naturalist* and which I have always—with no justification whatsoever—presumed to be the same St. Mary's in Chapel Lane in which James Connolly was 'read out from the altar', in the presence of his wife and children, for his godless communism.

Interestingly, Hewitt's moment in church is identical to the point at which that conservative intellectual, John Henry Newman, found the answer to his post-Oxford Movement quest, "in the unlettered crowd before the altar". But Hewitt is not, it might seem, as easily deceived as Newman: he considers that he might have the right to light a candle here, not to the painted Godhead

> ... but single flame to sway with all the other
> small earnest flames against the crowding gloom

Of course, the sentiment combines despair with a world at war and identification with the (albeit unlettered) aspirations of fellow humans, but the text combines the Confucian notion of a small gesture against the darkness with Newman's line "Lead kindly light, amid th'encircling gloom". Hewitt, however, suppresses the fancy cynically (he says) and leaves, resuming the discussion of how different this faith is in its ritual, symbolism, even décor, from the faith of his fathers (again his words intertextually acknowledging Father Faber's hymn to English Catholic martyrs).

It is unlikely that Hewitt was unaware of the Confucian parallels. It would also, however, be tempting to suggest that he was familiar with Newman's line from what is not generally regarded as a 'Catholic' hymn since it predates his conversion. Certainly, when Newman proceeds with "Pride ruled my will" and Hewitt confesses his "yawning want;/too much intent on what to criticise", both seemed to be singing from the same hymn sheet.

Hewitt resolves this apparent flirtation with a religion that is diametrically opposed both to that of his Protestant forebears and to his own free-thinking socialism, with the couplet, worthy of Newman, Father Faber or indeed any English recusant family:

> ... that which endures the tides of time so
> cannot be always absolutely wrong ...

It is a justification that is a trenchant definition of conservative thought. The confessional mode, the regret that "Pride ruled my will", is more evident still in the closing lines of this narrative:

> The years since then have proved I should have stayed
> and mercy might have touched me till I prayed.

Prayed? John Hewitt? It is hard to envisage the conductor of humanist funerals and avowed opponent of cant and superstition in this supplicant mode—although even Newman, like Hewitt, could excoriate the hypocrisies of Rome and Irish Catholicism when required. This is, naturally, strong stuff for those who have used Hewitt to validate anti-Catholic rhetoric; and, I may say, equally disappointing stuff for those who object to Hewitt as being irredeemably opposed to Catholicism *per se*.

Hewitt commented on his distance from—and acceptance by—the people of the Glens in many poems, but it is in the context of religion, rather than dialect, rural skills and local wit, that he feels this gulf most completely. Consider the story in 'The Hill Farm' of his arrival at a farmhouse where the rosary is being said. He listens and pictures the devotion within (note the imagery of light and darkness again):

> ... yet with a sense that I still stood
> far from that faith-based certitude,
> here in the vast enclosing night,
> outside its little ring of light.

This, then, is the same Hewitt who, in his famous *apologia*, 'The Colony' (1950), went so far as to suggest:

> I find their symbols good, as such, for me,
> when I walk in dark places of the heart;
> but name them not to be misunderstood.

Cautious indeed, that qualifying "as such", conceding everything and nothing, and the polite refusal to "name them" which speaks volumes on the judgemental contexts within which he operated.

It is fair to say, however, that Hewitt is not alone on the political left in this awareness of a "yawning want" and the consciousness that religions, however aesthetically tacky their plaster saints, relics, icons, prayer wheels, rosaries, *pietàs*, litanies or mantras, offer something to the supposed beneficiaries of humanist utopias that the utopias themselves—and the evidence in the former Soviet Union and the eastern bloc generally is not wanting—fail to provide.

The left in England owes its existence, of course, not to atheism, by and large, but to Methodist self-improvement, to Jewish intellectuals and to the vast numbers of starving Irish Catholic workers who flooded England's industrial cities in the mid-19th century following persistent government indifference and venality in the face of the potato murrain (at much the same time as the similar influxes into Belfast and Baltimore with their different political consequences). The legacy is there in England in the names: O'Connor, McGill, Noonan, Larkin, Connolly, Burns (and later Callaghan, Healey, McGahey, Gormley, MacNamara); in Cardinal Manning's successful intervention on behalf of his (Irish) flock in the 1889 London docks strike; and, indirectly, in the influence that the Burns sisters had on Engels and, therefore, on Karl Marx.

So perhaps, if it is stretching credulity to claim Hewitt for the Pope's legions, it may be more useful to identify the passage in 'Freehold' as a felt personal experience of Marx's view of religion, but not, I hasten to add, of the *Marxist* view of religion which invariably appears as 'Religion is the opium of the people', implying that all organised churches are an anaesthetising chicanery perpetrated on the proletariat by a capitalist establishment. What Marx actually maintained (in his *Contribution to the Critique of Hegel's Philosophy of Right*) was that religion is "the heart in a heartless world, the sigh of an oppressed people; it is the opium of the people". And one has to understand even the reference to opium contextually here as a legitimate palliative; think, for example, of Augustus Carmichael in Virginia Woolf's *To the Lighthouse*.

Marx saw religion as an inevitable stage in his programme of societal development—religion, atheism, communism, perfection of humanity—a progress to which he was unwilling to prescribe a predetermined timescale, unlike too many of his would-be followers whether in Russia, China or the British left. In this, Hewitt's more tolerant approach to the beliefs of ordinary people, while it sits uneasily with his distrust of hierarchical and authoritarian religion, follows an authentic socialist tradition.

Perhaps all we have found is a little *quasi*-religious chink in Hewitt's secular, free-thinking armour, even if it places him more correctly with Marx than with the pieties of Newman or Heaney. But the legacy of religious toleration for which the north of Ireland was once famous when it welcomed Huguenots, Baptists, Moravians, Quakers, Old and New Light Presbyterians, and all manner of Anabaptists, Ranters and many-hued antinomians, finds a secure echo both in Hewitt's criticism of the pomp and ritual of both sides and in his recognition of the "yawning want" that lies in the over-intellectualised world of the humanist, the secularist, the atheist.

Little wonder, then, that religion in its more exalted and arcane forms survives in the more oppressed parts of the world—Latin America, Poland, Russia today, Ireland in the 19th century—and that Hewitt should wish, however briefly, that he had lit his penny candle in common with all the others. Little wonder, too, that his Marxist (or crypto-Newmanian, if you will) narrative carries the apparently sentimental title, 'The Lonely Heart'. If the rationalist and free-thinker rejects the sentimentalism and credulity of the "unlettered crowed" in favour of his own tradition of "unfettered thought" and, as it were, places a "lifted hand between" the heart and mind, Hewitt is all too ready to identify in himself and in his background the want in such rigid barriers.

The Liberal Imagination in Northern Irish Prose

Patricia Craig

If you think of Belfast in the 30s and 40s, there are three centres of liberal thought that immediately spring to mind. The first is the Linen Hall Library, still sticking to its egalitarian principles after a century and a half of ups and downs (though it's true to say that its most exciting phase occurred early on in its existence, with the librarian and one of the earliest members hanged, and half the committee in gaol at one point). Davy McLean's socialist bookshops—one in Howard Street and one in Union Street—provided another haven, around 1940, for those averse to atavistic allegiances; while Campbell's Café, opposite the City Hall, was the third refuge of the level-headed. "Imagine a sunny morning in Campbell's coffee house towards the end of World War II ..." writes Robert Greacen, before going on to enumerate a few of the more prominent frequenters of this non-sectarian spot. First comes Denis Ireland, whom Greacen describes as a white blackbird—"that is, an Ulster Presbyterian with strong Republican sympathies, a sort of throwback to the 18th century." We all know what happened to Presbyterian republicanism after 1800; how it underwent various transformations until the term itself had become something of an oxymoron. Did Denis Ireland succeed in restoring to it any of its old authenticity? Another Campbell's regular and committed socialist, John Boyd, considered Ireland's liberalism hopelessly antiquated in the early 40s, though he has nothing but praise for the older man's courage in making a stand against the unionism of his background—doubly difficult since, at the time of the First World War, he'd been a British officer to boot.

Denis Ireland claimed to have made an honest man of himself by discarding the British uniform for ever, though he didn't underestimate the difficulties confronting him in his effort to achieve a balanced attitude to the question of national identity. According to Ireland

> ... it is easier for the proverbial camel to pass through the eye of a needle than for the son of the Ulster Protestant industrial ascendancy to orientate himself in relation to his country's history. All his early training is against him; so much so that he never begins to understand his surroundings and background until he makes a clean break not only with his own education but with the social standards of his class ...

This is characteristically perceptive, though not to any remarkable degree. Here we have an intermittently evocative writer who never seems to have felt the need to make any kind of sustained creative effort. What his literary output amounts to is a succession of spirited autobiographical jottings, sometimes mannered (especially in his later years), often illuminating about himself and his position within the liberal tradition, and nearly always interesting. There's a short quotation which gives the flavour of his prose. He is writing about some Jubilee Night celebrations in Belfast:

> What a strange world it is! A world full of flood-lighting, cheap electricity, new clothes, cigarettes, silk stockings, sixpenny seats at the cinema, and apparently endless leisure. I think of my dead father, now three years in his grave in the mountain-side above the city; how he toiled and moiled through the gas-lit decades of the Victorian era, and now we are all walking about in brilliant clean-swept streets, wearing new flannel trousers and smoking endless cigarettes, criticising European pictures, listening to wireless bands from the ends of the earth—a bright, clean, hard world in which gifts are showered on us in endless profusion, in which everything behind the illuminated plate-glass windows steadily cheapens, but in which one has only to step out of the main street in order to see the grey, pinched faces of men, women and children starving in the back alleys. A mad world, for all its concealed lighting, flood-lighting, and electric profusion.

There is something in this, I think, which sums up the whole rather tawdry and distant atmosphere of 30s modernism—but once he gets on to the back alleys, one can only say that Denis Ireland falls somewhat short as a commentator on social inequalities, becoming merely perfunctory and ineffective. He was, by all accounts, a vivid and entertaining talker, and liked to hold court at Campbell's Café before an appreciative audience—though at least one member of that audience, John Boyd, wasn't bowled over by his jokes about the back streets of Belfast and the attitudes prevailing there. Not, he concedes, that the least trace of snobbery underlay Denis Ireland's exuberant anecdotes, merely a robust enjoyment of working-class quirks. Still, they sometimes jarred with a listener whose experience of the working class wasn't confined to an uninvolved scrutiny.

The second volume of John Boyd's autobiography, *The Middle of My Journey* (1990), gives a very resonant and engaging account of the war years and their aftermath, when everyone was trying to write the great proletarian novel and onslaughts on Ulster philistinism were coming from all sides. Belfast has always been sympathetic to democratic ideas, ever since the days when the *Northern Star* circulated among its more enlightened inhabitants; and it has always had a horror of anything flashy or pretentious. The outlook resulting from these characteristics found expression in a number of novels either written or set during the wartime period, and it's worth looking at one or two of these in detail. But first, a slight digression.

John Boyd's friend and fellow socialist Sam Hanna Bell was another of the literary practitioners and coffee-drinkers who congregated upstairs at Campbell's Café. Since he died a year or two ago, I suppose it's reasonable to try and sum up his literary achievement. Certainly, his historical trilogy, which was published between 1951 and 1987, is a very ambitious undertaking—you might almost say his aim was to examine the moral history of his country (that is, Northern Ireland). I don't think he brought it off, but he deserves credit for the largeness of his objective. The first of his historical novels, *December Bride*, is generally agreed to be the most satisfactory of the three. Set in the County Down countryside around the turn of the century, it touches on such issues as illegitimacy, violence, social and religious prejudices and impropriety in clergymen. If it has a single theme, it might be identified as rural intractability. The second novel in the trilogy, *A Man Flourishing*, concerns the rise and industrialisation of Belfast, employing its central character, a one-time United Irishman and clerical-student-turned-businessman, to illustrate the shift from radicalism to respectability which overtook Presbyterian Ulster after the failure of the '98 Rebellion. You can see and appreciate what Sam Hanna Bell is trying to do in this novel, but in fact his plot, as it turns out, is simply too skimpy, and at times too melodramatic, to match up to his exacting intention (that is, to draw a parallel between one man's vicissitudes and the development of a whole pragmatic, rather than idealistic, community).

Part three of this historical trilogy, *Across the Narrow Sea*, goes right back to the time of the Ulster plantation to show the origins of the divisiveness that's bedevilled the province ever since. It's a perfectly agreeable and well-researched work of fiction—but, unfortunately, while the author's objective gets larger and larger the further back in history he goes, his method becomes increasingly facile. It's fine to try to reduce the charge in 'Protestant' or 'Catholic' ideas of history, as he does, but not if it means the acceptance of a kind of storybook romanticism. This is a far cry from his only other novel—and the one most relevant to my purposes here. *The Hollow Ball* was published in 1961 but it is set during the 30s, when Belfast was plagued to an even greater than usual degree by unemployment, and membership of trade unions was on the increase. Like all Sam Hanna Bell's fiction, this book follows a simple plot-line and the style is plain almost to the point of being pedestrian—but, nevertheless, it conveys a strong sense of Belfast's red-brick streets and the dismal prospect of finding oneself without an income, thereby pinpointing a fruitful interaction between social conditions, location and behaviour.

The Hollow Ball is about a couple of boys, friends, employed by a clothing manufacturer in Belfast's High Street. One of these boys, David Minnis, is at the centre of the novel, and one of the problems is that the author can't quite make up his mind as to whether he approves of this character or not—or even if he doesn't think it a bit frivolous of him to indulge his talent for football, which ensures that he at least won't starve, even if everyone else goes to the wall. To get where he does at the end of the book, David Minnis is obliged to carry out a number of small betrayals, including the betrayal of his friend Bonar McFall, who fails to make a trade union convert of him. David is found wanting when it comes to solidarity. On the single occasion when he's persuaded to attend a socialist meeting in Belfast, he finds the place chock-full of ideologues whose diverging principles keep them from achieving any consensus of opinion. Incidentally, at this point in the novel I think John Hewitt and his wife, Roberta, put in a personal appearance. Says Hanna Bell:

> A pretty woman in a headscarf followed by her stout escort in tweeds carried her argument in a high cultivated voice down the hall and into the benches... When they were seated her companion leant his head attentively towards her, folded his arms, sucked his pipe, and nodded understandingly as he let his thoughts wander off.

This pair is in decided contrast to many other people in the hall, who come decked out in duncher caps, or carry the scars of a clash with the police during a Glasgow dock strike. Another of the problems with the novel is that as Bonar McFall fades out of the picture, once he and David have become estranged, reports of his activities indicate that he is in many ways the most significant character in the book. His complicated allegiances, principled existence and violent end all raise compelling issues which are never tackled with the necessary degree of cogency.

It was a commonplace of the day that socialism—which breaks down into Marxism, trade unionism, anti-sectarianism or whatever—presented a rational alternative to unthinking tribal allegiance, Orange or Green. This was the time when it looked for a moment as though Catholic and Protestant working classes might join forces within the labour movement, which would have brought about an erosion of sectarian hostility. Of course, what actually happened was the other way round, with that hostility harnessed to keep each faction loyal to caste rather than class. In *The Hollow Ball*, Bonar McFall, whose father is something of a working-class intellectual (and something of a figure of fun to David Minnis), has inherited a socialist cast of mind and allows this to carry him to an extreme that readers may or may not consider logical. Recently, I was reading an account of this novel by a well-known critic, and I was surprised to find him referring several times to David Minnis's 'Catholic' friend Bonar McFall. Apart from the unlikelihood of a Catholic being named after Bonar Law, the prominent British unionist and leader of the Conservative Party, the fact that he is Protestant is important to the scheme of the novel. It allows him to renounce the working-class unionism of his background, putting trade unionism in its place; though, like many another social agitator, it is possible that he goes too far along the line of recantation. It isn't long before Bonar's socialism has shaded into nationalism and then republicanism; by the time of his death, on active service with the IRA, his name is given in the following way, which is rich in ironic implication: Bonár Lách Mac Phóil.

I suppose it's possible to agree that socialism in Northern Ireland in the mid-century provided a kind of middle ground, attractive to those of an unfanatical disposition as long as it was associated with pacifism; but that it all too easily accommodated the possibility of militant action in defence of some cherished principle. Bonar McFall, in Sam Hanna Bell's novel, represents a kind of Protestant republicanism, a bit further down the social scale, that harks back to the end of the last century and the writings of 'Ethna Carberry' and

Alice Milligan, editors of the nationalist newspaper the *Shan Van Vocht* and authors of some rather bloodthirsty verse of the "Oh God that my curses were embers, to fall on each Saxon head!" variety, very much in contradiction to the liberal spirit—even though these ladies would certainly have considered themselves enlightened in the democratic sense. There are other social reformers, though, who preferred to proceed along the lines of reasoning rather than extermination. It is one thing to react against the biases and limitations of an Ulster Protestant upbringing, as Alice Milligan did, and another to opt for the inflations of an opposing ideology. But this is a very tricky matter. What we have here, indeed, is Romantic nationalism, the allure of the lost cause, and the unquestionable rectitude of allying oneself with the underdog, in any situation.

The struggle in Ireland, though, had many different interpretations, and perhaps the most compelling of these was, and is, the struggle against sectarianism. There are those who would argue that the socialism of the 30s and 40s was a new force in northern Irish life, detached from any political tradition existing in the country and opening up a number of attractive possibilities, including the prospect of acquiring an international, as opposed to a provincial, outlook. But, on the other hand, we might look back to Dr. William Drennan, James Hope, the weaver-poets of the 18th and 19th centuries—all John Hewitt's "brave old pre-Marx Marxists of Ireland", indeed, who testify to a kind of continuity within the movement for social justice and egalitarianism, going right back to the mid-18th century. Or William Carleton, who wrote in 1860: "I have never entertained any ill-feeling against the people on either side; it is their accursed systems which I detest." In Carleton's day, the accursed systems were the Orange Order and the Ribbon movement—and, by extension, corrupt Protestantism and corrupt Catholicism—which kept the people of the Clogher Valley at one another's throats. When he wasn't at the business of converting peasant disabilities and discontents into the stuff of melodrama, Carleton took time off to exploit the farcical element in sectarian inflexibility, as we find in the very pointed set-piece in his novel *Valentine McClutchy*, in which a Protestant convert comes face to face with his Catholic counterpart. Both men are bursting with new-found zeal; however, in the course of their argument, each finds himself reverting to his original faith. The ex-Orangeman atavistically curses the Pope, while the ex-Catholic comes out as a papist partisan. By now a crowd of supporters has gathered, an equal number of Catholics and Protestants, and, Carleton tells us, "the

Catholics, ignorant of the turn which the controversy had taken, supported Bob and Protestantism; while the Protestants, owing to a similar mistake, fought like devils for Darby and the Pope". It is hard to think of a more telling indictment, or one more drily expressed.

The notion that Orange and Green fixations are interchangeable also finds expression in George A. Birmingham's splendid novel of 1912 and the home rule crisis, *The Red Hand of Ulster*, which tackles in a very ironic spirit the absurdities arising from unrestrained political feeling. It is only the author's incorrigible amiability that keeps this novel from turning into a satirical *tour de force*—it lacks the edge of ferocity or disquiet that might have transformed it. But as it is, it's both amusing and instructive. Following an impeccable logic, Birmingham turns every conceivable standpoint on its head. For example, an ardent Sinn Féiner, having looked around for the most potent source of rebellion against Britain and locating it among the unionists of the north, finds himself accepting the editorship of a loyalist newspaper; while loyalists tie themselves in knots in the effort to assert their loyalty to Britain. It isn't an unconditional loyalty, though, as it turns out: and once the refusal of home rule is backed up by a demand for a complete British withdrawal from Ireland, a state of semantic deadlock is brought about, and the author has tremendous fun with this and all the other pungent contradictions which make up his theme. Both he and Carleton in their different ways—one rowdy and the other playful—are poking fun at the sectarian instinct, and this, of course, is the best thing to do with it.

Another of Birmingham's novels, though a much more conventional one, is *The Northern Iron*, which is set at the time of the '98 Rebellion. I think Tom Paulin was right when he pointed out, in a radio broadcast about *The Red Hand of Ulster*, that as far as Birmingham was concerned, what the loyalist rebellion of 1912 amounted to was a distorted expression of the northern radicalism which flourished during the 1790s. This force, as I've suggested, was first modified and then became subterranean, though it never died out entirely throughout the course of the 19th century—and, indeed, it gave both a form and an ancestry to the liberal Protestant standpoint. As the historian Hugh Shearman has put it, "the moderate Ulster Protestant position was closely related to the tradition of democratic radicalism which formed a large part of the Ulster past". Birmingham himself—who lived from 1865 until 1950—relates in his autobiography how an attitude of mild defiance was inculcated into him in Belfast, around 1868, by an Orange clergyman, a Dr. Drew, who made him learn by heart the inspiriting line, "No Pope, no Priest, no surrender, Hurrah!" "I was never an Orangeman," he says, "and for a great part of my life have been in opposition to the political opinions held so firmly by my fellow Protestants of Northern Ireland ..."; yet he can't regret the independence of spirit which is a hallmark of Protestantism ('Protestantism' with a small 'p') at its most attractive, embedded in that unabashed saying of Dr. Drew's.

There are many ways in which the Catholic and Protestant churches may be found uncongenial—all of them anathema to the liberal-minded. To quote Hugh Sherman again:

> If we look at the worst aspects of each side, vulgar, ranting, drum-beating Protestantism on the one hand can be matched on the other by a sinister Roman Catholic fanaticism which was animated by all that was bad in the Counter-reformation spirit, and nothing that was good.

It's hard to think of anyone who embodied the Irish liberal mind more agreeably than George A. Birmingham (the pen-name of James O. Hannay), or anyone who deserved less to come up against religious prejudice (as he did) in an extreme form. As a Church of Ireland clergyman, whose ministry was in Westport, Co. Mayo, he fell foul of the local Catholic priest who got it into his head that he'd been caricatured in a Birmingham novel (this wasn't true), and stirred up his parishioners against the inoffensive author to such an extent that they burnt him in effigy in the streets. A lot of people who'd never read him were persuaded that George A. Brimingham went in for 'immoral' writing—the most ludicrous of charges, considering the unassailable innocence of his literary imagination.

This disgraceful episode shows the Catholic Church, or a few of its representatives, in an unfortunate light: wrong-headed and authoritarian. In its other most deplorable incarnation—as a reactionary force—that church has had an intensive airing in literature, from George Moore on. One rather underrated novel of 1934, Peadar O'Donnell's *On the Edge of the Stream*, for example, concerns an archetypal clash between backwardness and enlightenment—or, to be specific, between the Catholic Church and the co-operative movement in a remote part of Co. Donegal. What do we have? A practised socialist agitator, on the one hand, lately returned from Scotland with a message for the townlands; and, on the other, the usual bourgeois alliance of church, shopkeepers, schoolmasters, attorneys and so forth. When Phil Timony sets up a co-operative store in a barn, the whisper starts up against him that it's some considerable time since he darkened his chapel door, and this grows in force until he becomes the object of a religious procession, ostensibly designed to reclaim him for Catholicism. We hear the voice of the author, full of scorn and mock amazement: "Could it be that the whole parish was coming to sing hymns around Phil Timony's? In dry and sober daylight, grown-up men and women singing hymns around a neighbour's house ..."

There they stand, priests, nuns, Children of Mary, all the upright for miles around, singing in unison, "I am a little Catholic" ... But a bull gets loose and disrupts the mood, and the whole thing dissolves in an outbreak of hilarity. Then the bull falls sick and superstition flares. But the day is saved for socialism when it turns out that the animal was poisoned by someone with a vested interest in faking a piece of divine retribution. This act stands for radical corruption in the novel, and the effect of its exposure is to separate genuine integrity, in the author's view, from moral posturing: "The poor see a shelter in the rich man's piety when they are in the rich man's power; God help them." Peadar O'Donnell's strength, in this novel as in all his novels, lies in the firmness of his purpose—to show up the flaws in any kind of activity (including republican activity) not grounded in proper socialist principles.

This talk was supposed to be about the people who met at Campbell's Café and a few of the ideas generated there, and we seem to have got rather a long way from this significant starting-point—or perhaps not as far as all that. For all I know, Peadar O'Donnell and George A. Birmingham may have made a beeline for the place, as a haven of tolerance and lively debate, when they found themselves in Belfast. One person who definitely might have been seen on the spot, looking like Charlie Chaplin in his ARP trousers, was the 17-year-old Brian Moore—at least if we're to take his novel *The Emperor of Ice-Cream* as being autobiographical, which I believe it is:

> It was an Indian summer's day, warm, wet and close and the university students, as they passed through Campbell's ground-floor bakery shop and started up the stairs towards the coffee room, began stripping off their raincoats and long woollen scarves. In the coffee room the only male still wearing his raincoat was Gavin, sticky and ill-at-ease in a window seat, his steel helmet and gasmask hidden under his chair ...

Gavin Burke, as we all know, is about to find his feet and perform very creditably once German bombs start falling on Belfast, but, just for the moment, he's a prey to adolescent embarrassments and uncertainties. The fact that he has joined the ARP at all is construed as an affront by his nationalist family—"Gracious God," declares his Aunt Liz in the opening pages, "did I ever think I'd live to see the day when my own nephew would stand in this room dressed up like a Black and Tan"— while for Gavin this attitude typifies everything that is hidebound about Belfast. What exasperates him in particular is the failure of his elders to adapt to changing circumstances, their adherence to a formula that might have had some relevance once, but doesn't any longer. Gavin stands for the undirected but liberal-minded young, for whom a strong attachment to Ireland's cause—or Ulster's cause, for that matter—is associated with the previous, boring generation and their current idiocies: in Gavin's case, his father claiming to prefer Hitler to Churchill, his vehement Aunt Liz and all the rest of them. As far as he's concerned, over-consciousness of nationality is just a part of the terrible provincialism he has to contend with; and when he gets a glimpse of a richer kind of life, surprisingly going on in his own dull city, it's the 'Protestant' aspect of the set-up that strikes him: "Why was it that no Catholic could grow up in an interesting atmosphere?" You didn't catch Catholics, in other words, burning joss-sticks, writing poetry or building puppet-theatres—though Gavin, as it happens, is a bit taken aback when it dawns on him that homosexuality goes with the rest of the bohemian package.

At this point in the novel, Brian Moore imports a minor character directly from life. The puppet-maker, Maurice Markham, was in reality Terence Pim, the manager of Davy McLean's Union Street bookshop and also one of Belfast's few and flamboyant homosexuals, who used to strut around in enormous polished-leather boots, and often bleached his very dark hair, on a whim.

Pim, with his *bon mots* ("I like to picture Henry James drowning himself in his golden bowl"), was among the more colourful frequenters of Campbell's Café, and it's easy to see why the young, forward-looking Brian Moore should have found him fascinating, if only for a moment. Another figure to be admired was the parson in his novel known as "the Red Reverend"; and this character probably owes something, though not everything, to another real-life Campbell's *habitué*: the unofficial pastor to the intellectual set and outspoken opponent of sectarianism, vulgar prurience and narrow-mindedness of any sort, the Rev. Arthur Agnew. It's encouraging to know that Belfast threw up the occasional liberal cleric to balance all the noisy dogmatists.

Brian Moore, I think, is among those authors who perceived

Northern Ireland as a product of bad policies and fixed attitudes; and he's the first Catholic novelist, as far as I am aware, to write in a knowing and dispassionate way about the particular balefulness of Belfast. If one of his persistent themes is provincial inertia, however, he tackles this with such vitality and good humour that he ends up exhilarating, rather than dispiriting, his readers (this is especially true of his third Belfast novel, *The Emperor of Ice-Cream*, which, unlike its two predecessors, is constructed in a mode of comic realism). I'd like to look for a moment at another Catholic writer, one "seldom seen" at Campbell's Café, according to John Boyd; however, we may take that to mean that he did put in an appearance occasionally. "At McL's"—that is McLaverty's—"home in the suburbs", writes Denis Ireland: "There is a kind of creative warmth about everything he says ..." And of his stories set on Rathlin or in Donegal: "There is a clear white intensity about them, an incandescent clarity." This judgement may have been true in 1935, when it was written—indeed in many ways it remained true until 1942 and the novel *Lost Fields*, with its strong working-class atmosphere and Belfast street lore. Certainly, McLaverty's earlier novel, *Call My Brother Back* (1939), is a work of great charm and unpretentiousness, which evokes a rather more simple and decorative Belfast than the city recalled by Brian Moore—all holy-water fonts and plaster statues, brickfields and dumps and factory chimneys, ill-lit churches and deprived children hawking bundles of sticks in battered prams from door to door. The year is 1921, when it wasn't unusual to hear bullets whizzing along the side streets of the Lower Falls; in a single week of June that year, five men were assassinated by B-Specials, 11 people shot dead during street riots and 150 Catholic families driven from their homes. Between July and December in the same year, 174 people lost their lives in political confrontations. McLaverty has assimilated all this into the framework of his novel, though he never moves beyond the child's-eye view which determines his literary method.

All this is fine—however, as I've implied, after 1942 it was downhill all the way as far as McLaverty's talent as an author was concerned. When you call Brian Moore a Catholic writer, it's simply to indicate a fact about his background, of no particular importance to his development as a novelist; whereas with McLaverty the same tag signals a particular temperament and outlook, and not a very liberal one—which perhaps explains his separation from the Campbell's Café set. He turned himself more and more into a purveyor of Catholic family romances of the most frightful banality. What these later novels convey is a kind of stupefying dullness, with priests for ever uttering platitudes, dreary courtships going awry, and women getting it in the neck for failing to be enthralled by the simplicities of cottage life. On top of the other prejudices displayed in McLaverty's later work, we find a most shocking, though probably unconscious, anti-feminism—as in the following observation from the novel *In This Thy Day*: "...somehow a girl was made for one spot. When she starts the roaming she's like a dog that goes after sheep—never contented." And as for the treatment of Vera Reilly in *Truth in the Night*—well, because this character hankers after a fuller life than the one available to her on Rathlin Island, the author condemns her as morally suspect, and proceeds to punish her by killing off first her young daughter, then her unborn child and finally Vera herself. This is sensation fiction without the *frisson* engendered by the competent sensationalist. (Incidentally, notable women seem to be conspicuously absent from the Campbell's group—Janet McNeill must have gone there I suppose, since she mentions the place in her novel *The Maiden Dinosaur*; and I've heard May Morton—schoolteacher, poet and secretary of the PEN Club—referred to in this connection, but that's about it.)

Sectarian exclusiveness, whether Catholic or Protestant, was among the most egregious obstacles the social reformer was up against. Denis Donoghue's memoir, *Warrenpoint*, is a wonderful book, elegant, thoughtful and austere; but it contains one very alarming pronouncement which show the extent of the segregation prevailing in Northern Ireland in the late 30s. "A Protestant was as alien to me as a Muslim," Denis Donoghue writes—and this was a boy whose home was a police barracks, which presumably accommodated a fair number of non-Catholics, at least during the day. But clearly a Christian Brothers training debarred one from having any social contact with, or imaginative understanding of, other denominations. Sticking to your own, looking after your own: this is a very unattractive Northern Irish trait which has long had a hold in the province. Everyone knows the famous assertion made by Sir Basil Brooke, then Minister of Agriculture, in 1933, to the effect that no Catholic need seek employment about his place—"Catholics are out to destroy Ulster with all their might and power." This was a clear directive to "the Protestant people" to practise bigotry to their hearts' content, and those who resisted, from whatever social stratum, deserve the greatest credit. In 1936, an enquiry into the purpose and effect of the Special Powers Acts, published by the National Council for Civil Liberties, found that, among other things, "the Northern Irish Government has used Special Powers towards securing the dominion of one particular political faction and, at the same time, towards curtailing the lawful activities of its opponents ..." and that one inevitable result of this had been "to encourage violence and bigotry on the part of the Government's supporters as well as to beget in its opponents an intolerance of the 'law and order' thus maintained. The Government's policy is driving its opponents into the ways of extremists." The government of Northern Ireland, in other words, was very much to blame for battening on existing tensions and animosities instead of taking steps to minimise them. Not that extremists on either side required much prodding. As early as 1919, the historian James Winder Good made the following observation:

> Belfast's sudden relapses into savagery are a feature of its record much more characteristic that its commercial progress ... When it emerges into the light of general history it has been as the storm-centre of upheavals that stopped just short of revolution.

He knew what he was talking about. Between 1857 and 1912 there were seven serious outbreaks of sectarian rioting, probably caused by the considerable increase in the numbers of Catholic workers flocking into Belfast—though it's hard to know whether sectarian acts come under the heading of symptoms, or causes, of social disorder. In any case, the addiction to faction-fighting goes back a long way, and has resisted a good many efforts to eradicate it; indeed, in the view of some commentators, it is part and parcel of an indigenous disposition which includes the much-paraded energy and enterprise peculiar to the north.

In an essay on Ulster prose, written in 1951, John Boyd comments on the interaction between literature and history, and in particular social history; and certainly Belfast's persistent sectarianism offered the strongest stimulus to social critics of all kinds. (Just in passing, I should like to say that the anti-sectarian impulse, while praiseworthy in itself, sometimes found an outlet in the most terrible prose: I am thinking, for example, of a novel like Anne Crone's *Bridie Steen*—about the miseries of a cross-bred orphan in Co. Fermanagh, if I remember correctly, and no doubt written from the highest of motives—but unfortunately overdrawn, lurid and trashy.) As well as the fiction-writers, you had poets, painters, essayists, historians, actors, BBC men, businessmen and all among the *avant garde* of Belfast who gathered upstairs at Campbell's Café, all doing their bit to keep up a decent standard of liberalism. In the matter of social progress, though, things often become abstract and open to argument. If we turn to Robert Greacen again, we find him recalling a lively conversation in which it was agreed that the centre of Belfast should be demolished forthwith and rebuilt "in a contemporary architectural idiom". I don't know if the architectural historian Denis O'D. O'Hanna ever visited Campbell's Café, but I wish he had been there at that moment to argue the case for conservation. As far as I am aware, he was among the earliest to appreciate the glories of the northern Irish architectural heritage, including a good many of the buildings of Belfast—though it was left to his successor in this line, C.E.B. Brett, to enumerate these buildings and to reach the conclusion, at the same time, that the outline of the Georgian town was still discernible behind the industrial overlay. Moreover, "Up until 1966," wrote Brett, "Royal Avenue presented a totally unspoilt image of Belfast as an important Victorian city ... it represented a very deliberate exercise in streetscape-planning; building lines and elevations were carefully harmonised throughout its length; and the ultimate result was consistent and integrated." I mention this, in passing, partly because I've got a bee in my bonnet about pernicious redevelopment, and partly to suggest that Ulster philistinism, which may well be diminishing in other areas, is forging ahead in this one. It seems that this quality has to find an outlet somewhere, and just at present a widespread environmental unsightliness is filling the bill. My own view is that not enough has been made of the connection between social malaise and an aesthetically poor environment—I don't mean just something as obviously appalling as Divis Flats, though God knows such constructions deserve to be condemned as loudly as possible, but the whole tendency to knock down perfectly serviceable buildings and replace them with something as hideous and gimcrack as it can be made, and then ignore the effect on the people obliged to live with it.

Of course, I am half joking, though only half, when I look askance at that "contemporary architectural idiom" which was mooted at Campbell's Café in the mid 40s by Robert Greacen and his friends; I'm aware that what looks progressive from one angle may start to look fearfully retrogressive from an different perspective, or as one issue takes precedence over another. The public architecture of Belfast, in the mid-century, was strongly associated with that 'Ulster Protestant industrial ascendancy' from which Denis Ireland, for one, took such pains to detach himself—and associated, by extension, with the whole 'Ulster Protestant' mentality which all liberals repudiated. I suppose the point I am making here is that repudiation, like acquiescence, can go too far—that there comes a time when it is necessary to take stock of what exists, and to cherish such assets as an irreplaceable building heritage, a local dialect, a particular storytelling tradition, or whatever. We are all agreed that the most formidable antidote to intolerance is knowledge, knowledge of other person's customs, beliefs and so forth; and in this respect a great stimulus to liberal thought came also from fieldworkers, scholars, investigators, meticulous recorders and classifiers like Lloyd Praeger and Estyn Evans, or pioneering photographers such as R.J. Welch, Rose Shaw and Alex Hogg—all those who made information, and pride in local peculiarities and achievements, available to the public. I think it's fair to claim that the outstanding practitioners in any field, including literature, are those who approach their subject, whatever it is, holding as few preconceived opinions as they can manage. The others, those who—like Michael McLaverty—remain hidebound and, in a sense, anti-intellectual, will pay for it in the weakening of their capacity to exercise their gifts. I am sure that this was acknowledged, in some measure, by those who congregated at Campbell's Café during the period in question, and that the diversity of opinion prevailing there was a productive, and never a self-defeating, diversity.

Uladh, Lagan *and* Rann

The 'Little Magazine' comes to Ulster

Tom Clyde

Uladh, Lagan and *Rann* are three of the most important and influential literary magazines to have been published in Ulster. Aside from the high quality of many of the contributions (and the later stature of many of the contributors), the period between the first issue of *Uladh* (November 1904) and the last *Rann* (June 1935) neatly marks a transitional phase in the development of literary magazines here which mirrors the passage of the province itself from a pre-independence, pre-partition, colonial state to a semi-detached, more culturally confident region.

First, though, I think it is important to point out that *Uladh* was not, as is widely thought, Ulster's first literary magazine. In fact, out of just over 70 such magazines to date, some 30 were published before *Uladh*. Among the earliest was the *Publick Register*, published in Belfast in 1741. To put this in context, the earliest proper newspapers and journals of any kind first emerged in Ireland in the 1640s, and the first literary publication was the *Examiner*, run by Jonathan Swift and others in Dublin in 1710. These earlier magazines fell into a number of distinct categories, the flavour of which can, I think, quickly be indicated by some representative titles. First, we have *The Comet: A Belfast Journal of Fun, Frolics and Literature* (1849-50); secondly, *The Young Gentlemen's and Ladies' Monitor* (Belfast, 1788); thirdly, *The Irishman, A Weekly Journal of Irish National Politics and Literature* (Belfast, 1858); and, finally, the *Belfast Advertiser and Literary Gazette* (1847). Outside these four broad categories there are, of course, a number of titles ranging from the hard-to-classify to the plain eccentric (see the *Larne Literary and Agricultural Journal* [1838-40]).

What these have in common, which distinguishes them from *Uladh* and identifies it as something new, is that literature is not central to their identities or purposes. The first two are concerned with entertainment—one for the plebs, the other for the toffs; the third is primarily political; the last is a purely commercial venture. In all of them, the literary element is to a greater or lesser extent subordinate to the main business of the magazine and, although they contain some contributions from serious writers such as Carleton and Ferguson, these are clearly an adjunct, used for light relief or to draw in readers. As a result, these titles all tend toward balladry, tales and anecdote.

Despite not being the first—more like the 31st—an essential truth about *Uladh*'s novelty and importance in the context of Ulster literature is revealed by its almost mythic stature: like *Finnegans Wake* or *War and Peace*, it is referred to by many more people than have actually read it. Its impact and influence far outweigh the number of readers, either at the time of publication or since. What marks *Uladh* as a decisive break with what had gone before is that it was, like *Beltaine* and other journals associated with the Irish Literary Revival in the south a few years earlier, among the first of Ireland's Little Magazines. This is a technical term, and one which needs some explanation.

The origins of the Little Magazine seem to lie in the United States. There were a few false starts in the mid-19th century, including the grandparent of them all, Emerson's *Dial* (1840-44), but they really took off in the last decade of that century and the first decade of this. By the end of the World War I, there were dozens, including *Poetry, Voices* and Margaret Anderson's *Little Review*, from which the term Little Magazine seems to be derived. Already in this first flush, we can find the three underlying phenomena which have found expression in the Little Magazines of every country—the *avant garde* in art; political radicalism, particularly of a left-wing or libertarian hue; and regionalism, the urge of areas like the American mid-west to free themselves from cosmopolitan domination.

As by-products of that vast phenomenon known as Modernism, and of its many sub-movements (Symbolism, Imagism, etc.), these Little Magazines embodied the principles of the sects which spawned them and acted as manifestos. These manifestos fell into two broad camps: the explicit, tied to a particular movement and, typically, deliberately calculated to cause shock and outrage (the classic example of this being Tristan Tzara's *Dada* magazine); and those publications whose programmes were more subtle and expressed implicitly, into which category *Uladh* and, I feel, most Irish Little Magazines fall. These created "a comprehensive aesthetic environment in which new developments in writing and visual arts compound to distil an attitude, a distinctive graphic and typographic complex".[1] A typical example is the *Yellow Book*, published in England in 1894. Perhaps it says something about Irish society, and the place of the artist within it, that the vast majority of our Little Magazines falls into the second type, quieter and more cautious, rather than the revolutionary first type.

Another way of looking at this new type of magazine is as a kind of privatisation of publishing, a new mode more in keeping with the new century than the decidedly public Great Reviews which held sway in the Victorian era, and the converse of their seriousness and occasional solemnity. The Little Magazines, with their (deliberately) limited but (supposedly) discriminating readership, were more specialised than those they replaced, and often (as our three Ulster titles all show to varying degrees) determined to bring the various arts together, combining poetry, layout, typefaces and illustrations to make a unified artistic statement. By the end of the 19th century, these magazines were a crucial part of the artistic scene and the main channels of expression for the new movements in literature and criticism. They serve as a unique barometer of the general level, range and vitality of artistic activity in each country and region.

Obviously, they varied a great deal, but the new magazines were usually physically smaller than the standard 19th-century production; their rise saw the gradual emergence of the A5 format as the standard. They were also little in that they had much smaller circulations, minute bank balances, and shorter lifespans. My calculation is that the average Irish Little Magazine could count itself lucky if it reached issue 15. There are lots of possible reasons for this, including the fact that anything so intimately tied to fashion must die when the fashion changes; the editors' lack of, and disdain for, commercial sense; their consequent lack of hard cash; lack of interest among the general population; quarrelling and ego clashes among the editorial staff (none of whom would be professionals); the fact that most editors are artists who will fold a project and move on the instant they feel staleness or repetition creeping in; and finally censorship or persecution, though these have been surprisingly rare in Ireland, at least as regards purely literary publications.

The obverse of this is that they frequently have ludicrously large-scale ambitions, a sense of their own uniqueness and of their mission to nurture literary talent in a subtler and more vital fashion than the large-scale, commercial press is capable. Consequently, most have an air of arrogance which is usually a direct expression of the editor's own, necessarily forceful, personality.

Taking into consideration the role they play, '*avant garde* magazines' might be a more accurate description. This leaves the bigger magazines and reviews as the rear guard, less responsive (if not openly hostile) to the latest developments, or simply unaware of their existence. It is only after the Little Magazines have broken the ice that the more self-important reviews will accept new writers and movements. It could be said that publishing a grand review, such as the *Dublin University Magazine*, or any of the four magazines this century called the *Irish Review*, is a critical endeavour, while publishing a Little Magazine is an artistic one. This division of roles became established very early this century, with the Little Magazines as the recognised arbiters of taste and the accepted route of entry for new writers. In 1946, Hoffman, Allen and Ulrich estimated that these magazines first published some 80 per cent "of our most important post-1912 critics, novelists, poets and storytellers"[2], and this is a role they still play today. They illustrate the importance of these Little Magazines:

> Hemingway publishes his first story in *The Double Dealer* in 1922. Assume that the editor and a few other people read this story and like it. These people talk enthusiastically of the story and perhaps twice as many read the next Hemingway offering. Soon many admirers are talking—a snowball is rolling in the advance guard. A half-dozen Little Magazines are printing Hemingway stories and he has several thousand readers. An obscure, non-commercial press in Paris publishes his first thin volume, *Three Stories and Ten Poems*. The snowball rolls into the Scribner's office. Finally in 1926 comes *The Sun Also Rises*.[3]

The point is that we accept this today as the natural way of things; but, before the advent of the Little Magazines, it wasn't. They played an essential role in the democratisation of literature, carrying a little further the torch first lifted by the mass-circulation magazines of the 19th century which began the process of widening access to the practice of literature beyond the charmed circle of the wealthy, urban *élite*. The massive strides forward in both literacy and the technology of printing and distribution meant that it was now feasible for quite a wide range of people from the middle classes to consider starting their own magazines.

As I mentioned earlier, the Little Magazine came to Ireland at the end of the 19th century as a by-product of the Irish Literary Revival; it is fitting then that its first appearance in Ulster should come from the echo of that revival in the north, the Ulster Literary Theatre. Magazines like *Beltaine* in Dublin were a manifestation of that regionalist drive which has been identified as one of the underlying forces behind the Little Magazine movement, and they acted as a proving ground on which the gradual forging of a separate cultural identity for Ireland was worked out. They also attracted predictable criticism from the London literary establishment, the cosmopolitan *élite*, for doing so. In its turn, *Uladh* played an identical rôle, though this time the poles were Belfast and Dublin. As a first, abortive manifestation of Ulster's equivalent urge to build its own distinct cultural identity, *Uladh*, with sad inevitability, attracted criticism from our own but newly-instituted literary establishment in Dublin.

Despite being produced over a period of half a century, and by editors and artists with widely varying positions on art and politics, we can easily trace the common lineaments of the Little Magazine through the pages of *Uladh, Lagan* and *Rann*. All were founded and edited by visionaries, by artists and activists rather than academics, critics or businessmen. Bulmer Hobson and David Parkhill, fresh from the perhaps predictable failure of their Protestant National Association, started the Ulster Literary Theatre and then *Uladh* along with Francis Joseph Bigger, Robert Lynd and John and Joseph Campbell; *Lagan* was edited entirely by writers, principally John Boyd, but also Roy McFadden and John Hewitt; while *Rann*'s editors were Barbara Hunter and, again, McFadden. All attempted to combine the various disciplines of poetry, typography and illustration. *Lagan*, presumably due in part to wartime restrictions, is perhaps short on the latter, but *Rann* and, above all, *Uladh* are aesthetic triumphs, with layout, headings, typefaces, editorials, poems and illustrations combining to form a closely integrated whole, each issue a cultural artefact evocative and representative of its time and place.

Certainly, each editorial team proudly displayed the required arrogance, the blithe confidence in their own uniqueness and significance. If the similarity between Hunter and McFadden's statement "that *Rann* is the first magazine of its kind to appear in this province is a fact which need not be stressed" and Boyd's "introduction to this anthology—the first of its kind to appear in Ulster" is almost comic, then W.B. Reynold's opening editorial for *Uladh* innocently crosses that line with its assertion, regarding previous literary journalism in Ulster, that it

> ... expresses nothing, means nothing; it aims at being sixpence worth. We do not aim at being sixpence worth; we aim at being priceless ...

This hubris can almost be forgiven because in all three cases it is almost justified. *Uladh* was the first Little Magazine to come from Ulster; *Lagan* was first to embody and expound a mature regionalist outlook; *Rann* was the north's first ever magazine devoted entirely to poetry. The standard of work published in all three was remarkably high. Above all, they more than fulfilled their role as platforms for writers, the local *avant garde* who otherwise would have found it difficult, if not impossible, to get into print without a substantial degree of compromise and self-censorship. These magazines also attracted writers from outside their own circle of believers, including more established figures who had been drawn off to London or Dublin, and who often disagreed with the magazines' (not so) hidden agendas, but who were nevertheless excited and challenged by these signs of cultural life in the province. And so *Uladh* included contributions not only from Hobson, Lynd, Bigger and the Campbells, but also from AE, Alice Milligan, Padraic Colum and James Connolly. *Lagan* published not just the newcomers McFadden, Hewitt and Bell, but also Richard Rowley, Forrest Reid and Joseph Tomelty; while *Rann*, with the least dogmatism and the broadest agenda, published everyone from Hewitt to Yeats and from May Morton to Michael McLaverty. *Rann* also bolstered its claim to uniqueness in Ulster, if without realising it, by being the first magazine to publish substantial amounts of poetry by (mostly Ulster) women—Morton, Barbara Hunter herself, and Meta Mayne Reid.

The one Little Magazine component which these three seem to lack is an overt political standpoint. *Rann*, above all, seems almost without politics; knowing what we do about the editors (and indeed most of their contributors), we might be tempted to search for hidden clues, but that would be unwise. *Lagan* is only a little more committed, with the left-wing assumptions of its progenitors revealed in a way not open to the all-poetry *Rann*. Its stories and articles, choice of subject matter and sympathies, its general tone and positions strongly remind one of *The Bell*, its Dublin contemporary. It is, however, no subversive tract. The strongest political stance is taken by *Uladh*, as we might expect given Hobson's later exploits in the Gaelic League, IRB, Sinn Féin and Irish Volunteers, although even here the nationalism of the founders is expressed more in the determinedly Irish look and feel of the journal than in its content. The closest we come to an overt political statement is in an article 'Literature and Politics' by 'Connla' (a pseudonym of James Connolly). He describes unionism as

... a narrow and barren creed, which would exclude all native beauty in art and literature, because it was native; a little cell built round on all sides, with a loophole towards London, and wherein the mind starved for want of native provender, or grew sickly with imported rubbish.

But even here, he chooses to end on a conciliatory note:

> But a brighter day is dawning for Ulster and Belfast; a fairer life is drawing breath. Without fear of compromising their political opinions, nationalist and unionist are preparing to co-operate in many things, not least in literature, for the honour of Eire.

It is an astoundingly stupid view of Ulster on the verge of the home rule crisis, but it is the strongest political statement in four issues of *Uladh*.

The real politics of *Uladh, Lagan* and *Rann* were subsumed in the last major Little Magazine characteristic, an almost instinctive regionalism. In the US, the Little Magazines began to shift the focus of literary activity away from the east coast and to give a voice to the mid-west and the south. In late 19th-century Britain, they had contributed to Ireland's definition of itself as an independent region; as the 19th century progressed, they began to spring up in Cork and Galway, Wexford and Limerick, but nowhere was their regionalist message so strong as in Ulster. In his editorial for the first issue of *Uladh*, Reynolds proclaimed: "Ulster has its own way of things, which may be taken as in great contrast to the Munster way of things." However, regionalism did not even exist as a recognised term in 1904, and as dedicated Irish patriots and nationalists the staff of *Uladh* were halting and unsure in their defence of regional loyalties. Note the slight lameness of Reynolds' assertion that, while having the greatest respect for the work of Yeats and Hyde in Dublin:

> We in Belfast and Ulster also wish to set up a school; but there will be a difference. At present we can only say that our talent is more satiric than poetic. That will probably remain the broad difference between the Ulster and the Leinster schools.

Even this half-hearted declaration of independence was enough to bring down the wrath of the Dublin *élite* on his head, and his editorial reply in the second issue of *Uladh* is even more defensive:

> We have not striven to erect a barrier between Ulster and the rest of Ireland; but we aim at building a citadel in Ulster for Irish thought and art

achievements such as exists in Dublin. If the result is provincial rather than national it will not be our fault.

The collapse of *Uladh* and the Ulster Literary Theatre, and the cataclysms which followed, meant that this *proto*-regionalist voice was almost forgotten. But when the dust settled and *Lagan* was published, it re-emerged with greater strength and clarity. In his first editorial, Boyd launches straight into an analysis of the problems of the Ulster writer, of the lack of tradition or an audience, and the drift to London and Dublin also described by Reynolds 40 years before. In another direct echo of that first *Uladh*, Boyd writes that "the first job of Ulster writers is to make a clearing: to satirize, to parody and to ridicule". But his regionalism is vastly more confident and mature:

> An Ulster literary tradition that is capable of developing and enriching itself must spring out of the life and speech of the province; and an Ulster writer cannot evade his problems by adopting either a superimposed English or a sentimental Gaelic outlook. His outlook must be that of an Ulsterman. He must, therefore, train his ears to catch the unique swing of our speech; train his eyes to note the natural beauty of our hills and the unnatural ugliness of our towns: above all, he must study the subtle psychology of our people.

These editorials, plus of course the choice of contents and subjects in the main body of the two magazines, point to a fundamental difference in the regionalisms expounded: remembering the sad Ulster joke about Protestant and Catholic atheists, we might see the staff of *Uladh* as Irish regionalists and that of *Lagan* as British ones.

After this, *Rann* might appear as something of a climbdown; there are no crusading editorials or articles, and the subtitle of the magazine quickly retreated from 'A Quarterly of Ulster Poetry' to 'An Ulster Quarterly of Poetry', but this would be a misreading. As the culmination of that transitional phase referred to in my opening remarks, during which our literary journals reflected the emergence of the cultural identity of the province itself, *Rann* has no need to wear its heart on its sleeve any more than the *Honest Ulsterman* or *Gown*. It is totally confident of the ability, of the right, of an Ulster magazine to present the literary world from its own standpoint. From its cover illustrations to its reprints of poems by Allingham and the Rhyming Weavers, *Rann* has no need for histrionics; its Ulster regional identity is implicit and assured, and marks very clearly an important turning point in the cultural life of the province. An Ulster Quarterly of Poetry indeed.

Notes

[1] Malcolm Bradbury and James McFarlane, 'Movements, Magazines and Manifestos', in *Modernism 1890-1930* (Harmondsworth, 1976).
[2] Hoffman, Allen & Ulrich, *The Little Magazine* (Princetown: Princeton University Press, 1946).
[3] Ibid.

Socialism in Ulster

Henry Patterson

In present circumstances, in Northern Ireland and further afield, it might seem that 'Socialism in Ulster' is a topic redolent of nostalgia or, what is probably the same thing, an inability to face realities. Talk of reality in this context means the conflict of nationalities, of ethnicities, cultural traditions, and so on. Are those who, as historians or political activists, still take an interest in the history of the labour movement in Ulster, its past and its possible future, not in danger of letting their interest or commitment to a minority tradition, albeit one which has attracted some individuals of stature like John Hewitt, cut them off from the realities of communal division which have marginalised class politics and which must be dealt with in their own right?

My response to this is that it stems from a defective knowledge of the history of Ulster. A recent example of the underestimation of the significance of labour in the history of Northern Ireland is the introductory essay by Paul Arthur and Brendan O'Leary to a volume of essays on possible futures for Northern Ireland, in which they refer to:

> ... labourist movements which briefly threatened to transcend sectarianism in the 1930s and in the late 1950s and the early 1960s. This threat was easily handled by the Ulster Unionist Party. Explicit accusations of disloyalty, reminders of the dangers in splitting the unionist cause and overt renewals of sectarian appeals elicited the required responses.[1]

A similarly dismissive approach can be found in J.J. Lee's recent history of modern Ireland.[2]

Such arguments are quite simply empirically wrong and have been demonstrated to be so in a number of historical studies.[3] I still remember the surprise I felt when I came across the files of the *Workers' Bulletin* in the Henry Collection in the library of Queen's University in the early 70s. This was the document produced by the General Strike Committee which led the major shipyard and engineering workers' strike in Belfast in January 1919. The strike, which involved 40,000 workers directly and another 20,000 indirectly, was a massive eruption of class conflict, creating fear and insecurity amongst the Protestant *bourgeoisie* and the unionist political leadership. Although it was defeated by state authorities and by much vaunted instruments of social control, such as the Orange Order, the recently formed Ulster Unionist Labour Association and the unionist press were practically helpless before this assertion of industrial power.

This labour militancy and its political payoff—the labour municipal election victories in January 1920—would soon be submerged in a tide of sectarianism and political violence which culminated in the shipyard expulsions of July 1920. An American political scientist, convinced of the essentially colonial nature of the conflict in Ulster, provides this description of the expulsions and their significance:

> Facing unemployment, Protestant workers decided that if work had to be lost, it was better that Catholics lose it. In July 1920 they forced 10,000 of Belfast's 90,000 Catholics from their jobs and allowed the Unionist Party, which championed the expulsions, to restore its leadership over them.[4]

In fact, the figure of expelled workers was 7,500, of whom about one quarter were so-called 'rotten Prods'—active trade unionists and socialists.[5] Austen Morgan in his recent important book on the Belfast working class refers to this group as "almost the entire *cadre* of working-class leaders in the industrial and political wings of the labour movement".[6] This formative conjuncture needs to be read in a more discriminating way, for it reveals much about the dynamics of socialism and sectarianism in Ulster. From the nationalist point of view, the shipyard is a bastion of Protestant exclusivism, and all the figures for Catholic representation in the workforces of the two yards demonstrate clearly the basis for this view. Yet if we look at the shipyard workforce from the point of view of the *bourgeoisie* and the unionist political leadership of the time, we see a threat, a social force that may become a political one and against which an intense ideological campaign is waged using institutions like the Orange Order and the Ulster Unionist Labour Association.

Both views are part of the truth about the expulsions. The shipyards were sites of class conflict and of the reproduction of sectarian ideologies, and the balance between them was constantly shifting. A crucial determinant of these shifts was the perception of the workers as a balanced force in the political conflict between the British state and the political and military forces of republicanism. Workers, like members of other classes, whether they are Protestant or Catholic, do not have a set of primordial national, sectarian or class identifications which remain unaffected by history. In the history of Belfast, as Maurice Goldring has recently established, nationality, ethnicity and sectarianism are concepts which reflect the formation process and subsequent reproduction of the working class.[7]

Given the colonial origins of our present conflict (I need hardly state that origins can never provide more than part of the explanation of any phenomenon), the development of industrial capitalism could not be unmarked by the hierarchies of the colonised countryside. But although the logic of capitalist relations of production and that of sectarianism—in this case the demand for Protestant privilege—are not totally conflictual, there was not an easy congruence: witness the formation of the Orange Order itself, which emerged as a plebeian organisation aimed at stopping the employment of Catholic weavers by Protestant linen capitalists. Throughout the 19th century, sectarian violence in the workplaces in Ulster was often provoked by groups of Protestant workers who disputed the right of their employers to employ Catholic workers. For some workers at particular times, class interest was defined by communal exclusivism.

Here we come to a whole set of debates and problems which centre on the place of the ideologies of 'natural' communities—such as the nationalities and ethnic groups—within social discourse. The optimism of the *Communist Manifesto* has cast a long shadow:

> ... subjection to capital, the same in England as in France, in America as in Germany has stripped him (worker) of every trace of national character ...
> National differences and antagonisms between peoples are daily more vanishing owing to the development of the *bourgeoisie*, to freedom of commerce, to the world market, to uniformity in the mode of production and in the conditions of life corresponding thereto.[8]

It has become a truism that Marxism and, perhaps, much of the socialist tradition ignores or is at least incapable of explaining national conflict. Different reasons are provided for this weakness. Gerry

Cohen has suggested that the problem lies in Marx's philosophical anthropology, which treats human beings as essentially producers who realise themselves through the full use of their capacities:

> ... there is a human need to which Marxist observation is commonly blind, one different from and as deep as the need to cultivate one's talents. It is the need to be able to say not what I can do but who I am, satisfaction of which has historically been found in identification with others in a shared culture based on nationality or race or some slice or amalgam thereof.[9]

But, as Alex Callinicos has pointed out, while it may be the case that such a need exists and that nationalism may be one form of fulfilling it, the need for identity cannot be used to explain national divisions without committing the naturalistic fallacy—essential to all nationalist explanations of nationalism—that nations are pregiven natural entities. As Ernest Gellner, no friend of Marxism, has pointed out, "nations are not inscribed in the nature of things", nor are nation-states the "manifest ultimate destiny of ethnic or cultural groups".[10]

Marx's own difficulty with the question stemmed from the degree to which his own theoretical framework remained heavily influenced by 19th-century liberal ideology, with the result that he assumed that the world market operated over the heads, rather than through the hands, of the major states. This proved to be a serious misconception because the world market of his time was first and foremost an instrument of British rule over the expanded European state system. The reason why the socialist tradition has been, with the exception of the work of the Austro-Marxists, so deficient in the analysis of nationalism, lies in this down-playing of the role of states in the process of capitalist development. The development of the capitalist world economy, since the 16th century, has taken the form of a social system of which the key political units have been the states. Although looking at the development of the working class economically, as a 'class-in-itself', we can abstract from these political units, it is impossible to consider the process by which different working classes have moved towards that type of political consciousness identified by Marx as a 'class-for-itself', without bringing the state in to the centre of the analysis:

> ... a class *fur sich* is a group that makes conscious claims of class membership, which is a claim to a place in a particular political order. Such a class therefore could only grow up in relation to a given political entity.[11]

Exactly the same thing could be said of ethnic/national groups: they have defined themselves in relation to specific state structures. Too much of the writing about nationalism, and particularly about the class/nation, class/sectarian interfaces, focuses on questions of identity and ideology to the neglect of politics and the state. Just as classes as political actors have to be created through processes of mobilisation and political struggles, the 'nationalist people' or the 'loyal workers of East Belfast' are the products of political interventions as much, or more than, more primordial forces.

Bringing the state back into our analysis of the history of labour in Ulster helps to make sense of the major outbursts of class conflict which punctuated the history of the state. Before partition, particularly before 1914, the state framework was very clearly an imperial one. This was even the case for the Catholic minority of Belfast's working class whose support for home rule was not incompatible with Ireland's continued participation in the UK and imperial framework. For Unionist Labour, economic and social advance for the working class was seen almost as a by-product of the development of a Labour presence in the House of Commons, and home rule was portrayed, not unrealistically, as an economically retrogressive development. Thus, as part of the Ulster Unionist mobilisation against the third Home Rule Bill, a group of trade unionists made an appeal to their counterparts in the rest of the United Kingdom for support in their struggle against home rule:

> We are certain that the granting of Home Rule to Ireland must be fatal to the best interests of trade unionism in this country and would be a deadly blow at the solidarity of the movement.
> Our leading trade organisations are branches of the great British unions. The establishment of Home Rule will be followed by the setting up of rival and independent Irish unions.
> We have won improved conditions because the workers of the three kingdoms were able to exert joint pressure on the Imperial Parliament. To leave us to the consideration of a parliament with crippled finances, elected mainly from agricultural constituencies, will deprive us of participation in those further benefits which British workers are certain to secure from the Imperial parliament in the near future.[12]

These sentiments were commonplace in unionist ideology before partition and would be repeated for decades afterwards. They were based on an important element of truth—the Irish Party at Westminster had just ensured that the health provisions of Lloyd George's National

Insurance Bill were not extended to Ireland.[13] The mystificatory aspect of the ideology lay in its location of social and economic conservatism in the south. For, as would become very clear after partition, solid class pressure for reform—let alone for socialism—was largely a Belfast phenomenon. Connolly had opposed partition because it would lead to a "carnival of reaction". Unionist Labour supported it for the same reason. The difference lay in their respective expectations of the likely balance of political forces in a home rule parliament for the 32 counties. The weakness of the Unionist Labour position was in ignoring the fact that, even with partition, labour in Ulster could find itself overwhelmed by rural and small town conservatism.

Here the political form of the Northern Ireland state is important. Devolution represented a very different sort of alliance between the classes in the Protestant community from the one which existed before 1914. Pre-1914 unionism had been based—in its relationship to the working class—on what can be described as an expansionary hegemony; relying on the notion of a *bourgeois* leadership which would provide the political and social conditions of participation in an imperial economy. This was a hegemony that left the material conditions of the working class up to market forces. Labour in Belfast, as in the rest of Britain, accepted the separation of economics from politics. This was to change in Belfast and Britain because of the war. As Alastair Reid has argued, state intervention during the war had a major impact on labourist ideology, as the basis of industrial relations in Britain became a bargaining table between the unions and the state, thus eroding separation of economics from politics.[14] But, in Belfast, hegemony was recast in a repressive and sectarian direction. The violence and sectarian polarisation of the period of state formation intertwined with the onset of a major and secular crisis in the core industries that had previously been the mainstay of Belfast's economic leadership on the island. Departing from their emphasis on the integration of labour in Belfast with that in the rest of the UK, unionism now set out to stress the advantages of the responsiveness of local governing institutions.

The nature of the political alliances in the Protestant community was transformed. Although the institutions of devolution had little substantive capacity to deal with the structural problems of the decline of stable industries, they did possess the powers to take the logic of discrimination to the centre of state calculation and hence political life. The disintegration of the international economic system provided a backcloth for a set of manic involuted roads to national salvation. The "Ulster Way" was what Bew, Gibbon and I termed the populist strategy followed by the dominant group in the Unionist cabinet from 1921 through to World War II.[15] It was the threat of intra-Protestant class conflict that determined the adoption of this strategy: its major objective was not the destruction of republicanism, but the establishment of a relatively secular Protestant labour leadership.

The repression and dispersal of that leadership in the early 20s from the core workforces of Belfast, and the Unionist government's decision to get rid of proportional representation, first in local government and then in elections for the Northern Ireland parliament, would in themselves have done much to dissipate the threat of a repeat of 1919—as did the high unemployment which characterised Belfast throughout the inter-war period. But we also need to look at the political horizons of the labour movement itself. Here there was a strong sense of dissatisfaction that state power was in the hands of those who were seen to have had direct responsibility for the pogroms of 1920. The strength of anti-partitionism in the 20s and 30s thus reflected more than a commitment to a republican-socialist perspective on the part of some labour leaders. Amongst a broader sector, it reflected a moral and democratic refusal of the nature of the state's communal logic rather than a nationalist ideological commitment. But such a version of anti-unionism could—logically at least—have just as easily and, perhaps, more easily been part of an integrationist position. That, in point of historical fact, it was not reflects the sea-change in relations between Ulster unionism and the core British *élite* that the war and the Irish revolution of 1916-21 had brought about.

The assumption made by labour leaders like William Walker, before 1914, that the progress of socialism in Ireland would be an integral part of the ascent of Labour in Britain, was much more difficult to validate in the inter-war period. Northern Ireland's insulation carried on apace after 1921. In a period of economic crisis for staple industries throughout the United Kingdom, the flows of capital and labour which had integrated Belfast into the triangular relationship with Liverpool and Glasgow dried up. The financial provisions of the Government of Ireland Act, which saw a Northern Ireland state with the responsibility for balancing its budget (although in practice this proved impossible and a British Treasury subvention became essential to the existence of the state) did allow unionist ideology to emphasise the independence of the state and to build up the illusion of a federal, rather than a devolved, relationship with Westminster. The construction of an increasingly provincial frame of reference had damaging implications for the labour movement and socialists. Tom Nairn has described Ulster as "More like a city state than a territorial nation".[16] In fact, it was precisely because in electoral terms even a strong performance by the Northern Ireland Labour Party and other labour groupings would have been swamped by the traditionalism of rural and small town Ulster, that the provincial frame of reference was inherently a depressing one for the left. In reality, the question of socialism in Ulster had been a tale of two cities—Belfast and London. Labour as an economic and political force has been a Belfast phenomenon and this had resulted in its marginalisation, even when it had become a major force in the politics of the city.

One of the reasons why it is so easy for the significance of labour to be underestimated is the uneven nature of its implantation in the Northern Ireland political system. Thus, if we look at 1962—the high point of labour success in the history of the state—we find that the NILP won 4 seats out of 52 in the Stormont elections. However, this bald and dispiriting figure obscures more than it reveals. The NILP vote in 16 Belfast constituencies was 58,811 while the total Unionist vote for the same constituencies was 69,069. If to the NILP vote we add the 16,359 votes cast for a number of Irish and Republican Labour candidates, we get a total left vote in Belfast of 72,160—in this aggregate sense, the Unionist Party lost Belfast.[17] What these figures reveal is a constituency for politics of a labourist sort which is imprisoned by the dominant political framework in Northern Ireland.

Throughout the history of the state, a minority of socialists in Ulster, of whom Hewitt was a part—at least when he wrote his article on the United Irishman, James Hope, in 1941—looked to a joint anti-capitalist/anti-imperialist struggle with the working class in the Free State to overthrow both states. Elsewhere, I have analysed this social republican tradition at length, so all I will say here is that its possibilities of appealing outside a small minority in the Protestant working class were slim.[18] But the alternative possibility—breaking out of provincial isolation by linking up with the British Labour Party—has had to face obstacles which appear every bit as insuperable.

In the inter-war period, as Paul Canning shows very clearly, the leaders of both the Conservative and Labour parties in Britain had little sympathy with what was clearly seen as the obduracy of the Ulster Unionists. In the 30s, the predominant British concern ceased to be constitutional and economic aspects of British-Irish relations and became defence: to secure Britain's rear against Hitler, a general settlement with Ireland was needed. Appeasement of De Valera became part of British strategy. Influential British civil servants, like Sir

Warren Fisher of the Treasury, were sympathetic to the cause of Irish nationalism and deeply antagonistic to the Unionists.[19] The Labour Party had long had a sympathy with the Irish nationalist case, although Canning claims this was obscured in the 20s by Ramsay MacDonald's sympathy for the Ulster Protestants.[20] After his resignation, Labour returned to a more traditional position.

In Britain, apart from the *Manchester Guardian*, the only real support in the press for De Valera's anti-partition campaign came from Labour-supporting papers like the *Daily Herald*. The effects of this were evident in what Canning describes as "The first and last serious attempt by a prominent member of the British Labour Party to mobilise support against the Unionist Party in Northern Ireland ...".[21] This was the visit to Belfast in September 1937 by Sir Stafford Cripps. The accounts in the press of the time would not support the description of this as a serious attempt at anything. Lecturing on 'Socialism and Imperialism', he explained to his audience that the BLP "would like to see a united Ireland because they believed it would be the ultimate solution of the economic difficulties, both in the south and in the north". Eventually, he hoped that federal Ireland "might be part of the Empire and would be treated as part of Great Britain".[22] While recommending an end to partition, which would have meant absorption into a protectionist Ireland, he also attacked economic nationalism and added "the great shipbuilding and linen industries depended on associations with other people and other countries". A large section of the labour leadership appeared to have absented itself from the lecture and Canning reports that Cripps departed "embittered never to return". Cripps was not the first, and would not be the last, British Labour leader to combine blithe ignorance of Irish realities with a colonialist impatience with the views of local labour leaders. As one southern labour paper noted of the lecture: "Whatever may be said about his position and policy in British politics we fear that Sir Stafford Cripps does not show a very deep understanding of the situation in Ireland."[23]

World War II produced a significant alteration in British *élite* attitudes to Northern Ireland, at the same time as it allowed a strong Labour challenge to the Unionist *régime*. The rigidities of the local *régime* laid it open to a challenge that combined class and a sense of Britishness betrayed by provincial conservatism. Now it was the Unionist *élite* and the *bourgeoisie* that could be charged with disloyalty to the overriding national task of defeating fascism. One of its candidates in the Protestant constituency of Bloomfield got 5,802 votes—36.7 per cent of the total vote. In East Belfast, the Communist Party could run a bookshop and pay a full-time organiser and, in one street off the Beersbridge Road, a wall slogan proclaimed 'God bless a guy called Joe Stalin'.[24] In the 1945 Stormont election, the various labour parties managed a total vote of 113,413, 31.9 per cent of the total, again very largely in the Belfast area.[25]

With the exception of the 'Chapel Gate' election of 1949, the vote for the left never fell back to inter-war levels from 1945 to the mid-60s. This shift upwards may, in part, reflect the improved economic conditions of the post-war period. But these, in themselves, were also a product of the economic and social policies of British social democracy, which continued the process of the deinsulation of the province instigated by the war.[26] Such policies significantly dented the semi-sovereign pretensions of some aspects of unionist ideology. Labour in the north could again hope to integrate its own struggles into some broader vista of progress. The Conservative Party's acceptance of a large element of the social democratic consensus meant that this emphasis on progress within a UK context was possible, even when the Labour Party itself was out of power.

The Unionist government's inability to prevent the sharp rise in redundancies in Belfast industries at the end of the 50s did much to swell the NILP vote in the 1958 election. This was in part the result of the new prime minister, Terence O'Neill, and his commitment to economic modernisation. But it was also due to his unwillingness to endorse more atavistic themes in relation to the recently-elected Labour government. Sam McAughtry, who campaigned actively for the NILP at the time, is our best source on the double-edged relation of Belfast to British Labour:

> Wilson had a slipstream that stretched across the Irish sea. There was a boom in industry. When we knocked on doors we were talking to people who never in their lives had contemplated socialism. We were able to say for the first time—"Look, there's a factory opening in Dundonald that wouldn't be opening up but for Harold Wilson not allowing it to open in Welwyn Garden City."[27]

But, at the same time, McAughtry records the outrage of labour activists at O'Neill personally campaigning against sitting NILP MPs and using the issue of Harold Wilson's alleged anti-partitionist sympathies. Of course, such themes were not new—when Ramsay MacDonald was William Walker's election agent for the North Belfast by-election in 1905, which he nearly won, the unionist press focused on the ardent support for home rule of leading members of the British Labour Party.[28] However, the general disfavour with which the southern state was regarded by the British political *élite*, because of its wartime neutrality, had produced a post-war Labour administration which was pro-unionist and was seen to have solidified the link with Northern Ireland through the 1949 Ireland Act. Also in the 50s, the NILP had followed a strategy of building itself up as a provincial and clearly pro-union party, in order to consolidate itself securely within the Protestant working class and make future progress less susceptible to sectarian retrenchment. As Bob Purdie comments: "For it to proceed much further it would have to clarify if it was a Protestant and Unionist Party or a secular party trying to transcend the divisions between Orange and Green."[29]

In the early 60s, it was beginning to raise a number of the key issues that would be at the heart of the subsequent civil rights movement. This new agenda would cause its own tensions in the NILP where it intersected with internal conflict over the 'Sunday Swings' issue. The NILP's dilemma was acute—its muted civil rights strategy depended for success on an incremental approach, but one that demonstrated results. Harold Wilson gave it the worst of all possible worlds. His surrogate Irish nationalism gave grist to the mills of the unionist press while, in practice, he exerted little real pressure on O'Neill to introduce the reforms which might have avoided the civil rights mobilisations and the disintegration of the state. One of the foremost champions of a high NILP profile on civil rights issues, Charles Brett, has recorded the disgust he felt at the lethargy of successive Labour home secretaries with regard to the issues he was raising. Roy Jenkins put in a particularly lackadaisical performance, but Labour's responsibility for generating the crisis is also evident in the fact that, between its return to office in 1964 and the outbreak of serious disorder in August 1969, only one minister, Home Secretary Frank Soskice, visited the province and that was for a single afternoon. This after Harold Wilson's letter to the McCluskeys, founders of the Campaign for Social Justice, promising that a Labour government would implement large-scale changes in Northern Ireland.[30]

The Wilson government's record in Northern Ireland was all the more undistinguished, given the evidence that James Callaghan, at least, had briefly considered sponsoring a Labourist modernisation of the province. In July 1969, he wrote to the general secretary of the Labour Party: "The path to peace in Northern Ireland and to good relations with the government of the Republic lies in bringing together in one party the Protestant and Catholic working class."[31] The British party should therefore, in his view, have provided the NILP with financial, organisational and moral support. In fact, earlier that year, a special delegate conference of the NILP had voted to support plans for a merger with the British party and there had been subsequent discussions between officials of both parties. But, as with previous attempts in 1942 and 1949, the proposal was turned down by the National Executive Committee of the Labour Party without wider discussion.

Hugh Roberts, a champion of electoral integration, writes of the decision:

> The NILP disintegrated fast after the Labour Party's leadership's refusal to affiliate or incorporate it in 1970. It had obtained no fewer than 98,193 votes (12.6 per cent of the total vote cast in Northern Ireland) in the 1970 general election, despite the disabilities it laboured under and the three years of sectarian polarisation since late 1967, but the BLP's refusal to support it in the rapidly deteriorating situation in Northern Ireland was the last straw for the NILP leadership.[32]

This oversimplifies in attributing the NILP's decline largely to the failure of British Labour to deepen its involvement in Northern Ireland. Other factors, including the degree to which some of its strongest areas of support had been devastated and polarised by violence and intimidation, the massive movements of population which took place in the early years of the 'troubles' and the intensification of the decline of those traditional industries whose workforces had included a significant number of NILP supporters, must also be taken into account.

Nevertheless, acknowledgement of these other factors does not remove the strength of the case that Roberts and others make for the Labour Party to organise here. In a book which was published in 1985, Paul Bew and I argued for a reformist social democratic agenda of economic regeneration and structural reform in Northern Ireland.[33] Implicit in this was a rejection of the case for the Labour Party organising here. The Anglo-Irish Agreement has radically altered the state framework and demands a revision of this position. If the positive features of the Agreement—'Direct Rule with a green tinge'—are to be consolidated, then the whole set of economic, social, security and equality issues needs to be separated from the agenda of creeping unification. For the medium term, and possibly considerably longer,

Northern Ireland's state structures will have a hybrid British/Irish nature. If this is to be compatible with the requisite degree of stability in popular expectations, without which no form of progressive politics can flourish, then the Labour Party should make it clear that it will support the union plus the Agreement, along with new cross-border institutions in areas such as energy and tourism, and some form of internal governmental structures based on power-sharing. The decision to organise here would give a clear signal to the unionist community that, while the party might be in favour of a radical reformist agenda for Northern Ireland, it is not in favour of expelling them from the UK.

The radical changes in economy and society in Northern Ireland since the 60s have effectively destroyed the labourist tradition which has been the subject of this paper. The attempts by various political groupings to resurrect it in whole or in part—the struggles of the Workers' Party/Democratic Left and Labour 87, for example—have failed. If the many progressive features of that tradition are to be recreated in any form, then the decisive impetus will have to come from outside the depressing stalemate of our local political arena.

Notes

[1] Paul Arthur & Brendan O'Leary 'Introduction' to John McGarry & Brendan O'Leary (eds.) *The Future of Northern Ireland* (Oxford: Oxford University Press, 1990) pp. 24-25.

[2] J.J. Lee, *Ireland 1912-1985 Politics and Society* (Cambridge: Cambridge University Press, 1989).

[3] Peter Gibbon, *The Origins of Ulster Unionism* (Manchester: Manchester University Press 1975), Henry Patterson, *Class Conflict and Sectarianism* (Belfast: Blackstaff Press, 1980), Graham Walker, *The Politics of Frustration Harry Midgley and the Failure of Labour in Northern Ireland* (Manchester: Manchester University Press, 1985), Austin Morgan, *Labour and Partition* (London: Pluto Press, 1990), Maurice Goldring, *Belfast: From Loyalty to Rebellion* (London: Lawrence & Wishart, 1991).

[4] Michael MacDonald, *Children of Wrath: Political Violence in Northern Ireland* (Cambridge: Polity Press, 1986) p. 59.

[5] Morgan, p. 269.

[6] Morgan, p. 270.

[7] Goldring, *Belfast: From Loyalty to Rebellion*.

[8] Marx & Engels, *The Communist Manifesto* in Marx & Engels, *Selected Works* (London: Lawrence & Wishart, 1908), p. 51.

[9] Alex Callinicos, *Making History, Agency, Structure and Change in Social Theory* (Cambridge: Polity Press, 1987) pp. 157-158.

[10] Callinicos, p. 158.
[11] Giovanni Arrighi, Terence K. Hopkins & Immanuel Wallerstein, *Antisystemic Movements* (London: Verso, 1989), p. 23.
[12] Patterson, p. 86.
[13] Morgan, p. 87.
[14] Alastair Reid, 'Skilled Workers in the Shipbuilding Industry, 1880-1920' in Austen Morgan & Bob Purdie (eds.) *Ireland Divided Nation, Divided Class* (London: Inklinks, 1980).
[15] Paul Bew, Peter Gibbon & Henry Patterson, *The State in Northern Ireland: Political Forces and Social Classes 1921–72* (Manchester: Manchester University Press, 1979).
[16] Tom Nairn, *The Break-up of Britain* (London: Verso, 1977) p. 235.
[17] Sydney Elliott, *Northern Ireland Parliamentary Election Results 1921–71* (Chichester, 1973) p. 43.
[18] Henry Patterson, *The Politics of Illusion: Republicanism and Socialism in Modern Ireland* (London: Hutchison/Radius, 1990).
[19] Paul Canning, *British Policy Towards Ireland 1921-41* (Oxford: Clarendon Press, 1985).
[20] Canning, p. 232.
[21] Canning, p. 232.
[22] *The Irish Times*, 3rd September, 1937.
[23] *Labour News*, 11th September, 1937.
[24] Alan Grattan, *The Majority's Minority: A Sociological Analysis of Socialism within the Protestant Working Class of Northern Ireland*. D.Phil University of Ulster 1988, p. 245.
[25] Terry Cradden, *Trade Unionism, Socialism and Partition* (Belfast: December Publications, 1993), p.49.
[26] Bew, Gibbon and Patterson, especially Chapter 4.
[27] Grattan, p. 326.
[28] Patterson, pp. 59-60.
[29] Bob Purdie, *Politics in the Street: The Origins of the Civil Rights Movement in Northern Ireland* (Belfast: Blackstaff Press, 1990), p. 65.
[30] Paul Bew & Henry Patterson, *The British State and the Ulster Crisis from Wilson to Thatcher* (London: Verso, 1985), p. 11.
[31] Bew & Patterson, p. 24.
[32] Hugh Roberts, 'Sound Stupidity: the British Labour Party System and the Northern Ireland Question' in McGarry & O'Leary, p. 105.
[33] Conclusion in Bew & Patterson.

A Very English Socialism and the Celtic Fringe, 1880-1911

James D. Young

The brotherhood of man is no mere fable,
We are all brothers, just like Caan and Abel.

—Hugh MacDiarmid

When I received an invitation at the beginning of 1991 to address the John Hewitt International Summer School, I was involved in a very private process of reassessing my own life as a socialist. A serious illness following a heart attack had stimulated me to re-examine my own decades-old experience as a socialist activist and historian.

As I was feeling that I just might be living through my own penultimate chapter, I began to read John Hewitt's *Ancestral Voices* and to explore the origins and development of an Ulsterman's long and enduring interest in literature, history, politics, and socialism. As I was growing up in a working-class community in Grangemouth in the 30s, Hewitt, the young Ulsterman, was moving towards the Labour Party and the Left Book Club. By the late 40s, I took a similar route, though the recent feeling of reaching the end of the journey between two eternities has rather obscured the memory of those years.

But at least two things stand out in my memory with crystal clarity: the discovery of the Utopian novel, *News from Nowhere*, by William Morris, and the new conviction of the importance of the common ownership of the means of production, distribution and exchange as the foundation for human liberation. In 1950, I gave a talk at the Falkirk branch of the Labour League of Youth on William Morris, the great English socialist. So, when I discovered Hewitt's conviction of the critical importance of the common ownership of the means of production, distribution and exchange, I could empathise with this

Ulsterman's authentic regional socialism.[1]

Before 1980, I would not have had any real difficulty (as distinct from unease) in accepting John Hewitt's conceptualisation of British working-class history. When he published the essay 'No Rootless Colonist' in 1972, the accelerating break-up of Britain was much less obvious than it is today. Therefore, the really counterfeit concept of 'the British radical-democratic tradition' could still be accepted without question in the most left-wing socialist circles. This was what he said:

> My mother tongue is English, instrument and tool of my thought and expression. John Ball, the Diggers, the Levellers, the Chartists, Paine, Cobbett, Morris, a strong thread in the fabric of my philosophy, I learned about in English history. There are many others, but these epitomise for me the British democratic tradition. I also draw on an English literary tradition.[2]

This statement by John Hewitt was an approximate description of my own attitude towards the British socialist tradition as I understood it in the late 40s, except that I was a Scot rather than an Ulsterman. At a very early stage of my evolution as a socialist activist, I began to develop the historian's cast of mind by asking new questions of the past out of the experiences of the present.

John Ball did not excite me at all; it was, I suppose, because I simply could not find a Scottish historical equivalent. But, although I was very interested in the Levellers and the Diggers, they were not capable of firing my socialist passion or imagination. In cycling up to the Covenanters' graves near Carron Glen with other members of the Labour League of Youth, I was already vaguely aware of the Covenanters' absence in the 'British' democratic tradition. It was not, however, until the 70s that I discovered the communist sects within the Covenanters' mass movement.[3]

From the very beginning of my evolution as a socialist activist into a socialist historian, I was much happier with "the Chartists, Paine, Cobbett and Morris".[4] Even so, without any real education I was already worrying over such problems as how one could criticise morally an inevitable historical process. Though I did not have the language to formulate the question in that way in the late 40s, the question owed something to my unorthodox Presbyterian background.[5] What worried me even more was the place of Scotland within the British democratic tradition.

Two books played a critical role in stimulating an inarticulate sense of unease with what I knew about the traditions of British socialism.

Both *From Cobbett to the Chartists* (edited by Max Morris) and *Labour's Turning Point, 1880-1900* (edited by Eric J. Hobsbawm) gave me some insight into the English domination of British socialism. But they at least persuaded me of the value of Cobbett, the Chartists, and Morris.[6] So, when T.C. Smout, the chief representative of the tradition of English imperialist historiography in Scotland, published his book, *A History of the Scottish People, 1560-1830*, in 1968, I was not too upset by his reconstruction of Cobbett's denunciatory comments on "Scotch feelosophers".[7]

By then, I was teaching in a Scottish university and, being cursed with an active and enquiring mind, I began to read the original sources of English radicalism. As a Scot—or as an internationalist who spoke in a Scottish idiom, a cultural but not a political nationalist, for I was not really a Scottish nationalist—I found some of the comments in the *Black Book or Corruption Unmasked* rather surprising. Cobbett's attack on the dying Scottish Enlightenment was inspired by an obvious English chauvinism; and the English radicals' attack on the Celtic fringe, though short, nasty and brutish, put them in my black book. As John Wade asserted in the *Black Book*, the Scots and the Irish were parasites on the glorious British Empire:

> Scotland has benefited by the Union: her soil has been fertilised by our capital, and her greedy sons have enriched themselves by sinecures and pensions, the produce of English taxes; but what has England gained from the connexion? The generous and intellectual character of the Saxon race has not been improved by amalgamation with Scotch metaphysics, thrift, and servility. Again, what benefits have we derived from the conquest of Ireland? Her uncultivated wastes, too, will be made fruitful by English money, unless the connexion be prematurely severed: but what boon in return can she confer on England? Her miserable children have poured out their blood in our wars of despotism; our rich Aristocracy have been made richer by the rental of her soil; and the aggregate power of the Empire has been augmented: but we seek in vain for the benefits communicated to the mass of the English population.[8]

Those blistering comments on the Scots, the Irish and "Scotch metaphysics", appeared in the later edition of the *Black Book or Corruption Unmasked* in 1835, not the first edition of 1820. The implications of the English radicals' attacks on the Scots were particularly revealing. In the great libertarian book, *The Making of the English Working Class*, where Edward Thompson's admirable sensitivity towards the Scottish national question was crystal clear, there occurred a well-known passage:

> We had no peasantry in England comparable to the Highland migrants. And the popular culture was very different. It is possible, at least until the 1820s, to regard the English and Scottish experiences as distinct, since trade union and political links were impermanent and immature.[9]

By the 1830s, however, the world of William Cobbett, Richard Carlyle and John Wade was fraught with national tensions and antagonisms.[10]

By evading some of the critical questions about the relationships between English, Scottish and Irish democratic class-struggle movements in the 17th, late 18th and early 19th century, T.A Jackson could insist that:

> The true patriotic and nationalist tradition in England, Scotland, and Wales, is identical with the democratic tradition—the tradition of militant, self-reliant, resistance to oppression and unremitting endeavour towards liberation which is the historical heritage of the proletariat in Britain.[11]

In the early 70s, John Hewitt grappled with the question of how the Ulster identity fitted in with the "romantic nationalism" of James Connolly and international socialism. In offering an honest account of how his generation of Ulster socialists responded to the world of the 20s and 30s, he said: "Yet our politics looked beyond to the world. Sacco and Vanzetti were, for us, far more significant than any of the celebrated 'felons of our land'."[12] This was a more realistic, internationalist and almost imaginatively prosaic comment than what the Welsh historian, Gwyn Williams, said when he joined the British Communist Party in, I think, the late 70s: "I am a communist first and a Welshman second." If there had been a continuity of unproblematic British radicalism and socialism, it would have been relatively easy to be a communist first, last and always.

The English domination of radical and labour movements in Britain, and the presence of English cultural imperialism within those movements, was not at all accidental. It was no accident that the continuity of an abundance of English socialist literature on the Levellers and the Diggers existed at the expense of research on the Covenanters. Towards the end of his long and fruitful life, the great Fenner Brockway published a study of "the Levellers, Agitators and Diggers of the English revolution" in 1980 titled *Britain's First Socialists*.[13] But some of the left-wing Protestant sects in Scotland had a better claim to the title of 'Britain's first socialists'.[14] To raise such a question in a nominally Scottish university was sufficient to invite the appellation 'trouble-maker'.

In case I should be suspected of reading the British radical past through the lens of the present, I ought to come clean. As E.H. Carr argued in his book, *What is History?*, an audience should always ask a historian about his own history. Within my own immediate family background in the 30s, the names and deeds of John Maclean and James Connolly were the common currency of intimacy and warm approval. So, when I had to listen to the lectures of Billy Hughes, the Principal of Ruskin College, Oxford, between 1953 and 1955, I could not really enthuse about Bagehot's English Constitution or the (English) Constitutional law of Jennings.

But, although I would never have talked during a lecture, shuffled papers, or expressed any sort of disapproval of what was being said, I was full of a peculiarly Scottish resentment. Ruskin College—the so-called workers' Ruskin—did not have much to say about my concerns as a socialist internationalist of Scottish orientation. Even the great G.D.H. Cole, whose study group for socialist undergraduates I belonged to with Raphael Samuel, turned out to be a great disappointment. And this led me to write a well-known letter to the Scottish socialist newspaper, *Forward*, in 1954, in which I criticised Cole for his utter failure to mention "the great John Mclean" in his extensive chronicle, *A Short History of the British Working-Class Movement, 1789-1947*.[15]

Although I was not aware of it until the late 1960s, some of the leaders of the First International had been hostile to Marx's agitation for Irish independence. As Julius Braunthal put it:

> Thomas Mottershead spoke strongly against Irish independence. An independent Ireland, he argued, owing to its geographical position between England and France, would threaten the security of England. An English withdrawal from Ireland would be followed by a French occupation. At a subsequent meeting, a letter from the Chartist veteran, George Julian Harney, who had emigrated to Boston, was read out, in which he protested against the attitude of the International to the Irish Question: 'Ireland', he wrote, 'is an integral part of the British Empire.'[16]

In a very different way, the Scottish dimension of 'British' radical-democratic struggle did not gain much recognition from the dominant tradition of labourist historiography.[17]

Why, then, were the national dimensions of Scottish and Irish workers' history ignored by British radical and socialist historians? Without addressing this question at all, Raphael Samuel touched on the critical aspect of the neglect of Scottish and Irish labour history before 1980, when he argued that:

> In Britain, Marxist historiography was chronologically preceded by, and has always had to co-exist with a more broadly based, if theoretically less demanding 'people's history', radical and democratic rather than socialist in its leading concepts, yet providing very often the groundwork on which Marxist historians have built. Thus Marxist work on the 17th century is heavily indebted to a long line of English and American liberal-radical scholars, while the recovery of Winstanley's communism, so far as the labour movement was concerned, was the work of the old Radical journalist, Morrison Davidson.[18]

For the moment, I will pass over the fact that Davidson was also a Scottish nationalist and author of *Scotland for the Scots*.[19]

But inside the world of British socialist historiography, the word 'British' simply meant English. In moving from his vivid description of Marxist historiography to a general discussion of the 'people's history' of England without an easy transition or acknowledgement of the four nations within Britain, Raphael Samuel could offer a really lyrical analysis without any apparent awareness of the dimension of British/ English imperialism. In a most remarkable paragraph of his path-breaking essay titled 'British Marxist Historians, 1880-1980', he observed that:

> One of the more ambiguous legacies of radical-democratic history is that of English nationalism—the notion that the English people have been somehow singled out for a special place in history, that the English language is superior to others, and that the liberty of the individual is more secure in England than it is abroad. It forms the very ground work of J.R. Green's *Short History of the English People*, with its brilliantly chosen but utterly arbitrary starting point of the 'free' Anglo-Saxons. It is tentatively present in the historical work of H.M. Hyndman; it finds fugitive echoes in the work of the early communist writers, notably T.A. Jackson.[20]

When I took the 120th anniversary issue of the *New Left Review*, in which Raphael Samuel's essay figured very prominently, to Terre Haute, Indiana, in the summer of 1980, I told every historian I encountered about the astonishing perceptions developed by the founder of History Workshop. Being rather less critical of Samuel's essay than I am now, I had to confront American scholars who were not impressed at all. Gail Malmgreen, who was working on the project to collect everything written by Eugene Victor Debs, the legendary American socialist-humanist, brought me down to earth by insisting that: "He is like me a Jew, an outsider. It is relatively easy for those who are culturally alienated to develop such perceptions." Far from being alienated from the dominant culture of the British/English Left, Samuel's perceptions had been developed within the British Communist Party's Historians' Group.

It was significant that Raphael Samuel did not acknowledge the national question in Scotland, Ireland or Wales. In his ultra-long, brilliant, wide-ranging and important essay, there was a strange—a peculiarly English—insensitivity towards the distinctiveness of the national history of the Scottish, Irish and Welsh workers' movements. It took a rooted Ulsterman, John Hewitt, to acknowledge the internationalists' contribution to British socialism. As he put it:

> It was a dead German Jew who gave me my guidelines. It was an English poet who, for me, most movingly evoked the quality of the Good Society in his *News from Nowhere*.[21]

By contrast, Samuel characterised British Marxian socialism as being legitimately English and very Protestant, when he said:

> The radical-democratic strain in English Marxism was powerfully, and to some extent deliberately renewed in the 1930s with the Popular Front turn in communist politics, and it is indicative that A.L. Morton's *People's History of England* (1938), the first systematic attempt to offer an overall reading of national history, not only took its title from J.R. Green's *Short History*, but also—on Morton's own testimony—was in some sort modelled on it. Communists, in this period, set about deliberately fostering a sense of democratic heritage, and in those 'March of History' pageants which the Party organised in 1936, Cromwell's portrait was borne proudly aloft along with those of John Ball and Wat Tyler.[22]

Throughout the years between 1880 and 1980, the cultural traditions of the Left in Britain developed within the framework of English imperialism. This century-old tradition of British socialism depicted by Raphael Samuel had crystallised within a world circumscribed by the British empire. From the very beginning, therefore, British socialism was a peculiarly English socialism. From H.M. Hyndman, Ernest Belford Bax, Tom Mann, William Morris, Sidney and Beatrice Webb and Robert Blatchford to Raphael Samuel and Eric J. Hobsbawm, British socialists and labour historians had always been preoccupied with the Englishness of the historical origins and growth of socialism in Britain. In articulating the inherited culture of Hyndman, Bax, Mann, Morris, Blatchford and the Webbs, the Communist Party Historians' Group began in 1946 to develop "a profound sense of Englishness" and "called for a major reassessment of English culture and political history from the 17th century onwards".[23]

It took almost a decade after the publication of Raphael Samuel's seminal essay, within a new context of a revived Thatcherite British imperialism, before some English socialist historians would analyse their own history and attitudes more critically than ever before. Thus in the 65th Conway Memorial lecture, delivered in London in April 1989, Christopher Hill transcended his own history as an English leftist historian when he confessed to a need for a new assessment of England's imperialist role in British history. As he put it:

> Even more obvious is England's historic responsibility for the present situation in Northern Ireland. Whether we blame the potato famine, or William III, or Oliver Cromwell—or go further back—the current war in Northern Ireland is England's historic responsibility. Oliver Cromwell proceeded in suppressing Ireland on the basis of cost-effectiveness. 'If we should proceed by the rules of other states,' he told his government by way of explaining his massacres of civilian populations, getting towns to surrender would cost more. He hoped 'through the blessing of God, they will come cheaper to you'. Other chickens are coming home to roost more slowly. Scotland was bribed and swindled into union with England in 1707, and for two centuries, on balance, she did well out of it. But now? Scotland shares the depressed state of the North of England. We should clarify historically our view of and attitudes towards Scottish nationalism.[24]

During my 18 months' membership of the Oxford University branch of the British Communist Party in the 50s, Hill and Samuel were very hostile to the Scots aspirations for self-government.

The continuity of English imperialist historiography in the Scottish universities from the 18th-century enlightenment onwards was at least partly responsible for Christopher Hill's antipathy towards the Scottish national question before 1989.[25] But, although some of the evidence of the nationalism of the Scottish radicals existed in the archives, it was not available to Hill or most other people.

Indeed, in a powerful booklet, *The Political Progress of Britain*, James Thomson Callender offered the only sustained Scottish interpretation of British history from 1688 to 1792. A Jacobin, a Scottish nationalist and a fine writer, he had to escape to America after the authorities issued a warrant for his arrest. And no wonder they were upset. In addition to Thomson Callender's highly-developed Scottish nationalist denunciation of William III, the *Political Progress of Britain* contained two remarkable statements: a savage indictment of the role of English imperialism in Africa and Asia and a nationalist interpretation of Scottish history.[26]

The belated, though very welcome, acknowledgement of the role of Cromwell in Ireland and the Union of Parliaments of 1707 within "the British radical-democratic tradition" was the cumulative outcome of the break-up of Britain. But just as the English radical opponents of 'Old Corruption' denounced the Scots, the Irish and "Scotch metaphysics" in 1835, so the descendants of those radicals would later on offer the Scottish and the Irish left the consolation of playing a not insignificant role in the British radical and socialist movements. From Roy Pascel in the 30s through to Ron Meek in the 50s and Royden Harrison in the 60s, the so-called unique distinctiveness of the Scottish enlightenment was employed as a compensatory consolation for general social and economic "backwardness".[27]

British socialism was always a very English—or a peculiarly English—movement of men and ideas; and at the heart of British thought and behaviour was the tacit assumption of English socialists' hegemony over the British radical and socialist movements. This thought-world—the world of inherited English cultural superiority—began with a celebration of 'the free-born Englishman', came near to perfection in the commemoration of Britain's first socialists, and culminated, I suppose, in the British Labour Party's English rose. But the cultural tradition of British radical-democratic thought had always articulated a peculiarly English generosity towards the subordinate Celts, and especially the Scots and the Irish. There were compensations for being a subordinate part of the British labour movement provided the dominant hegemony was not challenged. Even movements representing the exploited and the oppressed often develop their own informal, unofficial and tacit rules about unquestioning obedience.

The inordinate English—or English-inspired—focus on the Scottish enlightenment was seen in the famous dispute between E.P. Thompson and Perry Anderson over "the peculiarities of the English". Unlike Thompson's attempt to glance at least at the role of the Scots within the context of the historical origins of the making of the English working class, Anderson simply ignored the Scots and the Irish altogether in *Arguments within English Marxism* and in *Considerations on Western Marxism*. He did not rate John Maclean as an important

Marxist, and James Connolly's contribution to Irish socialist historiography was unworthy of recognition.[28] But the subordination of the Scots and the Irish to English hegemony inside the British workers' movement was discussed by H.M. Hyndman when he wrote about Scotland—"by far the best educated portion of the United Kingdom"—as "the country in which the independent Labour movement began". But, although it had soon "fallen back into the old muddy ways of capitalist Liberalism", Scotland had completely dominated the British labour movement up to the First World War.[29] And as early as 1896, he had denounced the "ultra-revolutionary Irish press", its hostility to the British government, and its reactionary nationalism. Besides, there were "none so brutal in their denunciation" of the Paris Commune and the Chicago martyrs as "the Irish Romanists".[30]

The English socialists' texts have always been motivated within a hidden context: a context in which the quintessential Englishness of the British workers' movement was always assumed without any sustained challenge or debate. Eric Hobsbawm reflected this inherited cultural tradition less uncritically than Edward Thompson. In the book, *Industry and Empire*, which was published in 1968, Hobsbawm devoted a small chapter to what he called 'The Other Britain'. When he discussed the history of Scotland, Wales, and Ireland in a few pages of quite a large book, he gave very vivid illustrations of the very Englishness of the British labour movement.

Though there was no evidence that he had borrowed any ideas from Hyndman, Hobsbawm insisted that, by 1900, the Scots were chalking up considerable achievements by turning the world of British Labour upside down. As he put it:

> For the first time the Scots labour movement not only took a serious hold on its working class, but established a sort of (political) hegemony over the English. Keir Hardie became the leader of British socialism (and his Independent Labour Party had its firmest base on the Clyde), James Ramsay MacDonald became the first Labour Prime Minister of this country, and Clydeside became, during the First World War, the synonym for revolutionary agitation, and helped to give the post-1918 Labour Party a slant to the left and the Communist Party a core of leaders.[31]

Furthermore, the Irish seem to have exercised a sort of ideological hegemony over Labour in Britain, at least according to Hobsbawm's analysis. As he argued:

They provided the British working class with a cutting edge of radicals and revolutionaries, with a body of men and women uncommitted by either tradition or economic success to society as it existed around them. It is no accident that an Irishman, Fergus O'Connor, was the nearest thing to a national leader of Chartism, and another, Bronterre O'Brien, its chief ideologist, that an Irishman wrote 'The Red Flag', the anthem of the British labour movement and the best British working-class novel, *The Ragged Trousered Philanthropists.*

It is equally not an accident that he did not mention the distinctive Celtic socialism of John Maclean, James Connolly and Jim Larkin and their suppressed anti-British critique of the Englishness of British labour.[32]

On the rare occasion when the militants' Celtic socialism was acknowledged, it was dealt with in a very dismissive way. There was a certain irony that the Englishness of British socialism was defended, in 1975, by the Welsh establishment historian, Kenneth O. Morgan, in a celebratory biography of *Keir Hardie: Radical and Socialist.* As he put it:

> In any case the Clydesiders had (during the First World War) become identified with a distinctively Scottish position: Hardie had since 1892 been linked with British socialism, not with the Glasgow parochialism of the Clyde or the Celtic communism of John Maclean.[33]

As an important voice of British labourism and its historiography, it was not an accident that Morgan was quick to sense the Celtic fringe's innate threat to the 'integrity' of Britain.

Yet in labourist, as well as in socialist historiography, there was seldom any recognition of the existence of Scottish home rule or pre-1916 Irish socialist republicanism before 1980. In *Fifty Years' March: The Rise of the Labour Party,* Francis Williams did not acknowledge the disaffection of at least some Scots and Irish socialists in the late 19th and early 20th century. In *Scotland for the Scots* published in 1902, Morrison Davidson criticised "the vile herd of Anglicising traitors" in Scotland. Unlike Francis Williams, however, such an outsider as the Australian, A.M. McBriar, had the perspicacity to give his brilliant study of Fabian politics the apposite title *Fabian Socialism and English Politics, 1884-1918.*[34]

With great brotherly love, Morrison Davidson claimed that his brother Thomas had been the founder of the London-based Fabian Society. As he asserted in his book, *The Annals of Toil*: "The Fabian Society was founded in London in 1883. Its virtual founder was my brother Dr. Thomas Davidson of New York." It would not have been an irony of history if a Scot had been responsible for the foundation of the Englishness of the Fabian Society. Fortunately or unfortunately, Dr. Thomas Davidson "did not'', according to McBriar, "even virtually, found the Fabian Society".[35]

In any case, I agree with Christopher Hill rather than Royden Harrison that, though it is permissible for historians to ask new questions of the past out of the experiences of the present, socialists should not offer the answers of the present to questions about the past. In turning the world of British Labour historiography upside down (at least if we ignore the unique title of McBriar's book on the Fabians), Harrison was obviously motivated by the collapse of state socialism in eastern Europe when he attempted to provide a fragmented European left with the model of 'A very English Socialism: the Fabians, 1880-1914'.[36] Perhaps it was just as well that Thomas Davidson was not a founder of the Fabian Society. If the new emphasis on the Englishness, rather than the Britishness, of the Fabian Society was born in a context of the break-up of east European communism, the innate constitutionalism of English Fabianism will have less appeal to the Celtic fringe.

To avoid acknowledging the *disruptiveness* of the socialists of the Celtic fringe towards English constitutional socialism (or the fact the Scots and the Irish were sometimes to the left of their English counterparts), Patrick Renshaw, the English historian would, in 1967, argue that:

> The Industrial Workers of Great Britain was not strong in England as such. Its advocates were either Scottish, Irish, or Welsh, the 'immigrant' workers from the Celtic fringe ... The English cities, like Liverpool and Birmingham, where the IWW was active, had large Irish minorities. Liverpool was known as 'the capital of Ireland' and Jim Larkin had been born there.

Rather than discuss the possibility that the English workers were less receptive to radical ideas, he escaped behind the formula that "the most significant feature of Wobbly activity in Britain was that it took place in the same culturally alienated groups who found direct action most attractive on the other side of the Atlantic".[37] They were not, of course, alienated from their own (as distinct from English) culture.

From the heights of their Olympian objectivity inside the Fabians' HQ of the British labour movement, Sidney and Beatrice Webb, I'd like to suggest, were both anti–Scottish and anti-Irish.[38] In their shared condescension towards the socialists of the Celtic fringe, including the Welsh, they did indeed articulate the traditions and culture of a very English socialism. Although they could not be expected to empathise with John Maclean or James Connolly, perhaps more sympathetic sensitivity might have been expected from William Morris and H.M. Hyndman. But both the Social Democratic Federation (SDF) and the breakaway Socialist League founded by William Morris in 1884, belonged to the socialism of John Bull. Scottish socialists were attracted to Morris because of his warmth, literary and artistic interests and militant internationalism. At the very beginning of the foundation of the Socialist League, the Scots were nevertheless upset by the League's refusal to recognise the distinctiveness of socialism in Scotland. In a letter that James Mavor sent to London on behalf of the Scots, he argued that:

> We formed ourselves into a branch of the Scottish Land and Labour League (the Scottish section of the Socialist League). In these circumstances our executive did not see any necessity for seeking authorisation from your executive.[39]

Moreover, in a letter that A.K. Donald, the secretary of the Edinburgh branch of the Scottish Land and Labour League, sent to the secretary of the League in London, he objected to the manifesto drawn up without any consultation with the Scots. As Donald argued:

> In religious Scotland you may rest assured that the first point I have referred to will create unnecessary bitterness against us; it appears to several members of the League possible to be a socialist without being a materialist or an atheist.[40]

Before the disruptive Scottish Marxists in the SDF broke away to form the De Leonist Socialist Labour Party (SLP) in 1903, the Scots' uncompromising commitment to class-struggle socialism and rejection of the Parliamentary socialism of Hyndman and Bax did not fit in with the peculiarly English historiography of the British. At the annual conference of the SDF in 1901, William Gee, the anti-Hyndmanite Scottish organiser, told the delegates that "in spite of the canting, hypocritical gang of Presbyterians in the Land of Cakes, yet in the near future Scotland is destined to take a more prominent place under the Red Flag than England has".[41]

During the hundred years since the foundation of the Democratic

Federation the precursor of the SDF, in 1881, there have been many breaks in the continuity of socialists' consciousness of the history of their own movement. Thus, although John Maclean did not become a Scottish Republican until after the critical years of 1916-1917, he joined the SDF in 1901 before the 'impossibilists' broke away to form the De Leonist SLP. Unaware of the discussion of the peculiarities of Scots socialists in the British workers' movement, he had to grope his way around the question of the Scottish national identity. In 1912, he articulated his peculiarly Scottish discontent with Hyndman's new creation—the British Socialist Party—in sharp words:

> It is bad enough for Parliament to allot only a day and a half to Scotland; it is worse still to have a British Socialist Executive without a representative from Scotland.[42]

One of the hidden and critical aspects of the relationship between English Marxism and the Marxism of the Celtic fringe was the American De Leonists' sympathetic understanding of the distinctiveness of Scottish and Irish socialism. What is, however, absent from the dominant British historiography was the dispute about the militant socialism of the Scots and the nationalism of the Irish in the 1890s and early 1900s. A constant theme of Daniel De Leon's writings was the peculiarly English imperialist mentality of men like H.M. Hyndman.[43]

De Leon and the American SLP were very sympathetic towards the Irish Socialist Republican Party. In a letter to Henry Kuhn, the national secretary of the American De Leonists, James Connolly insisted on the importance of Irish sentiment in the struggle for international socialism as early as 1896. As he put it:

> We recognise the enormous importance of being duly represented among our countrymen in America, and we also hope you will perceive how much it would help you, to assist the socialist movement in Ireland. Irishmen are largely influenced by sentiment and tradition, and therefore a word from what they affectionately call 'the auld sod' will far outweigh any amount of reasoning applied to the discussion of American issues only. Show them that socialism has a definite message from Ireland and you awaken their sympathy immediately.[44]

Henry Kuhn, De Leon and the Americans were sympathetic to what Connolly was suggesting, and they readily agreed to sell *Erin's Hope* by Connolly within America.[44] Furthermore, in the fullness of time, De Leon would publish an article, titled 'The American Flag', in which he spoke about the Union Jack with "its Three Crosses quartered" and "symbolising the practically forceful annexation of Scotland and Ireland to England".[45] When the Irish Socialist Republican Party was founded in Dublin in 1896, H.M. Hyndman was less than enthusiastic. In a long account of his attitudes towards Connolly's nationalism, he reported that:

> Some of our friends in Ireland, fearing that national prejudice would be too strong for them, if they attempted to form a branch of the SDF there, have started a national socialist movement, which they call the Irish Socialist Republican Party.

He then went on to say that:

> National differences are always to be deplored, and one cannot but regret that our comrades should not have been able to establish in the Emerald Isle an outpost of the organisation whose flag has for so many years braved the battle and the breeze directed against it from all quarters. But it is curious that the patriotic sentiment is always strongest in a subject nation, and I am quite convinced that under all the circumstances our friends are adopting the wisest course in avoiding a conflict with that nationalism which, however strong it may appear to us, creates a prejudice in the mind of every Irishman against anything English, and which will never disappear till the English domination of Ireland is destroyed.

The critical thing was that English oppression in Ireland would require to be destroyed by *British* labour. Hyndman therefore concluded his critique of the manifesto of the Irish Socialist Republican Party by saying:

> Socialism teaches the interdependence of nations as well as of individuals, and therefore to talk of winning complete separation from all connection with the British Empire seems a bit out of place in a socialist manifesto.[46]

James Connolly's strategy for disrupting the British empire was much more acceptable to Daniel De Leon than Hyndman; and, when the Irish Socialist Republican Party tried to affiliate to the Second International in 1896, he persuaded the International Bureau to reject the application.[47] At the beginning of November 1897, D. O'Brien, the secretary of the Irish Socialist Republican Party, wrote to Henry Kuhn in New York:

I have been requested by the Party to write re a certain remark in your address to the Irish working class in the States, printed in *The People*. It is where you refer to the capitalist Home Ruler collecting money from the Irish servant girls in the States. Now this is a phrase coined by our bitterest enemies—the jingo London press, and such being the case, it stinks in the nostrils of all Irishmen. We are of the opinion it would do more harm than good, and think it would be well if you altered it.[48]

And they did. But, although the American De Leonists and the Irish Socialist Republican Party grew closer as the SDF's imperialist attitudes and support for 'revisionism' in the International became more and more obvious, there were internal conflicts in the Irish Socialist Republican Party, too. In September 1902, O'Brien informed the Americans of their disputes with Connolly. Before he went to America in 1903, Connolly had been expelled and reinstated as the editor of the Irish Socialist Republican Party's newspaper.[49]

Before the break-up of the Irish Socialist Republican Party in 1903, James Connolly won a major battle against Hyndman's attempt to deny Ireland's existence as a separate nation. In recounting a conversation with Connolly, T.A. Jackson said:

In 1900 owing to a split in the French party each 'nation' was given two votes. Connolly representing the Irish Socialist Republican Party refused to be included in the 'English' delegation where, as it chanced, a majority were either sympathetic to Ireland's claim, or (what came to the same thing on a decision) hostile to Hyndman as chairman who opposed the claim on legalistic grounds. Anyway on a vote Hyndman was over-ruled and the British delegation endorsed Connolly's claim, which was accordingly conceded.[50]

The break-up of the Irish Socialist Republican Party ensured that the Irish question was kept off the agenda of the British workers' movement until the Easter Rising in 1916.

The great and unending British crack-up began in 1916 and John Maclean and Jim Larkin were soon at the heart of it. The periodic crises in British workers' history have always been reflected by Fabian/ labourist historians. When W.P. Ryan's book, *The Irish Labour Movement*, was published in 1919, an anonymous reviewer in the *New Statesman* said:

Those agitators of the 20th century, Connolly and Larkin, could claim as their compatriot William Thompson—landlord, by the way, the 'most eminent founder of scientific socialism'... We find, on the other hand, that so genuine an Irishman of race as O'Connell vehemently took the part of the masters in the industrial disputes of his day. History repeated itself during the Larkinite strike of 1913-14; for the leaders of Dublin trade unionism in O'Connell's period have been condemned even by English socialist historians as 'impossibilists'. As in 1913-14, and in the thirties of the last century, the Irish workers displayed a revolutionary tendency and an indisposition to concentrate, like their English comrades, upon the more definite grievances of their class.[51]

And 66 years later, Kenneth O. Morgan would laud Keir Hardie's contribution to British socialism at the expense of John Maclean. As he put it:

But it was clear that his (Hardie's) horizon was extending far beyond his native Scotland; his instincts were naturally outward-looking, in contrast to John Maclean and the later generation of Glasgow socialism after 1917.[52]

I began by speaking about the dialectic of change and penultimate chapters. Spiritually speaking, there were not—and are not—absolutes or ultimate chapters. As we confront and struggle to transcend the ultra-serious crisis of contemporary socialism, it is useful to recall what E.H. Carr said:

Pregnant failures are not unknown in history. History recognises what I may call 'delayed achievement'; the apparent failures of today may turn out to have made a vital contribution to the achievements of tomorrow, prophets born before their time.[53]

Notes

[1] John Hewitt, Tom Clyde (ed.), *Ancestral Voices: the Selected Prose of John Hewitt* (Blackstaff Press, 1987). I wish to thank my friend Bob Purdie for introducing me to the writings of John Hewitt.
[2] Hewitt, *Ancestral Voices*, p. 148.
[3] My youngest brother, George, stimulated me to probe more deeply into the history of the Covenanters. For evidence of their communism, see James D. Young, *Women and Popular Struggles* (Edinburgh, 1985), pp. 11-36.
[4] See James D. Young, 'The Rise of Scottish Socialism', in Gordon Brown (ed.), *The Red Book on Scotland* (Edinburgh, 1977), pp. 282-88.
[5] See James D. Young, *Making Trouble: Autobiographical Experiments and Socialism* (Glasgow, 1987), chapter 1.

[6]Max Morris (ed.), *From Cobbett to the Chartists, 1815-1848* (London, 1948); Eric J. Hobsbawm (ed.), *Labour's Turning Point, 1880-1900* (London, 1948)
[7]T.C. Smout, *A History of the Scottish People, 1560-1830* (Glasgow, 1969), p. 506.
[8]Anon., *The Black Book or Corruption Unmasked* (London, 1835), p. 380.
[9]E.P. Thompson, *The Making of the English Working Class* (London, 1963), p. 13.
[10]James D. Young, 'Scottish Radicalism Revisited, 1778-1820: Confessions of a Revisionist Historian', at Conference of Scottish Labour History Society, and report by Ian S. Wood, *Journal of the Scottish Labour History Society* 22, 1987.
[11]T.A. Jackson, *Trails of Freedom*, quoted Raphael Samuel, 'Sources of Marxist History', *New Left Review* 120, 1980, p. 42.
[12]John Hewitt, *Ancestral Voices*, p. 150.
[13]Fenner Brockway, *England's First Socialists* (London, 1980).
[14]For evidence on the Lollards and their Covenanting descendants, see Patrick Tyler, *History of Scotland* (Edinburgh, 1841), Vol. 14, pp. 32-38; James Anderson, *The Ladies of the Covenant* (Edinburgh, 1850), Vol. 1, pp. 512-516; and James K. Hewson, *The Covenanters* (Glasgow, 1913), Vol. 1, pp. 6-9.
[15]Quoted in Nan Milton, *John Maclean* (London, 1973), p. 12.
[16]Julius Braunthal, *History of the International, 1864-1914* (London, 1966), p. 167.
[17]See my article, 'Cultural Imperialism and Labour History', forthcoming in *Journal of Historical Sociology*.
[18]Samuel, 'Sources of Marxist History', *NLR* 120, 1980, p. 37.
[19]John Morrison Davidson, *Scotland for the Scots* (London, 1902).
[20]Samuel, 'Sources of Marxist History', *NLR* 120, 1980, p. 41.
[21]John Hewitt, *Ancestral Voices*, p. 152.
[20]Samuel, 'Sources of Marxist History', *NLR* 120, 1980, p. 41.
[23]Bill Schwarz, '"The People" in History: the Communist Party Historians' Group', in Richard Johnson and others (eds.), *Making Histories* (London, 1982), p. 52. (Emphasis in original.)
[24]Chistopher Hill, *History and the Present* (London, 1989), p. 26.
25James D. Young, 'Marxism and the Scottish National Question', *Journal of Contemporary History* 18: 1, 1983; and 'National, "Marxism" and Scottish History', *Journal of Contemporary History* 20:2, 1985.
[26]James Thomson Callender, *The Political Progress of Britain* (Edinburgh, 1792). It was confiscated by the authorities even before Callender escaped to America, where he worked with Thomas Jefferson. My efforts to persuade publishers to publish Callender's booklet have been successful.
[27]See my article, 'The Scottish Enlightenment, the Highlands and Plebeian Radicals', in Dan Gillis (ed.), *The Year of the Sheep* (Philadelphia, forthcoming).
[28]Perry Anderson, *Considerations of Western Marxism* (London, 1976), pp 1-125.
[29]H.M. Hyndman, *Further Reminiscences* (London, 1912), pp. 242-43.
[30]*Justice*, 12th July, 1896.
[31]Eric J. Hobsbawm, *Industry and Empire* (London, 1968), p. 265.
[32]*Industry and Empire*, p. 267.

[33] Kenneth O. Morgan, *Keir Hardie: Radical and Socialist* (London, 1975), p. 45.
[34] A.M. McBriar's book almost certainly inspired the title of the fine essay by Royden Harrison, 'A Very English Socialism: the Fabians, 1880-1914', *Socialismo Storia*, 3 (Milan, 1991).
[35] A.M. McBriar, *Fabian Socialism and English Politics, 1884-1918*, pp. 1-2.
[36] Harrison, 'A Very English Socialism' (see n. 34). Unlike some other English labour historians, Harrison remains in the camp of militant democratic socialist internationalism.
[37] Patrick Renshaw, *The Wobblies* (London, 1967), p. 279.
[38] For their disapproval of the nationalism of the Irish labour movement, see Sidney and Beatrice Webb, *History of Trade Unionism, 1666-1920* (London, 1920), p. 473.
[39] Socialist League Archives, K. 2219/3, International Institute of Social History, Amsterdam.
[40] Socialist League Archives, K. 1219/1.
[41] *Justice*, 10th August, 1901.
[42] Gael [John Maclean], 'Scottish Notes', *Justice*, 25th June, 1914.
[43] A detailed discussion of Daniel De Leon's criticisms of the English imperialism of H.M. Hyndman, Belfort Bax and John E. Ellam can be found in my 'Cultural Imperialism and Labour History', forthcoming in *Journal of Historical Sociology*.
[44] Socialist Labour Party Archives, Box 14, folder 4, State Historical Society, Madison, Wisconsin, USA.
[45] Daniel De Leon, 'The American Flag', *Weekly People*, 4th July, 1914.
[46] Tattler [H.M. Hyndman], *Justice*, 30th June, 1896.
[47] T.A. Jackson, *Solo Trumpet* (London, 1953), p. 80.
[48] William O'Brien to Henry Kuhn, 7th November 1897, Socialist Labour Party Archives as above.
[49] On 15th September, 1902, O'Brien wrote again to Henry Kuhn: Socialist Labour Party Archives as above.
[50] Jackson, *Solo Trumpet*, p. 80.
[51] *New Statesman*, 19th July, 1919.
[52] Morgan, *Keir Hardie*, p. 284.
[53] E.H. Carr, *What is History?* (London, 1972), p. 46.

Though they have produced less of a distinctively Welsh historiography than the Scots or Irish, the Welsh left was more assertive than the rest of the Celtic fringe before World War I. As one Welsh socialist pointed out: "The Fabian Society very wisely publishes Welsh tracts, and there is now a Welsh pamphlet explaining the aims and objects of the Independent Labour Party": E. Morgan Humphreys, 'Socialism and Welsh Nationality', *Socialist Review*, October 1909.

Internationalism & the Civil Rights Movement
An Epitaph[1]

Bob Purdie

The Northern Ireland civil rights movement was international in two senses. First, it was inspired by international developments, principally the black civil rights movement in the United States; secondly, it relied on an international network of supporters, whose involvement influenced the direction which it took.

Internationalism implies a politics of respect for the rights and welfare of all human beings, regardless of incidental differences between them. It also implies a common struggle of oppressed groups. But, in practice, the international links of the civil rights movement were mainly with the Irish diaspora which was not an oppressed, but often a highly-privileged, group. This obliged the movement to accommodate political preconceptions and priorities which weakened its internationalism. Moreover, its international support network, instead of aiding the movement, helped to catalyse and exacerbate its internal differences over strategy and political outlook.

When the issue of civil rights in Northern Ireland burst upon the world in October 1968, there was already a well-organised network of Irish nationalist groups scattered around the English-speaking world. There was also an entirely different international network of the new left. Both, for different reasons, were inspired by the upsurge in Northern Ireland, so that the civil rights movement's supporters consisted of two distinct groups—Irish nationalists and Marxist revolutionaries.

The new left was shaped by the revolutions in China, Algeria, Cuba and Vietnam, and by the disintegration of orthodox communism following the discrediting of Stalin. Many young people of Irish descent were involved, and they greeted with joy the proposition that

Ireland might be the focus for a revolutionary confrontation with the state. The new left had a politics of solidarity. It would bring the revolution back home through support for struggles against imperialism in the third world. These concepts, of solidarity and imperialism, were used to interpret the civil rights movement in Northern Ireland, which meant that the new left regarded what was happening as, at least potentially, a revolutionary class struggle. But, for immediate purposes, the new left took up the perception of the Irish question which was prevalent amongst the old left—which was that it was about partition, and that the solution was a united Ireland.

The politics of the Irish diaspora were more directly formed by anti-partitionism; by the doctrine that the artificial political division of Ireland had been imposed by Britain and that a withdrawal of British support for Ulster unionism would result in the collapse of the Northern Ireland state and the integration of its territory with the rest of Ireland. Although it perceived itself as traditional Irish nationalism, anti-partitionism was actually of relatively recent origin. It only became fully formulated in the late 40s as a reaction against the Ireland Act of 1949 which, for the first time, gave the Northern Ireland parliament a right to veto Irish unity. De Valera's world lecture tour of 1948, in which he "put an anti-partition girdle around the world", helped mobilise the Irish diaspora into the ranks of the anti-partition campaign.

Although it spanned a remarkably wide spectrum from the extreme left, in the shape of the Communist Party, to the extreme right in the shape of the Catholic corporatist *Ailtirí na hAiséirghe*, the anti-partition campaign failed to achieve any concrete results, apart from a substantial victory for the Unionist Party in the 1950 Northern Ireland general election. By the mid-60s, it did not provide anyone with a basis for practical politics, and it had ceased to be a coherent political force amongst nationalists in Ireland. New forces within Irish nationalism, such as the National Democratic Party and the New Ireland Society of Queen's University, Belfast, and the republicans of the Wolfe Tone Society in Dublin, were looking for alternative strategies. The civil rights movement had its origins in these new forces, which were explicitly, or implicitly, critical of anti-partitionism.[2]

The anti-partition movement had agitated about discrimination in Northern Ireland. At one level, this was tactical: it hoped that the agitation against discrimination would influence liberal public opinion in Britain and wrong-foot unionism. It was also strategic: by mobilising external pressure to reform Northern Ireland, they could undermine unionist domination. Irish unity might then arise as a logical corollary of the collapse of unionism. Alternatively, the two parts of Ireland might come together through reforms which would erode the differences between them. The civil rights movement drew on the older propaganda material about discrimination, but it did not associate the issue with partition. This was a tactical route around the difficulties of anti-partitionism rather than an open breach with it, but it meant that allies elsewhere could see the civil rights movement as simply a new way of challenging partition.

In Britain in the early 60s, anti-partitionist groups like the United Ireland Association, the republican front group *Clann na hEireann*, and the Connolly Association, together with the Campaign for Democracy in Ulster, which was neutral on partition, formed the basis for a solidarity movement which also had the support of older movements like the Hibernians and the county associations. They supported organisations set up in solidarity with the civil rights movement, like the Northern Ireland Civil Rights Association and the Birmingham-based Campaign for Social Justice in Northern Ireland. In the United States, there was the Ancient Order of Hibernians, the venerable *Clan-na-Gael* and the American Congress for Irish Freedom (ACIF). This had been formed in 1966 to demand a British withdrawal from Northern Ireland and to organise a boycott of British goods.

In the USA of 1968, there was a new left, created in response to the Vietnam war, the upsurge of black militancy and the May-June events in Paris of that year. This new left gave its support to the National Association for Irish Justice (NAIJ), which had been initiated by supporters of the republican movement in the USA. In Britain, too, the anti-Vietnam war movement had given rise to a new left, and had also boosted the membership of established far-left organisations like the International Socialists and the International Marxist Group. They supported the Irish Civil Rights Solidarity Campaign (ICRSC).

Both generations of civil rights supporters saw events in Northern Ireland as part of the historic national struggle. The ACIF congratulated the civil rights movement on "a degree of solidarity and success not seen in Ireland since 1916-21".[3] Rick Hyland, a reporter on the left-wing magazine *Ramparts* hoisted a tricolour on the British consulate in San Francisco, which he proposed to send to NICRA for use on its next march. One of the earliest organisations set up in Britain to support the civil rights movement called itself 'The Irish Unity and Civil Rights Committee'; one of its aims was to get partition recognised as the root of the problem in Northern Ireland. In the left-wing newspaper *The Black Dwarf*, an English supporter, Dave Kendall, wrote that "The Irish working class must struggle for genuine independence, for the final expulsion of Britain from Ireland"; and called for "a people's struggle against imperialism".[4] In the same issue a report on the Irish Civil Rights Solidarity Campaign listed, as one of its demands: "The setting up of a constitutional conference between Westminster, Dublin and all tendencies within the civil rights movements, the trade unions and all Northern Ireland political parties; leading to self-determination for Ireland."

The civil rights movement's international supporters, therefore, had aspirations beyond and at odds with those of the movement. When one takes into account the sheer disparity in size and resources between the civil rights movement and its supporters in the Irish diaspora, it is easy to see how the movement could be effectively pressurised and channelled. There was also a significant disparity between the economic and political strength of the diaspora and the political and economic weakness of the Northern Ireland minority community.

A further complication was that the Marxists hoped, through solidarity activity, to exploit the resources of the Irish diaspora. Since most exiled Irish nationalists were fervently anti-communist and suspicious of left-wing infiltration and manipulation, this made strife amongst civil rights supporters inevitable. This became a serious problem for relations between the civil rights movement in Northern Ireland and Irish Americans.

In the USA, old anti-partitionists and young new leftists agreed on tactics like calling for a boycott of British goods. They also agreed on giving unconditional support to the civil rights movement; but they had profound differences about almost everything else. The ACIF picketed Harold Wilson in 1967, demanding that he get British troops out of Northern Ireland and British merchant ships out of Haiphong harbour. They claimed that Britain was supplying about 50 per cent of the armaments going into North Vietnam and tried to mobilise patriotic support for the US forces in Vietnam behind an anti-British movement. The other main group, the NAIJ, had its headquarters in the premises previously occupied by Eldridge Cleaver's Peace and Freedom Party, an offshoot of the Black Panthers. The avowed aim of the NAIJ's organiser, Brian Heron, was to move the Irish community in the USA over from the right to the left. On the two great issues then racking American society, the war in Vietnam and the upsurge of black militancy, the ACIF and the NAIJ took different sides.

The significance of the USA for the Northern Ireland civil rights movement can hardly be exaggerated. The very term 'civil rights' came from the black civil rights movement. As in America, in Northern Ireland the demand was that uniform standards of civil rights should prevail for all citizens. The strategy implied a willingness to put aside longer-term aspirations for a united Ireland in favour of unity around basic demands for equal treatment. Supporters in the United States, however, did not always grasp this subtlety.

A letter to the chairman of NICRA, Frank Gogarty, from a Belfast-born teacher living in New York, described the way in which the aims of the civil rights movement were being lost in the "eternal playing of the border record" by its American supporters. His wife and a nephew had gone on a vigil at the United Nations building in September 1969, but left after an hour because they felt like aliens. "The Falls, Belfast, Derry and the Bogside were not even mentioned. The cry was, 'Get the British troops out of Ireland'." He had been contacted about the formation of a local NAIJ group and had told them that he was only interested in civil rights and that if the border were made an issue he would "stampede the meeting in protest". He had not heard from them since.[5]

There were also problems with internal American issues, such as race. The civil rights movement in Northern Ireland saw itself as part of an international liberation movement which included black people in the USA and South Africa. This international perspective was one of the most significant shifts to have occurred within oppositional politics in Northern Ireland. But the race issue was a genuine moral dilemma for many Irish-American civil rights movement supporters. A Rhode Island activist noted the lack of response from local Irish-American politicians and attributed it in part to a "fear of criticism about not showing much concern for the American Negro, but now for the Northern Irelander". His local Committee for Justice in Northern Ireland had collected clothing for homeless black and white victims of a hurricane in the south and he hoped that, "we will build that bridge somehow! ... We have a rather deep guilt feeling about our indifference to the black man"[6].

Bernadette Devlin, during her tour of the USA in August and September 1969, made a point of linking the Northern Ireland struggle to the struggle of black people in the US. This did not go down too well with some of her listeners. One was reported as saying "everybody's got freedom in this country. You've got equal rights for anybody who wants to use their rights. A lot of 'em are too damned lazy to use them".[7] There were political and practical difficulties in making links with the black liberation movement. When Devlin visited a local black people's project in Los Angeles, she received a rather off-hand welcome. An education worker who was showing her round said, "No one was hippin' us that this chick was comin'". Devlin kept making comparisons with Northern Ireland, but her guide commented, "Her cause is probably cool, but we have other things to do".[8]

The attempt to link up with the black struggle never got beyond symbolic gestures, such as when Eamonn McCann, visiting the USA in 1970, presented to the Black Panthers a golden key to New York which Mayor Lindsay had given to Bernadette Devlin. He also attacked Senator Edward Kennedy for getting one hundred Congressmen to sign a petition in support of NICRA. He suggested that Kennedy should mind his own business and settle the Vietnam war. This provoked an exasperated protest to Frank Gogarty from a New York *Clan-na-Gael* leader. But it also discomfited some NAIJ activists, one of whom wrote to Kevin Boyle pointing out that the Black Panthers represented only a very small proportion of Black Americans, and that his action had taken no account of the much larger groups, such as the National Association for the Advancement of Coloured People, and Martin Luther King's Southern Christian Leadership Conference. He had also associated civil rights in Northern Ireland with the violent rhetoric of the Panthers.

Gogarty, for his part, regarded many Irish-American supporters of the civil rights movement as tainted by racism. Notes he seems to have made at the NAIJ conference in November 1969 referred to named individuals as, for example, a "Minute Man who supported KKK"; "campaigned for Governor Wallace" (the Southern racist presidential candidate); "member of the John Birch Society" (the far-right political organisation); and "known racist".

There was some evidence for this. One ACIF leader contrasted Harold Wilson's policy of "civil rights for Negroes in Rhodesia", with his denial of civil rights to "white men in Ulster". James C. Heany, the president of the ACIF, in a letter to the secretary of NICRA, said, "I might add that there is not a single Irish American group in the United States which has worked with the coloured civil rights movement, including Heron. So don't expect this of any of us".[9] Eugene J. Byrne of the New Jersey AOH, noted NAIJ activist Lennie Glaser's name and, to underline his Jewishness, respelled it, 'Glazer'. He also noted that another supporter, Jessica Mitford, had used the name 'Dora Treuhaft'. On the other hand, Heany called the B-Specials the "local Ku Klux Klan", and compared the situation in Northern Ireland with Nazi

Germany. Irish Americans like Heany, like most of his generation, were ambiguous on the race issue; they were small 'c' conservative northern Democrats, who had voted for JFK and went along with Lyndon Johnson's Great Society programme. They were insensitive on racial issues and regarded black militancy with horror, but few were out-and-out racists. The civil rights movement in Northern Ireland, however, demanded higher standards than that.

The ACIF was a serious embarrassment for other reasons. In July 1969, Paddy Devlin attacked it for a leaflet it had issued urging American businessmen not to invest in Northern Ireland. He accused it of being "parasitic" and "bigoted", and said that the civil rights movement had disassociated itself from the ACIF because of its failure to help American black people or to help end the Vietnam war.[10] The National Treasurer of the ACIF, Thomas A. Enwright, responded in hurt bewilderment to the condemnation by NICRA. He pointed out that, since 5th October, they had set up 20 chapters across the USA, sent out over 5,000 letters and 200 telegrams. They had also appeared on 8 hours of prime television and 50 hours of radio time. They had gone out in the rain, the snow and the heat collecting funds. He "humbly and respectfully asked" the NICRA Executive to reconsider.[11]

The Congress was a prime example of, to use Yeats' term, "ignorant goodwill". Its propaganda systematically exaggerated discrimination in Northern Ireland and transformed matters of degree into absolutes. For example:

> Public housing is closed to Irish Catholics and Irish Protestants who remain outside the Unionist Party, which is the political arm of the London government. The Unionist Party is unique in the United Kingdom in that it has its own private army, called the 'B-Specials' ... Government employment is closed to Irish Catholics and Irish Protestants opposing the British government, and employment in private industry is also closed to a large extent ... because of the British government's policy of discrimination ... An important phase of London's policy is the 'Special Powers Act'. This permits imprisonment without charge or trial, seizure of bank accounts ... and censorship of the press, radio and television ... British policy is aimed at driving all political opponents from the country ... Those who stay face imprisonment and repression.[12]

Kevin Boyle, of Peoples Democracy and the NICRA executive, wrote to James C. Heany about the inaccuracies in their propaganda and the difficulties this caused for the civil rights movement. He pointed out that only some civil liberties were infringed and that, for example, *habeas corpus* was still available. In reply Heany, who was a lawyer of Derry Protestant descent, confessed the difficulty he had experienced trying to convince people in Northern Ireland that they were living in a police state. He construed the situation from his reading of the Government of Ireland Act and the Special Powers Act. He seemed to think that because the latter could potentially suspend all civil liberties, they had in fact been suspended. When Boyle criticised the ACIF publicly, Heany attacked him as a "red Tory".[13]

The majority of the NICRA executive favoured the NAIJ over the ACIF, but the former caused problems too. Its national organiser, Brian Heron, had only been in the USA for five years, but he seems to have become absorbed into the culture of the new left. He was described as wearing the battered clothing of American radical students and behaving like the young, single minded, revolutionaries who were upsetting their elders all over the world. He had supported the black civil rights movement and worked for César Chavez and the Mexican-American Farm Workers' Union. His propaganda material was replete with clenched fists. Politically, he stood with the leadership of the republican movement which was trying to turn the IRA and Sinn Féin into the vanguard of the Irish working class. At the time he was, at best, delphic on the subject of whether money collected during Bernadette Devlin's tour of the USA would go to the IRA or to welfare, as she had pledged, although later he fervently denied that any of the money had been diverted. In any case, he helped to create sufficient mistrust in her mind to induce her to cut her tour short, and return to Northern Ireland.

The divisions between the various factions of civil rights supporters in the USA was nowhere more conspicuous than during and immediately after Devlin's tour. The cleavage between left and right gives no adequate concept of the fine grain of the disunity. One of the NAIJ people involved with the tour was Lennie Glaser. His diary of the tour recounts that Devlin was met at Kennedy Airport by Peter Cush, a Peoples Democracy member then living in the USA, and Phil Tracy of the NAIJ. They then made strenuous efforts to avoid meeting Brian Heron, who was also at the airport. Tracy later phoned the NAIJ office to arrange tour bookings, but gave Glaser a false return number. Tracy was a supporter of the radical Democratic Party politician, Senator George McGovern; Heron was a supporter of the Irish republican movement and Glaser was a supporter of the Trotskyist organisation, the Socialist Workers Party.[14]

Often the divisions were simply between individuals and groups vying for part of the action. At Devlin's first public meeting in the USA, the veteran Irish American Michael Flannery, of the Irish American Action Committee, complained about the monopolisation of her tour by Brian Heron and the NAIJ. The fact that Heron was James Connolly's grandson cut no ice with Flannery. In Boston, in early 1970, three different groups set up meetings for three different civil rights movement leaders on the 15th, 17th and 19th of the same month, and refused to get together on their plans. All the groups bombarded NICRA officers with requests and demands that they be recognised as official representatives of the Association in the US.

There were similar problems with supporters in Britain. When, in 1969, the Irish Unity and Civil Rights Committee wrote to Frank Gogarty asking to establish liaison, they complained that four different people, none of whom had known each other, had approached them in the past ten days, all claiming to be official representatives of NICRA. In Birmingham, the local Campaign for Social Justice took pains to stress that it had no connection with any other civil rights body in the city. The two main organisations in London were the London NICRA, which limited its aims to supporting the civil rights movement, and the Irish Civil Rights Solidarity Campaign, set up following a speaking tour by Devlin and supported mainly by the far-left International Socialists (now the Socialist Workers Party).

Devlin's endorsement of the ICRSC caused considerable bitterness on the part of the London NICRA, since she had at first appeared to be supporting them and then, without informing them, had helped set up the ICRSC. She attacked the London NICRA for containing 'Green Tories', by which she seemed to mean members of the Irish Club. The ICRSC also claimed to support the aims of the civil rights movement, but it tended to give more publicity to Peoples Democracy. The London branch of PD, however, attacked both organisations for their "broad front politics". It quoted PD leader Michael Farrell as wanting Irish groups in London to organise the Irish workers, as an immigrant community, against "both bourgeois states" and to link up Irish and British workers in the fight against exploitation on building sites and factories.

Left-wing British supporters were, at times, distinctly confused about the situation. The International Socialists proposed to organise an Easter demonstration from Belfast to Dublin, passing through "poverty stricken" towns like Newry and Dundalk, and culminating in the re-occupation of the GPO. They seem not to have consulted anyone in Ireland about this, nor to have considered the wisdom of warning the Gardaí of their intentions. Following a march in London in January 1969, International Socialists, quizzed by Irish journalists, were confused about whether withdrawal of British troops should include the Irish regiments permanently based there. The most prominent leader of anti-Vietnam war protests in Britain, Tariq Ali, speaking in Queen's University in January 1969, said the upsurge in Northern Ireland was the "most political and politicised struggle that had taken place in this country" because workers had followed the lead of students. He didn't say which country he meant, but he did suggest that the civil rights activists replace *We Shall Overcome* with the *Internationale*, upon which the 650 students in his audience burst into the revolutionary anthem.[15]

Problems with supporters in Britain were never as acute as those in the USA. Northern Ireland was geographically closer and Irish exiles had better first-hand knowledge of conditions. In addition, British groups like the Campaign for Democracy in Ulster and the Connolly Association had helped to initiate the civil rights movement, and to shape its strategy. In Britain, the various organisations tended to get on with their own campaigning and largely ignored each other, but in the USA, the unstable mixture between right and left created bitter antagonisms and, more seriously, led to intervention by American groups in the civil rights movement in Northern Ireland.

The biggest solidarity event to be organised in the USA was the NAIJ conference in New York in early November 1969. About 40 groups were represented and the Association had affiliates in New York, Long Island, Chicago, Boston, Philadelphia, San Francisco, Washington DC and other places. The NAIJ had originated with a tour of the USA by Austin Currie of the Northern Ireland Nationalist Party, Gerry Fitt of the Republican Labour Party, and Roddy Connolly (the son of James Connolly and uncle of Brian Heron) of the Irish Labour Party. At this time, Heron had been leading an active group in San Francisco called Citizens for Irish Justice. The Irish folk singers the Clancy Brothers and Tommy Makem had helped to raise funds for Heron to tour local groups, co-ordinating them into the NAIJ. On a visit to Belfast, he obtained the endorsement of the NICRA. Heron subsequently moved the national headquarters of the NAIJ to New York, where he worked as full-time organiser.

The affiliated groups were mainly support committees set up in localities or colleges, rather than established Irish-American organisations. A proposed constitution submitted to the conference gave as its purpose the enlistment of aid from the American people for civil rights and freedom in the 32 counties, and as its aims the advancement of the political and economic unity of Ireland.

The style of organisation and the rhetoric of the NAIJ was derived from the current anti-war movement rather than from Irish-American traditions. It shared with that movement a deep internal confusion about the nature and purposes of a single-issue campaign. The anti-war movement was a focus of radicalisation on broader international and domestic American issues, and its participants could never agree about the extent to which the movement itself ought to take up these wider issues. Motions submitted to the NAIJ conference reflected a similar ambiguity. The NAIJ was urged to oppose the Vietnam war and the Russian invasion of Czechoslovakia, and to recognise the similarity between the Black American and Northern Ireland civil rights struggles. There was a call to oppose the Nationalist Party in Northern Ireland and to support 'Republican liberties' for the Irish people. Another motion accepted the CRA's non-violent strategy, but supported the principle of "armed self-defence in exceptional circumstances".

Much of this went beyond solidarity and amounted to political and strategic advice to the civil rights movement. The steering committee recognised the problem and proposed a broad statement of policy:

> The National Association for Irish Justice supports the struggle to achieve equal rights for all people. It also supports the right of every man to a standard of living which allows him to live in dignity. Finally the NAIJ supports the right of every nation to self-determination and reiterates its opposition to all form of economic, political or military imperialism.

This was too anodyne for the more radical elements, who were hypersensitive about association with 'green Toryism', and it did not conciliate the anti-communists, particularly as local affiliates were left free to take up other issues if they chose.

Frank Gogarty and Kevin Boyle from NICRA and Eilish McDermott of PD were invited to address the conference. Gogarty complimented the Association on its "splendid work", but warned that the danger of internal conflict, which threatened to split the movement in Northern Ireland, had been transplanted to the USA. He said that the NAIJ must be an umbrella group, and confirmed that it had been mandated to be the NICRA's voice in the USA. The notes from his speech indicate that he had intended to stress the key role of the republican movement in the civil rights struggle, but had changed his mind. Kevin Boyle stressed that politics had changed in Ireland and that Irish-American notions about "occupied Ireland", partition, and the character of the south, all had to be revised. Eilish McDermott spoke about the growing sectarian polarisation in the north, and the need to unite Protestant and Catholic workers on economic issues.

The conference was also addressed by Maire Martin of London NICRA, who disavowed any aims other than those of the civil rights movement in Northern Ireland. Cathal Goulding, chief of staff of the IRA, said that the IRA supported the civil rights movement, but retained the ultimate objective of a 32-county republic. None of these speeches could have helped much. Gogarty was too vague and emotional, Boyle was too cerebral, and Martin too apolitical. Goulding would have reinforced the link in the delegates minds between civil rights and republicanism, and McDermott would have reinforced the tendency of the radicals to interpret a purely civil rights focus as one which favoured green sectarianism.

In his report to the NICRA executive, Gogarty backed the claims of the NAIJ, but said that he had spoken to other groups asking them to affiliate. One correspondent, writing to Eilish McDermott, said that he had caused problems by giving non-NAIJ groups in Boston and Philadelphia the impression that they were recognised by the NICRA. The visit was also dogged by a hostile letter from Patricia McCluskey, which had been circulated to Irish-American groups, and a similar diatribe by Máire Ó Scanlain of New York, denouncing Brian Heron and PD and demanding that NICRA dissassociate itself from leftists.

The conference stoked the fires of an internal struggle between left and right amongst civil rights supporters in the USA. In July 1969 James C. Heany of the ACIF had written to Peter Morris, secretary of NICRA, saying that they had definite information that the civil rights association was being infiltrated by communists. He claimed that Brian Heron of the NAIJ was a member of the radical campus movement, Students for a Democratic Society, and had confessed to Heany that he was a communist. He warned that Scotland Yard would learn about this through the FBI and would use it to brand the CRA as a communist organisation. Most of the letter, however, was concerned with belittling the size and influence of the NAIJ, and it was redolent of factional jealousy.

In October 1969, the *New Jersey Hibernian* published an article by the state president of the AOH, Eugene J. Byrne, attacking the communist and radical associations of the NAIJ. This was written in the style pioneered by that other great Irish American, Senator Joseph McCarthy. It showed a diligent reading of the left-wing press in order to list contacts and activities of Brian Heron, Lennie Glaser and Bernadette Devlin, together with a total failure to discriminate between, for example, the Communist Party, the Trotskyists, the Black Panthers and César Chavez's Farm Workers' Union. With a sure grasp of the cultural norms of his audience, Byrne noted the fact that Heron was divorced and remarried, and that Devlin's associate, Loudon Seth, was being sued for divorce.

In November, Byrne issued a press release warning the American Irish not to become involved with the NAIJ and attacking its invitation to Bernadette Devlin, Eamonn McCann, Michael Farrell and Kevin Boyle to speak at its conference. Amongst the evidence arrayed against Devlin was the favourable coverage her tour had received in the communist press, her left-wing rhetoric, her clenched fist salute at a rally in Berkeley, California, and the sponsorship of her fundraising by Jessica Mitford, formerly a prominent member of the San Francisco Communist Party.

The dispute amongst Irish Americans had repercussions in Northern Ireland. In early 1969, notes for a speech by Gogarty show that he was angry at what he called a "whispering campaign" in the USA and that some people were advising that all money raised there should go to the McCluskey's Campaign for Social Justice and not to NICRA. A telegram to Mrs. McCluskey in May 1969, from James C. Lavery of the Citizens for Irish Justice, about a split with the "disruptive radical elements" in San Francisco, shows that she and her husband were in the confidence of factions in America. A letter to Conn McCluskey from James C. Heany in September 1969, bitterly attacked Frank Gogarty for his support of Heron and the NAIJ. He warned that if Gogarty sent over "the reds", they would have to attack them openly in the press and elsewhere. They had no intention of allowing a communist takeover of the civil rights movement in the USA or Northern Ireland.

Another source of aggravation was money. Large sums were raised at emotional public meetings in the USA and in Britain. Very little of this was accurately accounted for, inevitably some went astray, or was perceived as having gone astray. Rumours were rife about the use to which money, intended for welfare, had been put. NICRA simply did not have the apparatus or the expertise to keep control of it. The fact that Irish-American groups had raised so much money tended to give them a proprietorial sense which sharpened their attacks when they perceived the civil rights movement taking an unacceptable direction. James C. Heany, in particular, was not slow to point out that his critics in the movement were spending ACIF money.

In the meantime, the civil rights movement in Northern Ireland was experiencing its own divisions between left and right. In March 1969, four members of the Executive—John McAnerney, Fred Heatley, Betty Sinclair and Dr. Raymond Shearer—had resigned in protest at a NICRA agreement to support a PD march to Stormont, which would have passed through Protestant east Belfast, alleging that PD was trying to infiltrate the NICRA and take it over. However, this could hardly give rise to an anti-communist witch-hunt, since Betty Sinclair was Northern Ireland's best known Communist Party member. McAnerney later issued a statement, headed 'Petit Livre Rouge', in which he attacked PD for being "more inspired by Mao than by the lack of rights for the minority".

However, it would be misleading to think of this as an ideological dispute between left and right. In essence, the disagreement was about tactics and PD's style of politics, which some civil rights activists considered dangerously provocative. PD wanted to confront sectarianism, as it had done on its Belfast to Derry march in January 1969, in order to force confrontation in which the British government would either have to intervene to protect the civil rights marchers, or be exposed as supporting sectarianism. Their opponents in the movement feared that these tactics would unleash an uncontrollable confrontation between the two communities. Behind this, there was also a difference over lessons to be learned from the black civil rights movement in the USA. PD based their strategy on Martin Luther King's Selma-Montgomery march, which had forced the federal government to intervene in the south, while their opponents emphasised the constitutionality and moderation of King's approach.

In an essay about Ireland and Scottish politics, I tried to get to grips with the meaning of sectarianism in Northern Ireland:

> Many of the most striking aspects of sectarianism in Northern Ireland—residential segregation, divining the other person's religion from discrete signs, involvement in different sports and social activities, informal restriction of different occupations to Protestants or Catholics—are control mechanisms, which limit the contact between members of the two communities. When they do come into contact there are elaborate, but unwritten rules of conduct about not giving offence. This is why Northern Ireland people are constantly protesting to outsiders about how well they get on with each other. Sectarianism is a means, precisely, of ensuring that this will be the case. But it is a dangerously flawed mechanism for maintaining peace. It perpetuates ignorance and prejudice within each community about the other, it perpetuates inequality, with Catholics relegated to a less

favoured position, and it breaks down from time to time because existing custom and practice are not strong enough to maintain the balance between the two communities when some new and unexpected challenge to the status quo appears. In this way, it perpetuates violence and the potential for violence.[16]

For the opponents of PD on the NICRA executive, sectarianism was dealt with by silence, by avoiding confrontation and by accepting the limitations it put upon your behaviour. As Seamus Heaney put it, "whatever you say, say nothing". In this, they showed how little they had succeeded in detaching themselves from their culture and how insular their outlook was. But PD leaders were no better; they refused to consider the actuality of sectarianism in Northern Ireland. They thought it was a trick by the Unionist government which could be exposed and discredited. They refused to consider its deep roots in society and the dangers which were posed by provoking it so thoughtlessly.

The chairman of NICRA, Frank Gogarty, was a staunch defender of PD and the two pioneers of the civil rights movement, Dr. Conn and Mrs. Patricia McCluskey of Dungannon, were their strongest critics. These internal differences were to be exacerbated by relations with their American supporters. In February 1970, Conn McCluskey, together with two other members of the executive of the NICRA, Brid Rogers and John Donagh, issued a statement criticising the majority of the executive for its handling of relations with American groups.

They complained that they had not been informed about the decision to recognise the NAIJ, nor even that it was on the agenda of the executive meeting which had taken the decision. They were similarly unaware of the decision to send Gogarty and Boyle to attend the NAIJ conference. These accusations were probably justified, but they arose from the informal and *ad hoc* nature of NICRA, of which they must have been aware. Conn McCluskey told one researcher that the "Belfast tail wagged the country dog", because meetings could often go on until 2.00 am.[17] In a situation of political turmoil, expectations of formal agendas and rigid procedures were bound to be disappointed. They also complained that, although NICRA members voted to exclude politics from civil rights platforms, Eilish McDermott had been allowed to make an hour-long political speech at the conference. Since she was representing PD, not NICRA, the complaint had little substance, and it revealed a rather nit-picking attitude on their part.

Other complaints replayed the right-wing Irish-American attacks on the NAIJ; but there was a revealing phrase. The New York conference was described as "small". Since there had been no larger gathering in support of the civil rights movement, one might question their standard of measurement. They cited several solidarity groups which were not part of the NAIJ, but it is a moot point whether these represented larger numbers than the NAIJ: the movement in the USA was too amorphous to establish the facts. But they did cite the "Ancient Order of Hibernians (membership 250,000 in USA and Canada)", as one of the groups which had been alienated by NICRA endorsement of the NAIJ. The conference was "small", therefore, in relation to the bulk of established Irish-American organisations, to which they looked for support.

The disagreement revealed by this document was not about left-wing or right-wing politics, but about the kind of support the movement in Northern Ireland ought to seek from supporters elsewhere. The majority of the executive wanted political support, which required close interrogation of the attitudes on domestic political issues, of those offering solidarity. The minority, carrying over expectations from the anti-partition movement, looked in the main for financial support. As we have seen, this actually caused problems for NICRA and weakened it, rather than augmenting its strength. What is more, in repeating right-wing Irish-American attacks on the left, they were pursuing issues which were not only divisive, but ultimately irrelevant, to the crisis facing the civil rights movement.

In my history of the origins of the civil rights movement, *Politics in the Streets*, I characterised the period when all this was happening:

> The CRA was also being obliged to elaborate and extend its demands by changes in the political situation. O'Neill's promises of concessions on the franchise and housing, the abolition of Londonderry Corporation and his public relations successes, together with the emergence of strong anti-O'Neill forces within the Unionist Party, created a more complex political situation. It was no longer a simple confrontation between the civil rights movement and an intransigent and insensitive government. NICRA was not prepared to accept O'Neill's promises and it wanted to keep up the momentum of its campaign. This made it necessary to make more radical demands and to enter qualifying clauses on its former simple and clear-cut aims.[18]

This process of adaptation sparked off a confrontation between right and left within the movement. This was disruptive and futile, but probably inevitable. It served, however, to mask the nature of the real division which was opening up in NICRA, which was not between left and right, but within the left.

By the spring of 1969, it was clear that elements in the Fianna Fáil government and party in the Republic were intervening in Northern Ireland. This led ultimately to the Dublin arms trial of September 1970, which revealed that funds, originating with the Irish government, had been used to supply arms to groups in the north. The left in NICRA was unanimous in denouncing this, and in characterising it as an attempt to impose a green sectarianism agenda on the civil rights movement. One aspect of this intervention was a newspaper, *Voice of the North*, which was published in Dungannon, but funded from the Republic. For the left, this newspaper reflected the kind of politics which they had condemned amongst Irish Americans.

Voice of the North certainly was anti-communist, and it opposed the elements in the republican leadership which had been influenced by communist politics. It was natural, therefore, that it would not welcome the announcement in 1970 of the setting up of the Communist Party of Ireland, created as a merger between the Communist Party of Northern Ireland and the Irish Workers' Party in the south. It editorialised:

> The point to remember is that the Communists do not give a tinker's damn about civil rights, or housing, or jobs, or about the unity of Ireland. They are intent only on causing anarchy. And with their pink friends, they are campaigning hard for the retention of Stormont and the so-called constitutional position of Northern Ireland. Partition suits their purpose since it is a running sore that divides the Irish nation and gives them scope for agitation and promoting class war ...[19]

The regular columnist, Sean Mac Bradaigh, elaborated:

> People do not want an authoritarian socialism, which claims for itself the status of a religion ... and that all persons and existing institutions must fit themselves into the mould or be smashed. This is the type of socialism being preached by China and Russia and Cuba in different degrees of intensity. It leads to a totalitarian state.
> This type is being proclaimed in a more harmless way by Miss Bernadette Devlin herself, who is repeating what is put into her mouth by cleverer companions—(the courageous little girl has not a clue what it means in theory or in practice) ...[20]

There are two crucial distinctions being made here, which were completely absent from the anti-communist polemics of the Irish Americans. First, communists are not only bad in principle, but they are specifically bad because they want to reform and retain the Northern Ireland state; secondly, not all leftists are to be tarred with the communist brush. Devlin was OK, because she didn't really mean it: at heart, she was a nationalist and an anti-partitionist, and, of course, was only a "little girl" who couldn't be held fully responsible for her actions.

This was the first gentle hint of the real division which was about to appear within Northern Ireland politics. Tomás Mac Giolla, president of Sinn Féin, issued a 'Republican Statement on the Northern Crisis', in August 1969. This document deserves close scrutiny. The style is militant; it denounces 50 years of British Rule, and warns that the "Irish people cannot be expected to stand idly by". The question was no longer civil rights, but British rule. There is a list of demands, including that the Dublin government make representations to the British government, demanding a withdrawal of troops, the immediate granting of civil rights demands, and the holding of an all-Ireland election under UN supervision. It goes on:

> British troops never brought peace to Ireland, and those who think that their use in the present situation could help matters are cherishing an illusion. Neither must there be any reversion to direct rule of the north by Westminster; direct rule by Westminster as during the 19th century is no solution to either Ireland's or the civil rights problems.

Most of the document was huffing and puffing. The key point was opposition to direct rule, which implied retention of the Northern Ireland state, albeit reformed, pending achievement of unity.

This is elaborated in a statement by the Dublin Wolfe Tone Society in April 1970. This organisation had been the first to propose a civil rights movement, and it was the most important intellectual focus of the communist-influenced strategists of the republican movement. In the mid-60s, the Society had concluded that developments such as the Anglo-Irish Free Trade Agreement and the opening up of political and economic links between north and south represented a deep-laid British plot to draw the whole of Ireland more firmly under its influence. It warned, therefore, that "Irish Democrats" had to be very careful not to do anything to advance this imperialist plan. It went on to explain:

> Paradoxical as it may seem ... the most favourable conditions from Britain's point of view ... require the abolition or at least temporary suspension of the Stormont Parliament in Belfast and the imposition of direct rule ... as has already been suggested by Enoch Powell and others. Such a step would be a blow to Craig and Paisley and the right-wing Unionists, but it would strengthen the union overall. For the north would then become a morsel to tempt the south into an Anglo-Irish Federation; there would be changes in some of the forms and institutions of Partition and the Border would basically remain and the whole of Ireland would be under greater British control than ever.

The significance of this for the left in the civil rights movement is explained in a commentary in the Irish news magazine *Nusight*, about the situation in the autumn of 1969:

> Sinn Féin had always been opposed to PD. The ideologists of the Wolfe Tone Society ... saw the CRA as a means of destroying sectarianism by attracting Protestant moderates and middle class support. PD hoped to effect the same change by radicalising the Catholic working class ...
> PD reasoned that with the imposition of direct rule from Westminster the whole unionist machine would collapse when the easy flow of patronage dried up. Sinn Féin ... denounced this as Left Wing Adventurism and instead called for the implementation of Article 75 of the Government of Ireland Act and for the formation of a progressive bourgeois coalition government.[21]

On one side of the division were those who wanted to confront and bring down the Northern Ireland state. This line led, eventually, to the Provisional IRA campaign. On the other side were those who wanted to retain a devolved parliament and administration in Northern Ireland on the basis of the abolition of sectarian discrimination. This line led to the constitutional politics later manifested in the SDLP, the Official Republican Movement, and its offshoots the Workers' Party and the Democratic Left.

At the time, this was very unclear because the official republican movement juggled with confused images of romantic guerrillaism and rhetorical leftism, which seemed to combine the most militant elements of republicanism and communism. A time traveller going back to 1969 would easily have mistaken Brian Heron (a staunch supporter of the Officials), with his clenched fist and Easter Lily and his support for the Black Panthers, for a 1990s Provo. PD, for its part, combined frenetic leftism with bitter opposition to Irish nationalism. The emerging

Provisional movement at first spoke in the conservative language of Catholicism and nationalism, in terms which were similar to those of the right-wing Irish Americans. No one foresaw the eventual line up, which only fully emerged after Bloody Sunday in Derry in 1972, when NICRA was displaced by the Northern Resistance Movement, which combined the Provos and PD.

NICRA was the only organisation which might have challenged the Provisionals for leadership of the militant nationalist areas of Northern Ireland. But when it came to the decisive moment, it had been weakened by the departure of the moderates, who had helped to create the civil rights movement, but who mistook the Official republicans and the Communist Party for a subversive threat. Conn McCluskey, for example, misread the take-over of NICRA by these organisations at the February 1970 AGM. In a circular issued by his Campaign for Social Justice following the meeting, he wrote:

> The new executive will be regarded as hardline, and will completely repel Protestant opinion as well as, of course, moderate Catholics. With a million Protestants here we just cannot make any headway without their goodwill. To expect a united Ireland without their approval, and that of the fifty million British is, in my opinion, pie in the sky.

This is true, except that he had failed to notice who the hardliners were. He fought like a tiger against recognition of the NAIJ, and was deeply upset that traditional Irish-Americans would be alienated by the fact that it contained individuals like Lennie Glaser, who had a drug conviction (for possession of cannabis). When the real business started, many of these Irish-Americans ignored left-wing political rhetoric, and exotic personal lifestyles, and concentrated on helping those who were killing British soldiers.

This is not to condemn McCluskey and the other moderates. They could not have been expected to have foreknowledge of the coming war, nor to have teased out the complexities of republican and left-wing politics. The tactical and strategic adaptations, necessary in the rapidly changing situation after August 1969, were being made by an inexperienced civil rights leadership which was internally divided, and under pressure from the explosive developments in Northern Ireland. Relations with its supporters outside Northern Ireland, particularly in America, made their situation more difficult.

The traditional nationalists put the civil rights movement under pressure to live in their insular dream world of a heroic struggle against British domination. The new left tried to direct them to the real struggles, like those of the American black people; but the Northern Ireland civil rights movement, like the new left, could only make symbolic gestures towards those whose struggle had inspired it. What internationalism demanded was an understanding of the internal logic of the black civil rights struggle, a grasp of the historical and societal context in which it operated, and how its philosophy and methods could be translated into a very different context in Northern Ireland. But the civil rights movement never made a serious study of the black movement, but only imitated certain of its actions. This was an intellectual failure, and it was also a failure to develop a practical internationalism.

This led to another failure. This was an insufficient grasp of what was particular about Northern Ireland. This could only have been overcome by understanding how it compared with a range of other societies; but, in the 60s and 70s, the only points of reference were Britain and the Republic, and all they revealed was that Northern Ireland diverged from their norm. We had to wait until 1989 for Frank Wright's *Northern Ireland: A Comparative Analysis*[22], and until after its author's tragic death for its significance to begin to sink in.

That is why their internationalism could only be imitative. Unionists and nationalists, in disputing the ownership of their territory, have blinded themselves to the way in which it has been shaped by both communities. They could never be internationalists, because their insularity prevented them from understanding their own society. Their Northern Ireland is an unreal and imaginary construct in which the other community has no significance. It is tragic that the civil rights movement, although international in spirit, perceived internationalism as an escape from Northern Ireland, not as a way of seeing it more clearly. That is why it failed to be truly internationalist, and that is its epitaph.

Notes

[1] A shorter version appeared in *Irish Studies Review*.
[2] For a discussion of the anti-partition movement, see the author's 'The Irish Anti-Partition League, South Armagh and the Abstentionist Tactic 1945-58', *Irish Political Studies*, 1986.
[3] *Irish Weekly*, 8th February, 1969.
[4] 26th October-15th November, 1969.

[5] D3253 (Gogarty papers in PRONI).
[6] Ibid.
[7] Quoted in Sara Davidson, 'Bernadette Devlin: an Irish Revolutionary in Irish America', *Harpers Magazine*, January 1970, p. 78.
[8] *Irish Weekly* 19th October, 1968.
[9] Gogarty papers *op. cit.*
[10] *Irish Weekly* 29th March, 1969.
[11] Gogarty papers *op. cit.*
[12] D3297 Kevin Boyle Papers, PRONI.
[13] *Irish Weekly*, 26th July, 1969.
[14] This organisation has no connection with the British SWP, mentioned below.
[15] *Irish Times*, 15th January, 1969.
[16] 'The Lessons of Ireland for the SNP', in Tom Gallagher (ed.), *Nationalism in the Nineties* (Edinburgh: Polygon, 1991), p. 81.
[17] James Thompson, *The Civil Rights Movement in Northern Ireland*, M.A. Thesis, Queen's University of Belfast, 1973, p. 137.
[18] Belfast: Blackstaff, 1980, p. 222.
[19] 29th March, 1970.
[20] Ibid.
[21] October 1969.
[22] Dublin: Gill & Macmillan. I would like this essay to be my tribute to Frank's memory. I am glad we were able to meet for the last time at the John Hewitt International Summer School at which I first read this paper.

Eiresponsiblities
Rhythm and Revolution in 'The Rime of the Ancient Mariner'

Derek Franklin*

The following remarks are excerpted from a shorter lecture delivered at the John Hewitt International Summer School at Garron Tower, Co. Antrim, on 1st August, 1991. The lecture was delivered as a companion piece to a talk given earlier that day. The fundamental assumptions behind the earlier lecture were that all poems are written in a particular time and place, and that all poetry may therefore be said to be politically conditioned.

Born in 1772, Samuel Taylor Coleridge could not have been unaware that the year 1800 would occur in his lifetime, if he lived to be 28. But in 1772, neither the then-suckling Coleridge nor his future readers could have predicted the impact that late 18th-century Irish politics would have upon the emerging poet and his poetry.

Earlier today, a lecturer who shares my interest in politics and poetry addressed the closing lines of Coleridge's 'Frost at Midnight':

> Therefore all seasons shall be sweet to thee,
> Whether the summer clothe the general earth
> With greenness, or the redbreast sit and sing
> Betwixt the tufts of snow on the bare branch
> Of mossy apple tree, while the nigh thatch
> Smokes in the sun-thaw; whether the eave-drops fall
> Heard only in the trances of the blast,
> Or if the secret ministry of frost
> Shall hang them up in silent icicles,
> Quietly shining to the quiet moon.
>
> (ll.65-74)

He correctly concluded that these lines are no mere lullaby addressed to the poet's infant son, but an expression of Coleridge's profound discomfort over the perturbations of 1798, and that we might even see the word 'quiet'—twice iterated in the closing line, albeit once in adverbial form—as the poet's forward glance to his hope for a refuge in the less troubled harbours of Anglicanism.[1] Agreeing with this as I do, I was troubled by the ensuing general discussion, which fanned out to take account of Coleridge's 'The Rime of the Ancient Mariner', but failed to take account of its political implications. For if 'Frost at Midnight' may be said to be a political poem, 'The Rime of the Ancient Mariner' may be said to be Irish.

According to the shorter edition of *The Norton Anthology of Poetry* (New York, 1970), Coleridge commenced 'The Rime of the Ancient Mariner' in 1798 and finished it in 1817 (p. 275). This is an apparently lengthy spot in time; and it would be all too easy to claim that Coleridge exhausted too much of his not inconsiderable talent by devoting nearly two decades of his creative life to a poem that is simple to the point of transparency.

But in the final analysis, there is little that is either simple or transparent about Coleridge or the 'Rime', particularly when the poem is properly relocated in the Irish dimension out of which it came.

At first glance, there may appear to be little reason to regard Coleridge as an 'Irish' poet, let alone as an 'Irish poet'. Yet even the internal evidence of the 'Rime' is compelling on this point, all but inexorable.

The justly famous opening line—"It is an ancient Mariner"—clearly marks the speaker of the poem as the quintessential Englishman, since England was then the most powerful—hence the dismissal of the past tense, and the subtle choice of "is"—of the nations that might justly be described as both "ancient" and "maritime". From here, it is a short step to the realisation that the second line of the poem—"And he stoppeth one of three"—refers, not to Scotland or Wales, but to Ireland; for the poem abounds with references to the island that Coleridge perceived as England's belaboured, but defiant, brother to the west. It is no accident, for instance, that the ice that threatens the ancient Mariner's symbolic ship of state is "As green as emerald" (l. 54), or that the water-snakes that later surround the ship are sketched as "Blue, glossy green, and velvet black" (l. 279). These were the colours that had originally been proposed for the flag of the United Irishmen, the revolutionary group that had been founded a few scant years before Coleridge began his 'Rime': as the old saying had it, "blue for our undivided sky, green for our divided fields, black for our living dead". Nor is it any accident that Coleridge's narrator comes to love these politically-charged snakes in all their "rich attire" (l. 278):

> O happy living things! no tongue
> Their beauty might declare:
> A spring of love gushed from my heart,
> And I blessed them unaware.
>
> (ll. 282-85)

or that he immediately thereafter retreats, not towards Anglicanism, but into the more blatant forms of Mariolatry:

> O sleep! it is a gentle thing,
> Beloved from pole to pole!
> To Mary Queen the praise be given!
> She sent the gentle sleep from Heaven,
> That slid into my soul.
>
> (ll. 292-96)

For Coleridge had become a convert to the cause of the United Irishmen, and his 'Rime' expresses his hatred of English policy towards Ireland as thoroughly as the works of an equally famous author whose works have also been co-opted into the 'English' canon. I mean to say that Coleridge's condemnation of England was as sure as it was Swiftian, and that it announces itself in terms no less decisive that those the Dean might have chosen. Consider, for instance, the central image of the albatross.

Deeply encased in the emerald ice and facing death by starvation, the Mariner and his British shipmates are liberated from the ice-field only after they encounter the albatross and not only permit it to eat "the food it ne'er had eat" (l. 67), but hail it "As if it had been Christian soul" (l.65). The subtext here speaks for itself. The reference to "the food it ne'er had eat" carries us back to the then-fresh memories of starvation and famine in Ireland. The reference to the "Christian soul", tempered though it is by the phrase "[a]s if", is nonetheless obviously meant to counter early 19th-century English views of the Irish as sub-human, or at least sub-English. And, lest the force of these ironies be lost, Coleridge, who was generally more perceptive than the narrators of his poems, goes on to deny his English sailors the liberating vision that he hoped to inspire in his English readership: despite the fact it had been their Christian hailing of the albatross that had brought the "good south wind" (l. 71) that freed them from their glacial racialism, both the sailors and, at this stage in the poem, the Mariner himself, remain pig-ignorant about the political sources of either their blessings or their woes. While they correctly associate the bird with "fog and mist" (ll. 100-102), they fail to make evident the connection between these baleful weather conditions and Ireland. Ultimately, then, their failure is a failure to read the text of the world aright; they see the redemptive bird simply as a bird, and want it slain. And the Mariner naively complies.

To be sure, it was Swift who first took the image of an ingenuous English seafarer and turned it as a mirror towards the English; but Coleridge's poem in a sense completes the work begun by Swift, representing as it does the first and only gest in literature in which a gull kills an albatross. Nor do the Swiftian resonances subside with the death of the bird. Inevitably, the Mariner is draped not with the Cross—that most traditional of English symbols of redemption—but with its Irish equivalent:

> Ah! well-a-day! what evil looks
> Had I from old and young!
> Instead of the cross, the albatross
> About my neck was hung.
>
> (ll. 139-42)

Here I want to resist the traditional interpretations that point to Coleridge's awareness that *Alb*ania (my emphasis) was an ancient name for Scotland, and insist instead on his awareness that 'Alba'— alternately, 'Elba' or 'Eire'—was one of the original eponyms of his persecuted island neighbour. And in thus glossing 'alba-(t)ross' as 'Elba-(c)ross', we can point to something more than Coleridge-as-etymologist. Until now, I have relied primarily on textual evidence to make the case that Coleridge's 'Rime', like the works of most authors, can best be understood when relocated in the context of Irish politics. But sound as that evidence may be, we need not place our reliance solely on the internal. Indeed, we may turn, as well to the form of evidence that is—too loosely—classified as 'historical'.

Ultimately, the Mariner is shrived by the "Hermit good" who "lives in that wood/ Which slopes down to the sea" (ll. 514-15). The exact location of his home is encoded in the quatrain that follows those lines directly, wherein we discover that the Hermit

... kneels at morn, and noon, and eve—
He hath a cushion plump:
It is the moss that wholly hides
The rotted old oak stump.

(11. 519-22)

Aside from Coleridge's evident gesture of deference to the Irish monastic tradition, these lines contain a covert reference to Derry— in Irish *Doire*, or the oak-wood—as a place which the Mariner—and by implication, the English race he represents—must take into account in their quest for forgiveness. The old oak-wood is now a "rotted" oak "stump", a fit image of what Catholic Derry had become under the aptly named Sir Henry Docwra, who had firmly established English rule in the city between 1570 and 1603. But the city remained a central symbol of Irish resistance to English rule, as witnessed by the green moss that has made so heroic a comeback that it now not only "wholly hides" a woeful history, but serves the Hermit as it might well serve the Pope: a cushion "plump". The city would thus be a place that the Mariner, who is to the albatross what Docwra was to Derry, would turn to all but perforce; and, as Coleridge came to discover, the city had also been the home of Seamus MacNamara (1765-1798).

Before his mysterious death in 1798 in a pub in Castlebar, MacNamara would have had ample opportunity to meet Coleridge; but, in all likelihood, they first encountered each other in 1797, or shortly before Coleridge began 'The Rime of the Ancient Mariner'. In his unpublished journal, now in the archives of the Linen Hall Library in Belfast, MacNamara writes:

> 1st July, 1797. Met another English poet in London today. Place is full of them. None of them write, but all are said to be 'working on something' and all beguile unwary foreign visitors into the purchase of ceaseless rounds of drink. This one claimed to be a University man. I was told he was working on dreary naive sonnets, I think about falconry in the middle ages. Quote me the first two lines: 'That bird so good you may believe I slew/For slain it was, and by my own crossbow'. Pronounced last word 'crossboo', said it was 'of the folk'. Told him to give it up.

Here follows a gap on the page of the journal which suggests that MacNamara's attention had been temporarily distracted, a suggestion reinforced by the fact that, when the entry resumes, the next few lines of script are so difficult to read that one can only assume they are in some kind of code. The entry then concludes in block letters: 'TOLD

HM (*sic*) TO REALLY WRITE OF FOLK SHOULD USE OLD TUNES & SANG HIM TUNE WE WILL SING WHEN WE MARCH. VIOLATED PLEGDE. (*sic*)'

As we shall see, the "pledge" that MacNamara sees himself as having "violated" no doubt has to do with his disclosure of the secret song of a secret society; and in any event, it is clear that the poet he was referring to is Coleridge, and not simply because of the coincidence between the verses he has quoted and the narrative line of the 'Rime'. For, in his brief span of 33 years, MacNamara had acquired a substantial following, not only among English poets in London, but more expectedly in Rome and his native Derry. As a leader of the United Irishmen and a man preparing for revolution, he had adapted an ancient song from the Gaeltacht as the "tune we will sing when we march". Its opening bars ran thus:

And Coleridge, to his credit, not only absorbed MacNamara's message but was transformed by it. His original plan for a sonnet was shed as surely as the albatross itself; and MacNamara's radical Irish politics were paid an explicit tribute by a radical English poet, nowhere more movingly than in the famous verses—meant to be sung, not read—in which Coleridge imagines an England which has been spiritually dehydrated by its colonial policies and which, more pointedly, will someday have to face the moment when the colonised retrace the sea-paths traversed by their monster, and appear in frightful form in the English proper:

> Water, water everywhere,
> And all the boards did shrink;
> Water, water, everywhere,
> Nor any drop to drink.
>
> The very deep did rot: O Christ!
> That ever this should be!
> Yea, slimy things did crawl with legs
> Upon the slimy sea.

(ll. 119-126)

The fact that the entire 'Rime' may be sung to this Irish melody allows us to withdraw entirely from argument about the melody's source; it is the tune that MacNamara sang on that fateful day in London, and the tune that Samuel Taylor Coleridge hummed as he composed. In its refusal of iambic pentameter, 'The Rime of the Ancient Mariner' betrays itself as a poem that cries against the traditional rhythms of English verse; and it thereby establishes itself as a political refusal of the pentameter line, the beast with five feet.

It also, and happily, establishes itself as a political refusal of English politics, at least as those politics applied to Ireland. There have been complex explanations offered as to why the Mariner's tale is parenthetically enclosed by a wedding feast, and why the Wedding Guest is denied admission. But questions as direct as these invite responses that are themselves direct, and the poem itself responds to these particular queries in strokes both bold and plain.

I have already suggested that the Ancient Mariner may be read as an emblem of England, specifically the England that had 'slain' Ireland and that, in Coleridge's view, could be forgiven only after it had understood the consequences of its actions and repented. From here, the reader may move fluidly to the realisation that the Wedding Guest is in turn emblematic of William Pitt (1759-1806), and that the Mariner has prevented him from attending the wedding feast because he realises that the Guest has failed to understand the most fundamental of all concepts that form the underpinning of a marriage. At the end of the day, after all, a wedding is nothing if not an act of union; and while Pitt had been the prime mover behind the passing of the Union Bill of 1800, Coleridge clearly felt that this marriage between England and Ireland had been both forced and false. Hence the propriety of barring the Guest from a celebration of the wedding, since in Coleridge's view there is little to celebrate. The marriage was to prove an unhappy one for both parties involved, and a disaster for their offspring.

Finally, the end of the poem. In his attempts to secure the Act of Union, Pitt had gained the support of the Irish Catholic Church by promising that the passage of the Act would be accompanied by Catholic emancipation in Ireland. But once the Act had gone through, George III stoutly refused to grant the emancipation Pitt had pledged; and though the Act he had pressed so hard for was barely in place Pitt promptly resigned as Prime Minister. There are resemblances between this sudden action by Pitt and the sudden moment of revelation accorded the Wedding Guest, who turns "from the bridegroom's door" (l. 621) even as the wedding feast is reaching its climax:

> He went like one that hath been stunned,
> And is of sense forlorn:
> A sadder and a wiser man,
> He rose the morrow morn.
>
> (ll. 622-25)

But if we are to find in these lines even the sketch of a gesture of forgiveness for Pitt, must we not then find in them a melodic echo of tribute to a sad, wise man who turned his back on his feast years before? His tomb is unscribed, his memory in oblivion. Yet he laid down his life for the cause of Irish freedom in Castlebar in 1798; and a scant year earlier, he had no less surely laid down the line for one of the most famous of all the poems that England has unwittingly claimed for its own. It is time that his epitaph be written. Ladies and gentlemen, it is time now.

Notes

[1] The ironic issue of all this is well known. Coleridge was buried, after his death, in St. Michael's in Highgate, a church whose location on a hill leaves it "stand(ing) higher than any other church in London", but which nonetheless—in the playful words of its own current tour guides—is "neither high nor low but Church of England". For details, see Sir James Brown, *St. Michael's, Highgate* (London, n.d.), which is my source for the first citation in this note (p.1).

*Derek Franklin was a pseudonym for the late Frank Kinahan.

The Big Elsewhere & the Wayward Hyphen
Further Gleanings from the Clarity Archive

George O'Brien

Professor F. X. Clarity
Dean of Humanities and Communication Skills
Central State University
Murpheytown
West Virginia

Dear F. X.,
Delighted to hear from you and to know all goes well out there in "the big elsewhere" (I see you haven't lost your touch for a phrase). So— the fish are jumping out at Yellowwood Lake? That's grand. You didn't say if the cotton was high. Do you have cotton where you are, or is it gone the way of the plantation, the minstrel and the cakewalk, and given over entirely to the Asiatic mode? I really admire the way you can get rid of unwanted baggage out there.

That pen-picture of the trip to Yellowwood was a treat, particularly the view from the interstate—the fathomless ocean of the bottle-green pines, the wave upon wave of ridge after ridge, the solitary houses stark white in the hanky of clearing, are a view of that great country of yours which is not very much considered here. The continental sweep is difficult to appreciate, and the whole idea of land that's hardly been touched and whose history is either unwritten, forgotten or irrelevant, is unimaginable. An elsewhere, indeed. It makes me understand, in some small way, why you'd have to have guns and every other sort of machine known to man to be able to deal with it at all.

But what made your picture complete was the portrait of yourself barrelling down the road in your Chevy S10 Blazer 4x4 with the Seldom Scene blasting out of the old CD player. Yes, I remember the

Seldom Scene, and the night we had in Clifden when you played the tapes to us. (Will you ever forget it? Everyone was expecting a lecture; several members of the clergy experienced strong weaknesses when you produced the jew's-harp). If that night didn't make a convert of me, nothing would, though I wouldn't mind sampling it with you in what seems to be a chariot of fire of a pick-up truck. Interesting what you brought out in your memorable—what shall we call it?—illustrated talk. I always thought that Bluegrass was too fidgety, too full of squirrels in the treetops and turkeys in a tizz, to have anything to do with us. Hornpipes on speed, eh? And true enough, a lot of the songs are very lonesome. Your point of view about the kind of numbers called 'Breakdowns' was also most intriguing, though I'm not sure I quite grasped the etymological range you were proposing regarding the breakdown connoted by emigration, and the dancing at American wakes being engraved and later being resurrected at moments of communal witnessing in the new world ... We must go into that another time. Meanwhile, I'm sticking to my James Last. You may call it 'elevator music', but I get high on it.

There's no denying, though, that you would not be the daring scholar we all know and value if you didn't march to the beat of a different drummer, as you say yourself. And speaking of scholarship: what a summer you're having! Typically, rather than take a well-earned rest after that wonder of the world, your conference, 'Ireland 2000', on you go again, dashing and daring. I'm sorry, though, that we weren't more closely in touch in the final stages of the conference planning. I might have saved you from the misstep of inviting Jack Charlton to be your closing speaker. I do see the sense of such an invitation, from one point of view. And I take your point about diversity and keeping options open. Indeed, I'm sympathetic to your plan to have a raffle for tickets to some Irish soccer match, somewhere. Finding funds, I agree, is very much a Dean's role. And holding the closing ceremonies in the Central Mountain stadium with pricey tickets from far and wide certainly has a logic to it. And yet, and yet ...

Of course, not even I could have foreseen the reaction your Charlton invitation provoked. And before saying anything more, I want to make clear that, in this matter, you would have, and do have, my full support and sympathy. To think of their being such opposition to what, at the very least, was an absolute winner of an idea as far as publicity is concerned—and there's no doubt about it: as you say, creating such ideas is very much the role of a Dean ... And the invitation spoke with a certain tacit eloquence to your new research departure regarding the Diaspora, too. I totally agree with your position that somebody given the freedom of Dublin could at least be relied on not to let the side down. The response of that *alumni* ginger group, CID—*Caritas Incipit ad Domus*, indeed!—that Dublin could get stuffed and that it was the freedom of Ireland that you should be thinking of, casts, I'm afraid, in a rather poor light the claims of these people to be educated. But, of course, you mentioned to me before their role in getting gay marches banned. You didn't say what Pat Buchanan's Commencement address was like. I'm sure, though, that, as ever, he knew his audience and played to them accordingly.

Still and all, as you rightly point out, such irritations quickly fade and die once the life of the mind is resumed. And is it really true what you tell me—the great work is complete at last? The long wait is over, and the song of Barney Stubble will be loud in the land. Allow me to be among the first to congratulate you. When you first presented the poems of Barney Stubble at that plenary session in the AOH Memorial Hall, Akron, you could literally hear a pin drop. Few, if any, had suspected the existence of an Irish cowboy, despite—as you cogently pointed out at the time—O'Neill, Nebraska; Kennedy, Nebraska; Duff, Nebraska. The question, for us, is not *what* are they, but *who*, for us, now, at the very moment in history when we rejoin the world and articulate our own idiomatic contemporaneity, our soccer, our pop, our *Commitments*? Even more so, you went on, isn't the need to know them greater than ever now that, in the words of Mike Curran, ex-mayor of Green Harbor, Massachusetts, "'we've just *fallen apart*, my friend'" (George V. Higgins, *Kennedy for the Defence*, 1980). How many must be effaced, you asked, before their presence claims us?

To say that, and no more, would have caused stir enough. But when you demonstrated that Barney was such a gifted poet, well, what can I say? You were there: you know what I mean. Something along the lines of terrible beauty, eh? Let's not be modest now!

> Hard chaw north of Omaha—
> Snow deep, no sleep—
> Horse dead, sky lead—
> And I have promises to keep.

A shiver went through the Akron assembly. Not a dry eye in the house after your most trenchant rendition of that poor cowpoke's grizzled plainsong. I know I'm not alone in saying that the prospect of a complete annotated edition of the poems of Barney Stubble is joyous news indeed. The patience of *cloinne Bháirní*, in which I am delighted to number myself, formed that unforgettable night in Akron and pledged further awareness and information regarding one of the more notable variants on so many of our hallowed literary traditions—the *spailpín*, the wanderer, the man of no property, cousin german to the poor scholar, Christy Mahon, and Molloy—is the last rewarded, and I'm greatly looking forward to receiving my copy. What do people at Deadwood Stage say the publication date is to be?

Just one word, if I may, in response to your remarks in passing about the critical apparatus. I can certainly understand why you would say that your introduction to this landmark publication will simply consist of an amalgamation of your Stubble articles. This is a sensible and economical use of resources, and particularly acceptable in this case, in view of the exciting demands of your new project. I, for one, however must express my regret that those magisterial articles of yours are now going to seem subsidiary. 'A Tale of Two Barneys: Wattletoes, Stubble and the Discourse of Class Aphasia in the Rural Literature of the 19th Century' would certainly suffice as an introduction as it stands. If reproduced as such it would sustain the status of 'Barney Stubble, Matt the Thresher and Tradition', as one of the true collectors' items in this field. As you very well know, ever since its first publication in *Les Amis de la Terre: Journal de la société pour Sang et Sol*, it has gripped the hearts and minds of everyone who's read it. And as you were telling me when we appeared together as guest speakers at the Stradbally Ploughing Week, the sudden disappearance of this periodical, under unexplained circumstances, has increased the value of everything that appeared in it. By the way, still no word I suppose from Père Maurice, M. le Directeur, since that postcard from Tangier?

I'd have thought, though, that bringing this work to fruition would have tempted you to rest on your laurels. But not a bit of it, evidently. And pleased as I was to hear that Barney Stubble was about to be given to the world, you won't mind if I say that the best news of all is the project on which you've now embarked. A *Dictionary of Irish-American Scenes, Portraits and Other Representative Appearances*! Yes, I agree, it does make a very appealing acronym. And, of course, you are absolutely right, their name is legion. Talk about from Dunkirk to Belgrade (that's Dunkirk, New York and Belgrade, Montana) ... And their presence is spectral, no more visible in the big story than the hyphen that defines them, yet to all appearances ineffaceable.

I for one am still haunted by the "fine womanly Irish features" of Mr. Roche, Converse's landlord in Robert Stone's *Dog Soldiers* (1974). It's too early to be thinking of epigraphs, I suppose, but the mention of Stone puts me in mind of that line of drunken Callaghan, the mercenary, in *A Flag for Sunrise* (1981): "'In the words of the great Irish wit ... it's not enough to opt for silence. You have to consider the kind of silence.'" One type of silence will perhaps be audible in your treatment of the same novel's Sister Justin Feeney, while a more profound type will be reserved, no doubt, for her equal and opposite in the story, Father Egan.

How to gloss the ruminative Richard Nixon's unbuttoned recollections, in *The Public Burning* by Robert Coover (1977), of his father's "Black Irish temper" and the rods and leathers with which he set his sons' asses "on fire" still stings, or reminiscing about poor Pat (*née* Ryan): "My Wild Irish Potato"? I see by the way, that Haldemann's recently-published *Diaries* presents the prince of our disorder brooding on the "need to build our new coalition based on Silent Majority, blue collar, Catholic, Poles, Italians, Irish. No promise with Jews and Negroes."

And, of course, you have to find a place for Terry Leary, the cop in Thomas Maxwell's *Kiss Me Once* (1986), whose Uncle Paddy—"the priest, not the Jersey City hooch runner"—secured for him promotion to detective in the days when "the New York Police Department was very Irish, very Catholic, and it seemed like most of the gents at the top of the heap had initials like F.X. One Francis Xavier after another".

No doubt about it, that hyphen is a deceptive yoke. It may look like a straight line, but it's by no means the shortest distance between two points. Nor should it be confused with the equal sign. It unites and separates in the one gesture, and the entities to which it does that only *appear* to have their feet on the ground. You never know when it's going to crop up, or the peculiar vectors, pointers and odd angles that slink around in serpentine squirms (as though with knowledge to impart!) behind its unassuming face. Simplest of brands, knottiest of histories. And, as the *Dictionary* will undoubtedly demonstrate, why should not the history of Irish-America be as complicated and as multiform as that of anything else? I remember looking weak at you when you told me about the radio show you did one Patrick's Day on WRC, and Bev Smith, the show's Black hostess telling you while the ads were on that she was part Cherokee and part Irish, as well as African-American. "We all have our troubles," I recall you saying, soberly. 'Yet, interestingly, while I could obviously see she was Black, and infer the Native American from her cheekbones, where was she Irish? And why did she want to hold onto it?"

This anecdote, and indeed some of the textual citations which, as I say, unnervingly remain with me—these emblems of so many that have gone, so many stories untold and untellable—came up, don't you remember, at the Ballindine Vegetable Carnival that summer we were invited to debate 'Potayto-Potato: The Limits of My Language Are the Limits of My World'. Another memorable night! Next morning—stop: the pair of us were under the wheel of the steamroller, and no mistake. Nothing would do us, of course, but to try and insert spirit of potayto-potato into juice of tomayto-tomato, the bottle knocking on the glass like an alarm clock, and you singing to wake the dead: "Bloody Mary from Argyll ..."

Then the next thing I knew, you had commandeered the only hackney car in the seven parishes thereabouts to drive you to Waterford (all the other honoured guests had to wait for the bus). I won't ask what that cost. The driver only had to take one look at you to know not to ask either. That was the year you were on the Ford Foundation grant, wasn't it? Right go wrong, you insisted on seeing those mean streets, as you called them, down which respectable Raymond Chandler walked as a boy. Why only this and nothing else would do you, I never understood, until your news of the *Dictionary*, even though I checked on Chandler afterwards, and sure enough his mother's people hailed from old *urbs intacta*. Of course! *In vino* ... That was the instant of your inspiration. You didn't care how far away Waterford was, off with you, heading off for the new territory, leaving me with a tongue like a tramdriver's mitten, bewailing my fate. Cripes, you're as American as the Americans themselves.

And leave it to you. It comes as no surprise at all to hear (by way of an overture to the great work, I presume) that, if ever there was an example of how unpredictable and ill-behaved an article that hyphen is, sophisticated, successful, well-educated, Raymond Chandler is its victim. Whether the thing is a cosh, a riding crop, Cupid's arrow or a pint, as it must appear when you're falling, it seems like it got him good. I couldn't get over what you cite of that letter of his to Mrs. Knopf, wife of his first upmarket publisher. He's correcting the 'natty' dust-jacket biography which was to appear on his second novel from that house, *Farewell, My Lovely*:

> Fourth point, and one I'm sensitive on, but one which is difficult to make other Americans understand. I am not an Irish-American in the sense commonly understood. I am of Quaker descent on both sides. The Irish family my mother belonged to had not a single Catholic relative or

> connection, even by marriage. Furthermore, the professional classes in southern Ireland are and have always been largely non-Catholic. Those few Irish patriots who had the brains as well as spite have also been non-Catholics. I should not like to say that in Ireland Catholicism reached its all-time low of ignorance, dirt and general degradation of the priesthood, but in my boyhood it was bad enough. It does the Irish great credit that out of this flannel-mouthed mob of petty liars and drunkards there has come no real persecution of the non-Catholic element.
> —Frank McShane (ed), *Selected Letters of Raymond Chandler.* New York: Columbia University Press, 1981, pp. 15–16

Now, as you make abundantly clear, there's at least one very good reason that Americans might find it difficult to understand this point of his. That reason is Rusty Regan. Of course, I remember him. He's the basic cause of the kerfuffle in Chandler's first novel, *The Big Sleep*. Trying to track him down is the reason Philip Marlowe gets involved with those two nasty Sternwood girls. And Rusty's misfortune was that he became more intimately entangled with the same pair. The girls are daughters of General Sternwood, who took quite a shine to Rusty, so much so that he's willing to pay money to have him run to ground. He explains:

> I'm very fond of Rusty. A big curly-headed Irishman from Clonmel [near Ballyporeen, indeed: but what there might be in a name must await the *Dictionary*], with sad eyes and a smile as wide as Wiltshire Boulevard ... He was the breath of life to me ... He spent hours with me, sweating like a pig, drinking brandy by the quart and telling me stories of the Irish revolution. He had been an officer in the IRA. He wasn't even legally in the United States ...

One soldier to another, all very man-to-man. The family retainer tells Marlowe how the General relished Rusty's "youth ... and [his] soldier's eye." It doesn't matter that Rusty's looks and professional expertise seem to have qualified him for the New World calling of bootlegger. What matters is that there's a man around the house. The house itself is a monument, of sorts, to an archetype of The Man, or at least The Male. Portraits of the General's military ancestors adorn the vestibule, and Marlowe is very conscious of running the gauntlet of their ironsided poses. But the General himself is the last of the line. And he is not only moribund physically—fathering daughters shows how comprehensively things have gone to the dogs.

And there is poor Rusty. As a Clonmel man, he probably would be able to tell greyhounds apart, and there's some slight evidence that making such distinctions might well have been a feature of Rusty's pillow talk. Vivian Sternwood, his ex-wife, says "Rusty was earthy and vulgar at times, but he was very real". In the heel of the hunt, though, he was pretty much a rabbit to the creatures who sank their southern Californian teeth into him. Another good man gone west, and as decent an IRA man as ever wore a trenchcoat. But innocent, God love him. A greenhorn, out and out. No match for sexual terrorists like Vivian and Carmen Sternwood.

Race, gender and class—far away from them Rusty must have thought he was born. Gender was what the General wanted to give him, but the women wouldn't have it. Class came with the marriage, but it dissolved with the marriage too. Even Rusty's Christian name identifies him as a man of no property. This being an American tale, only race remains: "an Irish face that was more sad than merry and more reserved than brash." But ineffaceable, as said before. When Marlowe leaves Sternwood acres, having these unhappy deeds related, "after the rain, the terraced lawns were as green as the Irish flag"—that pure and unhyphenated green, though, of course, to grow a front that green in such a desert a hybrid seed would probably be required.

And, of course, that's one of the things that attracts me so much to the *Dictionary*. It will show all the confusions and contortions of the diasporic presence at large and the diasporic trauma within. Anyone can see that inside the shell that's Rusty, and the tics of the unfinished businesses it contains, the fatal clashes of virility and victimology, innocence and bad blood, sexual violence and the other—more cleancut? more uniform?—variety; the greenness of faraway hills. It's all twitching away like the legacy of an amputation, the finality and its double, the unforgettable.

It's true that in Chandler's particular case he tries to write it off. Next time out, in *Farewell, My Lovely*, Moose Molloy, the hapless missing person (and what a diasporic metaphor that is!) is a Rusty clone; if anything, a more conspicuous innocent, all man and with nothing but emasculation for a story. It's not Moose that you'll be attending to (Chandler just lets the name hang there silently). It's Anne ("call me Annie") Riordan. Marlowe falls: "'Your hair's red ... You look Irish.'" Plus she's a cop's daughter. Of course there's that "'So what?'" of hers, in response to Marlowe's ethnic gambit. But you will not be put off so easily, eh? And, in fact, Chandler can't let go at that either. Annie doesn't deny who she is. Marlowe is the one who does that. Glad as he is of her embrace, he denies himself commitment, and instead resumes his life of sexual exile, the life he shares with his investigations' victims. The private eye, viewing himself without illusion, and looking for a landscape that will bear out what he sees ... The diasporic one.

Can't you feel the old hyphen flexing, the compass needle forever seeking its true north, the divining rod unpredictably prospecting for sustenance and solace? It's all there, F.X. boy! And, as the *Dictionary* will confirm, mostly in the least expected places. There's that one bit of gristle, it seems, some knuckle or nodule no bigger than a hyphen that never melted, no matter how well-stocked the pot or how vociferously the recipe called for reducing. Didn't, wouldn't, or couldn't melt. The off-chance, the unexamined, the superfluous, the marginal—those are the occasions when the hyphen buckles, and the tensions it tries to mask (race, gender, class) helplessly break through. It makes sense, in a way. "Patsy Caliban, our American cousin": you won't rest till you get to the bottom of what Joyce meant by that, will you? Well, fair play to you. Ride that hyphen! No better man to chart the lonesome trail of loss and turmoil it disguises so demurely. And remember, if you don't—well, in the words of Eddie Mars, the crook in *The Big Sleep*, "'you'll wish your name was Murphy and you lived in Limerick'".

Again, without wishing to take one whit away from your Barney Stubble achievement, I have to say that for all that edition's undoubted significance and certain success, you're really going to make hay with the *Dictionary*. The sales!—and which of us, unworldly as our vocation calls on us to be, will deny that sales are the essence? The publicity! The grants! I wouldn't mind betting there'll be money for a centre, and maybe even a new building in this, before all's said and done.

And quite apart from the interest you're bound to excite far and wide over there (think of the genealogically-inclined!), the appeal on this side of the water alone is going to be mighty.

I know that will probably sound strange to you, in view of the somewhat skewed perspective each side of the hyphen has of the other. But there's always a very simple reason why I say it. Indeed, with diagnoses and analyses of traditions and identities currently taking place in the lounge bars of every summer school in the country, it behoves me to point it out. The fact of the matter is that we're all as hyphenated as bedamned over here as well, and anything that helps us to see the dash in our own eye is greatly to be commended. Anglo-Irish? Man alive, you haven't heard the half of it. Even before history, the Belly Men must have known the Parthalonians. Then, Celts made free with all in sundry. Vikings on top of that. Normans, Scots, Welsh, in no particular order. The Armada. Jews. Huguenots. People of the Palatine. The blow-in tradition. Travellers, if you'll pardon the euphemism. *Droit de seigneur* and *Lex primae noctis* (why pretend?). Don't be talking. Our family tree's the hyphen. A many-branching artifice, with nests for all, especially the ones we'd rather call cuckoos and quare hawks. Who're we trying to cod? "Crazily tangled as the Book of Kells," as the fella said. But sure someone such as yourself, F. X., old stock, could name them out in a song. And will, with the help of God and the three Ryans, Tom, Mick and Gillicks, as my poor grandmother used to say, herself lineally descended from a Cromwellian soldier and mad Fianna Fáil. Modern before our time—our curse, our glory. Now and in time to be ... So who better to speak for us than an American? Tell it like it is, F.X.

And if you need a hand over here getting shopkeepers, heritage centres, and so on, interested in the finished product—anything at all in that line, really—remember, I'm your man.

The Parish and The Dream
Heaney and America, 1969–1987

Michael Allen

"Here no elsewhere underwrites my existence." So wrote Philip Larkin, who had left Ireland for England—"home"—in 1955. The implied aesthetic is akin to (and roughly contemporaneous with) Kavanagh's assumption that creative potential has its tap-root in the "parish" of one's deepest allegiance. But despite the importance of Kavanagh for Heaney's art, such a stance was not empowering for Heaney's generation of Irish poets. On the first occasion that they read together in the mid 60s (in Glengormley, Mahon's "home ground"), Longley, Heaney and Mahon were celebrating a poet, MacNeice, for whom all places were potentially elsewhere. Robert Frost and Theodore Roethke as well as Ted Hughes show, through their influence on the early Heaney, that his writing was not immune to the stimulus of other parishes than rural, regional Ireland. And from his second book to his seventh, as we shall see, America's intermittent presence in Heaney's poetry, alongside England and Ireland, almost suggests that the verse itself was searching out some kind of hegemonic support there.

Vincent Buckley (in *Memory Ireland*) and Dillon Johnston (in the *Colby Quarterly*, 28, 4, 1992) have illustrated how America has figured "in the finances and poetic forms" (Johnston's phrase) of recent Irish poets. Heaney's long-standing respect for two older writers in particular, Kinsella and Montague, suggests that they may have offered him a precedent in seeking such support. It is significant that not just these three, but almost all the writers cited by Johnston as attracting American patronage, and achieving American audiences, come from the Catholic/nationalist tradition (south and north of the border); it was only for such writers that the prospect of a symbiotic relationship with American readers would seem realistic. They shared with

Americans in general an ideological distrust of the colonial power. Moreover, Catholic Irish-Americans, the core of the diaspora for whom President Mary Robinson keeps a light in her window, had established a powerful and distinctive American sub-culture, equating Irishness, for the wider American public, with Catholicism and nationalism. A premium was thus placed on a 'green' Irish identity in American literary circles and may have been augmented by widespread Irish-American recruitment to the teaching and graduate study of Irish writing in the USA. By 1983—when Heaney's American reputation was really catching on—it was by no means only his Irish readers who would respond enthusiastically when he insisted in his Field Day pamphlet 'An Open Letter', "My passport's green".

So it is not surprising that, apart from some stylistic indebtedness to Hart Crane, there is little American presence in the early poetry of Longley and Mahon. Whatever the pan-Irish notions they might have picked up as students in Dublin, they were excluded at the outset from a Hiberno-American rapport by their northern Protestant cultural antecedents. When America does figure in their later poems, it is merely as a place of exile or a launching-pad for home. On the economic front, Mahon has quite recently entered Dillon Johnston's list of major recipients of American patronage and employment with a Lannan Foundation Award; but it is interesting that he does so at a time when he has changed his attitude to Irish poetic locale, rejecting the northern literary regionalism he was still displaying in an interview in *Poetry Ireland Review*, 14, 1985, in favour of the Dublin-centred literary nationalism editorially shared with Peter Fallon in *The Penguin Book of Contemporary Irish Poetry* (1989).

Heaney's way of broaching the possibility was, from the first, very different from that of Montague (who then provided the most notable example of poetic success—particularly in the mid-west—for an Irish poet in America). Brooklyn-born, Montague uses America either autobiographically, as Dillon Johnston has shown, or else to emphasise his place in the cosmopolitan tradition of Irish poetry instituted by Denis Devlin and Thomas MacGreevy. California, in a poem like 'All Legendary Obstacles', functions very much as does Paris throughout *A Chosen Light* (1967), to confirm the mobility and high-cultural credentials of the speaker. These tendencies are merely modified where the poetry is packaged in a more explicitly political way: on the back cover of *The Rough Field* (1972), the prestige of place is given a veneer of radicalism to link Paris, Northern Ireland and Berkeley in 1968:

...the New Road I describe runs through Normandy as well as Tyrone. And experience of agitations in Paris and Berkeley taught me that the violence of disputing factions is more than a local phenomenon.

In contrast, Heaney has always resisted the cosmopolitan self-image. He tends to present himself as the humble worker-craftsman, whether as iconic poem-maker, autobiographical poet, critic or man of letters. His first invocation of America, as he says himself in the essay 'Feeling into Words' in *Preoccupations*, grew out of working assumptions about American literature and culture natural to a teacher of modern literature in higher education in the 60s (though there is no doubt that they would have a special potency for an Irish writer of Heaney's tradition). The concept of the 'American Dream', which extrapolated itself into the teaching situation in Belfast in those days out of texts like *The Great Gatsby* and *Death of a Salesman,* takes on a triple resonance in his work: the phrase is redolent of the emigrant experience (travelling west to the land of opportunity is a powerful idea for an Irish imagination); it accommodates the frontier experience ("Go West, Young Man!") which was rejuvenated in the 60s when space became the New Frontier (the moon-landing occurred in the same year as the publication of Heaney's second book); and, finally, these locational and spatial metaphors shade into the dream of upward mobility, of rags to riches, whereby every Irish-American boy can be president.

In 'Bogland' the final poem of that second book, *Door into the Dark* (1969), Heaney seems to be mediating Kavanagh's inward and "parochial" aesthetic to a potential American audience in Frontier terms: "We have no prairies/To slice a big sun at evening—..." he says and later in the poem "Our pioneers keep striking/Inwards and downwards". The key verbs here, "slice" and "striking", display the kind of ambiguity which the influence of the English poetry of the 60s encouraged in Mahon and Longley as well as Heaney: the incipient violence is extended—in terms reminiscent of the "snug ... gun" of 'Digging'—so that the bog "keeps crusting/*Between the sights* of the sun" (my emphasis). The machismo of the "slightly aggravated young Catholic male," as Heaney called his younger self in an interview with Seamus Deane in 1977, is here offering tribute to that involved in the 'winning' of the West (Heaney's own formulation, as we shall see later). In so far as the imagery resembles that of 'Digging' (or 'The Forge' from which the book's title is taken), the poem is suggesting that violent energies should be harnessed into a creative process of orgasmic potency which may be extrovert (America) or introvert

(Ireland). It is revealing that the "downward", "wet", "soft" qualities on the Irish side of the equation, though easy to interpret, provoke only the most clichéd of implied alternatives on the American side, as though Heaney is saving the obvious binary opposites of these qualities so that he can attribute them to England at the end of the 'Belfast' section of *Preoccupations*.

The poem is, nevertheless, more open to its transatlantic materials than its surface assertiveness would suggest. Its rudimentary plot follows the American settlers westward, with mid-Irish parallels at every point. "*Our* unfenced country" (my emphasis) is the bog; instead of the buffalo, 'we' have "the Great Irish Elk"; instead of Nevada gold, "Butter sunk under" the bog is "recovered". Finally, "waterlogged trunks/Of great firs" are dug up: "logged", in its place in the line, hints at "logging" and the geographic logic of the poem could suggest California Redwood. This narrator, despite the inevitably static Kavanagh aesthetic which he claims to be promoting, has itchy feet. What is more, perhaps tactically, the speaker does not insist that the crowded archaeology of forerunners he has inherited is preferable to the exploitable virgin land (conveniently empty of native Americans), which his imagined New World shares with the last pages of *The Great Gatsby:* "Every layer [our pioneers] strip/seems camped on before." But there is no way of getting him on to the western trail he surreptitiously hankers after: the emigrant first stage of the journey is missing. These submerged frustrations are accommodated, to some extent, in the expressed hope that "The bogholes might be Atlantic seepage". The poem is hinting that commitment to a regional and local culture need not preclude alien modes of apprehension, a culture-flow from elsewhere.

The so-far missing strand in Heaney's version of the American Dream, the emigrant strand, opens up in the final poem of *Wintering Out* (1972), his third book, with the speaker on his way to a residency at Berkeley and the style, under the influence of Gary Snyder, relaxed, narrative and associative, rather than cryptically linguistic. 'Westering' is sub-titled 'In California', to show how far you can go terrestrially in that direction. But the opening lines intimate the larger imaginative dimensions of the journey through the suggestion, in the word "Official", that the moon is now American territory, won as the West was won. And where the infatuated speaker's poetic journey began, how far he has come (in achievement) since his first success as "parochial" poet with the frogs of 'Death of a Naturalist', is also accommodated:

> I sit under Rand McNally's
> 'Official Map of the Moon'—
> The colour of frogskin,
> Its enlarged pores held
>
> Open ...

What have been left behind on this revelatory journey are the reduced "parochial" circumstances of rural Ulster, so dilute in comparison to the present experience that what illuminated the earlier scene hardly seems the same moon:

> my shadow
>
> Neat upon the whitewash
> From her bony shine,
> The cobbles of the yard
> Lit pale as eggs.

When he looks back from this new point of vantage only a "shadow" is left to represent the poet. There is a studied reference in the last two lines here to an earlier page of the collection and to the yard where the 'Servant Boy'—in what was probably Heaney's last unconditional celebration of the Kavanagh aesthetic—came "resentful/and impenitent,/carrying the warm eggs" (emblems of parochially-derived poems).

The journey by road to Shannon, embarkation point for the American west-coast airport where the poem is set, passes through middle Ireland, Kavanagh country, a now "empty amphitheatre", and the travellers seem to leave behind the repression central to its culture: "congregations bent/To the studded crucifix." (I say "seem" because the point-of-view of the "congregations" is also represented: "we drove by/a dwindling interruption", we are told earlier.) The inward pioneering ostensibly evinced in 'Bogland' has been replaced by a more extrovert journey, which seems on the whole to envisage with gusto the dropping away of the Irish Catholic heritage of suffering and repression: "what nails dropped out that hour?" asks the speaker, patently identifying his own 'rooted' predicament with that of the figure on the studded cross. By the end of the poem, however, it is clear which nails have not dropped out. Euphorically, the speaker can "imagine untroubled dust,/A loosening gravity": see the degree of his freedom from the in-turned and rooted Kavanagh aesthetic in terms of the moon as destination. But he (and Jesus) are still only footloose: the hands ("Between my finger and my thumb/The squat pen rests", as the early poem, 'Digging' proclaimed) are still under coercion. Indeed, the apparently colonised moon of the airport map itself bears the stigmata and it suddenly seems possible that, like the Jutland traveller earlier in the volume ('The Tollund Man'), this westward, moon-ward voyager may find himself "lost, unhappy and at home."

These irresolutions are unaddressed in the next book, *North* (1975) which concerns itself with Ireland in its European historical context and with the northern Irish issue. But the kind of north American support and attention that Buckley and Johnston see as available can be read as a sub-text to the subsequent development of the verse. This is apparent at the most basic level in the way that American journals and publishers bulk much larger in the 'Acknowledgements' listings of the volumes from *Field Work* (1979) on, than in *North*. Poetry in the mid-70s is becoming ever less iconic, ever more an extension or equivalent of autobiography. In a poem addressed to Seamus Deane in the earlier volume (published as Heaney prepared to take up an academic post in Dublin), the year in California is given a retrospective aura of intellectual glamour:

> ... Then Belfast, and then Berkeley.
> Here's two on's are sophisticated,
> Dabbling in verses till they have become
> A life ...
>
> ('Singing School')

Field Work looks both back and forward. The dedication of the 'Glanmore Sonnets' (to "Ann Saddlemyer, our heartiest welcomer") is a tribute to the way that (Canadian) scholar made a work-place in Wicklow available to the poet in the three years after he gave up his previous academic post in Belfast. And Heaney's 'Elegy' for Robert Lowell, in the same volume, implicitly recognises that the route to a New England sphere of influence and the possibility of a ready audience for his learning and his poetry at Harvard in this period were opened up in his mind through his friendship with that poet.

Such transatlantic presences, like the hegemonic possibility they represented, must have seemed unproblematic compared with the irreconcilable tensions of the Irish situation. *Wintering Out* (1972), despite its recognition of the need to "uproot" ('A Northern Hoard'), was powerfully committed to the imaginative resources of its region, scrupulous in its ecumenical good-will; but this did not mean that Heaney, as a liberal nationalist, could respond positively when one of the two Protestant dedicatees of that book, Michael Longley, invited him, in a verse letter published a year later, to share the benefits of the Act of Union. On the other hand, *North* (1975) openly committed itself to a liberal nationalist agenda; and, two years later, in an interview with his former schoolmate in *Crane Bag*, Seamus Deane, the dedicatee of the book's central statement of literary fraternity, 'Singing School', was demanding that Heaney adopt a more radical nationalist position. Such pressures seemed to imply two alternative hegemonic possibilities—alignment with the "...Northern Irish 'Renaissance'", as it was later to be represented in England by Morrison and Motion's *Penguin Book of Contemporary British Poetry*, or with the radically nationalist Deane-centred Irish groupings which energised *Crane Bag* and Field Day. The Kavanagh parochial aesthetic (essentially apolitical as Heaney himself noted, when writing in *Preoccupations*, about 'The Sense of Place') offered one way of temporising with these extremes. The American option provided another, a kind of adjustable counterweight to either or both of the opposed cultural imperatives which haunt the prose and verse of the time.

In the 'Elegy' for Robert Lowell, we see the American poet's influence at both intertextual and autobiographical levels launching the speaker on his most substantive westward journey so far, "fear of water" paling into insignificance beside the euphoria with which the verse responds to the communicated rhetoric of the 'Dream':

> As you swayed the talk
> and rode on the swaying tiller
> of yourself, ribbing me
> about my fear of water
> what was not within your empery?
> You drank America
> like the heart's
> iron vodka ...

The word "America" functions here with the enigmatically liturgical force that it always carries in the literature of the Dream: at the end of Bellow's *The Adventures of Augie March* for instance. So advocated, and by such an inspiring patron, the potentially emigrant journey was made to seem no more terrifying than the familiar archipelagic crossing in the opposite direction (cf. Mahon, *Night Crossing*) from Belfast to Liverpool:

> You were our night ferry
> thudding in a big sea,
> the whole craft ringing
> with an armourer's music
> the course set wilfully across
> the ungovernable and dangerous ...

The suggestion is still that violent energies are to be harnessed and that the courage and determination which might be required of a "slightly aggravated young Catholic male" on the home front are also required on the westward journey. Heaney could valorise the *quasi*-emigrant entrepreneurial impulse because professional success for the northern Catholic has political significance. It represents a triumph for the liberal (non-violent) nationalist cause in demonstrating, within the Catholic community, that social and economic advantage can be gained in peaceable and constitutional rather than revolutionary ways.

The next book, *Station Island* (1984), seems to take several steps backwards (a frequent strategy with Heaney), relocating the vocational quest—wherein the protagonist is allowed a childlike earnestness—among the penitential rituals of middle Ireland out of which Kavanagh had fashioned *Lough Derg*. It is not surprising, however, if one looks back to 'Westering', to find the Irish/American cultural tensions I have been following dramatised in a key poem. There is a conflict of loyalties, for the poet-speaker of 'Making Strange', between the embarrassed incoherence of his Co. Derry farmer-father and the sophistication of a literary visitor from America, Louis Simpson. Just as it was important that Lowell featured as the initiator of a stylistic trend that Heaney was momentarily following, as well as an inspiring friend, so it is important that Simpson, while he provides in poems like 'American Poetry' and 'Walt Whitman at Bear Mountain' a distinctive American idiom for Heaney to play off his own style against, can still, by insisting that America is his adopted country, as he does in the Preface to his *Collected Poems*, offer Heaney a possible alter-ego in his *quasi*-emigrant quest.

The speaker in 'Making Strange' is initially paralysed by the need to introduce "the one with his travelled intelligence" to "the other" (his father) and to his own "parish", to "these eyes and puddles and stones". The poem itself is an uneasy blend of the iconic and the autobiographical and, in an improbable mode directly inherited from Kavanagh's poem, 'Temptation in Harvest', a mediating voice comes out of "the field across the road", urging Heaney on the one hand to "Be adept and be dialect,/tell of this wind coming past the zinc hut ..." (i.e. continue to capitalise on the "parochial") and on the other hand to "love the cut of this travelled one" (a poetic equal this time rather than a genial patron like Lowell). At first sight, Heaney might seem to be indulging here in the kind of aestheticised cosmopolitanism one sometimes finds in Montague. But the naivety with which he characterises his speaker is balanced, through adjective and simile, with elements of the 'noble savage' in the American visitor: "[his] tawny containment,/his speech like the twang of a bowstring." The speaker's first need in realising their potential equality is (as in 'Elegy') for courage to transcend the tried parochial aesthetic:

> Go beyond what's reliable
> in all that keeps pleading and pleading
> these eyes and puddles and stones,
> and recollect how bold you were
>
> when I visited you first
> with departures you cannot go back on

says the Muse. The "making strange" (which, in the vocabulary of an Irish family, would be a phrase describing a child behaving peculiarly in the presence of a stranger) is reversed in its implication by the requirements of a relationship with the representative of another culture:

> I found myself driving the stranger
>
> through my own country, adept
> at dialect, reciting my pride
> in all that I knew, that began to make strange
> at that same recitation.

The materials of the poetry may still be "my own country", "all that I knew" (cf. 'The Forge': "All I know is ..."), but access on equal terms to a new audience (of which Simpson is here representative) is recognised by the poem as necessary to produce new "departures", an adjusted aesthetic.

The adjustment in question had been in process from about 1979, when Heaney began teaching creative writing at Harvard for one semester a year (spending the rest of his time in Ireland). He was publishing widely in American journals and, at once, cementing literary relationships and confirming a New England audience through his association as contributor and guest-editor with a New England magazine, *Ploughshares*. In 1984, he became both Boylston Professor of Rhetoric at Harvard and presented there, as his Phi Beta Kappa offering, the poem 'Alphabets' (later to appear in *The Haw Lantern* [1987]). At the centre of the poem, and treated with some irony, stands the prospective Boylston Professor of Rhetoric:

> The globe has spun. He stands in a wooden O.
> He alludes to Shakespeare. He alludes to Graves.

The first sentence, despite the irony, is not entirely free from portentousness. It encapsulates at once the speaker's westward journey from the Co. Derry "parish" of the earlier poetry, and his journey in time from an education at the hands of a teacher who is recognisably "Miss Walls" of 'Death of a Naturalist'. As in 'Westering', the image of the moon-journey enhances the speaker's vertiginous sense of his own spatial and social transportation from Co. Derry farmyard to Harvard lecture-hall:

> As from his small window
> The astronaut sees all he has sprung from,
> The risen, aqueous, singular lucent O
> Like a magnified and buoyant ovum-
>
> Or like my own wide pre-reflective stare
> All agog at the plasterer on his ladder
> Skimming our gable ...

But the "parish" as a reservoir of mimetic possibilities (which made Heaney modify rather than jettison the Kavanagh aesthetic in 'Making Strange') is now seen as a total anachronism:

> Time has bulldozed the school and school window.
> Balers drop bales like printouts where stooked sheaves
>
> Made lambdas on the stubble once at harvest
> And the delta face of each potato pit
> Was patted straight and moulded against frost.
> All gone ...

And, interestingly, with the "parish" gone, the idea of an American 'elsewhere' ceases to be pressing. Implicit and exemplified in these lines is the shift to the non-mimetic and self-reflexive aesthetic which governs the recent poetry. It is as though the poet has here lifted out a strand in his own development, contemplated it, refocussed it, and turned from the subject entirely.

It was at about this time that one of Vincent Buckley's informants found the opinion common back in Ireland that Heaney was "not an Irish poet; he's a Yank now". Buckley himself formulates a contrary, but equally unsubstantiated view, that Heaney, like other Irish poets, was exploiting in America his 'native' Irishness to achieve a social elevation comparable with that from working class to upper middle class (together with a sophistication which was continental and the experience and income to match). In 1986, Terence Brown suggested in *Poetry Ireland Review* that Buckley's general thesis (that the complex fate of such Irish poets as Heaney and Montague was "not to become Americans but to be Irish in relation to America") deserved exploration. But it probably reflects little more than a knee-jerk response to reports like this from the US Information Service's international magazine, *Dialogue* (76, 2, 1987):

> It was a pleasure, too, last spring, to join the annual dinner of the Signet Society, a 116-year-old club for undergraduates and professors. The guests sat back at their tables in the Faculty Club—pale faces, red faces, elegant shocks of white hair, the half-childlike faces of adolescents, a colourful punk hairdo or two, and everyone in evening clothes—and listened silently to a string trio of superb undergraduate musicians.
>
> Later, the Irish poet Seamus Heaney, Harvard's Boylston Professor of Rhetoric, recited some of his verses, which sounded as if Yeats had come back to life; and then Helen Vendler, a professor of English, told everyone what Heaney meant. At one point, a great silver bowl of champagne went around the room, and hundreds of people sipped from it. And still later, at the Signet's clubhouse, the undergraduates got intelligently rowdy. They obviously felt, as such undergraduates do, that they were special, as they were.
>
> And Heaney spoke the first lines of his poem on Harvard:
>
> A spirit moved. John Harvard walked the yard.
> The atom lay unsplit, the west unwon,
> The books stood open and the gates unbarred.

My own interest here is in how the passage from an (uncollected) poem, recited in such circumstances, shows Heaney in the American 80s (when the whole concept of the Dream has been transformed by the sense of America as a mosaic, a plurality of co-equal and hyphenated groupings) still tying together her westward journey, technological advance and (by implication) upward mobility, in a way conceived of in Ireland nearly 20 years earlier.

Foremost among the creative benefits to him of the on-going American experience (Heaney is reported as saying in 1987 in Thomas Foster's study of the poet) was the achievement of "a certain distance from your first self". What is more, Heaney argues that this is particularly necessary to a northern Irish poet, which is clearly how he still sees himself. It is interesting that Paul Muldoon, a younger northern Irish poet now resident in the United States, dedicates to Heaney a prefatory poem placed immediately before his own deconstructive version of the American Dream, 'Madoc' (1990). In it, a bustling, expatriate Muldoon, crossing New York, nearly loses his *eel*-skin briefcase (my italics) and the poem inside it. The briefcase symbolises the desire for upward mobility as patently as does the one in Ellison's *Invisible Man*: its sudden "supple" impulse to "strike out" for "the 'open' sea" by way of the East River, however, serves (like a great deal of sly intertextuality in the volume) to relate Muldoon to an undeniable poetic precursor who was also his predecessor on the transatlantic route. Muldoon, after all, began "parochially" writing out of his "own little postage stamp" of Co. Armagh (though it has to be said that it was sometimes unaccountably tinctured with American images and *mores* from the very start). His career, from rural beginnings to university in Belfast to Faber/Farrar, Straus, Giroux publication, to employment by American universities has closely paralleled Heaney's.

The eel to which our attention is being drawn appears in the older poet's 'Beyond Sargasso' (1969), and has a homing instinct which inevitably leads it back to Lough Neagh, a landmark of Heaney's "parish":

>   he drifted
> into motion half-way
> across the Atlantic,
> sure as the satellite's
> insinuating pull
> in the ocean, as true
> to his orbit.

It appears again in *Station Island* (1984) to suggest a "parochial" colouring to the "signatures of your own frequency" which the poet hopes to transmit: "elver gleams in the dark of the whole sea". Muldoon, while sharing with Heaney an underlying readiness to reverse the upward and Westward direction of the Dream is eager to register his vote (in characteristically oblique fashion) against the inexorable "pull" of any "parish"; hence the force given by the emphatic syntax, its final position in the poem and its intertextual quotation marks to "the 'open' sea":

The Briefcase
for Seamus Heaney

I held the briefcase at arm's length from me;
the oxblood or liver
eelskin with which it was covered
had suddenly grown supple.

I'd been waiting in line for the cross-town
bus when an almighty cloudburst
left the sidewalk a raging torrent.

And though it contained only the first
inkling of this poem, I knew I daren't
set the briefcase down
to slap my pockets for an obol—

for fear it might slink into a culvert
and strike out along the East River
for the sea. By which I mean the 'open' sea.

Derek Mahon's Cultural Marginalia

Colin Graham

> The beyond is neither a new horizon, nor a leaving behind of the past ... Beginnings and endings may be the sustaining myths of the middle years; but in the *fin de siècle*, we find ourselves in the moment of transit where space and time cross to produce complex figures of difference and identity, past and present, inside and outside, inclusion and exclusion.[1]
>
> —Homi K. Bhabha

Derek Mahon's poetry can be read as an examination of movement—from the centre to the periphery, from here to elsewhere, from culture to literature. However, his poetry's ambivalence at "the question of belonging"[2] becomes neither a 'leaving' nor a 'beyond' but a circulation around 'identity', a revelation of a reluctance to sacrifice the securities of the 'inside' in 'the middle years'—and, ultimately, an argument over the existence of a *fin de siècle*.

Mahon's 'Glengormley' is at the core of his initial restlessness, the beginnings of "anthropological concerns"[3] which eventually knot themselves inexorably into his epistemology:

> 'Wonders are many and none is more wonderful than man'
> Who has tamed the terrier, trimmed the hedge
> And grasped the principle of the watering-can.
> Clothes-pegs litter the window ledge
> And the long ships lie in clover. Washing lines
> Shake out linen over the chalk thanes.
>
> Now we are safe from monsters, and the giants
> Who tore up sods twelve miles by six
> And hurled them out to sea to become islands

Can worry us no more. The sticks
And stones that once broken bones will not now harm
A generation of such sense and charm.[4]

Civilised irony is the necessary trope of the second stanza, as 'us' and the (so far) implied 'I', belonging and self, are strung on the tension between cultural place and displaced individual. In Bhabha's terms, 'Glengormley' holds its beginnings by notionally making them endings: the myths which 'we' are—but only ironically—"safe" from are thus both origins and continuities. The poem's historical teleology is able to self-authenticate itself in the 'ethnicity' of history while playing on the banality of modernity.

  No saint or hero,
Landing at night from the conspiring seas,
Brings dangerous tokens to the new era—
Their sad names linger in the histories.

"Linger" drawls here, as an act of conservation and preservation, an avowal of history as place, where the "new era" both is and is not pieced together from those ambivalent "dangerous tokens" (the 'paradox' history sees in myths as empowered falsehoods). History as "an impossible condition and a salutary irony"[5] is 'resolved' in a juxtaposition of savage/nostalgic past against bourgeois/impersonal present; a cultural tension which is a partial recipe for an ethnic history theme park.

'Glengormley', in its titles as in the poem, knows its circumscription; 'I' and 'we' jostle and compete without fear of the ground shifting beneath them. "By/Necessity, if not by choice, I live here too", confirms the space ("here") and solidifies the perpetual dialogue of I/ we ("too") on this particular territory. Yet 'elsewhere', other spaces, are glimpsed in 'Glengormley'; the "conspiring seas" serve at once as defining boundary and an insistent reminder of the other, the margin at which even the implication of the continual movement from instance to generality must check itself (Mahon's use of the sea as boundary, void *and* place is discussed further below).

While 'Glengormley' is central (to the process of self-preservation in a context of marginalisation), Mahon subsequently moves to margins the better to see centrality. 'The Chinese Restaurant in Portrush' is one of few poems that looks to apparently unco-opted cultures as light on the cultural dialogics of Northern Ireland[6]:

> Before the holidaymakers comes the spring
> Softening the sharp air of the coast
> In time for the first 'invasion'.
> Today the place is as it might have been,
> Gentle and almost hospitable.[7]

The almost-Betjeman is almost a pose, but the "coast" and "'invasion'", the quaintness of "holidaymakers", cement the new nostalgia for post-war simplicity, itself undercut with a half-critical nod towards its own forms of knowledge ("might have been" ... "almost hospitable": these can in turn, however, be used unproblematically to constitute the world-that-[never]-was). The first section of the poem delineates its historical knowledge through this remembrance, perhaps hinting only at the mythologies inherent in 'Glengormley' in the "old wolfhound [dozing] in the sun"; it is then a possibility which only the reader can dare wake into significance.

The cultural provenance in this first section of 'The Chinese Restaurant in Portrush' is hardly removed from that of 'Glengormley', but it serves to reiterate before the movement in the second section:

> While I sit with my paper and prawn chow-mien
> Under a framed photograph of Hong Kong
> The proprietor of the Chinese restaurant
> Stands at the door as if the world were young
> Watching the first yacht hoist a sail—
> An ideogram on sea-cloud—and the light
> Of heaven upon the mountains of Donegal;
> And whistles a little tune, dreaming of home.

The final "home" catches hold of and encircles the shifts these lines describe. But what places does the restaurateur have? In the scheme of "I sit", "he stands", how is 'I' redefined (he, after all, is ultimately defined only by not being 'home')? The lines "An ideogram on sea-cloud—and the light/Of heaven on the mountains of Donegal" pull together the two voices. On to the cultural context of the "ideogram" are added the clipped sounds of "ideogram on sea-cloud", with a missing definite article which leaves the phrase unhappily poised over 'poetic' Chinese or pidgin English. The caesura is significantly weighted against the open sounds and stretched rhythm of the enjambement from "and the light" to "Donegal". The poem thus structures itself around these clear definitions of I/he, in terms of language, poetics and culture and hence leads very deliberately to the final two lines forcing "Donegal" and "home" to stare at each other, challenged to fit the dichotomies set up ahead of them, or define the gap between them. The result is prosaic enough, but confrontational and essential; from the logic of this perspective what can be seen from the doorway is the 'home' of the 'I' who sits under the "photograph of Hong Kong". Truly displaced is the restaurateur, who has merely a representation of "home" (and a second-hand representation in Mahon's poetics). For this "I" there is a logic at work which sees Donegal inevitably as "home". A crucial issue, and pushed further in the worlds "heaven" and "dreaming"—is Donegal available, resolvable, only in the currency, to borrow a phrase, of "the shadow and sheen of a moleskin mountain"?[8]

Following the "conspiring seas" in 'Glengormley', the coast in 'The Chinese Restaurant in Portrush' signifies "'invasion'". Having gone to the land borders the sea remains ("The kettle yearns for the/Mountain, the soap for the sea"[9]), and Mahon's 'North Wind: Portrush', from *The Hunt by Night* (1982), turns to this dissolving and threatening 'presence'.[10]

'North Wind: Portrush' rehearses the traits of 'Glengormley', the "wrapped-up bourgeoisie" battered on "this benighted coast". The wind

> ... works itself into the mind
> Like the high keen of a lost
> Lear-spirit in agony
> Condemned for eternity
>
> To wander cliff and cove
> Without comfort, without love.

It may be over-reading to see, in this tragic figure of dispossession in his own land (King Lear), a paranoia underlying the ideological ethos of the *bourgeoisie* the poem describes, through the 'alienation' of Ulster Protestantism which has become a commonplace in Irish political science.[11] The cliff is, of course, in literary terms, at Dover, and the intertextual web is further complicated in 'Brighton Beach' which, in turn, alludes to Matthew Arnold's 'Dover Beach'. The notion of the edge of the land as the place where tensions are tested, where ideological and cultural cohesions undergo a meteorological and metaphorical tempest (Prospero and King Lear appear, the deceived and the declining) is encapsulated in what is shored against the ruins:

> The wrapped-up bourgeoisie
> Hardened by wind and sea.
> The newspapers are late
> But the milk shines in its crate.
>
> Everything swept so clear
> By tempest, wind and rain!
> Elated, you might believe
> That this was the first day—
> A false sense of reprieve,
> For the climate is here to stay.

The MacNeicean detail of the materialities which modernity produces as ineffective ammunition to slow its own 'progress' ("the milk shines in its crate", against the newspapers being late) is a contradiction implying a new kind of teleology which continually reabsorbs 'history'; for this reason, it is rejected. If "the climate is here to stay", there is still the natural, the original, the environmental, to stand over against material culture. And so the circle of 'Glengormley', re-positioned but undisrupted, could perpetuate, holding grimly to the "sustaining myths of the middle years", except that 'North Wind: Portrush' does involve a momentary breach of that encapsulating perspective:

> Then, from the ship we say
> Is the lit town where we live
> (Our whiskey-and-forecast world),
> A smaller ship that sheltered
> All night in the restless bay
> Will weigh anchor and leave.
>
> What did they think of us
> During their brief sojourn?
> A string of lights on the prom
> Dancing mad in the storm—
> Who lives in such a place?
> And will they ever return?

And in keeping with the wrench in achieving this perspective from the blurred places beyond the definitions of the land, the poem's certainties fade, the land becomes a ship, the "they" in the final quoted line needs re-reading to establish it as the 'unfortunates' of the now Titanic-like cultural *malaise* which the actual ship observes. The price of being prised off the land's culture embeddedness is that the backward look dissolves the stabilities which "wrapped-up" and "hardened" (again MacNeicean).

The Hunt By Night could be read as a movement beginning with 'North Wind: Portrush', touching the microcosmic 'Rathlin Island' ("the whole island a sanctuary", and where there is a "bleak/Reminder of a metaphysical wind"[12]) and moving to the marginal space beyond (at least physically) the Irish context in 'Brighton Beach'.

'Brighton Beach' utilises the same tropes of northern Irishness underpinning 'Glengormley', 'The Chinese Restaurant in Portrush' and 'North Wind: Portrush':

> Remember those awful parties
> In dreary Belfast flats,
> The rough sectarian banter
> Of Lavery's back bar,
> The boisterous take-aways
> And moonlight on wet slates?

It also revisits the discomfort of Donegal raised in 'The Chinese Restaurant in Portrush':

> Remember the time we drove
> To Donegal and you talked
> For hours to fishermen
> You had worked with, while I,
> Out of my depth in these
> Waters, loafed on the quays?

And Donegal here becomes the epistemological insecurity which was previously only the sea's ("Out of my depth in these/Waters"), continuing as a source of cultural schizophrenia by nestling in the 'authenticity' of stanzas beginning "Remember ...", "Remember ...", "Remember ...", and the triumvirate of dreary-rough-lovable Belfast, muddy-Muckamore, in-touch-with-itself-Donegal (urbanity/rurality/the west).

Again, the structure of the poem depends upon a second part which 'revises', looking towards "a thousand *deux-chevaux*" in France from Brighton beach:

> Europe thrives, but the off-shore
> Islanders year by year
> Decline, the spirit of empire

> Fugitive as always.
> Now, in its rancorous peace,
> Should come the spirit of place.
>
> Too late, though, for already
> Places as such are dead
> Or nearly; the loved sea
> Reflects banality.

Matthew Arnold similarly placed himself at the point of descent where the knowledge of what once was ("The Sea of Faith"; in Mahon, "the spirit of place") can only be utilised as a necessity for what is needed now:

> ... now I only hear
> Its melancholy, long, withdrawing roar
> Retreating, to the breath
> Of the night-wind, down the vast edges drear
> And naked shingles of the world.[13]

And, as Arnold retreats into "let us be true/To one another!" against the tide when "ignorant armies clash by night", so Mahon's aesthetic, poetics and literariness pit the faint possibilities nostalgia lives on against displacement, disruption and difference:

> Too late, though, for already
> Places as such are dead
> Or nearly.

The deliberate deflation of the half-line is careful not to overstate to the point of resurrection the ideal which still mouths, Demosthenes-like, at 'history'.

Mahon's poetry can be placed at the intersection of what Bhabha calls "the middle years" and the *fin de siècle*—not specific points in history, but states of ideology, understanding and culture. The perceptible movement in Mahon's poetry from centrality to marginality, played out on the imagined and real borders and the seashores is rehearsed in 'The Last Resort' (the title itself an Arnoldian stand against time):

> Years later, the same dim
> Resort has grown dimmer

As if some centrifugal
Force, summer by summer,
Has moved it further
From an imagined centre.[14]

Here, at least (at last), the "centre" is "imagined", but it holds tenuously and crucially in many of Mahon's poems, so that past is valorised over present, inclusion over exclusion, identity over difference and, in peculiar forms, myth (as origin and authenticity) over history (as modernity, even postmodernity). And the apparently inverted valorisation of literature over culture works only because 'culture' is material modernity, literature originary and unmolested, standing on the shore with Arnold and Mahon:

Prospero and his people never
Came to these stormy parts:
Yet, blasting the subtler arts,
That weird plaintive voice
Choirs now and for ever.[15]

Notes

[1]Homi K. Bhabha, *The Location of Culture* (London: Routledge, 1994), p. 1.
[2]Kathleen Shields, 'Derek Mahon's Poetry of Belonging', *Irish University Review*, 24:1 (1994), 67-79 (p. 67).
[3]Eamonn Hughes, 'Introduction: Northern Ireland—border country' in *Culture and Politics in Northern Ireland* (Milton Keynes: Open University Press, 1991), pp. 1-12 (p. 5).
[4]Derek Mahon, 'Glengormley', *Poems 1962-1978* (Oxford: Oxford University Press, 1986), p. 1.
[5]Edna Longley, *Poetry in the Wars* (Newcastle-Upon-Tyne: Bloodaxe Books, 1986), p. 204.
[6]See, for example, Frank Ormsby, 'Street Life: 1 Near Windsor Park', 'Home' in *A Northern Spring* (London: Secker & Warburg, 1986), pp. 48 & 54.
[7]Mahon, *Poems 1962-1978*, p. 100.
[8]Louis MacNeice, 'Neutrality', *Collected Poems* (London: Faber & Faber, 1979), p. 202.
[9]Derek Mahon, 'Nostalgias', *Poems 1962-1978*, p. 68.
[10]Derek Mahon, *The Hunt By Night* (Oxford: Oxford University Press, 1982), p. 12.
[11]See especially Steve Bruce, *The Edge of the Union: The Ulster Loyalist Political Vision* (Oxford: Oxford University Press, 1994). A wider context is given by

Feargal Cochrane in 'Ourselves Alone', *Fortnight* 326 (March 1994), pp 16-18.
[12] Derek Mahon, *The Hunt By Night*, p. 16.
[13] Matthew Arnold, 'Dover Beach', *Arnold: Poems*, selected by Kenneth Allot (Harmondsworth: Penguin, 1985), p. 181.
[14] Derek Mahon, 'Autobiographies: 3 The Last Resort', *Poems 1962-1978*, p. 90.
[15] Derek Mahon, 'North Wind: Portrush', *Poems 1962-1978*, p. 13.

Shaping Special Worlds
Louis MacNeice's Anti-Parables

Kathleen McCracken

> If this story is a parable, perhaps everyone takes his own meaning from it and reads his own life into it.
> — John Steinbeck, *The Pearl*

One of Louis MacNeice's favourite sayings was "If you always see through things you never see into them". R.D. Smith has suggested that this distinction in ways of perceiving corresponds to MacNeice's 'split' personality: the acute analyst, scrutinising surface realities, and the creative maker, endeavouring to order discord and construe connections between the specific and the universal.[1] Smith's schematic is constructive, insofar as it locates in the complex divisions which informed MacNeice's life—national, religious, political, philosophical—an argument between the opposing concepts of an absolute first principle and continual, inimitable flux. While MacNeice may have wished for the certitude of the former, he found in reality 'parables' of the latter. This paper argues that MacNeice's experiments with parable writing for radio and the stage are literary constructions which explore this pervasive dualism in a concrete form.

MacNeice's choice of the term parable as opposed to symbolism, allegory, fable, fantasy or myth to describe the kind of writing he set out to discuss in the 1963 Clark Lectures[2], may appear arbitrary, largely because it is not 'scientifically' generic, but it does in fact carry important connotations and supports the claims specific to his usage. He expresses misgivings about taking up the term because "it suggests something much too narrow for my purposes, namely the parables of the New Testament" (*Varieties of Parable*, p. 1). Yet part of the reason he selected it was to challenge the 'enigmatical' or 'dark' quality traditionally associated with parable. His insistence on *this* term has to do with parable's formal characteristics. In his poems and in his plays, MacNeice had espoused a type of double-level writing suitable for the expression of his 'sceptical beliefs'. He was searching for a label to identify a quality which he felt his work shared with other writers from Spenser to Golding. Parable, MacNeice discovered, allowed him to develop a fictional narrative and, at the same time, to make serious topical statements in a way that the prescriptive format of allegory could not.

The identifying attribute of the MacNeicean parable is the fabrication of what he described as a "special world". The use of the adjective 'special' to signal the concrete level of parable, while it indicates the doubleness of the narrative, reveals little or nothing about the world it refers to other than that it is—probably—fictional. It does, however, assume a specific denotation: multivalent allegory declared as such by reduction, removal of detail and strange juxtapositions which demand critical activity by the reader. The label is deliberately equivocal, drawing attention to the story without assigning it definite dimensions, and must be questioned when, in the majority of MacNeice's parables, that world remains largely realistic. Yet if it is an evasion, it is also a means of expanding the possible significance of the fictive world, making the reader, and not the writer, responsible for drawing and acting upon conclusions.

What features constitute MacNeice's parables? In what respects are they derivative of, or distinct from, traditional or surrealist parables? The basic criteria to which a work must conform if, in MacNeice's view, it is to be considered a parable are threefold: it must operate on two levels continuously and consistently, the surface or story level must be a projection of a special world which bears some relation to the real world, and it must proclaim the writer's "belief-experience-attitude" (p. 22). These attributes, however, disclose little about MacNeice's concept of parable and point to the central problem in his discussion of the form: the lack of a single, clear definition of what a parable is. At times it appears interchangeable with allegory (pp. 26-7); elsewhere allegory seems to provide a framework for a series of parables (pp. 34-41). MacNeice's indecisiveness about the nature of parable is reflected in his own plays. *The Dark Tower*, subtitled 'a radio parable play', might be construed as allegory, although MacNeice argues that one-for-one correspondence is here surpassed by the concrete quality of the story.[3] Other plays, including *The Careerist*, *One Eye Wild* and *One for the Grave*, are classified as "psycho-morality", "a romance in commonplace" and "a modern morality".[4] Apart from uncertainty, this inexactitude suggests that MacNeice intended his usage of the term to have a general, as opposed to a narrow, application. By virtue of its elusiveness, parable could become a singularly inclusive genre.

MacNeice comes closest to defining his brand of parable writing when he states:

> ... one very valuable kind of parable, and particularly so today, is the kind which on the surface may not look like a parable at all. This is a kind of double-level writing, or, if you prefer it, sleight-of-hand. It has been much used by poets and one could make out a case that all worthwhile poetry involves something of the sort.
>
> (pp. 2-3)

If it does not "look like a parable at all", how is it to be identified? One response MacNeice might have given is by its form. The form will necessarily be double-level, a pronounced plot-line as opposed to character development giving shape to the writer's beliefs. The subject will be appropriate to this structure, consisting of a manifest and a latent value. MacNeice stresses that these two planes (story and theme, image and significance) must be inseparable. The special world and the system of beliefs it represents are held in equilibrium, so that on the surface the work "may not look like a parable at all".

The argument in *Varieties of Parable* and in MacNeice's second major critical study, *Modern Poetry*[5], emphasises that a precise balance must exist between form and the writer's beliefs. Beliefs, he asserts in an article entitled 'The Poet in England Today', are an intrinsic part of life and thus of poetry. But he repeatedly warns that beliefs must not be allowed to monopolise poetry, turn it into an instrument of propaganda. Although he skirts the seemingly unavoidable issue of whether certain historical or cultural settings (the context for a system of beliefs) exist for parable as they do, for example, for blank verse, the epistolary novel or the travelogue, his contention that the form cannot, nor should it be, neatly disengaged from beliefs is sound.[6]

In *Varieties of Parable*, MacNeice does as original writers often do: he creates a theory by which his writing can be enjoyed. In attempting to assess works which may or may not be parabolic, he is in fact devising a personal aesthetic which provides the intellectual groundwork for his poems and plays. Thus, in selecting those works scrutinised in the Clark lectures and in calling many of his own pieces parables, he bends the genre to suit his purposes. What we discover in *Varieties of Parable* is an appropriation and redefinition of the term 'parable'.

MacNeice's attraction to double-level writing began at an early age. In his autobiography, he recounts how as a child he created fantasy worlds to share with his sister Elizabeth, and immersed himself in reading fairy tales.[7] Some of his earliest poems and stories, printed in the Marlborough school magazine, are youthful essays in the direction of parable writing. By 1946, however, his poetics had been firmly established. The introductory note to *The Dark Tower* reads as a manifesto on parable writing. He renounces single-plane writing as an inexact representation of complex physical and psychological worlds:

> My own impression is that pure 'realism' is in our time almost played out, though most works of fiction of course will remain realistic *on the surface*. The single-track mind and the single-plane novel or play are almost bound to falsify the world in which we live. The fact that there is method in madness and the fact that there is fact in fantasy (and equally fantasy in 'fact') have been brought home to us not only by Freud and other psychologists but by events themselves. This being so, reportage can no longer masquerade as art ... Man does after all live by symbols.[8]

What is meant by "single-plane" is not entirely clear. MacNeice seems to have in mind writing which offers simply to represent, the nearest example being newspaper reportage or documentary. The fallacy in this argument, however, is that all writing is to some extent dual-plane. What *is* obvious is that, for MacNeice, parable-art offers a useful mechanism for the investigation of states of mind, in particular subversive or irrational states of mind, rather than a means of advertising political ideology.

MacNeice is commonly regarded as the 'apolitical' element in the MacSpaunday group. While he was not without political opinion (as poems like 'Valediction' and 'Neutrality', or the plays *The Dark Tower* and *Traitors In Our Way* indicate[9]), the catalogue of contemporary 'isms' provided no philosophy to which he could comfortably subscribe. In the present context, MacNeice's "sceptical vision" gives rise to a crucial question: what sort of parable is likely to be produced when a writer eschews strong personal or commonly-shared beliefs? I would suggest that the answer is something which can be called, with some precision, *anti-*parable, a genre which in MacNeice's usage is designed less to impart a particular moral or meaning than to question and analyse existing systems. His considered adoption of parable may be seen as evidence of the *desire* to write literature of conviction under the pressure of the acknowledged impossibility of achieving precisely that end. And this desire corresponds to an impulse, implicit in much of his writing, to hold faith in a divine 'other', an absolute principle that—tragically and ironically—is inevitably negated at the moment of its inception.

Anti-parable, as I apply the term in this study, does not denote a parable without meaning, that is non-instructive or consistently unresolved. Instead, it implies a shift in emphasis from result to process, from conclusion to question, from uncritical acceptance to acute response. While the intrinsic interest of the surface story initially engages the listener's attention, the recovery of meaning through a correlation of secondary world and primary content becomes the real object of the drama. Yet because a single correct reading of this type of parable will be impossible (and, indeed, undesirable), the attempt to impose precise meaning becomes a 'meaningless' response, an ironic re-enactment of the human condition. To be content with, and to delight in, the pluralism and indefinability of life is the first 'lesson' the MacNeicean anti-parable seeks to impart.

In practice, MacNeice's dramatic anti-parables are a continuation of the dual-plane writing he had begun to experiment with in the stage plays of the early 30s. His concern in the radio plays of the 40s and 50s is not only to accommodate a larger and more popular audience, but to discover the possibilities afforded by adapting parable, traditionally a verbal mode of communication, to a medium for which it is pre-eminently suited.

Although MacNeice's first attempts at dramatising anti-parables were stage plays, the majority were written for radio. His involvement in sound radio was one factor which originally attracted him to parable writing:

> ... it was the medium itself propelling me ... sound radio, thanks to the lack of any visual element, is very well able, when attempting fantasy, to achieve the necessary suspension of disbelief ... it tempts one, more than the stage does, and far more than television, to experiment in modern morality plays or parable plays.
>
> (p. 9)

The chief advantage that radio has over the stage and television is that it is non-visual. In a video-orientated culture, this is more likely to be thought of as a disadvantage but, as MacNeice points out, once divorced from the physical interferences of sets and characters, and of the printed page, speech takes on a different dimension—it is intensified and purified.[10] And it is in this context that his frequent references to the parabolic story as a special world become meaningful. Because the listening audience is not provided with a ready-made theatrical environment, it is required to construct out of words and music alone a world that is unique, private and wholly convincing, that is indeed 'special'.

Speaking of the adaptability of particular stage plays to radio production, MacNeice notes that "the air brings out certain virtues in them which we are apt to miss when our eyes are working full time", and cites Sartre's *No Exit* as having "actually gained in horror ... because one could not see the victims".[11] Whereas the theatre must realise the fantasy element so literally that it risks making the special world comic, even ludicrous, the mental and subjective visualisation elicited by radio bolsters the analogy between actual and imaginary phenomena. Speaking of *The Dark Tower*, MacNeice has indicated how the transference of that radio play to screen or stage would detract from both its meaning and its success:

> Roland, my hero, as he sets out on his quest, meets an alcoholic solipsist who with the aid of music summons up a pub out of the air; I should not wish to see this transformation scene, the point being that the scene may be quite unsubstantial and imaginary, nor do I wish the solipsist himself to have a face ... The great appeal of radio is its purity. One is taking a chance on one's speakers and a decent production. One can in this medium come nearer perfection *in performance* than possibly anywhere else where executants are involved—except in music.[12]

Besides heightening the listener's imaginative participation in the story, radio is an apt medium for parable writing because it allows for a wide range of formal and contextual variations. A radio play can adopt almost any shape or subject, and it can accommodate sudden and varied spatial and chronological shifts in a way that the stage cannot. In a list of programmes better suited to radio than television, MacNeice names several kinds that he himself either wrote, adapted or produced. These include dramatised biography, history, fantasy, parable, internal drama and works which emphasise the 'physicality' of the words and music.[13] In his foreword to a posthumous selection of MacNeice's radio plays, Auden drew the same conclusion: "radio drama is an excellent, perhaps the ideal, medium for 'psychological' drama, that is to say the portrayal of the inner life, what human beings privately feel and think before and after they perform a public act."[14]

The technical approaches required by sound broadcasting—the

emphasis on vocal rather than facial expression or physical gesture, the greater significance of music and sound, the primacy of internal thought and soliloquy—encourage what MacNeice calls "intimate" drama. Because an audience's suspension of disbelief is likely to be greater when the action is heard and not seen, the whole of a radio programme could conceivably take place within a single character's mind. Dialogue, set and sound effects all contribute to the internal, parabolic worlds of his psychological portraits, dreamscapes and modern moralities.

To describe MacNeice's parables as realistic would be wrong; they are, however, closely-drawn representations of particular public and private concerns between the years of 1940 and 1960. One stage play in particular illustrates this point. *Traitors In Our Way* combines an obvious double-level structure with a more complex pattern of images, in much the same way as Canto XXVI of *Autumn Sequel*.[15] The surface story is realistic and easy to follow—one man's betrayal of his friend for political and personal reasons—but is offset by disturbing symbols of guilt and corruption: roses, dead nestlings, icebergs. "What I was interested in was the effect of ... a public issue upon people's private lives."[16] Yet, even in the revised version, the intended fusion of internal experience is awkward. It is more successfully realised in the radio plays *Prisoner's Progress* and *Persons From Porlock*[17], largely because the sort of play MacNeice was writing, as he quickly discovered, is better suited to radio.

Surprisingly few radio plays which could be called parables, or anti-parables, were written in the 30s. MacNeice began writing features and propaganda for the Overseas Department of the BBC early in 1941, and it is in this and the following year that what can be identified as his first original anti-parables for radio were broadcast.[18] MacNeice's initial dramatic anti-parables, however, were written for the stage during the previous decade.[19] As such, they reflect the political climate of the times as well as his ideas about what the theatre should and should not do. They are less 'intimate' than the radio plays, concerned more with outer than inner experience. Despite his aversion to the use of parable to propound any sort of ideology, MacNeice soon discovered that, particularly in the years between the wars, it was well nigh impossible *not* to touch on politics in some way. Even if he did not subscribe to their solutions, he was clearly aware of the inadequacies of existing political systems, and his excursions into writing for the theatre were no doubt prompted by the aspiration to expose what he felt were the major concerns of the decade to a larger, more immediate, audience than poetry was likely to afford.

Yet even at this early stage the focus is clearly the alignment of two or more levels of meaning. *Station Bell*, *Blacklegs*, *Eureka* and, to a lesser extent, a translation of *Agamemnon* and *Out of the Picture*, are all parables which attempt to illustrate contemporary social and political situations by means of a symbolic, often satirical, special world. Yet they are anti-parabolic in that they offer no remedies for the problems they point out. Contemporary events are depicted in terms of fantasy, partly because of MacNeice's conviction that realism was 'played out', but also as a way of evading explicit political statement. These stage plays were the workshop where MacNeice initially confronted the structural and thematic cruces he was to grapple with throughout his career. But as forays into the socio-political arena they are a less than satisfactory impetus for revolution, intellectual or otherwise. We are reminded of Auden's "poetry makes nothing happen ... it survives,/A way of happening, a mouth".[20] If MacNeice's anti-parables fail to offer viable political alternatives, if they refuse to be either rationalist or propagandist, their value survives in another form. As 'mouths', they respond to and transmit the challenge inherited by the modern dramatist to reassess traditional modes of discourse in the context of a radically altered social, political and literary environment.

Although few of the formal or thematic approaches characteristic of MacNeice's drama are ground-breaking, the technical strategies employed in the radio plays (internal voices, spatial and temporal transportations, flashbacks, sound effects) were to become standard practice. While the early stage plays are, in many ways, derivative of Auden and the political parables of the 30s, there is a distinctive strain of anti-parable in tension with predominantly realistic plot lines. Shaped by the experience of writing for sound broadcast, in the later plays realism gives way entirely to anti-parable in an effort to reproduce on stage and film[21] what had been achieved on the air. Although much of the rich ambiguity and prolonged suspension of disbelief of radio was lost, the advantage for MacNeice was that writing for the stage and television enlarged his workshop, making him critically aware of the limitations as well as the applications of double-level writing.

Taken together, the anti-parabolic aspects of MacNeice's radio and stage plays may be seen as indicative of the direction in which much post-modern drama would develop. More specifically, MacNeice's work has exerted a formative influence on contemporary Irish writing, particularly northern Irish writing, during the past three decades. We recognise in poems such as Michael Longley's 'The Fairground',

Derek Mahon's 'The Last of the Fire Kings', or Seamus Heaney's 'From the Frontier of Writing' and 'Parable Ireland', traces of the 'sleight-of-hand' MacNeice theorised about and practised.[22] The clearest connection, however, is between MacNeice and Paul Muldoon. In an essay examining their shared concern with parable, Edna Longley identifies several points of contact: figures and landscapes which are allegorical versions of a single persona or familiar locale; a syntax of dream logic; the revitalisation of structural and verbal clichés; a common interest in the *immram*.[23] The similarity between Muldoon's "subtle moralities" and MacNeice's anti-parables extends, as Longley points out, to "the quest for the self—rendered as pursuit and flight—[which] is currently a growth-point in Irish literature North and South".[24] MacNeice's metaphoric quests and dreams provide one possible source for the development of this pattern. For instance, a comparison of Muldoon's long poem 'Immram' and MacNeice's radio play *The Mad Islands*, discloses how Muldoon parallels and extends MacNeice's redirection of the Mael Duin legend.[25]

MacNeice's belief in the dramatic potential of double-level writing has been effectively realised in contemporary Irish theatre as well. Recent productions such as Tom Paulin's *The Riot Act* (a version of *Antigone*) and Derek Mahon's *High Time* (a translation of Molière's *The School for Husbands*)[26], achieve that balance between political parable and "adult make-believe" that MacNeice aimed for in his own rendition of *Agamemnon* and *One for the Grave*. MacNeice's inversion of parable provides a forum for talking about the divisions of self and nation experienced under the duress of civil war. Consequently, playwrights including Stewart Parker, Graham Reid and, in some measure, Brian Friel and Tom Murphy, have adopted MacNeice's methodology.

It is possible to read much post-modern literature as anti-parabolic in the sense in which the term has been applied in this study. This is not to imply that MacNeice is the inventor of contemporary double-level writing; rather, it is to suggest that his reinvention of a traditional form is representative of the reassessment of structural and thematic standards that characterises the modern period. MacNeice responded to Eliot's demand that modern writing be difficult, allusive and indirect, with drama which, if on occasion ingenuously simplistic, at its most accomplished challenges and ironically reflects preconceptions about and visions of ourselves. In '7, Middagh Street', Muldoon casts MacNeice in the role of "sleight-of-hand-man", leaving us with an appropriately ambiguous image:

the displacement of soap-suds in a basin

may have some repercussion

for a distant ship:
only last night I tried to butt the uneven

Pages of a *Belfast Newsletter* from 1937
into some sort of shape[27]

Notes

[1] RD Smith, 'Here Is A Man: A Talk on Louis MacNeice', audiotape, BBC Sound Archives, London. T44066
[2] Reprinted as *Varieties of Parable* (London: Cambridge UP, 1965).
[3] Louis MacNeice, introductory note to *The Dark Tower, The Dark Tower and Other Radio Scripts* (London: Faber & Faber, 1947), pp. 21-22.
[4] *The Careerist* was first broadcast by the BBC on 22nd October, 1946. *One Eye Wild: A Romance in Commonplace* was first broadcast by the BBC on 9th November, 1952. *One for the Grave: A Modern Morality Play* was first performed at the Abbey Theatre, 3rd October, 1966. It is published in *One for the Grave: A Modern Morality Play* (London: Faber & Faber, 1968).
[5] Louis MacNeice, *Modern Poetry: A Personal Essay* (London: Oxford UP, 1935; re-issue 1968).
[6] Louis MacNeice, 'The Poet in England Today', *New Republic* 25th March, 1940, pp. 412-13. Reprinted in *Selected Literary Criticism of Louis MacNeice*, Alan Heuser (ed.) (Oxford: Clarendon Press, 1987), p. 114.
[7] Louis MacNeice, *The Strings Are False: An Unfinished Autobiography*, 1965 (London: Faber & Faber, 1982), pp. 50-54.
[8] Louis MacNeice, introductory note to *The Dark Tower, The Dark Tower and Other Radio Scripts* (London: Faber & Faber, 1947), p. 21.
[9] 'Valediction' and 'Neutrality' are published in *Collected Poems*, ed. ER Dodds. 1966 (London: Faber & Faber, 1979), pp. 52-4, pp. 202-3; *The Dark Tower* was first broadcast by the BBC on 21st January, 1946 and is published in *The Dark Tower and Other Radio Scripts* (London: Faber & Faber, 1947), pp. 19-66, reprinted 1979; the stage play *Traitors in Our Way*, originally entitled *Nowhere Fast*, was first performed by the Ulster Group Theatre, 25th March, 1957, Belfast; unpublished.
[10] Louis MacNeice, introductory note to *The Dark Tower, The Dark Tower and Other Radio Scripts*, p. 12.
[11] Louis MacNeice, 'A Plea for Sound', *BBC Quarterly* 8.3 (1953), p. 131.
[12] Ibid., p. 134.
[13] Ibid., p. 132.
[14] W.H. Auden, Foreword, *Persons From Porlock*, by Louis MacNeice (London: BBC, 1969), pp. 7-8.

Auden's analysis of the closing scene of *Persons From Porlock* is an apt description of the modern morality method, and justifies MacNeice's transference of these strategies from stage to air: "Hank's death is a good illustration of a scene that would only be possible in a radio play. As he is dying, various characters who have played a part in his life appear to him and speak, helping him to arrive at a deeper self-knowledge. If one tries to imagine this scene in a stage play, one realises that it would not work. Firstly, while in the radio play one knows that the other characters are thoughts inside his head, if brought on to the stage they would be visibly external, so that the audience would be puzzled to know—a fatal dramatic flaw—whether they were 'real' or tiresomely 'symbolic'. Secondly, a dying man cannot 'do' anything: he can only lie there motionless, and on stage a motionless figure is an undramatic bore."

[15] For *Autumn Sequel*, Canto XXVI, see MacNeice, *Collected Poems*, pp. 435-9.

[16] MacNeice, 'Another Part of the Sea', [Introduction] *Radio Times* 2nd September, 1960, p. 2.

[17] *Prisoner's Progress: A Romantic Fable* was first broadcast by the BBC on 27th April, 1954. *Persons From Porlock* was first broadcast by the BBC on 30th August, 1963. It is published in *Persons From Porlock and Other Plays for Radio* (London: BBC, 1969), pp. 107-144.

[18] These include the "feature-historical-portrait" *Dr. Chekhov* (retitled *Sunbeams In His Hat*), first broadcast on 6th September, 1941, published in *The Dark Tower and Other Radio Scripts*, pp. 67-98; the satire *Calling All Fools*, first broadcast on 1st April, 1942, unpublished; and the historical parable *Christopher Columbus*, first broadcast on 12th October, 1942, published in *Christopher Columbus: A Radio Play* (London: Faber & Faber, 1944).

[19] These include *Station Bell: A Play in Three Acts*, written 1934-35, first performed by the University of Birmingham Dramatic Society, 1936, unpublished; *The Agamemnon of Aeschylus*, trans. 1936, first performed by the Group Theatre, 1st November, 1936, Westminster Theatre, London. (London: Faber & Faber, 1972); *Out of the Picture: A Play in Two Acts*, written 1936, first performed by the Group Theatre, 5th November, 1937, Westminster Theatre, London. London: Faber & Faber, 1937; *Blacklegs*, written 1939, accepted by the Abbey Theatre but never performed, unpublished; *Eureka: A Play in Three Acts*, written 1939, never performed, unpublished.

[20] W.H. Auden, 'In Memory of W.B. Yeats', *Selected Poems*, Edward Mendelson (ed.) (New York: Vintage, 1979), p. 82.

[21] MacNeice wrote a film script entitled *Pax Futura* in 1945. The film was never produced and the script is unpublished. His adaptation for television of the stage play *Traitors In Our Way*, retitled *Another Part of the Sea*, was broadcast 6th September, 1960, unpublished.

[22] Michael Longley, *Poems 1963-1983* (Harmondsworth: Penguin, 1986), p. 88; Derek Mahon, *Selected Poems* (London: Viking/Loughcrew, Oldcastle: Gallery Books, 1991), p. 58; Seamus Heaney, *The Haw Lantern* (London: Faber & Faber, 1987), p. 6, pp. 10-11.

[23] Edna Longley, 'MacNeice and Muldoon', *Poetry in the Wars* (Newcastle upon Tyne: Bloodaxe Books, 1986), p. 211.
[24] Ibid., p. 224.
[25] Paul Muldoon, *Why Brownlee Left* (London: Faber & Faber, 1980), pp. 38–47; Louis MacNeice, *The Mad Islands and The Administrator: Two Radio Plays* (London: Faber & Faber, 1964), pp. 11–69. *The Mad Islands* was first broadcast by the BBC 4th April, 1962.
[26] Tom Paulin, *The Riot Act* (London: Faber & Faber, 1985); Derek Mahon, *High Time* (Dublin: Gallery Press, 1985).
[27] Paul Muldoon, *Meeting The British* (London: Faber & Faber, 1987), p. 57.

Sent to Coventry
Emigrations and Autobiography

Eamonn Hughes

This paper will make some general points about autobiography, emigration, and place, before discussing John Hewitt as autobiographer. Given that I will be talking about various travels, I hope I can be excused if, instead of taking a straight and narrow path, I make my journey from this introduction to the elsewhere of the end of the lecture by a series of digressions.

> I will arise and go now, and go to Innisfree,
> And a small cabin build there, of clay and wattles made:
> Nine bean-rows will I have there, a hive for the honey-bee,
> And live alone in the bee-loud glade.

This is, of course, the opening of Yeats' 'The Lake Isle of Innisfree' written, as he explains in his draft *Autobiography*, in 1890 in London:

> ... I was going along the Strand and, passing a shop window where there was a little ball kept dancing by a jet of water, I remembered waters about Sligo and was moved to a sudden emotion that shaped itself into 'The Lake Isle of Innisfree'.[1]

There is a slightly, but significantly, different account of the poem's origin in Yeats' published *Autobiographies*:

> ... when walking through Fleet Street very homesick I heard a little tinkle of water and saw a fountain in a shop-window which balanced a little ball upon its jet, and began to remember lake water. From the sudden remembrance came my poem Innisfree, my first lyric with anything in its rhythm of my own music.[2]

The difference between these two accounts is very much in favour of the feeling of homesickness. The detail of where he is alters—is it the Strand or Fleet Street?—suggesting that he cannot be bothered to remember his precise location. More importantly, where he wishes to be becomes vaguer, as "waters about Sligo" changes to "lake water". What's left and emphasised is the emotion of homesickness and its expression. In the poem, too, the point of departure is the unlocated "roadway, or ... pavements grey". The poem then is an exile's lament, a piece of emigrant literature, as is much of Yeats' early writing, and it stands for one type of emigrant writing. He does not wish to return to Ireland, but to Innisfree, an island within an island. His longing is not for a real place and its society; instead he wishes, in the terms of my title, to send himself to Coventry, to exchange the society of London for the solitude of an archaic monkish existence in an imagined and static place. From this perspective, we can see that, for the exile, elsewhere can be an imagined Ireland.

By way of contrast to this imagined Ireland, we have the apparently more real Ireland in Patrick MacGill's *Children of the Dead End*. This Ireland is not a longed-for home, but rather a place which brutally expels people. So when the autobiographical figure of Dermod Flynn is 12 his mother says:

> 'Ye have to go out and push yer fortune. We must get some money to pay the rent come Hallow E'en, and as ye'll get a bigger penny workin' with the farmers away there, me and yer da have thought of sendin' ye to the hirin'-fair of Strabane on the morra.'[3]

Throughout the work, letters from home remind Flynn and us of the economic brutality of his Ireland. Eight years after going to the hiring fair, in which time he has been a farm labourer, a navvy and a tramp, Flynn becomes a journalist, and the letters from home reach their climax:

> Of my salary, now three pounds a week, I sent a guinea home to my own people every Saturday. Of course, now, getting so much, they wanted more. Journalism to them implied some hazy kind of work where money was stintless and to be had for the asking. My other brothers were going out into the world now, and my eldest sister had gone to America. 'I wish that I could keep them at home,' wrote my mother. 'You are so long away now that we do not miss you.'

(pp. 282-83)

So much for the Irish mother. Dermod then is being sent, we may say, to Coventry, and this reminds us that, despite Yeats' romantic view of Ireland, it is ultimately poverty that causes both Flynn and Yeats to be elsewhere. George O'Brien's statement that "If England didn't exist, they would have had to invent it"[4] is true for both Yeats and MacGill.

The question then is, are Yeats and MacGill different? Well, yes; but the difference is not as straightforward as one might expect. The Irelands presented in their work are very different: Yeats' Ireland is a Romanticised home; MacGill's is a place of economic deprivation. However, alongside the economic deprivation which pushes Flynn out of Glenmornan, there is also an affective insufficiency which leads him on a quest. So when his mother announces that he is going to the hiring-fair, he responds joyfully: "I had been dreaming of this journey for months before, and I never felt happier in all my life than I did when my mother spoke those words" (p. 26).

This quest aspect of *Children of the Dead End* is often overlooked, because readers of the work (myself included) want to believe that, despite its fictionality, it is authentic. We want to believe in MacGill/Flynn as the economic outcast. The idea of quest, that there is a voluntary aspect to his emigration, runs counter to this. If his quest were simply for wealth, which is one of its aspects, we could accommodate it. But Flynn seems to want more than that and so the quest takes a variety of forms. Its abiding manifestation is, however, the figure of Norah Ryan. She, too, is from Glenmornan, but they meet on the Derry boat when they are both part of a potato-picking squad. Her wish to return home prompts Flynn's promise that he will make his fortune and turn her into a great lady. This indicates what Flynn's quest really is; its endpoint, as represented in Norah Ryan, is, no matter how deferred, his point of departure.

Flynn's quest, like the work as a whole, ends only with Norah's death. As a symbolic figure, she stands for many things—Ireland, love, innocence—as well as being Flynn's last literal link to Glenmornan and a realistic depiction of the emigrant as victim. Her death then is the ultimate disillusionment of Flynn's questing, or rather an indication that, since the moment when a combination of economics and curiosity first made him think about elsewhere, his quest has been false. The economic determinants which forced him out of Glenmornan also exist elsewhere, and the idea that elsewhere can lead him home again is, therefore, mistaken.

If home is the elsewhere that will seemingly resolve Yeats' longings as an exile, elsewhere seems to be the place where Flynn can remedy the deficiencies of home. I do not want to be taken here as saying that Yeats and MacGill are similar writers. Rather, it is their very dissimilarity which I wish to use to make a point. While each produces very different pictures of home and elsewhere, they share an important feature. In both cases, home and elsewhere are relativised rather than differentiated. Instead of home and elsewhere being different locations with different functions, elsewhere is simply not where you are.

To explain this further, I want to turn to Coventry. 'Sent to Coventry', suggested itself as a neat conflation of what happened to John Hewitt on both the literal and metaphorical levels. It was to Coventry that he went as director of the Herbert Museum and Art Gallery, and it was into Coventry that he might be said to have been sent by those who failed to appoint him as Director of the Belfast Museum and Art Gallery. This metaphorical usage makes clear that, in discussing place, we are referring to what Oliver MacDonagh usefully calls "mental geography".[5] Coventry is not just a real place, it is also a condition. There are two speculations that I like to make about the phrase in relation to Hewitt. The first is to wonder if he knew the probable etymology of 'sent to Coventry' in the English Civil War; 'sent to Coventry' then referred to Royalists held there as prisoners of the Parliamentary forces. Secondly, it is possible that, with his knowledge of Ulster and particularly Antrim dialect, Hewitt, when moving to Coventry the place, may actually have thought of himself as being sent to Dinglety-cootch.[6] The condition figured in the phrase 'sent to Coventry' then has, depending on the place of origin, at least two linguistic, historical and geographical figurations.

Finally, 'sent to Coventry' has the added advantage of referring to the hometown (and I use that word very cautiously) of Philip Larkin, from whom the title of this summer school—The Importance of Elsewhere—is taken. Larkin's 'I Remember, I Remember' is about a chance return when his train stops unexpectedly:

> "Why Coventry!" I exclaimed. "I was born here." ...
> "Was that," my friend smiled, "where you 'have your roots'?"
> No, only where my childhood was unspent,
> I wanted to retort, just where I started ...[7]

Larkin might be said, in the light of such 'unrooted' remarks, to be someone for whom, since nowhere is home, everywhere is elsewhere. Hewitt, as we will see later, makes more effort to make Coventry home than Larkin ever does. And this is where I want to return to my point about the relativity, rather than the differentiation of home and elsewhere in the autobiographical writings that we have looked at so far. 'Elsewhere' does have a differentiated geographical value for Larkin and other English writers that it lacks for Irish autobiographers. There are two points I want to make about this. The first of these is about how the relationship between place and the psychological and social conditions associated with it is complicated in Ireland by colonialism. It is worth remarking that Hewitt is one of the few poets (rather than critics) to have made extensive use of the colonial model of Irish history and culture. The second point is about the sea.

We have, we share, a colonial inheritance and we also share the determinate consequences of that inheritance, including an uncertainty about place and one's relationship to it. We are all familiar with the idea that dispossession is a factor in the continuing dominance of the concern with place in Irish culture. But it is not only this aspect of colonialism which explains that concern. Certainly, it is not this aspect of colonialism with which Hewitt was primarily concerned.

Edward Said has written about "the ceremonies of bonding with the territory [which] ironically stimulate queries in the reader about the need for such affirmations".[8] In Hewitt's writing, such affirmations contest with his growing sense of himself as rooted and therefore we need to enquire about his need for these affirmations. Many commentators reject the colonial model as simplistic because it appears to challenge the legitimacy of the existence in Ireland of people like Hewitt. It is precisely this apparent illegitimacy which, it seems to me, much of Hewitt's writing addresses: think of the way in which he constantly attempts to establish rights to a place and you will see that this effort is grounded in a yearning to be legitimate. So far this conforms to the usual colonial model which, in slightly reductive terms, can be summarised as the conflict between the legitimate indigenous people and the illegitimate colonisers. The ground of that conflict is, of course, a place. But this is where the colonial model falls short. The most basic version of it is curiously ahistorical: it suggests that all three terms—the native, the coloniser, and the place—remain constant and unchanged; it implies that there is an original set of relationships between the native and the place which could be resumed if those perceived as interlopers left. History, in this view, is a blanket which covers but does not alter Ireland. If that blanket is removed, we may find what Daniel Corkery, an early proponent of this version, called the hidden Ireland. A slightly more sophisticated version of the model will allow for the impact of history on one term of the triad; the indigenous people in this version are altered from happy natives to oppressed victims; they become the unhappy and yearning MacGill. This version speaks of dispossession, discontinuity, and deculturation. Another, and so far the most sophisticated, version allows for change only in two terms of the triad; this version acknowledges that the colonisers too might be affected by history. This takes a rather patronising form by suggesting that the colonisers remain illegitimate only because they cling to a false position; if only they would recognise the falseness of their position they could then join a group of people who have, unlike them, moved on through history. Yeats' legitimacy, in this view, depends on him aligning himself with nationalism, and the patronising nature of this version is evident in the many challenges to Yeats' right to be considered Irish.

However, none of these versions allows for the fact that history changes not only people but also places. All of them suggest that the geography of the place remains constant; the borders, frontiers and lines of conflict may shift across it, history may blow over it, but the territory, the place itself, while being the ground on which the change happens, is not itself subject to change. One result of this supposedly unchanging nature of place is found in the continuing concern of much Irish writing with the rural.

We are aware, from the works of, for example, James Joyce and Ciaran Carson, of the urban place as constantly changing. Both writers have made us aware that urban maps are fragile things, always torn apart before completion. Our urban, psychological, affective, cultural, though not apparently our political, landscapes are always changing. The autobiography of emigration can be read in such a way as to suggest that all places are like this, that all places are unfinished because dynamic and subject to change. It is on this basis that places can be differentiated.

The most usual form of change in place to be found in autobiography, and an important reason why autobiography so often includes or culminates in emigration, is decline. This is different from MacGill's Ireland which is static; Flynn's misfortune is that he wants to change himself without any alteration in the place to which he wishes to return. So in Glenmornan people read only old newspapers.

The distance in time and space from the events described does in no way diminish the readers' interest in the stories. That they are so far removed from the world in which such things occur gives the people a certain amount of comfort. "Strange things are always takin' place in foreign parts," they say to one another. "It's good to be here where things like that never take place."[9]

George O'Brien has further pointed out that such a culture demands one thing only of its emigrants—that they too remain unchanged:

> "You'd swear she'd never been a day away." ... the greatest compliment an emigrant could be paid. To journey unscathed. To remain true. Exile as a myth of stasis. Emigration as fidelity's enriching rite.
> —*The Village of Longing/Dancehall Days* (p. 55)

Given this stasis, it is almost a relief to turn to the autobiographies of, for example, George Moore and Sean O'Casey, who insofar as they present an Ireland in decline are, at least, also presenting a place which is changing, even if only for the worse. Moore's *Hail and Farewell* considers at length his failure to write a novel, *Ruin and Weed*, about Ireland in decline. *Hail and Farewell* appears to be about Moore's return to Ireland, but is really about his reasons for ultimately leaving an Ireland which is an "untilled field", and in which Moore feels that he comes closest to being accepted only when he becomes impotent.

For O'Casey, too, the Ireland he leaves is one which is sinking into desolation: so in *Inishfallen, Fare Thee Well* the account of his flowering as a writer is contrasted with his memory of a young girl in Athenry as a "lone cherry-blossom thrusting itself shyly and impertinently forward through the ragged, withering foliage of an ageing tree".[10]

Moore and O'Casey at least acknowledge historical forces in Ireland, and, while the Ireland that each describes is blighted economically and culturally by the effects of colonialism, there is in each of them a sense that there is potential for a different type of change. It is perhaps glib to suggest that Moore's "untilled field" and O'Casey's "withering foliage" need only cultivation, but it must be said that each writer certainly leaves open the possibility that stasis and decline are alterable.

George Buchanan analyses the way in which stasis becomes habit-forming: "Submission brings routine. Routine carries a nibbling fear lest routine be disturbed. Behind static days something treacherous may hide, like rats in a wall."[11] He resists this by being aware of the changes which are happening in the landscape and is thus able to feel "well nourished with the familiar" (*Green Seacoast*, p. 61). This enables him to leave Kilwaughter at the same age, 12, that MacGill leaves Glenmornan; but with a greater security he can return, even though the place he returns to will not be the same as the place he is leaving. He also defines the "difference between fixation and fidelity". "Fixation is sticking to the same thing ... Fidelity means letting go, living new experience ... "Let go, let go" is the faithful way" (p. 123). Like Hewitt, Buchanan was influenced by Lewis Mumford and *Green Seacoast* proposes a dynamic regionalism.

Hewitt's thought seems to me to be less glib than Buchanan's because he is, at his best, aware both of how history changes landscape and of those forces which resist that change. In 'Once Alien Here', he can write that "Once alien here my fathers built their house,/claimed, drained, and gave the land the shapes of use", and therefore he sees himself as part of a history which changes place, without losing sight of "the sullen Irish" who had previously made the place their own. Similarly in 'The Colony':

> We laboured hard and stubborn, draining, planting,
> till half the country took its shape from us.
> Only among the hills with hare and kestrel
> will you observe what once this land was like
> before we made it fat for human use.

Again there is the sense that place has been changed and rights acquired thereby, but again there is tension caused by a line such as "for we have rights drawn from the soil and sky", in which the right seems to be based on a natural rather than a cultural claim. Places themselves, however, are not natural; they are cultivated as Hewitt knows, at times. If we consider Hewitt's favourite metaphor of 'rootedness', we can again see this tension. The most immediate connotation of rootedness is organic; it seems to imply a claim to have sprung from the soil that is much like the autochthonous claims of nationalism. But the opposition that Hewitt invokes is not nature *versus* culture, not rural *versus* urban. What is important for him, despite the organicist connotations of 'rootedness', is direction in history. The writer "must know where he comes from and where he is: otherwise how can he tell where he wishes to go?"[12] The issue then is not place *versus* placelessness; it is rather place in history and the possibility of change and development that Hewitt is discussing. His metaphor has to do with determinate development and growth. It is this tension in Hewitt that makes his work of interest to those who see value in the colonial model: his "ceremonies of bonding" are no simple assertion of right, but a consideration of the changes wrought in and on Ireland; they are, in the face of simpler models, a consideration of how Ireland itself becomes elsewhere through history. In Hewitt, at times, geography and history conspire to produce new mental maps.

It is at this point that I want to turn to the sea, for it is the sea which, as Oliver MacDonagh has argued, has allowed Ireland to be seen as unchanging:

> In one sense, the Irish problem has persisted because of the power of geographical images over men's minds. In particular, the image of the island, with the surrounding water carving out a territorial identity, has been compelling.
>
> —*States of Mind* (p. 15)

If the usual mental map of Ireland does not allow for change but only a sense of uncertainty and dispossession, then nowhere is elsewhere, since everywhere is a place of exile. The title of this year's School is taken from Philip Larkin for whom elsewhere can be defined as somewhere overseas. This is due to the role of the sea in English culture: it is the providentially-granted guardian of English insularity (and *there's* a piece of mental geography) and everywhere beyond it is elsewhere. 'Fog in channel; continent cut off' is the phrase to which this attitude can be reduced. Allied to this, and again connected to the imagined status as island folk, is the sea-faring tradition: Britannia rules the waves, and so on. The sea is then a providentially-granted opportunity for the examination of the individual, and latterly Protestant, conscience. From 'The Seafarer' through Coleridge's 'Rime of the Ancient Mariner' to the William Golding *Rites of Passage* trilogy, the sea acts as a location in which the individual can be alone with the metaphorical struggles with elemental forces which exemplify the workings of conscience. The ship at sea can, of course, also provide a microcosm of English society with the arrangement of ranks, decks and accommodation providing a neatly stratified image of the structure of class and authority.

Elsewhere, for the English, is then a differentiated place arrived at only after the passage, both physical and metaphorical, overseas. The puzzle to be addressed is the absence of any similar modern tradition of seafaring in Irish writing. There is, to be sure, the medieval voyage poetry, the last kick of which, it has been argued, may be seen in Swift's *Gulliver's Travels*. After this, there is little or nothing to compare with the riches of the English tradition. Mitchel's *Jail Journal* has some marvellous seafaring passages, but they exemplify Mitchel's struggles with the English class system. There is Liam O'Flaherty's account of his voyages in *Two Years*. There are also the Muldoon adaptations of the voyage poems, Heaney's Lough Neagh sequence and Joyce's rendering of the *Odyssey*, but these are all resolutely land-locked; Bloom approaches his Nausicaa from landward not seaward (I feel uneasy using such terms—they are nearly as esoteric to me as the terms of cricket). In the opening section of *Ulysses*, the attitudes to the sea are indicative. "Our great mother" Gogarty calls it, echoing the Greeks, but his swim is part-baptism, in a rite to which Stephen no longer adheres, and part-revelation of his West Briton status. Stephen leaves him and Haines to swim, while he goes off to define a pier as a disappointed bridge, disappointed because it is left stranded in the sea rather than having crossed the sea to its destination. The modern Irish, for all our actual insularity, are dockers, shipyardmen, and coasters rather than seafarers. If we venture onto the sea at all, it is like the chicken—only to get to the other side, not to engage in seafaring for its own literal or metaphorical sake. Paul Muldoon's line, "By which I mean the 'open' sea", emphasises this point in its stress on the word "open"; here, for once, the sea does not lead straight back to Ireland.[13]

The sea then cannot define elsewhere for us. This stems from emigration. Leaving and arriving, not travelling, are the important aspects of that experience; the sea is not a medium of exploration, but rather of communication. Perhaps we should be glad that there is one element in which the Irish are not forced to introspection about identity; perhaps we have been cast in the role of Caliban rather than Narcissus for so long that water does not help us to reflect upon ourselves. The English at sea are just that—at sea—while they contemplate their usual value systems. The Irish are not at sea at sea; rather, we are between relativised places where we feel equally and unchangingly dispossessed.

Louis MacNeice, champion of Heraclitus, flux, and dynamism is the sole autobiographical exception that I can think of to this rule. *The Strings Are False* begins on board ship with him returning from the known America to the newly-unknown England of wartime in 1940 and ends with him taking ship for America at the beginning of 1940. This circularity makes the autobiography a meditation at sea. The text functions on a dialectic provided by MacNeice in a parable about a boy living in his father's house, where everything is always the same, who is granted a wish to be somewhere different. Dissatisfied with that different place, he wishes again and "he was back in his father's house where everything had always been the same. But now everything was different".[14] MacNeice's sense of displacement is therefore not disabling because he recognises the need for such change, the validity of elsewhere. As he puts it, the desire to return to the womb may be there "but it can't be helped anyway" (*The Strings Are False*, p. 36), and flux is always if not preferable to stasis, then more realistic.

Hewitt also has some significant moments connected to the sea. His "first important words [are] Ship-Boat-Water ... Such an auspicious first declaration ought, by right to have proved prophetic. I should surely have run away to sea ... But, against the portent, I have remained a rooted person ..." (*Ancestral Voices*, p. 1). Another reference to the sea confirms this rootedness. In 'From Chairmen and Committee Men, Good Lord Deliver Us', Hewitt recounts what we can call his dis-appointment in the Belfast Museum and Art Gallery. For the first time ever he is then asked to travel to London on museum business and, on the trip over, he walks round the deck:

> Once I stopped at the rail and looked down at the troubled waters, sliding, folding over, and turning past and, for a minute or more, I was nearer suicide than I shall ever be again.
> —*Ancestral Voices* (pp. 54-5)

Once again, there is that tension I have already referred to in Hewitt's work. Here is an Irishman meditating at sea, but the focus of his meditation, and the cause of his thoughts of suicide seems to be a disabling feeling of displacement. This latter point becomes clear when we look at *A North Light*, his unpublished autobiography. I want to concentrate on that for the remainder of this paper, beginning with some brief remarks about Hewitt as an autobiographer.

In 'Welsh Rarebit', Hewitt tells of meeting Roy Campbell whose autobiography, *Broken Record*, he had read and admired: "So I was very properly amazed when he declared this to be largely fictitious, and, where not fictitious, in fact the life of another South African poet."[15] This implies that his own autobiographical writing will be straightforwardly accurate. But when reading *A North Light* or any of the other autobiographical materials, we should be wary of Hewitt's avowed reticence: "I remember once reading that before you give information to any man you should ask yourself 'Does he need to know?' And this has become my general practice regarding personal or confidential matters." Not the most helpful attitude for an autobiographer. However, against this we can consider his autobiographical material as part of his search for "my personal myth, my imaginative pattern of truth". It is this pattern that I want to consider in two ways. The first and smaller of these involves the chapters dealing with Hewitt's dis-appointment. Many of you will know about this episode from the published chapter 'From Chairman and Committee Men, Good Lord Deliver Us', but its context in *A North Light* is very important. *A North Light* is, by and large, a chronological account of Hewitt's time as a museum man, but there is a break in this pattern. Chapter 31, 'Annus Mirabilis', concerns a trip to Venice in 1949; Chapter 32, 'From Chairmen and Committee Men ... ', is about the events in 1953; and Chapter 33, 'Stanley Spencer', is mostly about a Spencer exhibition in 1958; chapters after that return to 1954, 1955 and 1957. This break in chronology forces us to read this part of his story through references to paintings and painters, (and, in general terms, *A North Light* is better read through painters and paintings rather than through writers and writing.)

Two paintings pattern Hewitt's feelings in regard to his non-appointment. In Venice, he is much impressed by Titian's 'The Presentation of the Virgin'; 'From Chairmen and Committee Men ...' opens with Roberta's comments on Hewitt's *naïveté*; and 'Stanley Spencer' is first mentioned in relation to his painting 'The Betrayal'. There is a satisfying, if not pleasant, arc described by these details: virgin, naïf, betrayal. The Venice and Spencer chapters, however, do more than this. Of Venetian paintings (especially Titian's), Hewitt remarks:

> Most forceful of all, the impression that so much Venetian painting was about Venice, the sacred subjects given the only setting worthy of their holiness; that pictures were still in the ambiance for which they were first intended. Titian's Presentation [of the Virgin] had been painted for that very wall.

It is the experience of this sense of rootedness elsewhere that helps to make 1949 "a year of marvels indeed", "for my adventures among pictures", and which therefore allows Hewitt to feel that, at this time, he is beginning to know something about pictures. For which modest comment, in context, read that he would have made a good director of the Art Gallery. The Spencer chapter is also a celebration of rootedness but with an ironic edge. The chapter is a consideration of Spencer as the English artist *par excellence*, and culminates in a visit in June 1958 (i.e. after the Hewitts' move to Coventry) to a Spencer exhibition in Cookham, Spencer's birthplace, his home for most of his life and the setting for many of his paintings: "Here at Cookham for a brief June afternoon, place, man, and work were held in a unity of being and feeling, an experience never likely to be repeated, but to be remembered as long as life." Again we have here, and in other details in the chapter, a sense of a rootedness which Hewitt has himself lost.

This brings me to the second pattern I want to trace in *A North Light*, that is the one which overarches the whole work. *A North Light* moves from 'How It All Started', in which Hewitt sees an advertisement for the job of Art Assistant, to 'Exeat' which takes him just to the brink of being interviewed for the job in Coventry. The typescript is divided into two volumes for convenience of binding, but there appears to be a significant split at that point in any case. Much of the early part of the first volume is about travel, and it is worth noting that the Hewitt family, especially compared to the MacNeice or Buchanan families, seem to have been comfortable and ready travellers. The "surprise of foreignness" is what makes the greatest impact on Hewitt on his first trip to the continent, but, thereafter, his concern is to judge local work by European standards in an attempt to diminish the gap he perceives between Northern Ireland and elsewhere. Despite this wide travel and Roberta's urging to think about moving elsewhere, Hewitt remains contentedly, it seems, in Belfast. It is only with the outbreak of war at the end of the first volume, that he can no longer supplement deficiencies at home with travel and thus turns, at the start of the second volume, to regionalism. The first volume then moves from travel to enforced enclosure, while the second volume moves from the rationalised enclosure of regionalism to the enforced travel of emigration. The whole work is caught in a tension between the idea of rootedness and the need for the wider perspectives of elsewhere.

The final chapter summarises the aspects of this tension. On his visit to Coventry for interview, Hewitt tries to respect its otherness, to recognise the advantages of this not being home. So he makes a virtue of the fact that those very political ideas which had disbarred him at home will not, in this new place, be a social and economic handicap. He also visits an eating house called Farmer Giles thinking it will be very English, but finds himself surrounded by Irish voices, for this is the Coventry not just of Hewitt but of Tom Murphy's *A Whistle in the Dark*, which is almost contemporary with this period of Hewitt's life, a Coventry of the Carneys, who were truly the dispossessed. This signals a homecoming for Hewitt and his closing words are a capitulation not to the "surprise of foreignness", but to its potential homeliness:

> Yet, seeing the surname [of the Lifford Hewitts who had gone from Coventry to Ireland in the 18th century] cut in stone and dated, I had an odd friendly feeling, as if, in some way, part of me had come home, that I

stood in that place with some sort of right, and, from that moment, I knew in my heart, that I should, later in the afternoon, be appointed the Art Director of the Herbert Art Gallery and Museum, Coventry, in the county of Warwickshire, England.

For all of the qualifications in this last paragraph, the desire for rootedness overrides the knowledge of place as Hewitt lays natural rather than cultural claim to Coventry. For that reason, I want to end by taking issue with the editors of the proceedings of the first three Hewitt schools. Instead of *The Poet's Place* the proceedings should, of course, have been called *The Poet's Places*. Those places with which Hewitt is most closely associated have each had many different existences, as his best work acknowledges. The poet's places, then. Nor is this, it seems to me, just nit-picking, for what it allows me to do is to state that while Hewitt may have had knowledge of a variety of aspects of the places with which he is associated, we cannot say in the end that he knew his place, as his capitulation to Coventry as home rather than as elsewhere shows. After all, if we think of that famous central statement—Ulster, Ireland, Britain, Europe—we are listening to a series of displacements. Indeed, it is precisely because Hewitt did not know his place, in all senses of that phrase, that we still attend to him.

Notes

[1] W.B. Yeats, *Memoirs*. Denis Donoghue (ed.) (London, 1988), p. 31.
[2] W.B. Yeats, *Autobiographies* (London, 1980), p. 153.
[3] Patrick MacGill, *Children of the Dead End* (Dingle, 1982), p. 26.
[4] George O'Brien, *The Village of Longing/Dancehall Days* (Harmondsworth, 1990), p. 52.
[5] Oliver MacDonagh, *States of Mind: A Study of Anglo-Irish Conflict, 1780–1980* (London, 1983), p. 26.
[6] I want to thank Caroline Macafee of the Ulster Folk and Transport Museum for her assistance with this point.
[7] Philip Larkin, *The Less Deceived* (London, 1977), pp. 38-9.
[8] Edward Said, 'Narrative, Geography and Interpretation', *New Left Review*, 180 (March/April 1990) pp. 81-97, p. 96.
[9] Patrick MacGill, *Glenmornan* (London, 1983), p. 29.
[10] Sean O'Casey, *Inishfallen, Fare Thee Well* (London, 1972) quoted by Michael Kenneally, 'Joyce, O'Casey, and the Genre of Autobiography', in Diana A. Ben-Merre and Maureen Murphy (eds), *James Joyce and His Contemporaries* (London, 1989), pp. 105-110, p. 108.
[11] George Buchanan, *Green Seacoast* (London, 1959), p. 23.

[12] John Hewitt, 'The Bitter Gourd' in Tom Clyde (ed.), *Ancestral Voices: The Selected Prose of John Hewitt* (Belfast, 1987), pp. 115–7.

[13] Paul Muldoon, *Madoc—A Mystery* (London, 1990), p. 12. I am grateful to Michael Allen for this point.

[14] Louis MacNeice, *The Strings Are False*, E.R. Dodds (ed.) (London, 1982), p. 206.

[15] I am grateful to the Librarian and staff of the University of Ulster at Coleraine for allowing me to consult Hewitt's unpublished papers, including the typescript of *A North Light*, from which all subsequent quotations are taken.

Woman as 'Elsewhere'
Seamus Heaney's 'Feminine' Voice

Karlin J. Lillington

One can readily imagine 'the importance of elsewhere' for a writer: elsewhere, defined as an alternative physical location, may provide a changed perspective, a detachment, an insight into self or subject not available at 'home'. However, if one moves laterally and takes the definition of 'elsewhere' to mean a psychic space that may be explored just as readily as a physical space, elsewhere functions more clearly as 'other', with all the implications that term carries (thus signalling that perhaps the physical notion of elsewhere also has its implications). The dangers and limitations of a male writer co-opting one particular 'elsewhere'—the realm of what may be termed 'the feminine'—are readily apparent if one takes as example several of Seamus Heaney's poems. This is not to argue reductively that all of his large body of work can be implicated in this way, but many of what may be called the 'feminine-centred' poems in the volumes up to and including *North* are problematical.

Heaney's 'elsewhere' is very much the realm of the feminine. He is one amongst a number of Irish male writers (others include John Montague, Paul Durcan, James Joyce, and Brian Moore[1]) who have been lauded for their ability to articulate the feminine, and he has described the act of writing, of creating poems, as "a feminine action, almost parthenogenic".[2] His frequent use of gendered imagery, both in the writing of poetry and in talking about his own and others' writing in his essays and in interviews, has led critics to write about a 'feminine principle' or a 'feminine sensibility'[3] in his work. In an interview, he remarked:

> There's a kind of voice in the world that's deprived because it hasn't got

something feminine in it or about it. It's just a conviction I have that some kind of wholeness, of content, is a good thing ... A religion that has a feminine component and a notion of the mother in the transcendental world is better than religion that has a father, a man, in it. I also—just in my nature and temperament, I suppose—believe in humility and in bowing down, and in 'we' rather than 'I'.[4]

Heaney's voice, particularly in the poems up to and including *North*, has "something feminine in it or about it"—with qualifications. Not only his poetry, but his prose and interviews are heavily gendered as he works to incorporate a 'we' voice. However, this use of 'we' poses several difficulties. At the very least, one must ask who is doing the talking? And who constitutes the rest of this collective voice? Behind the plural 'we' is still the singular 'I' of the writing poet—what is being voiced can never be more than a writer's view of an-'other' perspective. The 'we' dissolves back into 'I' and 'you'; 'you', the 'object', is endlessly fixed and defined as 'other', but as 'other' also gives the 'I' its identity: the 'I' is what the 'you' is not. In this sense, 'woman' functions as 'other' and 'elsewhere' for Heaney, in much the same way as Edward Said argues in *Orientalism* that the east functions to the west: as an 'other' place defined in terms that, consciously or unconsciously, privilege the viewer rather than the viewed and allow the construction and shaping of one's own identity (individually or collectively), often in a highly manipulative way.[5]

In Heaney's writing, a close reading reveals the instability of the 'we', the assertion that the 'I' knows and can therefore define, represent, or speak for the 'other'. At the same time that Heaney works to incorporate this 'other' voice, trying to give it equal play or even, as some have argued, privileging it, his rhetoric subverts that aim. A deep anxiety underlies much of his highly-gendered, sexual, imagery, sometimes evincing a fear of masculine sexuality, as in parts of 'A Lough Neagh Sequence' and in 'Death of a Naturalist', but most frequently betraying a marked uneasiness with the feminine that is in direct opposition to the warm embrace of it which his poetry has been said to represent.

Readily apparent in the gendered imagery of the poems is a chasmic dichotomy between male and female. Masculine and feminine are distinct, oppositional categories; a curious sundering, if Heaney's voice as a writer embodies the blending of the two genders, and a clear mark of the disintegration of the 'we' into subject and object. From Heaney's first, surprisingly prescient poem, 'Digging', and throughout many of his books, the masculine is posited as central and centred, predominantly associated with mastery, power and control. Adept and capable fathers, grandfathers and uncles are admired as role models, even though Heaney has spoken of his upbringing as woman-centred, both in the strong mariolatry of the Catholic Church, and in the "intimate domestic warmth and affection"[6] of his childhood, created by two women, his Aunt Mary and his mother. Additionally, in the great number of his poems which are, on one level, about the act of writing/creating itself, the artist figure (sometimes fictional figures like thatchers, diviners or blacksmiths, sometimes the poet 'himself'[7]) is always male, often intensely masculine. A startling array of phallic imagery, frequently appearing in the form of various rod-like tools the male/creator will use—sticks, rods, pens, guns, spades—consolidates the masculine imagery.

In contrast, the female is non-central, dispersed, waterlogged and oozing, portrayed as a dark hole or space of womblike blackness, a squelchy bog, or as water in various forms (in 'Undine', sluggish and dirty until the male enables her to flow clear). Bog, clay, mud and earth are her avatars as earth goddess. Even when the feminine is ceded a tentative focus, that focus keeps threatening to dissolve: "The wet centre is bottomless"; "This centre holds and spreads." The role of the male artist/creator is to give meaning to, interpret, or shape this dispersed and shapeless femaleness. This task is eroticised, so that the interaction of masculine and feminine becomes a sexual coupling, literally a 'creative act', where the art object is the 'child'. Heaney has affirmed such a view of the writing process himself in his prose writings and lectures, particularly in *Preoccupations*: the poetry and prose comment on and reinforce each other, symbolically and thematically, in a most revealing way.[8] Repeatedly, in essays detailing his own creative process as well as his interpretations of others' work, he genders the creative process and sexualises it. The 'masculine' strain is described in terms of mastery, will and control; the 'feminine' strain is secretive and involves the non-rational, indefinite qualities of instinct, emotion, the unconscious, and chance. Writing poems:

> ... involve[s] craft and determination, but chance and instinct have a role in the thing too. I think the thing is a kind of somnambulist encounter between masculine will and intelligence and feminine clusters of image and emotion.[9]

However, as is clear especially in poems with an overt female presence (poems in which the female is identified as a concrete individual, a 'she', even if she is a personified object as in 'The Pump' or 'Victorian Guitar'), such a coupling involves, not an equal merging, but a conscious controlling of the female by the masculine: she has it done to her. The masculine dominates, the feminine remains passive; the female is controlled and defined by the masculine, and remains the powerless object of the erotic act. The erotic, most frequently the provenance of the male, is a function of patriarchal society, which has for centuries defined eroticism in terms of domination and control. As Catherine MacKinnon has noted, "The erotic sexualizes power differentials".[10]

This exhibition of masculine power from an ostensibly feminine voice is particularly apparent in this passage from *Preoccupations*, where Heaney's assertion that his categories lack 'sexist overtones' is at once negated by the rhetoric of the paragraph:

> So I am setting up two categories and calling them masculine and feminine— but without the Victorian sexist overtones to be found in Hopkins' and Yeats' employment of the terms. In the masculine mode, the language functions as a form of address, of assertion or command, and the poetic effort has to do with conscious quelling and control of the materials, a labour of shaping; words are ... athletic, capable, displaying the muscle of sense. Whereas in the feminine mode the language functions more as evocation than as address, and the poetic effort is not so much a labour of design as it is an act of divination and revelation; words in the feminine mode behave with the lover's come-hither instead of the athlete's display, they constitute a poetry that is delicious as texture before it is recognised as architectonic.[11]

Such attributes of male and female could hardly be more stiflingly Victorian: the masculine mode is vibrantly active, fit for grappling manfully with the outside, and speaks out, giving public utterance to private thought and, indeed, making the assumption that such thoughts are worthy of such publication, while the feminine is passive, at best exhibiting womanly intuition, limited to summoning the male to her, calling rather than speaking out. Her realm is small and private, not large and public. Even the act of writing is eroticised, the feminine words reduced to the role of sex object, limited to behaving seductively, awaiting possession rather than going forth vigorously as the athletic male words may. The feminine mode of poetry is itself erotic, its "delicious texture" orally and tactually stimulating.

Of course, such representations of the masculine and feminine conform to the binary oppositions noted by Sherry Ortner, Hélène Cixous, and others, where, in general terms, male *equals* culture and female *equals* nature.[12] Culture is always privileged over nature, and, thus, masculine over feminine. As Cixous notes, a vast array of binary terms can be slotted into this basic male/female opposition:

Activity/Passivity
Sun/Moon
Culture/Nature
Day/Night
Father/Mother
Head/Emotions
Intelligible/Sensitive
Logos/Pathos

Cixous asserts that even if the categories are reversed, one always is aware of which half of the pair is given dominance in positive/negative paradigm:

Nature/History
Nature/Art
Nature/Mind
Passion/Action[13]

That such oppositions are implicit in Heaney's poetry and prose has, significantly, only seemed to be a subject of dispute when the critic questions their use; the many articles which either merely note them or even endorse them go unremarked upon.[14] Typical of the latter type of criticism is this passage, in which the critic nicely sums up and, indeed, positively enthuses over stiflingly essentialist gender distinctions:

> Everywhere in his writings Heaney is actually sensitive to the opposition between masculine will and intelligence on the one hand, and, on the other, feminine instinct and emotion; between architectonic masculinity and natural female feeling for mystery and divination. It is the opposition between the arena of public affairs and the intimate, secret stations of 'all the realms of whisper'. He uses it to describe the tension between English influence and the Irish experience ... It underlies two different responses to landscape, one that is 'lived, illiterate and unconscious', and one that is 'learned, literate and conscious'.[15]

Two early Heaney poems from *Door into the Dark*, 'The Forge' and

'Undine', are examples of those poems which are about the act of writing/creating. In such poems, the creator is always male, the privilege of creating art, masculine. The poems demonstrate how firmly the female is indeed 'elsewhere', a worrying unknown that the poet attempts to shape and control within the parameters of art. In so doing, Heaney clarifies and affirms a masculine identity, as 'I', which is, perhaps, open to the feminine, but only within certain and constrained definitions.

In 'The Forge', artistic creation involves a subconscious confrontation with the mastery of the feminine, but the poet himself avoids the confrontation. Indeed, only the first line of the poem is the first-person, establishing the poet at the "door into the dark"[16], but he does not enter. Instead, he creates an almost grotesquely male figure to master the dark for him. The sonnet begins with one line in the first person, "All I know is a door into the dark", then shifts into the third person to describe the forge. The blacksmith becomes the symbol watched externally by the poet; he is hugely male ("leather-aproned, hairs in his nose", vulcan-like). The forge itself is ostensibly the subject of the poem, but the blacksmith fills its spaces, even though he is never identified as a specific person or even a blacksmith (in contrast to the title-as-definition of 'The Diviner' or 'Thatcher'); he suddenly appears, after the sonnet's turn, an anonymous 'he'.

With the opening line, the poet sets himself outside the action of the poem and becomes a kind of apprentice artisan. Almost childlike, he is poised at the entrance to the door, where he can't see clearly inside because of the darkness. He can only describe what he *imagines* to be inside, based on what he hears and what he knows of the blacksmith's craft. The darkness is associated with what is unknowingly, mysteriously, feminine and what is unknowable in the self. (Heaney's fear of the dark, womblike interiors is clearly articulated in his first two books in 'The Barn', 'Nightpiece', 'Gone', and 'The Outlaw'.)

The poem unconsciously voices an anxiety about sexuality and the creative process: the poet stands outside the doorway leading into the darkness, afraid to cross the threshold; the male afraid of the sexual act, the inception into female darkness. Yet creation requires facing the darkness, because it takes place within, or 'elsewhere'; here, the physical space as 'elsewhere', the forge, elides with the physical space, the 'feminine'. Heaney creates a tension between what is known (outside) and unknown (inside), and his own tenuous position in between, *via* the structure of the first three lines:

All I know is a door into the dark.
Outside, old axles and iron hoops rusting;
Inside, the hammered anvil's short-pitched ring ...

Heaney responds to this anxiety by deploying the reassuring masculine, placing the superbly male, anonymous figure, completely in control, at the very heart of that which is feared, in the centre of the darkness, at the anvil. Inside the forge, the blacksmith is the creator, a combination of brute force—he can "beat real iron out ... work the bellows"—and restrained artistry, at home in the darkness, yet able to move outside, away from it; and it is crucial to the blacksmith's function that, for him, the dark is *not* 'elsewhere', but 'home', quite literally the smithy of his soul. Heaney pictures him as creator of both objects and music; the hammering of metal against metal becomes a kind of music as he creates form; the music image further links the blacksmith to the poet, the writer of lyrics. The blacksmith is also mysterious, a leather-aproned priest within a kind of church of darkness with the anvil, the artistic template, a pagan altar.[17] The blacksmith's anvil is therefore located "somewhere in the centre"; even though the poet hasn't ventured into the dark, he knows the anvil "must be" there; reassuring, an anchoring presence, "immoveable". It is also magical, mystical, and phallically male, "horned as a unicorn". If Heaney may not himself be the blacksmith, at least it is reassuring to know that the blacksmith is there, mastering the darkness.

In 'The Forge' and other male-focused creativity poems (like 'The Diviner' and 'The Salmon Fisher to the Salmon'), although a sexual dichotomy is implied, phallic and masculine imagery predominate. The female element is particularly abstract, evoked through language but not concretely evident. 'Undine' is one of a series of poems in *Door into the Dark* in which Heaney begins to use an overt female presence. Written in the first person, as if spoken by the mythical undine, or water nymph, it is a very good example of a poem in which Heaney ostensibly (and literally) gives voice to the feminine, while a careful reading reveals suppressions and masculinist assumptions. In this series of poems, Heaney opposes the passive, biologically-determined female element to a variously-active, vigorous male in highly sexual poems about art and creativity. The female is peripheral, a facilitator or muse of the male's artistic act. Decentred and marginal, she is needed *for* the work of the poem, but is not part *of* the work (as the wife says in 'The Wife's Tale', "I'd come and he had shown me/ So I belong no further to the work").

Undine was a water nymph who had to marry a mortal and bear him a child in order to gain a soul, consequently losing her own immortality. Heaney transposes the myth to a rural setting: the handsome man and the lovely, bathing water nymph upon whom he stumbles are transposed into a farmer shovelling clear an overgrown waterway, and the waterway itself. The action of the man frees the nymph. Her passivity and helplessness are contrasted with his forceful activity; he gives her "right of way in [her] own drains". Heaney almost certainly intends that the farmer returns sovereignty to her; however, the lines easily slip into a statement of her resentment at his *invasion* of her sovereignty (they are *her* drains, clogged or unclogged). Interestingly, the 'voice' of the 'other' (as supplied by the poet) seems to try to subvert the text itself.

Heaney's language in this poem has obvious sexual connotations: the stream/Undine "ran quick for him", and she notes "He halted, saw me finally disrobed,/Running clear, with apparent unconcern./Then he walked by me ..." The unclear referent makes it uncertain whether the man or Undine shows "apparent unconcern". However, when he walks by, she tries to attract him, rippling and churning, until he responds. The moment at which the man becomes the mortal lover of the water nymph is phrased in erotic, violent imagery: " ... he dug a spade deep into my flank/And took me to him." Heaney echoes his male as creator and spade as pen(is) imagery of 'Digging'; he will return to this imagery in *North*, especially in the poem 'Kinship' (part III), where the poet finds a spade, "the shaft wettish/as I sank it upright"[18] into the earth/earth goddess.

In this poem, the female is wholly dependent on the male's action for her freedom: "I swallowed his trench/Gratefully, dispersing myself for love/Down in his roots, climbing in his brassy grain." The man is transformed into a tree, merging with the water nymph. He now needs her: " ... once he knew my welcome, I alone/Could give him subtle increase and reflection." Possibly, Heaney intends this to mean (male 'craft', female 'gift') each is necessary to the other. However, in this poem, Undine seems to give much more than she gets: "He explored me completely, each limb/Lost its cold freedom. Human, warmed to him." Freedom is freedom, cold or not; this line suggests, too, the "sad freedom" of the Tollund Man of *Wintering Out*, where there is a liberating aspect to his willingness to be sacrificed to the earth goddess—it is, after all, an honour of sorts, and he goes by choice. Nonetheless, he is losing his life. Undine is losing her independence and freedom in exchange for becoming (literally) joined to the farmer.

The disturbingly misogynist source myth for 'Undine', wherein the nymph cannot gain a soul without sexual union and childbirth, suggests that a woman's rightful role, the only one which makes her 'human', is to surrender her sovereignty to a man.[19] Heaney describes this poem, in the essay 'Feeling into Words', as "a myth about agriculture, about the way water is *tamed and humanized* when streams become irrigation canals, when water becomes involved with seed"[20] (emphasis added). In 'Undine', as in other poems, that surrender is a violent act. And throughout this poem, the 'we' voice of Heaney speaking through the feminine and thereby purporting to give insight therein, keeps dissolving into oppositions of male/female, I/you, subject/object, domination/submission—even when the subject voice, the 'I', is given to the woman.

Both of these poems lay down a foundation of attitude and imagery which finds its most intense (and, I would argue, often problematical) expression in Heaney's famous bog poems. Once the notions of squelchy bog, earth goddess, and territory possessed and repossessed, are folded into this basic recipe, Heaney has a resonant and powerful metaphorical concoction which is also dangerous poetry in that it has a seductive appeal to a wider audience. Stan Smith has noted "There is no such thing as an innocent poem"[21], and this beautifully-wrought poetry, in assuming a dismayingly essentialist view of gender, in consequence argues on behalf of it. One who speaks of 'elsewhere' by definition does so as someone who is outside, a visitor. This 'other' perspective may be constructive, revealing and insightful—but the speaking position of the viewer, the 'I', can never become a 'we'. This is especially true when, as is so often the case with the 'other', the viewed are not allowed to speak for themselves, but are instead voiceless, defined by the viewer. As Virginia Woolf most famously argued in *A Room of One's Own*, this has historically been the case between men and women. As feminist and post-colonial theorists (amongst others) have so persuasively shown, it is extremely risky and presumptuous to purport, indeed to assume, to speak for and on behalf of 'elsewhere'.

Notes

[1] One sometimes is led to wonder why more attention isn't paid to the female poets who do just this—and certainly one might expect that women can 'articulate the feminine' (in all its diversity) with particular accuracy. The

suspicion that one discourse is more privileged here than another is strengthened when one tries to recall a single woman poet or novelist who has been greeted with equal praise and fanfare for articulating the masculine.

[2] Seamus Heaney, *Preoccupations* (New York: Farrar, 1980) p. 83.

[3] See Carlanda Green, 'The Feminine Principle in Seamus Heaney's Poetry,' *Ariel* 14.3 (1983): pp. 3-13; and John Haffenden, 'Seamus Heaney and the Feminine Sensibility,' *The Yearbook of English Studies* 17 (1987), pp. 89-116.

[4] Seamus Heaney, interview, *Viewpoints: Poets in Conversation*, John Haffenden (ed.) (London: Faber & Faber, 1981), p. 61.

[5] Edward Said, *Orientalism* (1978; Harmondsworth: Penguin, 1985). Said's argument is precisely that 'elsewhere' *equals* other. See also recent post-colonial criticism which makes the same point in terms of national identity; Cairns and Richard's *Writing Ireland* specifically addresses the Irish context of this argument (Ireland as England's 'other'). The authors also note the way in which this opposition is gendered as England/Ireland; male/female.

[6] Neil Corcoran, *Seamus Heaney* (London: Faber & Faber, 1986), p. 12.

[7] Inasmuch as the poetic 'I' is ever actually 'the poet'.

[8] It is frequently the prose that confirms the subvertive/subverting voice that undermines the (apparent) intention of the poetry.

[9] Heaney, *Preoccupations*, p. 34.

[10] Catherine A. MacKinnon, 'Does Sexuality Have a History?' *Michigan Quarterly Review* 30.1 (1991), pp. 1-11.

[11] Heaney, *Preoccupations*, p. 88.

[12] Sherry Ortner, 'Is Female to male as Nature is to Culture?,' *Women, Culture, and Society*, Michelle Rosaldo and Louise Lamphere (eds.) (Stanford, CA: Stanford UP, 1974) pp. 67–88. As Ortner points out, this is not a strict equation: woman tends to be identified more strongly with nature and man with culture. Although I agree that these categories are a western construct and not necessarily valid across cultures and throughout time (as Carol P. MacCormack and Marilyn Strathern argue persuasively in *Nature, Culture and Gender* [Cambridge: CUP, 1980]), I do believe Heaney's own poetry, coming from a western, highly patriarchal society, both fits these categories and attempts to give validity to them.

[13] Translated by Toril Moi in *Sexual-Textual Politics: Feminist Literary Theory*, (London: Methuen, 1985), pp. 104-5.

[14] For example, Carlanda Green's relatively early article on 'the feminine principle' in Heaney merely observed the gendered aspect of poetry and prose and offered no critique (however, the article is sanctioned as the only 'feminist' essay in Harold Bloom's *Seamus Heaney*). Critical articles by Elizabeth Butler Cullingford, David Lloyd and Patricia Coughlan have drawn more ire.

[15] Elmer Andrews, *The Poetry of Seamus Heaney: 'All the Realms of Whisper,'* (Basingstoke: Macmillan, 1988), pp. 8-9.

[16] Seamus Heaney, *North* (London: Faber & Faber,1975) p. 19.

[17] Priest imagery also runs through another of these male-as-creator poems;

see 'The Diviner.'

[18]*North*, p. 42.

[19] Similarly, the feminised guitar of 'Victorian Guitar' is finally and belatedly given "the time of its life" (Heaney, *Door into the Dark*, p. 33) only when handled by the right man. This point is also noted by Patricia Coughlan in "'Bog Queens': the Representation of Women in the Poetry of John Montague and Seamus Heaney', *Gender in Irish Writing*, Toni O'Brien Johnson and David Cairns (eds.) (Milton Keynes: Open UP, 1991) pp. 88–111 (102), who stringently observes in a footnote: "Neil Corcoran severely understates the case when he say 'the poem has, like 'The Wife's Tale', its element of male presumption'".

[20]Heaney, *Preoccupations*, p. 53. Again, this is typical of the way in which Heaney seems unconsciously to undercut his own stated intention in a poem.

[21]He continues: "All poetry, at its deepest levels, is structured by the precise historical experience from which it emerged, those conjunctures in which its author was formed, came to consciousness, and found a voice." Stan Smith, *Inviolable Voice: History and Twentieth-Century Poetry* (Dublin: Gill & Macmillan, 1982), p. 1.

'Time that was extra, unforeseen and free'
Representations of childhood in the poetry of Seamus Heaney

Patricia Horton

In the introduction to her book *What is a Child? Popular Images of Childhood*, Patricia Holland makes the following point about modern-day representations of childhood:

> For all its modernisation, the nostalgic imagery of childhood refers overwhelmingly to a harmonious and comfortable world before industrial civilisation, where plenty did not depend on work or wealth. A rural idyll is pictured on milk cartons, bread wrappers, supermarket labels, advertisements for foodstuffs, and in high gloss magazines about country living.[1]

Holland is drawing attention to two things here—our continuing preoccupation with childhood and the pervasiveness of a certain kind of representation of childhood in our society. Certainly, this preoccupation is bound up with the fact that childhood plays a major role in the stories we tell ourselves to make sense of our lives. It is part of our impulse towards self-definition and self-understanding.

Any analysis of the past, however, tells us things about the present and about the self who is reconstructing it. As Carolyn Steedman puts it:

> ... the point doesn't lie there, back in the past, back in the lost time at which the event happened, the only point lies in interpretation. The past is re-used through the agency of social information, and interpretations of it can only be made with what people know of a social world.[2]

What she is seeking to highlight is how our interpretations of childhood are made *via* a web of associations which society has built up around this area of experience; associations which, at least partially, condition our own responses. These have tended to dehistoricise childhood by denying personal and historical particularity, absorbing the marginal into an official, central story. This 'official' story takes two forms. The first, as Holland points out, presents childhood as an idyllic rural past, a pastoral myth of uncomplicated certainties, contrasting forcefully with an industrial present, a world of adult complication and difficulty. The second—which Holland does not take into account, since the focus of her book is on representations of children in advertising—is the notion of childhood as a period which is pre-social and is therefore a threat to the civilised world. In the first, the child is an innocent, uncorrupted by society; in the second, the child is a savage, beyond the pale of the civilised world. Both representations help to perpetuate certain myths about childhood and serve to mask the real conditions in which children live. With this in mind, I will focus on Seamus Heaney's representations of childhood, the way that he uses this area of experience, the extent to which his 'story' colludes with or disrupts an 'official story', and the ethical implications that this has for his poetry.

Although the child has always featured prominently in literature, it is only with Rousseau that childhood begins to be regarded as a state having importance in and by itself. "Childhood," Rousseau said, "has its own ways of seeing, thinking and feeling; nothing is more foolish than to try and substitute our ways"[3]. He uses childhood as a means of protest, a way of expressing his dissatisfaction with the present world and society. The child is the innocent victim of a corrupting society and childhood is a paradisal state in which individuals can express themselves freely, where they are most truly themselves. Rousseau's is a theory constructed around the oppositions of nature versus culture, primitive versus civilised. He sees 'man' as naturally good, a free, whole human being who is at one with nature. Maturity and adulthood see the self gradually alienated from its true nature and forced to enter the 'civilised' world of politics and property. These notions are popularised in the poetry of Wordsworth. Peter Coveney, in *Poor Monkey: The Child in Literature*, nominates Wordsworth as one of the writers who helped to establish childhood as an independent and influential phase in the individual's life. Coveney has indicated why the child was such an attractive figure for writers:

> Through the child could be expressed the artist's awareness of human Innocence against the cumulative pressures of social Experience. If the

central problem of the artist was in fact of adjustment, one can see the possibilities for identifications between the artist and the consciousness of the child whose difficulty and chief source of pain often lie in adjustment and accommodation to its environment. In childhood lay the perfect image of insecurity and isolation, fear and bewilderment, vulnerability and potential violation.[4]

Wordsworth's preoccupation with childhood can be seen as a response to the developing industrialisation of the 18th and 19th centuries. The child's world, like that of the artist, is precarious and vulnerable because both are inexorably forced to cope with the constraints of a world which is at odds with their 'true nature'. The child, therefore, became a perfect symbol for the artist who felt increasingly alienated in a world where writing was coming to be dominated by the rules of commodity production. Wordsworth reinforced the notion that adulthood is bound up with property, production and the modern industrial society; and childhood, the source of identity and poetic creativity, a time of "uninhibited expression and activity"[5], where the subject is undifferentiated from nature. He describes his own childhood as a time "when like a roe/I bounded o'er the mountains, by the sides/ Of the deep rivers, and the lonely streams,/Wherever nature led".[6] It was a time of "aching joys" and "dizzy rapture" ('Tintern Abbey'). Although these first sensations give way to "a sense sublime/Of something far more deeply interfused", they are still "The anchor of my purest thoughts, the nurse/The guide, the guardian of my heart, and soul/Of all my moral being" ('Tintern Abbey'). The transition from childhood to maturity brings advantages, but it is on the whole portrayed as "an experience of declining power".[7] The "hiding places" of his power, Wordsworth claims, are buried in childhood, in those "spots of time". He sees in childhood "an unproblematic selfhood"[8], which is stable and unchanging and to which he can repair as a source of restoration and nourishment. This construction of childhood has persisted as a structure of feeling to the present day. Robert Bly, for example, writing in 1990 in *Iron John*, speaks of our search for the golden ball which "reminds us of the personality we had as children— a kind of radiance, or wholeness, before we split into male or female, rich and poor, bad and good. The ball is golden, as the sun is, and round. Like the sun, it gives off a radiant energy from the inside."[9] This is the great myth of childhood.

Images of the child and childhood in Irish writing are complicated by the political context and literary traditions of Ireland itself. Irish

Romantic nationalism and the Irish Literary Revival predicated the identity of the nation in the land and in an idealised rural past. Rural life is idealised and seen as giving access to a timeless, traditional and, above all, 'authentic' way of life. This is the true identity of the nation which has been replaced by an industrial England. This idealisation of the peasant and rural life is taken over from the 'cultural primitivism' of English Romanticism which, as M.H. Abrams has pointed out, was "Wordsworth's standard".[10] We see this in *The Preface to the Lyrical Ballads*, where Wordsworth, in attempting to trace the "primary laws of our nature" chooses to focus on "low and rustic life", because

> ... in that situation they can attain their maturity, are less under restraint, and speak a plainer and more emphatic language; because in that situation our elementary feelings exist in a state of greater simplicity and consequently may be more accurately contemplated and more forcibly communicated; because the manners of rural life germinated from those elementary feelings.
> (*Wordsworth*, p. 597)

The peasant, therefore, occupies a privileged position in Wordsworth's theories of human nature. He comes closest to embodying the essence of human identity. Like the child, he maintains some vital connection with the "primary laws of our nature" and, as such, is a potent source of inspiration for all of us who have lost touch with that source. These tenets are carried over into Irish Romantic nationalism via Arnold and Yeats. Arnold, in 'On the Study of Celtic Literature', characterises or caricatures the Celt as 'sentimental', "keenly sensitive to joy and sorrow" and having a "peculiarly near and intimate feeling of nature":

> The skilful and resolute appliance of means to ends which is needed both to make progress in material civilisation, and also to form powerful states, is just what the Celt has least turn for.

Identified with the feminine, the Celts are excluded from the masculine world of politics and relegated to a child-like state where they are undifferentiated from nature and are dependent on others for moral and political guidance. Yeats responded to this with 'The Celtic Element in Literature', turning Arnold's "natural magic", that sentimental emotional energy the Celts share in their response to the natural world, into the "ancient religion", that flood of "passions and beliefs of ancient times" without which "literature dwindles to a mere chronicle of circumstance, or passionless fantasies, and passionless meditations". Yeats tries to subvert Arnold's argument, but by remaining within the binary opposition Arnold sets up, he lends it validity. He gives the peasant privileged status, not because he finds in him the essence of human identity, but rather because he possesses the essence of Irishness. The peasant is pure and innocent, and has escaped the influence of modernisation and industrialisation. It is Wordsworth's Romantic matrix in an Irish context. Fintan O'Toole, in 'The Country and the City in Irish Writing', points to how

> ... this element of childishness in the portrayal of the idealised peasant of the countryside ... has been the crucial dimension of the myth of the country which is opposed to the city. Time and time again, the image of the peasant in modern writing, stemming from the revival, is an image of the child.[11]

By glorifying the peasant, and his primitive, instinctive bond with the land, Yeats and the writers of the Irish Literary Revival "nationalised colonial attitudes, internalising a process which belonged to the colonial mentality and selling it back to the outside world as a reflection of Irish reality."[12] Seamus Deane, in 'Civilians and Barbarians', sees the most dangerous aspect of this to be the internalisation of the colonial discourse which characterises Ireland as barbaric and ungovernable. Deane stops short at looking at how present-day Irish writers continue to collude in and thereby perpetuate such representations. The aim of this paper is to show, through analysing images of the child and childhood, how Seamus Heaney tropes these colonial stereotypes.

'Making Strange', from *Station Island* (1984), is a key text here. In the poem, the speaker faces a conflict between two selves, a former self who is described as "unshorn and bewildered/in the tubs of his wellingtons,/smiling at me for help" and a self who arrives "with his travelled intelligence and tawny containment,/his speech like the twang of a bowstring". The former is the archetypal childish peasant, helpless and inarticulate in the face of this sophisticated, intelligent and self-assured adult. The conflict is that of child versus adult, peasant versus cosmopolitan, and barbarian versus civilian. However, since both are adults, the poem replays an Arnoldian discourse which sees the Irish people as barbaric children, inarticulate and needing to be governed. This is part of an ongoing attempt in Heaney to reconcile two conflicting aspects of self, an original Irish identity and an educated acquired identity, a division which can only be healed by the "cunning middle voice" of poetry. His writing consistently locates childhood in a rural past, and identifies it with the feminine presence and finally with the "matter of Ireland" itself. It is part of the illiterate, the unconscious and the irrational, bound up with roots and origins. This identity is threatened by, yet must join with, the "masculine element" of "involvement with English Literature"[13], which is part of the public world of social and political reality, rational and responsible processes.

The dichotomy that is being set up is typical of those "patterns of tension between the country and city, with the country as the place of childhood, family and innocence and the city as the centre of sophistication, complication and adult difficulty"[14], which pervade Irish literature. The poetic act has the potential to build bridges between these, to wed these masculine and feminine worlds. In doing so, it heals the split subject and reaffirms the wholeness of the transcendent ego. Yet, if poetry is conceived of as a marriage of these two worlds then those worlds must remain as they are in order that poetry can continue to fulfil its function. Ireland must remain agrarian, associated with the irrational, instinctual and feminine. 'Authentic' Irish identity, like childhood must be located in a 'lost' world which only poetry can recapture. This idea is reinforced if we turn to Heaney himself. When, in an article in *The Listener*, he says "I think this notion of the dark centre, the blurred and irrational storehouse of insight and instincts, the hidden core of the self—this notion is the foundation of what viewpoint I might articulate for myself as a poet"[15], he is grounding his identity and his poetry in values which are associated with his rural childhood experience, in pre-reflective and pre-verbal stages of development. By implication, he grounds Ireland's identity in those same stages.

From the first, childhood has been a pervasive theme in Heaney's work. *Death of a Naturalist* (1966) shows the break-up of the child's world and his entry into the world of adolescence and adulthood. The poems present a Romantic view of childhood, where the child is seen to exist in a state of nature. Adulthood begins with the break up of that world by change and death. Thus 'Death of a Naturalist' and 'Blackberry-Picking' show how an awareness of sexuality and change disrupt the idyllic world of childhood and harmony with nature. This is in keeping with the kind of representations of childhood we looked at earlier and with those pastoral assumptions which are the central interpretative devices of Irish Romantic nationalism. Heaney speaks of his rural childhood in Derry as an "omphalos", a constant source of nourishment.

In 'Mossbawn', reflecting on the events of World War I, he talks of how "all that great historical action does not disturb the rhythms of the yard". His home stands outside history and his childhood forms part of the perfected world of pastoral convention which seeks to displace and idealise. Yet, as Carolyn Steedman pointed out, very often our stories are in "deep and ambiguous conflict with the official interpretative devices of a culture". Heaney's story is no exception. History invades the pastoral idyll in the imagery of war and conquest which permeates the collection. In 'Death of a Naturalist', we see it in words like "punishing", "invaded", "cocked", "obscene threats", "mud grenades", "vengeances". In 'Churning Day', the "four crocks" are likened to "large pottery bombs". In 'Trout', the fish is a "fat gun-barrel" that "darts like a tracer-/bullet". Such language undermines Heaney's portrayal of his childhood as a "completely trustworthy centre". Poems like 'Digging' and 'Follower' perform the same task, for they base a fully achieved independence upon a symbolic killing of the father.

If unity with the natural world constitutes childhood in Heaney's writing, then the severing of that bond is what constitutes adulthood. The adult must achieve transcendence and enter the realm of culture. Patricia Holland focuses on this as an element in the construction of images of childhood:

> The dichotomy child/adult is linked to other dichotomies which dominate our thought; nature/culture, primitiveness/civilisation, emotion/reason. In each pair the dominant term seeks to understand and control the subordinate, keeping it separate but using it for its own enrichment.[16]

This is precisely the dichotomy that is set up in *North* (1975), where we have the politicisation of childhood and adulthood in their use as metaphors to describe the England/Ireland conflict. In 'Antaeus', a figure with whom Heaney identifies himself and Ireland[17], the speaker has a filial relationship with the land. He is "cradled in the dark that wombed me/And nurtured in every artery/Like a small hillock". The move from this child-like state of reassurance and security to adulthood, the realm of nationality and culture, is envisaged as a severance of contact with the land. Colonisation by Herculean England precipitates by implication Antaean Ireland from childhood to adulthood. It is perceived as the 'fall' from innocence into experience, from irrationality and the instinctual life to the 'light' of intelligence, from the darkness of tribal affiliation into Enlightenment rationalism. It is, above all, an experience of "loss/and origins". This reading is endorsed by Heaney himself, who has said that "Hercules represents the balanced rational light while Antaeus represents the pieties of illiterate fidelity"[18]. The implications of this opposition are heightened when we consider Locke's theory of childhood. As David Archard has argued, Locke believed that "the exercise of reason qualifies an individual for the exercise of freedom"[19] and, since he regarded children as "not yet fully rational"[20], they were, therefore, incapable of holding citizenship. By presenting Ireland as a child within the political domain, Heaney is implying that it is incapable of holding citizenship and is in need of being governed, an argument which is part of the discourse of colonialism.

Heaney's later work, however, shows a development in his representations of childhood. In his early work, the child is often associated with the instinctual unconscious life, the buried life of the feelings, and the adult, by implication, with the rational and the conscious. Childhood is a dark creative storehouse deep in the unconscious. In the later work, those representations are still based upon the Wordsworthian "spots of time" model, but are now associated with the marvellous and wondrous rather than with fear and guilt. Heaney has thrown light on this development in an interview with Melvyn Bragg. Talking of 'Wheels within Wheels', a poem in *Seeing Things* (1991), he says "there is a sense that this child is being invigilated at a distance with affection and some kind of comprehension, whereas in 'Death of a Naturalist' one is much more close up, it was much more child's eye view, hot-breathed, closed-in"[21].

This 'detached' perspective signals a more conscious crafting, even manipulation, of representations of childhood by Heaney and this is borne out textually in his successful creation of a timeless, ahistorical childhood which papers over those ruptures we saw in the early poetry. More than any other, this a collection about transcendence. 'Markings', for example, concentrates on how children can play football in the dark, and how in that time they go beyond the limits of the ordinary and of history into "time that was extra, unforeseen and free". In 'Wheels within Wheels', the speaker remembers turning the wheel of his bike backwards, an experience which is "Like an access of free power". These childhood "spots of time" are Wordsworthian, the "hiding places" of Heaney's power. Yet Wordsworth's representations of childhood are often elegiac in tone. Maturity was for him an experience of "declining power" in terms of his creativity. This is not the case for Heaney in his latest collection. The "spots of time" he focuses on are not unique experiences, forever lost and never to be repeated. Thus the freedom and transcendence which the children experience in 'Markings' can be captured by the artist in the poetic act. In this moment, he is apparently able to transcend the constraints of time and place, entering free space that leaves him feeling "amplified" and "extended". So too in 'Wheels within Wheels', the sensations that this childhood experience produced are repeated again in a "circus ring" where the speaker sees another set of spinning wheels. The central thrust of these poems is that the freedom and freshness of vision that were part of our childhood are not lost to us. The emphasis on freedom from constraints, on transcending limits, and on escape into the extraordinary, all of this is part of an adult desire to evade the personal and social responsibilities that define adulthood. In effect, these poems imply that adulthood can be just like childhood.

All these representations of childhood—which we might categorise as the Wordsworthian, the political, and the anti-Wordsworthian—are nostalgic rather than historic, not part of a project to understand a personal and social history, but an attempt to escape from the personal and social responsibilities that define adulthood. Heaney's representations reflect, with increasing success, the myth that childhood is an idyllic uncomplicated time. In this respect, the politicisation of childhood in *North* is central, since it makes explicit what was latent in earlier representations and, by making them explicit, serves to shape later representations. The backward shadow cast by *North* means that the privileging of darkness in earlier collections is no longer simply an exploration of the unconscious, but the privileging of an authentic 'Irish' way of life. The same may also be true, in a different way, of *Seeing Things*, for if *North* casts a backward shadow, it might also be said to shape future collections. Before, Heaney privileged darkness in his poetry, associating it with creativity, childhood and Ireland. In his latest collection, however, it is light which is celebrated, though in *North* this was associated with rationality, adulthood and England. Now light symbolises the irrational. *Seeing Things* represents an attempt to depoliticise *North*, a collection which exposed a cultural unconscious of Romantic nationalism at work in Heaney's early poetry. The renewed preoccupation with childhood in his latest collection is a conscious attempt on Heaney's part to revise his own representations and to control readings of his own work.

Notes

[1] Patricia Holland, *What is a Child? Popular Images of Childhood* (London: Virago Press, 1991), p. 14.
[2] Carolyn Steedman, *Landscape for a Good Woman* (London: Virago Press, 1986), p. 5.
[3] Jean-Jacques Rousseau, *Emile*, trans. Barbara Foxley (London: Dent and Sons Ltd, 1974), p. 54.
[4] Peter Coveney, *Poor Monkey: The Child in Literature* (London: Rockliffe, 1957), p. xi.
[5] Jonathon Cooke, 'Romantic Literature and Childhood', in David Aers, Jonathon Cooke and David Punter (eds.) *Romanticism and Ideology: Studies in English Writing 1765–1830* (London, Routledge and Kegan Paul, 1981), p. 62.
[6] William Wordsworth, 'Lines written a few miles above Tintern Abbey' in *William Wordsworth*, Stephen Gill (ed.) (Oxford: Oxford University Press, 1984), p. 133. All subsequent references to this edition.
[7] Cooke, p. 62.
[8] Cooke, p. 61.
[9] Robert Bly, *Iron John: A Book about Men* (New York: Vintage Books, 1992), p. 7.
[10] M.H. Abrams, *The Mirror and the Lamp: Romantic Theory and Critical Tradition* (New York: Norton, 1958), p. 105.
[11] Fintan O'Toole, 'Going West: The Country and the City in Irish Writing', *The Crane Bag Book of Irish Studies* 9,2 (1985), p. 113.
[12] O'Toole, p. 113.
[13] Seamus Heaney, 'Belfast', in *Preoccupations: Selected Prose 1968-78* (London: Faber & Faber, 1984), p. 34.
[14] O'Toole, p. 114.
[15] Seamus Heaney, 'King of the Dark', *The Listener* (5th February, 1970), p. 181.
[16] Holland, p. 14.
[17] Seamus Deane, 'Unhappy and At Home', interview with Seamus Heaney in *The Crane Bag Book of Irish Studies* 1,1 (1977).
[18] Deane, p. 63.
[19] David Archard, *Children: Rights and Childhood* (London: Routledge, 1993), p. 6.
[20] Archard, p. 2.
[21] Seamus Heaney, in conversation with Melvyn Bragg, *The South Bank Show*, LWT, 1991.

Pictures, Singing and the Temple
Some Contexts for Hewitt's Images

Norman Vance

My title recalls the last line of "Because I paced my thought by the natural world", one of Hewitt's gently regretful poems (dating from 1944) describing his rather lonely creative and civic allegiances. For the rest of his life he stood by these allegiances, and by this poem, frequently anthologised, which provided the title and introduction to the Arts Council film about his work, *I Found Myself Alone*. His hope for the future, he says, depends on recreating a time and a place where art and letters vitally matter in the community, when there can be procession and celebration with "the picture carried with singing into the temple".[1]

This splash of colour amidst 40s austerities suggests southern climes and the artistically opulent city states of the Italian renaissance. Frank Ormsby, in his edition of Hewitt, has the poet's authority for referring us to the 16th-century Italian art historian Giorgio Vasari. Vasari describes the painter Cimabue's newly-completed Madonna, the Rucellai Madonna, being carried in triumphant procession through the streets of Florence from his house to the church of Santa Maria Novella, for which it had been commissioned. Processions and celebrations of creativity were part of the cultural and social life of medieval and renaissance cities, and Hewitt would have read about them, not just in Vasari but in Lewis Mumford's influential study, *The Culture of Cities* (1938).

But there is a more immediate source which would have been well-known to Hewitt, the art gallery man. Over the main entrance of the National Gallery in London, on loan from the collection of Her Majesty the Queen, there hangs Frederick Leighton's once-famous Victorian painting entitled *Cimabue's celebrated Madonna is carried in procession through the streets of Florence* (1855), closely based on the same passage in Vasari.[2] In the picture, the poet Dante stands pensively in the extreme right-hand corner, an onlooker complicit with, yet partly withdrawn from, the life of his city, perhaps prefiguring Hewitt's rueful self-image in the same poem: "I found myself alone who had hoped for attention."

The church for which the painting was intended is not shown in Leighton's picture. Hewitt the Methodist atheist, a dissenter even from dissent as he called himself, is happy to generalise the occasion and deconsecrate the Florentine church of Santa Maria Novella into a general-purpose, vaguely classical "temple". In much the same manner, William Morris, whom he so much admired as a writer, a socialist and an artist, was disposed to see churches as places of communal and artistic importance, rather than centres for institutional religion. The celebratory singing in which the poet can share like his predecessors in the tradition of poetry, the pictures cherished by the art gallery man, and the communal focus of the temple embodying a sense of secularised civic responsibility or civic humanism, represent the three main themes of this discussion, three contexts for Hewitt's images.

Singing seems to come first, a little unexpectedly. Hewitt's poems usually depend more on sense than on sound. With their quiet conventional rhythms and sober diction, they are not, on the whole, words for music, perhaps. But poets sing despite themselves: it is, after all, what they are for. Lyric poetry such as Hewitt's can enshrine emotionally-heightened celebration and exploration that go beyond the prose sense of the words. Furthermore, the strongly ethical, socially committed Methodism that Hewitt formally ceased to espouse, but never quite got rid of, was famously, even notoriously, "born in song" and ever since has sustained a vigorous hymn-singing tradition. Hewitt can be considered not so much a 'post-Christian' as a post-Methodist poet, with hymns and preaching still resounding in his head. It is only quite recently, in the last 30 years or so, that hymns have become respectable, academically speaking, as appropriate objects of scholarly attention. Cultural historians have now outgrown their adolescent anti-religious bias sufficiently to see hymns as repositories of enhanced shared images, communal and accessible assertions of values and social meanings. It has also been observed that hymns may formalise, and give a representative quality to, individual spiritual loneliness and conflict as in hymn-book versions of the lyrics of George Herbert (much admired by the Wesleys) and in the Psalms. Hymn-singing worshippers reach out from loneliness into joy and the consolation of shared experience: those with whom they are singing may have travelled the same hard road and can now share the same vision of glory.

For Hewitt, who found himself alone when he had sought attention, loneliness could be allayed by the writing and publishing of verse, to be shared by the verse-reading community at least. In a politically-radical tradition that he would have recognised, because it includes the United Irishmen and 19th-century Chartist poets, he is at times a post-Methodist secular hymn-writer, fired with the secular enthusiasm of humanity. With the distracting example of sentimental Victorian hymns in front of us, it is easy to think of hymnody as fuzzily irrational and slackly emotive, but scholars such as the post-Baptist literary critic Donald Davie[3] have drawn our attention to the extent to which the best 18th-century hymns have the linguistic and intellectual clarity and precision characteristic of the enlightenment. It is with the enlightenment, and with radical enlightenment intellectuals such as Thomas Paine, author of *The Age of Reason* and *The Rights of Man*, that Hewitt most naturally belongs.

One of Donald Davie's particular heroes is the dissenting scholar-poet Isaac Watts, whose hymns were much admired by the Wesleys and whose work underlies both Methodist hymnody and the *Songs of Innocence and Experience* of the revolutionary dissenter, artist and poet William Blake. Blake was one of Hewitt's heroes, an inspiring if faintly improbable role-model for a well-behaved municipal official. Like the Psalms, and like Watts' *Divine Songs for Children*, Blake's lavishly-illustrated lyrics depend on simple, familiar, traditional images: flowers, trees, lambs, shepherds, green pasture or the green fields of a vulnerable paradise; in the same way, Hewitt the nature poet depends on an accessibly public and familiar lexicon of images—flowers and trees again, sheep, if not lambs, hillsides, the pattern of fields, crops, birds, whin blossom, the effects of cloud and light.

The connection between the word 'image' and the word 'imagination' was of particular importance to Romantic poets such as Coleridge and Wordsworth, and when Hewitt describes himself as pacing his thought by the natural world, he is laying claim to a characteristically Wordsworthian mode of vision and understanding. But, of course, Wordsworth is no naïve watercolourist of Cumbrian landscapes, and Hewitt's nature poetry has ambitions which lie well beyond providing a kind of colour supplement to the tourist literature of the Glens of Antrim or the Mourne Mountains. The natural world provided him with a vocabulary for exploring personal and social themes. In a glum poem of the 40s, the poet grumbled that "I have turned to the landscape because men disappoint me" ('The Ram's Horn', *Collected Poems*, p. 67); but the human features of the landscape, the impress of the farmer or the planters or colonists from whom he claimed descent, were never far from his thought. And his landscapes were viewed honestly, rather than always romantically suffused with an ideal beauty. They participate in his own temperamental wariness. For Wordsworth, nature poetry is a process of interaction rather than simple reprographics, and that implies the possibility that the interaction may not work. In poems such as 'October-born' (p. 230), Hewitt ruefully concedes that the images he wants from the landscape, sustaining images of peace and consolation and wholeness, may be temporarily unavailable, autumnally absent, his fault as much as theirs. The stubborn evidence of the senses—guarantee of the integrity of the enlightenment rationalist in Hewitt—denies easy sentimental solutions to personal and social discord in a world without peace or justice, and without a transcendental sublime in the form of the Wordsworthian God. Wordsworth's poetry had depended on emotion recollected in tranquillity, we are told, but Hewitt in despondency could not always invent or project upon the landscape a tranquillity he could not feel. Wordsworth, like C.S. Lewis, could be "surprised by joy", and Hewitt tried to be. Sometimes it happens, as in the magical moment in wartime in 'Townland of Peace':

> Once walking in the country of my kindred
> up the steep road to where the tower-topped mound
> still hoards their bones, that showery August day
> I walked clean out of Europe into peace.
>
> (p. 642)

But such sudden joy cannot be relied on.

In some ways, the Suffolk poet George Crabbe, a contemporary of Blake and a *protégé* of Edmund Burke, is a less exacting and more satisfying model for Hewitt's nature poetry, though Hewitt would not relish the "miserable shore" of Aldborough which dominated Crabbe's imagination (*Conacre*, p. 11). In Hewitt's poem 'A Country Walk in May' (1960), Warwickshire landscape suggests that Crabbe's verses "closer match the stride/of one who danders through the countryside" (p. 520). It is not just a matter of the movement of Crabbe's verse: Hewitt the honest observer welcomed the unsentimental particularity of Crabbe's images. Crabbe characteristically reacted against the conventions of pastoral idealisation by specifying tangled weeds, blighted trees, blackened sheaves and slimy watercourses bounded by mud-banks. This suited Hewitt's wry intuition that nature, as well as men, can let you down. In a sonnet called 'Failed Image', nature fails to deliver the consummation and mellow fruitfulness of harvest. Crabbe helps Hewitt to subvert the conventionally consoling imagery of harvest, by supplying sharply disconcerting counter-images:

> But here, where we had pledged us to expect
> the harvest's image endlessly renewed,
> bright as the berries on the bird-rife thorn,
> through rotting sheaves the thistles of neglect
> thrust ragged spikes or, purple-crested, stood
> in the pale acres of unripened corn.
>
> (p. 234)

In establishing what the image of harvest ought to have been, Hewitt sardonically invokes the landscapes of Breugel and of Samuel Palmer, because for him painting is one dimension of his vision, part of the way he sees. Specific, detailed links between verbal and painterly images are, of course, very common—it has long been realised, for instance, that John Keats' allusions to Bacchus owe a lot to Titian's painting of *Bacchus and Ariadne*—but for Hewitt, as for Robert Browning, painting and poetry are linked in a more general and a more complex fashion. Leighton's painting of *Cimabue's celebrated Madonna* was much admired by his friend Browning. Like Leighton, Browning read his Vasari and found in him subjects for poems, rather than subjects for paintings. The vision of the painter and painterly constructions of reality served him as models or analogies for the procedures of poetry and for the ways of seeing and understanding life which his own poetry explored. The most famous examples are his poems about the lives, as well as the vision, of Fra Lippo Lippi and Andrea del Sarto.

Pictures, like poems, embody ways of seeing, of constructing a manageable reality. In a late poem entitled 'Bifocal in Gaza' (1985), which glances self-mockingly at Milton's description of the captured Samson "Eyeless in Gaza, at the mill with slaves", Hewitt describes a cataract operation and tries to come to terms with increasingly unreliable sight, finding in the history of painting styles images for the visual distortions he experiences. He acknowledges the centrality of the visual sense in his mental and imaginative life:

... the axle of my being
which pivoted, propelled my spinning wits.

(p. 395)

His new bifocals, fortunately, could "set in order all my rocking world", so treacherous and chaotic when seen out of focus. Finding an order for things, seeing the world in focus, developing well-defined images— this describes the activity of poetry as well as of clear vision.

But Hewitt's characteristic wariness and scepticism make him uneasy about the possibility of the value of absolute clarity of mental and moral vision, however desirable it might seem to be. The sharp-edged 'realism' and quasi-photographic perspective of 17th-century Dutch painting provide a case in point. The Viennese art historian and theorist Ernst Gombrich, in works such as *Art and Illusion: a Study in the Psychology of Pictorial Representation* (1960), has drawn attention to the way the eye, and the painter, actively order and construct, rather than passively register visual realities. This has implications for Hewitt's work as poet and art gallery man closely engaged with social and political realities, a man who, like so many of us, saw reality with the help of his optician.

Long before Gombrich, since the late 19th century, art historians interested in 17th-century Dutch painting have explored connections between the development of optical instruments or aids to vision and the achievements of Dutch realist painters, such as Vermeer. Ways of seeing—as observer, as moralist, as painter, as poet—are reviewed in a fine poem Hewitt wrote in the mid-50s, 'The Spectacle of Truth':

> A masterly lens-polisher,
> pride of his guild in Amsterdam,
> once linked two crystals rim by rim
> whose mutual strength should make all clear;
> and when he clapped them to his eyes
> they proved so purging to the sight
> that all seemed as the last Assize,
> in the strict justice of the light.
>
> He saw the burgomaster stand
> beneath the towering Westkirk's porch,
> and like a candle in a church
> he held his small soul in his hand:
> one housewife bent above her tub,
> one pinned white linen on the line,

and whether shift or bridal robe,
bright as their sheets their spirits shone.

He saw the flowering barges glow,
the men aboard seemed bowed in prayer,
and at the stalls across the square
where nameless figures come and go,
all stood for judgment, stirring not,
hand held to mouth or hand at side;
and he could tell from where he sat
that this was wicked, this was good.

Then while he marvelled at the sight,
a breathless moment or an hour,
his rocking heart grew still and sure
that charity was more than light,
that, gazed at through the perfect glass,
this shining scene was bright and false,
the men, the houses and the trees,
mere patterned shapes on painted tiles;

And while he fixed his mind on truth,
time and the world were ice and stone,
so if he'd have them move again
and air thaw out in noisy breath,
he'd have to lay the lenses by,
and turn once more upon the street
his old decaying mortal eye,
desiring it, despising it.

(p. 89f)

A trip to Amsterdam in 1954 suggested the setting, but the masterly lens-polisher comes straight from the 17th century. Spectacle-making, which included grinding and polishing the lenses, was a skilled and established trade in the Low Countries, and the 17th-century philosopher Spinoza worked as a lens-polisher in Amsterdam. Another Dutch lens-polisher, Hans Lippershey, discovered about 1608 that if you lined up two lenses you could get an enlarged image of a distant object. Optics was one of the great new sciences of the 17th century and the French philosopher René Descartes wrote a treatise on optics which provides a practical and objective commentary on his more abstractly philosophical first principle *cogito ergo sum*—'I think therefore I am'—and its implication that the physical world stands over against and separate from the world of thought. At first, the poem seems to go along with this. When the short-sighted lens-polisher claps the linked lenses to his eyes, the world around him stands out with awe-inspiring clarity, as if presented to the contemplation and judgement of an all-seeing and all-knowing God at the Last Judgement. The lens-polisher sees the kinds of images Dutch painters meticulously constructed, sometimes with the help of optical instruments. Every Dutch town had its big church and its marketplace with "the stalls across the square": in the National Gallery in London, you can see Gerrit Berckheyde's painting of *The Marketplace and the Grote Kerk at Haarlem* (1674), a masterpiece of perspective. In the same room, you can see Emmanuel de Witte's *Adriana van Heusden and her daughter at the New Fish Market in Amsterdam* (1661-3). Dutch townscapes such as Jan Vermeer's *View of Delft* (1658), or Rembrandt's etched *View of Amsterdam* (1643), commonly provide profiles of the town seen across a body of water with barge-traffic helping to supply the human dimension ("He saw the flowering barges glow,/the men aboard seemed bowed in prayer"). There are also more intimate Dutch paintings showing the sort of things that go on in people's back yards: Pieter de Hooch's *A Woman and her Maid in a Courtyard* (1660) offers a visual counterpart to Hewitt's sharply glimpsed housewife pinning white linen on the line.[4]

But there is something disconcerting and unnatural about the brightness of the housewife's sheets, the almost feverish glowing of the barges, the observer's judgemental sense of distance from and superiority to the small soul of the burgomaster. The masterly lens-polisher's breathless contemplative wonder is not entirely comfortable. Spinoza, the lens-polisher of Amsterdam, had felt uneasy about Descartes' logical separation of the conscious ego from the physical and material world and had distrusted Descartes' confidence that, through disciplined reflection, one could attain to "clear and distinct ideas" which would necessarily convey the truth about the world.[5] This godlike capacity to rise above the world and, as it might be, to sit in judgement upon it, had no appeal for Spinoza, who had abandoned the orthodox Judaeism of his upbringing, and no appeal for the decidedly ex-Methodist John Hewitt. For both of them, the mind cannot ultimately be separated from the world. It is part of the world: it must live in and participate in the only world there is, the material and physical world. The repeated "it", and the syntax of the last two lines of the poem, make it slightly unclear whether it is the street or the decaying mortal eye that is both desired and despised: quite probably both, but the point is surely that it does not matter, for both participate in the limitation and in the wonder, the absolute givenness of the world as it is. Hewitt, the man who found himself alone, could never really accept aloneness or separation from the social and political realities of his time; but, by the same token, he could not accept the 'holier than thou' judgemental superiority to mere mortals—characteristic of too many of his countrymen, not all of them churchmen. It is interesting that, while in 'Bifocal in Gaza' the optician's lens can order Hewitt's "rocking world", in 'The Spectacle of Truth' his "rocking heart" is disturbed, not soothed or stilled, by what he sees through the lens.

Hewitt's ultimate distrust of optical and moral clarities of vision might owe something to the art historian Erwin Panofsky's comment on the startling precision of surface in the earlier Dutch painting of Jan van Eyck:

> Jan van Eyck's eye operates as a microscope and as a telescope at the same time ... However, such perfection had to be bought at a price. Neither a microscope nor a telescope is a good instrument with which to observe human emotion ... The emphasis is on quiet existence rather than action.[6]

Action makes it possible to unfreeze the tableau of the last judgement, to work in and with the world as it is, the responsibility of the politician and the ethical humanist. Human feeling and charity which engages with the human world, rather than coldly judges it, are obviously better than inert images, "mere patterned shapes on painted tiles", which is Hewitt's ultimately merciless account of the painterly precision of the Dutch masters.

Hewitt returns to this theme of the gap between the surface vision of the image-making poet (or painter) and ethical and politico-economic understanding in a much later poem (1975), 'Below the Mournes in May' (pp. 244-5). Despite the poem's impressively painterly framing of the landscape, the studied precision of the imagery, the poet suddenly, if slightly boringly, "remembered that the nature-poet/ has no easy prosody for/ class or property relationships,/ for the social dialectic". Much less boring, much more understandable in this context, is his enduring admiration for the genre paintings of the Belfast artist William Conor, well represented in the Belfast Art Gallery where Hewitt spent so much of his working life. The ordinary life of Belfast streets and small houses comes across not with *quasi*-photographic precision, but with a kind of semi-impressionistic atmospheric warmth and breeziness. Conor developed an idiosyncratic *impasto* technique, using wax to provide a broken surface for the paint, often thickly and unevenly applied.[7] The images have the blurred edges of sympathetic identification and understanding, providing Hewitt with the secularist's equivalent of the Methodist hymn-singer's vision of glory. He describes Conor's vision with sympathy and love, assembling biblical qualities of mercy and humility in the same line:

> ... the women gathered at some neighbour's door,
> the shabby men against a windowsill—
> the pity and the laughter of the poor—
> stir the dull heart and prop the flagging will,
> by mercy made more humble than before.
>
> (p. 225)

For Hewitt, things and places seen with the poet's or the painter's eye have ultimate significance only in their human context. Cimabue's picture was carried with singing into the temple so that it could be looked at and play its part in the devotional and communal life of Florence. Hewitt's best nature poems were written in the 40s, when World War II and restricted travel turned his thoughts much more intensely than before to the landscapes of his native place; but that does not mean that the political activism which had involved him in the Peace Pledge Union and in socialist politics in the inter-war years immediately disappeared out of the window. Notions of poetry as a self-affirming discourse, as an aesthetic event complete in its own terms, had been the daring new dogmatism of Hewitt's youth in the 20s, drawing aid and comfort from Yeats and art for art's sake and the heritage of symbolism from which Hewitt's poetics never entirely escaped. But William Morris's socialist aesthetic had helped to inoculate Hewitt against taking such notions too seriously; they were soon overwhelmed by the social earnestness and sub-Marxian poetics of the 30s associated with W.H. Auden and his contemporaries. Hewitt himself had written poems in this new idiom, including 'Anti-Promethean Ode' (1932), which seeks to bring poetry down from the mountain-tops, to domesticate the Romantic revolutionary impulse stemming from Shelley and apply it to "fields and habitable places", to turn from the contemplation of "elemental skies" to the "hearts and faces of dull common people".

Such people are the vital element in the landscape in Hewitt's field of vision, and such people provided audiences for Hewitt's vigorous activity as a middleman in art and letters. In 1948, long before cultural critics had turned their attention to the darker side of the landscape and to the representation or marginalisation of working people in landscape painting, Hewitt had observed:

> For a countryman the living landscape is
> a map of kinship at one level,
> at another, just below this, a chart of use,
> never at any level a fine view ...
> landscape is families, and a lone man
> boiling a small pot, and letters once a year.
>
> ('Landscape', p. 67)

But though Hewitt could identify with the lonely countryman, being used to finding himself alone politically and ideologically, there is a poignancy about his relations with country people:

> even a lifetime among you should leave me strange,
> for I could not change enough, and you will not change.
>
> ('O country people', p. 73)

This can stand for other forms of reluctant alienation: the alienation of the liberal middle-class child and adult from grinding poverty and working-class life and struggles that troubled his conscience, the increasing alienation from the violent and embittered city and region he cared about so much, the lifelong alienation from that unembarrassed, unqualified, unproblematic sense of Irishness available to Gaels, but not to planters "once alien here".

This discussion began by mentioning Frederick Leighton's portrayal of Dante as onlooker rather than participant in the Florentine procession in which the painter's art was honoured. Leighton's later picture, *Dante in Exile* (1864), shows Dante even more alone in the midst of people. The final instalment of Hewitt's loneliness and alienation was perhaps his (much less drastic) exile in Coventry, from which, unlike Dante, he eventually returned. Again unlike Dante, Hewitt, the sceptical rationalist, could construct no master-narrative in which art and life, his city and his world and the world to come could be assimilated and reconciled in a transcendent order. A lyric poet, he could at least escape from loneliness in moments of vision: he could find and share images of perplexity and, more rarely, of peace and even joy. There is one such moment in a section of 'Variations on a Theme', a long poem first published in 1969, in which Blakean piping and joy unexpectedly resound through the temple-like solemnity of a municipal art gallery:

> One day, before a canvas crammed
> with country crafts and colours gay,
> a Slovak landscape diagrammed,
> across the sky a shepherd lay,
> his long pipe lifted up to play.
>
> I quizzed a group of children then
> with pointing finger, playing fair;
> they spelt each object back again,
> but none among them could declare
> what purpose spread the shepherd there.
>
> Then, after silence infinite
> I begged once more. A grubby boy
> cried: sir; he plays the tune of It!
> What better phrase could you employ
> to symbolise Art's instant joy?

(pp. 319-20)

In this brief, treasured, moment art speaks to its community: the picture and the singing have found their temple. Image and music, painting and poetry are conjoined in an act of celebration and creative joy.

Notes

[1] John Hewitt, *Collected Poems*, Frank Ormsby (ed.) (Belfast: Blackstaff, 1991), p. 60.

[2] For Frederick Leighton see Leonee and Richard Ormond, *Lord Leighton* (New Haven and London: Yale University Press, 1975); the *Cimabue* painting is discussed pp. 26-31.

[3] For dissenting culture and Wesleyan and other hymns in the 18th century, see Donald Davie, 'Enlightenment and Dissent' in *Dissentient Voice* (Notre Dame and London: University of Notre Dame Press, 1982), especially pp. 20-31; Martha Winburn England and John Sparrow, *Hymns Unbidden: Donne, Herbert, Blake, Emily Dickinson and the Hymnographers* (New York: New York Public Library, 1966), especially pp. 35-7, 44-6; George Lawton, *John Wesley's English* (London: George Allen and Unwin, 1962), especially p. 56; T.B. Shepherd, *Methodism and the Literature of the Eighteenth Century* (London: Epworth Press, 1940).

[4] For Dutch painting and optical devices, see Heinrich Schwarz, 'Vermeer and the Camera Obscura', *Art and Photography: Forerunners and Influences*, William E. Parker (ed.) (Chicago and London: University of Chicago Press, 1985), pp. 119-131; Svetlana Alpers, *The Art of Describing: Dutch Art in the Seventeenth Century* (London: John Murray, 1983), especially pp. 152-9 (for illustrated discussion of panoramic town views). For reproductions of National Gallery Dutch Paintings see Christopher Brown, *Dutch Paintings* (London: The National Gallery, 1983) especially Plate 3 (Berckheyde's *The Marketplace and the Great Church at Haarlem*), Plate 21 (De Hooch's *A Woman and her Maid in a Courtyard*) and Plate 40 (Salomon van Ruysdael's *A View of Deventer*).

[5] For Spinoza and Descartes, see Stuart Hampshire, *Spinoza* (1951) (Harmondsworth: Penguin Books, 1962), pp. 104-11, a source which could have been available to Hewitt when the poem was written in 1954.

[6] E. Panofsky, *Early Netherlandish Painting*, 2 vols, (Cambridge, Mass.: Harvard University Press, 1953), I, p. 182.

[7] For William Conor, see S.B. Kennedy, *Irish Art and Modernism* (Belfast: Institute of Irish Studies at the Queen's University of Belfast, 1991), pp. 33, 182f, 326f.

The Primitive Image
Tradition, Modernity and Cinematic Ireland

Martin McLoone

In 1990, *My Left Foot*, Jim Sheridan's film about the writer Christy Brown, won international critical acclaim and picked up two acting Oscars for Daniel Day-Lewis and Brenda Fricker. This success only confirmed what was already emerging as a trend in both American and British film-making anyway. Irish-theme films were becoming more common, both on television and in the cinema, and not only were they in demand on the international film festival circuit but they were also beginning to make money at the box-office as well. In 1993, moreover, the Irish government adjusted tax incentives to entice big-budget American films to use Ireland for locations and to encourage film production in the country generally. At the same time *Bord Scannán na hÉireann* (the Irish Film Board) was relaunched specifically to stimulate indigenous film production. The result has been the most prolific period of film-making in and about Ireland since the birth of cinema 100 years ago.

This gives rise to a number of interesting cultural debates. What images of Ireland have emerged from this recent wave of cinematic and televisual representation? What is their relationship to existing traditions of representation? What are their similarities and differences? How do the indigenous images differ from those originating outside the country? Most pertinently for the cultural life of contemporary Ireland, can these outsider images suggest the kind of film-making to which an indigenous industry should aspire? These are complex questions in themselves. However, they are further complicated when considered within those wider debates which dominate the cultural life of Ireland today—debates about national and cultural identity, revisionism and the interpretation of history, cultural traditions and pluralism, and, overlaying it all, the question of Northern Ireland, as influential when it is absent from debate as much as when it is present. These questions have dominated Irish culture for many years now, creating a cultural ferment at the interface of politics and both creative and critical activity. Perhaps, over the years, they have been more associated with literature and historiography. Nonetheless there are few critical or artistic practices in Ireland today which have remained untouched by them. They are, therefore, just as relevant to an understanding of contemporary audiovisual culture in Ireland as they are to any other discourse and are arguably more important in this popular cultural context, because it is here that they connect with popular audiences in a very direct way.

Yet, it would also be wrong to consider these recent images in isolation from the traditions of visual representation which have influenced them. Indeed, consciously or otherwise, many of the recent films echo, or reinforce, traditional representations, while others, again consciously or not, attempt to respond in a contemporary idiom to the dominance of older traditions. These traditions have had a long historical gestation, of course, which has allowed them to enter into common currency, their ideological assumptions and political implications long disguised beneath their surface 'naturalness'. Although, until relatively recently, there has been little in the way of sustained indigenous film-making in Ireland, nonetheless, 'cinematic' Ireland does exist, largely the product of American and British film industries and going back to the beginnings of the cinema itself. And yet this cinematic tradition, too, consciously or not, tapped into older forms of representation—literary, theatrical and visual—which stretch back through the centuries.

To unravel the contemporary significance of this long historical process, I want to discuss briefly the opposition between 'tradition' and 'modernity', considering especially the notion of the 'primitive' which, it seems to me, underpins such an opposition. The concept of primitivism has been a crucial debate in the visual arts over the last century or so. It has also been invoked in literary debates over the same period to illuminate, among others, the work of 19th-century popular novelists, D.H. Lawrence, the social-realist writers of the 50s and 60s, and, in recent years, many so-called post-colonial and Third World writers from a variety of cultural backgrounds. Likewise, I believe the concept of the 'primitive', when applied to pre-cinematic images of Ireland, provides a useful historical and cultural context in which to discuss the recent steady stream of Irish and Irish-theme films.

Primitivism: Modernity's Janus

In the conflict between tradition and modernity, primitivism seems to look both ways. Writing about the role of British ethnography in the construction of an imperialist sense of national identity, Annie E. Coombes discusses a curious and revealing aspect of the Franco-British exhibition held at the White City, London, in 1908.[1] This was one of a series of international and colonial exhibitions which were mounted as both popular entertainments and as forms of popular education. For Coombes, they were also celebrations of European (especially British) civilisation and its superiority over the primitive colonial cultures, whose artefacts were often displayed in reconstructions of 'typical' villages inhabited by the colonial subjects in their native lands. Professional performers from the countries represented acted out the native culture of these villages. The curious aspect of the 1908 exhibition was that, as well as the construction of primitive villages from various African and Asian countries, the exhibition contained both a 'typical' Irish and a 'typical' Scottish village.

This might strike us today as a rather contradictory practice. After all, the purpose of the exhibition was to celebrate and reinforce European superiority, not to admit that primitiveness could exist close to the heart of the most powerful empire in human history.

But, as Coombes points out, these villages performed an important ideological function. On one hand, the European 'primitive' provided a kind of historical and teleological perspective that actually reinforced the difference and distance between Europe and its colonies. Even European 'primitiveness' was inherently superior to that of the colonised races represented at the exhibition, and this was evident to the general public in the vastly more 'advanced' culture presented in the Irish and Scottish exhibits. And, of course, the relative primitiveness of its Celtic periphery only reinforced the high achievement of the Anglo-Saxon centre. Furthermore, as far as the construction of a particular 'British' sense of identity was concerned, the Irish and Scottish villages confirmed the rich folk tradition upon which the 'national' culture was being constructed, and helped to reinforce the illusion of a homogeneous British culture.[2] This is a primitiveness, in other words, which validates, and is in turn validated by, a specific form of modernity—that of imperial Britain.

These villages, of course, might also have performed another function, one associated with a Rousseauesque Romantic sensibility.

They can also look back at this imperial progress with a more critical gaze, suggesting in their authentic folk traditions, in their organicism and closeness to nature, the price which has been paid for such progress. The 'primitive', then, has two faces—the uncivilised barbarian and the noble savage.

It has to be remembered, though, that this duality has a long lineage in British representations of Ireland. Many commentators have noted the emergence of the negative stereotyping of the Irish as far back as the 12th century.[3] Gerald of Wales (Giraldus Cambrensis) accompanied the first Norman invasion of Ireland and wrote an account which was to have a profound influence on subsequent English attitudes to the country. Manuscripts of his *History and Topography of Ireland* were illustrated with images of the Irish as debauched and bloodthirsty savages. The object of his graphic depiction of Irish cruelty and lack of civilisation was to provide justification for the Norman conquest of the country and it is hardly surprising that, four centuries later, during the Tudor conquest, his original writings re-emerged to exert a profound influence on Elizabethan writers and illustrators.

It is important to note that this emerging tradition of representation in a 'pre-modern' era is, nonetheless, a response to the 'primitive' from a particular construction of progress and modernity. The negative imagery of the Irish was based on the assumption that the mission in Ireland was essentially a civilising one, in both a religious and a political sense. Nor was this kind of cultural response to conquest a peculiarly British one. Spanish culture of the time is similarly replete with accounts and illustrations of the barbaric nature of the native populations of South America, offering the same kind of justification for conquest (and, in the case of Spain, helping to disguise the lust for gold and silver which motivated the *conquistadores*). Finally, in both the British and Spanish example, the dual face of the 'primitive' was present, even in these early pre-modern times. Indeed, the influence of Thomas Moore's *Utopia* on 16th-century Spain allowed for a construction of the native as a possible utopian figure, living a pure and simple life that was almost divine in its Edenic simplicity. The seeming contradiction in this duality was resolved by drawing a distinction between the land and the people who inhabited it. The native was reassigned the role of the serpent in the garden and was systematically expelled or brought to heel under the civilising authority which would best realise the Edenic potential of the land.

It is hardly surprising, then, that the negative face of the 'primitive' dominates when the political tensions between the coloniser and the colonised are at their most intense and that the more benign face predominates at moments of relative political stability. This process can be clearly seen in the nature of British representations of the Irish during the 19th century. These long years of political and social turbulence coincided with the rise of cheap, popular publications and, in the pages of satirical journals and illustrated weeklies, images of the Irish as uncivilised and ungrateful barbarians reached new levels of graphic cruelty. The cartoons and caricatures in popular publications like *Punch, Judy, The London Illustrated Weekly* and *The Tomahawk*, were based on a particular reading of Darwin and on the *pseudo*-science of physiognomy to produce a simianised version of the brute Irishman. As Lewis P. Curtis has shown, this image of the Irish was also prevalent in the USA at the same time.[4] The result of this vicious stereotyping was to deny a political or social context to agitation in Ireland and to reinforce Anglo-Saxon superiority over Celtic backwardness. In his study of contemporary cartoons on the Northern Ireland crisis, John Darby notes the return of this Victorian imagery, applied equally to nationalist and unionist, as the political tensions and the violence increased.[5] Thus this long tradition of negative stereotyping has become a reservoir of images to be dipped into according to the ideological or political needs of the time.

However, it must be remembered that the more positive face of Irish primitiveness continued to co-exist with, and develop alongside, the Neanderthal Irishman. This version of Ireland as a potential Garden of Eden, populated by a simple, musically-gifted, loquacious and happy peasantry, bore as little resemblance to reality as the ape-man brute, but it was an important aspect of European Romanticism throughout the 19th century. The Celtic periphery of Europe continued to provide intimations of the sublime for this Romantic sensibility as a response to the increasingly urban and industrial nature of modernity and progress.

The irony, of course, of this Romantic primitiveness is that it became internalised in Ireland itself. The combination of a rural utopia, a simple but moral peasantry, and the intimations of the sublime, perfectly suited the religious/political alliance that fuelled Catholic nationalism towards the end of the 19th century.

Thus the image of the Irish that grew out of the Romantic imaginings of urban intellectuals and antiquarians, both inside and out the country, was used against them in the long struggle for national determination. Again, there is nothing unique about this process. The idea of the nation itself is a product of the kind of modernity that imperialism and colonialism promoted, and the search for the individuality that marked out one nation from another is a product of the Romantic sensibility that motivated the utopianism of the 'primitive'. The images and language of the coloniser became the weapons to overthrow him and, therefore, his imaginings became internalised. Nor did this process end with 19th-century nationalism. Compare this quote from Nigerian novelist, Chinua Achebe, writing about a symposium he attended in Dublin in 1988:

> We (Africans) chose English not because the British desired it, but because having tacitly accepted the new nationalities into which colonialism had grouped us, we needed its language to transact our business, including the business of overthrowing colonialism itself in the fullness of time.[6]

Similarly, in accepting and promoting a rural Romantic definition of Irish identity, the nationalist movement rejected the imperial definition of modernity. In doing so, it came to reject all definitions of modernity and contemporary Ireland is still involved in a process of coming to terms with this rejection. The duality of the 'primitive' may certainly have been the product of Britain's long association with Ireland but unravelling its political and ideological implications is a more complex question than this fact might suggest.

Cinematic Ireland: The Outsider's View

For a variety of reasons—economic, cultural and ideological—Ireland, until relatively recently, did not develop an indigenous film industry.[7] This has meant that, for most of the hundred years of cinema, cinematic Ireland has been dominated by images made outside the country, largely by the Hollywood or British film industries. These images can be categorised into two main types, approximating to the two faces of primitiveness that dominated pre-cinematic imagery. As John Hill has argued:

> On one hand, Ireland has been conceived as a simple, and generally blissful, rural idyll; on the other, as a dark and strife-torn maelstrom.[8]

Hill's focus is on the latter, especially those films over the years which have dealt with political violence in Ireland. He offers an exhaustive formal and content analysis of a number of key, largely British, films which have addressed the issue, including Carol Reed's *Odd Man Out*

(1947), Basil Dearden's *The Gentle Gunman* (1952) and a number of less celebrated examples—*Shake Hands with the Devil* (1959), *A Terrible Beauty* (1960), *The Violent Enemy* (1969), *Hennessy* (1975) and, finally, *The Long Good Friday* (1979).

The dominant theme of these films is that the cause of violence in Ireland lies with the Irish themselves. A propensity to violence is a national trait or 'curse' of the Irish, a tragic flaw that sees them struggling with their own basic instincts, caught up in an irrational cycle of violence or trapped forever in a Greek tragedy of their own making. The violent heroes of these films are either looming psychopaths or passive victims of fate. They are either sexually repressed or intellectually challenged, acting out a dance of death of utter pointlessness. Granted, there is no image here as grotesque as the simian caricatures of Victorian or contemporary cartoons. (Indeed, the matinee-idol good looks of James Mason in *Odd Man Out* were objected to by some commentators at the time of its release.) But the ideological effect is the same. As Hill argues, these cinematic images reinforce the stereotype of the irrational, violent Irish that first appeared with Gerald of Wales and dominated representations of political violence in Ireland right down to the 90s. These films make no pretence of exploring historical, political or social factors. The problem lies with the Irish themselves and Britain is exonerated from any responsibility in the human tragedies that unfold.

Interestingly enough, the new wave of films about Ireland in the 90s showed how this recurring theme continued to maintain its hold on the cinematic imagination. One of the recent Hollywood blockbusters to have addressed itself to an Irish theme was *Patriot Games* (1991) in which heroic CIA agent, Jack Ryan (played by current matinee idol Harrison Ford), struggled to save his family from the psychopathic revenge of a demented IRA man. The IRA there here is, of course, a convenient plot device. As the 'communist' psychopathic threat to the 'American family' has receded, other reservoirs of villainous imagery have to be dipped into.

However, political events in Northern Ireland since the republican and loyalist ceasefires seem to have overwhelmed this negative imagery. While the official government response to paramilitary violence was that it was motivated by psychopaths and criminals, this dominant cultural representation was convenient. But, as events have unfolded, we have seen the emergence, on television at least, of a significant modification. The image of the terrorist, for example, in the NIO advertisements for the confidential telephone, screened during the summer of 1993, went through a subtle but important change. These short films were shot with all the power and style of the best cinematic thrillers and represented violence in the graphic detail expected of the cinema. But the perpetrators of the violence had been humanised to some extent. They were shown in loving family situations and the effects of their violence on themselves and their own families, as well as on society in general were portrayed. But these were ordinary men in ordinary communities, not the faceless psychopaths of the dominant image. Their violence was extreme, no doubt, but the films seemed to suggest that they were motivated by ideals, not psychopathology, and this was a major change in what was, in the last instance, a piece of government propaganda. It was hardly a surprise that, by the end of the year, the government admitted that 'lines of communication' had been opened to Sinn Féin. The government could never talk to Neanderthal psychopaths. It could, however, talk to politically-motivated men of violence, no matter how repugnant that violence might have been.[9]

What has often been missed about this tradition of representation is the political effect it has had, until recently, on the paramilitaries themselves and the part it has played in the hold they have exercised on their host communities. While the political and social context of violence continued to be denied, the only choice available to understand the situation was that between 'terrorist' and 'freedom fighter'. This was and continues to be an inadequate paradigm and one which, for too long, limited the political options available. If it suited government policy for so long, it also suited the paramilitaries on all sides, and the complexities of the situation were disguised beneath a simplistic rhetoric.

And that is, surely, the point of Hill's critique of dominant cinematic images of political violence in Ireland. His was not a call merely for sympathetic portrayals of republican or loyalist paramilitaries. Rather, he argued, the continuing denial of the political and historical context of the violence operated as 'a bias against understanding' and merely exacerbated the situation. It was ironic, indeed, that the first popular images to recognise his point should have come from a series of government information films.

To turn to the more romantic face of Irish primitiveness in the cinema is to turn to a more attractive, but less disabling, visual legacy. The key film is John Ford's *The Quiet Man* (1953), a film which continues to exercise a substantial influence on audiences' imaginations even today. It is a perennial favourite on television across the English-speaking world and is one of the most successful films ever to be released on video. As Luke Gibbons points out, in Steven Spielberg's *ET* (1983) even the curious extra-terrestrial is shown to be watching *The Quiet Man* on television as he attempts to come to terms with human culture.[10] Spielberg, no doubt, was aware that this is the last film to look for the 'truth'. The appeal of the film lies in the manner in which it conjures up a blatantly fanciful world of whimsy and romance and does so with an almost disarming self-consciousness. This is the Edenic Celtic periphery of the Romantic movement writ large and the artifice of its creation is commented on throughout the film, almost as a conscious internal subversion. Thus when the film's returning Irish-American exile, Sean Thornton, sees the beautiful Mary-Kate for the first time, herding her sheep through the trees in perfect Arcadian splendour, he is moved to exclaim, "Is that real? She can't be!" His guide, Michaeleen, answers caustically, "Nonsense, man! It is only a mirage brought on by your terrible thirst". And, of course, so is the film itself. If the thirst which first willed such splendid utopias into existence was that of the urban intelligentsia of industrialised Europe, then the film suggests that the thirst is now that of the nostalgic Irish-American in complicity with the Irish themselves. In the late 50s, for example, the Irish tourist board sponsored a promotional film called *O'Hara's Holiday*, aimed at the American market. In the film, a New York cop visits Ireland to get away from the urban grind and leaves for home at the end of his holiday with his very own Mary-Kate in tow. Even today, the country continues to be sold abroad as a holiday destination very much in these terms.

In fact, this rural Romanticism goes back to the earliest days of the cinema. The first American films to be shot on location outside of the USA were made during three consecutive summers in Ireland from 1910-12 by the Kalem company, under the direction of Irish-Canadian Sidney Olcott. These films were to prove attractive to the large Irish-American audience back home and featured Irish tales of love and heroism set amid the rural splendour of Killarney. At times, the landscape seems to take over from the action, as the camera pans away from the characters to reveal the scenery, and inter-titles give the location details ('The Lakes of Killarney', 'The Gap of Dungloe'—as in the 1911 production, *Rory O'More*). Some of these short films had an overtly nationalist theme, celebrating the Irish struggle to free themselves from British rule, and their depiction of a rural community of freedom fighters, priests, lovely maidens and natural beauty was a winning combination in both America and Ireland. Thus only two years after the Franco-British Exhibition referred to by Annie E. Coombes, similar images of rural Ireland as those displayed in the 'villages' of the White City were being committed to celluloid for very different ideological reasons.

In the contemporary context, the appearance of 'primitive' images such as the whimsical *Hear My Song* (1989), the cleverly empty *Widows Peak* (1993) or the Tom Cruise blockbuster, *Far and Away* (1991) suggest that, as the political tensions in Northern Ireland ease, there is a real danger that 'Romantic Ireland' will re-emerge with force in a contemporary cinematic idiom, lacking even John Ford's mischievous self-consciousness as compensation.

There is surely another danger, though, in the continuing Romanticisation of Ireland. In his discussion of Robert Flaherty's 1934 film, *Man of Aran*, Luke Gibbon usefully points out that the pastoral *genre* has in fact two Romantic variations. Following the art critic, Erwin Panofsky, Gibbons refers to these as 'soft' and 'hard' primitiveness. Soft primitiveness is the mode of romantic representation most of us are familiar with and is best exemplified in the rural idyll of *The Quiet Man*. Hard primitiveness is more problematic, in that it casts a Romantic eye on the less attractive of landscape and rural life—it "conceives of primitive life as an almost subhuman existence full of terrible hardships and devoid of all comforts". This, as Gibbons points out, is a perfect description of *Man of Aran*.[11]

The problem is that, at the time of its release in 1934, the film was received as a realistic representation of the Aran Islands, its hard primitivist Romanticism mistaken for a slice of social realism. The image of the islanders that the film promoted no doubt dove-tailed with the prevailing ethos of Irish nationalism at the time and seemed to offer visual credence to de Valera's own vision of an Ireland of frugal self-sufficiency.

But the film is a very stylised affair indeed, and it is not necessary to know the details of the liberties that Flaherty took with the reality of life on Aran to be conscious of its epic artifice. The islanders are continually framed in heroic style against the skyline or shot from underneath to emphasis their strength and determination to overcome all that the elements can throw at them. Their struggle is elevated to the universal—humanity's struggle with nature—and, as is the case with the whimsical nonsense of the Ford film, the image created bears little resemblance to objective reality. The film's ending, visually linking the father with his son, intimates that this struggle will pass on from generation to generation as it has since time immemorial. As well as evacuating any reference to the actual material realities of the situation, the film also seems to deny the possibility of social change.

Man of Aran caused a critical controversy in its day, especially among those politically-committed documentary filmmakers who saw the film as a betrayal of the social and political concerns of the documentary form. When it went on to win the 'Mussolini Cup' at the 1934 Venice film festival, these same critics saw this as confirmation of the film's fascist aesthetic. This has always seemed a harsh judgement on Flaherty, who was certainly no fascist. He once said of himself that he was "first and foremost an explorer and incidentally a filmmaker". Certainly, I feel that it is more accurate to describe him as a 19th-century anthropologist who used the most advanced cultural technology of the 20th century to create his own images of the elemental 'noble savage'. But the accusation of fascist aesthetics does illustrate the danger inherent in the Romantic pursuit of essence, whether the essence of 'Man' as in Flaherty or the essence of the nation as in the many Irish nationalist readings of his film. The reviewer for the *Derry Journal* at the time wrote of his film, "Here is Irish realism at last—a grim, sad realism that grips at the heart of the nation". But if the Romanticism of Flaherty's film can be mistaken for realism what does this say about the conception of the nation which saw its image in the film?

In a famous essay on the German filmmaker, Leni Riefenstahl, Susan Sontag did attempt to define what fascists are and her, admittedly tentative, conclusions provide an interesting codicil to the debate on *Man of Aran*. Riefenstahl had made two notorious Nazi propaganda films for Hitler in the 30s, *Triumph of Will* (1934) and *Olympia* (1936)— which, incidentally, won the Mussolini Cup in 1938. In the 70s, she attempted to reinstate her artistic credentials through the publication of a number of photographic studies, and Sontag considered in her essay on Riefenstahl whether or not there was something in her work which might be considered inherently 'fascist'. She argued:

> National Socialism—or more broadly, fascism—stands for an ideal, and one that is persistent today under other banners; the ideal of life as art, the cult of beauty, the fetishism of courage, the dissolution of alienation in ecstatic feelings of community, the repudiation of the intellect, the family man (under the parenthood of leaders).

It may or may not be fair to level these characteristics at Flaherty's film, but it is an interesting insight into the possible destination of a concerted Romantic gaze that evacuates the material reality of existence and denies the complexity of human culture in the pursuit of an idealised essence. It is the legacy of such a Romantic gaze that has interested the small, but growing, indigenous film industry.

Cinematic Ireland: The Indigenous Image

It is tempting to think that the negative imagery of the outsider's view of Ireland—this primitivist view—would necessarily be challenged by indigenous film-makers. However, it is not that simple, as we have seen. Much of this negative imagery has been internalised and has played an important cultural role in the construction of one important definition of Irish identity. Only a critically-engaged cinema can mount such a challenge. It would be naïve, as well, to suppose that a fully-formed and recognisable film culture could emerge quickly in Ireland, given how little support there has been over the years for indigenous production. What we have seen so far is, in many ways, an exploration of the potential rather than a realised aesthetic. The most interesting films and film-makers continue to work towards a new cinematic sensibility, rather than attempting to ape the dominant forms of the international style. Indeed, I have described these films before as a kind of 'critical regionalism', where local preoccupations are tested against dominant themes and forms.[12] As part of this exploration, the best Irish films have attempted to address the deficiencies of the traditions of representation. While it is impossible to see clearly anything that resembles a coherent aesthetic, nonetheless I think that the themes and avenues of exploration are certainly emerging. Not surprisingly, these seem to be motivated by desire to interrogate the legacy of the Romantic past and to explore the possibility of either a more realist aesthetic or a more liberating imagining of the nation than that bequeathed by Romantic cultural nationalism.

This new imagining is being attempted in a context where a very different version of modernity is on offer than the British imperialist progress rejected by Irish nationalism earlier. The context now is a European one, and the kind of Ireland which is imagined into existence is as important for the future of this European identity as it is for the stability of the country itself. The emerging film industry is an important popular arena where these ideas can be explored—the starting point is, surely, to come to terms with the legacy of the past.

If one of the key concerns is to explore the legacy of Ireland's

Romantic past, then it is hardly surprising that many recent Irish films set out to interrogate the rural mythology which underpinned cultural nationalism and is encapsulated in the use of landscape. This continues to be an obsession in the films of Joe Comerford and Bob Quinn, both of whom have chosen to work largely in the west of Ireland and have attempted to lay bare the accretions of myth and cultural significance which the west has held in Irish consciousness. In *Reefer and the Model* (1987), Comerford, with an almost postmodern playfulness, subjects the landscape to an encounter with an array of miscreants and social outcasts seemingly devised for their perversity to the role models of Catholic nationalism. One of the most interesting visual reworkings of the Irish landscape, however, is in Thaddeus O'Sullivan's *December Bride* (1989) which populates the familiar scenery with a northern Protestant community and thereby challenges the audience's assumptions about both.

Recent Irish film-making has also been concerned to represent urban Ireland, largely absent from cultural discourse under the sway of cultural nationalism. Two films by Cathal Black in particular are of note—his 1984 feature, *Pigs*, set in a run-down Dublin squat, and his 1981 short, *Our Boys*, which looked at the kind of education which the Christian Brothers provided in an inner-urban school. This excellent short also probes other areas which have become a concern in recent work—the influence of religion in Ireland and, especially, the question sexual repression. These, not surprisingly, have been areas explored by women film-makers, though interestingly, these have come from the nationalist communities of Northern Ireland rather than from the south (Margo Harkin's *Hush-a-Bye Baby* [1989] and Anne Crilly's *Mother Ireland* [1988] from Derry and Pat Murphy's *Maeve* [1981] from Belfast). These films also address the politics of Northern Ireland and do so from the interesting perspective of the women's movement, providing a different analysis to that which normally emanates from the male discourse of mainstream nationalism or republicanism. In many of these films, there is also a concern with history, especially its role in the construction of identity and in its significance for contemporary Ireland. Finally, a number of recent Irish films have been concerned with film form itself and have begun an exploration for a cinematic aesthetic that will allow Irish film-makers to escape from the closed circuit of imagery which still binds and limits expression.

Despite the new optimism among film-makers in Ireland, there are still dangers and problems in trying to imagine a different, more liberating identity, than that which has frozen and polarised us for so long. Some of the disabling images of Ireland and the Irish, that have dominated cinematic representations for decades, still have the power to exert influence. In some cases, they have become so thoroughly internalised that they are no longer recognised for what they are—the tired failed imaginings of yesterday. Furthermore, as film-makers attempt to appeal to a wider, more international audience, there is the risk that, like some of the more British and American films, they will be obliged to dip into the reservoir of existing representations to ensure their 'recognisability'.

And, finally, there remains the major problem that film-makers in Northern Ireland have no easy access to the new funding arrangements in the south (some, of course, would not wish to access them anyway), and there is little in the way of British government support for film-making in the north. This is likely to exacerbate the problem facing film-makers from a northern Protestant background who remain largely absent from cinematic expression. This kind of new imagining I am talking about would require the northern unionist to begin to explore the disabling myths of his/her past in the way in which nationalist Ireland has begun to do and it is to be regretted that so far there is little evidence of this happening.

Notes

[1] Annie E. Coombes, 'Ethnography and National and Cultural Identities', in Susan Hiller (ed.) *The Myth of Primitiveness* (London: Routledge, 1991) pp. 189–214.

[2] Annie E. Coombes, 'Ethnography and National and Cultural Identities', pp. 206–7.

[3] See, for example, John Darby, *Dressed to Kill: Cartoons and the Northern Ireland Conflict* (Belfast: Appletree Press, 1983).

[4] Lewis P. Curtis, *Apes and Angels: The Irishman in Victorian Caricature* (Newton Abbot: David & Charles, 1971).

[5] John Darby, *Dressed to Kill*.

[6] Chinua Achebe, 'The Song of Ourselves' in *New Statesman and Society*, 9th February, 1990.

[7] The best historical overview is Kevin Rockett, 'History, Politics and Irish Cinema', in K. Rockett, L. Gibbons and J. Hill, *Cinema and Ireland* (London: Routledge, 1988), pp. 3–144.

[8] John Hill, 'Images of Violence' in K. Rockett *et al*, *Cinema and Ireland*, pp. 147-193.

[9] I discussed these films at the time in an article in *Fortnight*, no. 321, October 1993.

[10] Luke Gibbons, 'Romanticism, Realism and Irish Cinema' in K. Rockett et al, *Cinema and Ireland*, pp. 194–257.
[11] Luke Gibbons, 'Romanticism, Realism and Irish Cinema', pp. 197–203.
[12] For fuller discussion, see Martin McLoone, 'National Cinema and Cultural Identity: Ireland and Europe', in J. Hill, McLoone and P. Hainsworth, *Border Crossing: Film in Ireland, Britain and Europe* (Belfast: Institute of Irish Studies/ BFI, 1994).

Imagining the Titanic

John Wilson Foster

> "Any fate was titanic"
> — *Howards End* (1910)

I

The accidental collision of the Royal Mail Steamer *Titanic* with an iceberg on the evening of 14th April, 1912 made an impact not only in lives—in over 1,500 cases, a fatal impact—but also on culture. The astonishing cultural phenomenon of the ship's loss (and recent discovery) is an international one, of which the huge success of Stephen Low's remarkable IMAX Corporation film, *Titanica*, and Melissa Jo Peltier's two-part television documentary. for the North American A&E channel, are but the latest fragments of evidence. Even before her loss, the *Titanic* was of significance beyond the nation that built her. She was built, Low tells us in his film, "at the very leading edge of the Industrial Revolution". The *Titanic, Olympic, Majestic, Baltic,* and other liners designed and built by Harland & Wolff from 1870 (when the *Oceanic* was launched), charted an evolution in international shipbuilding.

Yet no North American I have asked (and who hasn't seen Low's film) has known that the *Titanic* was built in Belfast. The vivid compound imagery of the ship and the grim simple image of the city seem entirely unconnected. Even for those of us from Ulster, the ship and the city can seem strange bedfellows. There is a well-known photograph, taken by R.J. Welch, of Harland & Wolff workers leaving the yard with the embryo *Titanic* in the Great Gantry in the background. The workers have their backs to the vessel that was advancing shipbuilding technology, and are returning to their homely east Belfast kitchen houses without hot running water, bathrooms or indoor lavatories: the world of Inglis bread and the *Belfast Telegraph*, which a barefoot boy in the foreground is almost certainly selling.

Can we relate the two parts of this photograph, the international and the local, the technological and the domestic? At the time, this might not have seemed such a problem. "The ship was built in Belfast," J. Bruce Ismay (hapless manager of the White Star Line) told the U.S. Congressional hearing after her loss, "she was the latest thing in the art of shipbuilding"; it was as if the second fact were synonymous with the first.

Of course, some measure of engaging anomaly will always remain, even if we succeed in connecting the photograph's halves. The builders worked feverishly before the ship entered service. Walter Lord, in *A Night to Remember* (1955), recounts the anecdote of the masseuse at Southampton readying the Turkish bath on board and finding a half-eaten sandwich (somebody's 'piece') or empty beer-bottle in every nook and cranny. "The builders were Belfast men," she explained cheerfully, in a statement that is a humorous foil to Ismay's.

II

The international significance of the *Titanic* is hard to exaggerate. Not only the building, but also the loss, of the ship were important episodes in the ways of the sea. The sinking resulted in changes in maritime laws; ship design; transatlantic crossings were re-routed; safety at sea became an international priority. Decades later, the sunken ship became an incentive to deep-water exploration, exerted some small impact on oceanography, and stimulated the technology of submersibles and underwater video, culminating in Robert Ballard's discovery of the wreck in 1985. With the retrieval of objects and artifacts from the wreck, the ship became a laboratory for the study of sea-bed corrosion, a field that has grown important since containers of toxic and nuclear waste were dumped into the oceans.

The sinking itself was the greatest disaster in maritime history and still holds that grim distinction. Indeed, it remains an important episode in the history of disasters generally, a catastrophe that sharpened our sense of an ending and darkened the psychology of extinction. Wyn Craig Wade in *The Titanic: End of a Dream* (1979)—on which Peltier based much of her documentary—claims that "in America, the profound reaction to the disaster can be compared only to the aftermath of the assassinations of Lincoln and Kennedy ... the entire English-speaking world was shaken; and for us, at least, the tragedy can be regarded as a watershed between the 19th and 20th centuries". He adds, surely with some hyperbole, that not even the wars of the 20th century equalled the *Titanic* disaster in the breadth of its shock or the depth of its pathos, though that the event should invite such hyperbole is a measure of its magnitude. Like the assassination of Kennedy, the death of the *Titanic* seemed like the end of an era of confidence; in the ship's case, that of Victorian expansionism, both material and cultural.

An enormous quantity of literature, fictional and documentary alike, has been inspired by the death of the *Titanic*: histories, memoirs, novels, short stories, plays, poems. The international industry of books began the year the ship sank. Laurence Beesley, a survivor, published his eye-witness account, *The Loss of the RMS Titanic*, that same year. Before the year was out, Marshall Everett published *Wreck and Sinking of the Titanic*. A spate of books followed. After some years of leisurely flow, Robert Ballard's discovery of the wreck opened the sluice gates, with Ballard himself contributing a book and two lengthy *National Geographic* photo-essays.

Inevitably, the disaster set the poetasters early to work. Within a year, Edwin Drew had published *The Chief Incidents of the 'Titanic' Wreck, Treated in Verse* ("may appeal to those who lost friends in this appalling catastrophe"). But real poets too have been drawn to the subject, including Hardy (as quick off the mark as Drew), E.J. Pratt, Anthony Cronin and Hans Magnus Enzensberger.

If the poetasters were quickly on the scene of the shipwreck, so too were the songwriters of Tin Pan Alley, as Michael McCaughan of the Ulster Folk and Transport Museum has reminded us in his popular lecture, 'The Chocolate Mousse *Titanic*'. The first commercial song was copyrighted in the United States ten days after the sinking and sheet music and gramophone records followed in its wake. Much of the resulting noise was theatrically sentimental.

There have been innumerable paintings; and also films: most famously *A Night to Remember* (1958), adapted from Lord's book by Eric Ambler and produced by a remarkable Belfastman, William MacQuitty; but a host of others as well, everything from World War II German anti-British propaganda to Hammer horror. Low's film *Titanica* must be among the most striking of the numerous documentaries. It has the distinctive IMAX surround effect and is projected on a screen four storeys high: a hi-tech movie that is a salute to its own technology, as well as to the technology both of deep-water exploration and the

Titanic, a celebration of the fraternity of cutting-edge applied science.

The *Titanic* and its foundering quickly gathered meanings in the popular mind that found currency far beyond Britain and long after the decade that ought to have smothered them with the awesome events of World War I.

Still, the ship immediately became a symbol of the unique systematic inequality of British society, even though many of the wealthy aboard were American. Despite the presence of other classes aboard, the ship could be said to have represented one of those 'islands of money' that E.M. Forster has the Schlegel sisters guiltily inhabit in *Howards End*, a novel published in 1910 and full of intimations of disaster and finality that the *Titanic* tragedy fulfilled. The physical lay-out of the ship seemed like a blueprint of the British class system. The vertical system of decks, and social stratification (which we imagine as also vertical: the lower orders, the upper classes), seemed related; the distinctions were highly considered—third-class toilet bowls were iron, second-class porcelain, first-class marble. The bulkhead system, technically advanced, but ultimately unequal to the task of keeping the ship afloat, is another suggestive metaphor of segregation.

When we think of the highly charged world of the engine-room and boiler-rooms, with their infernal machinery, it is hard not to think of H.G. Wells' use of such imagery in *The Time Machine*, 'The Cone', 'Lord of the Dynamos' and other works, written a few years before the *Titanic* was built, and of which the technology of the ship is a curious and real-life enactment.

And there is another Wellsian connection. One of Wells' short stories is 'In the Abyss', the story of the disappearance of a bathyscape in deep water; the explorer fails to return, like the Time Traveller in *The Time Machine* (1895). The *Titanic*, found by submersible in a replay of Wells' short story, lies on or near the Sohm Abyssal Plain; and the Abyss is an image of the place the *Titanic* sank into: Stygian darkness out of all countenance. The fate of the *Titanic* brought to culmination the imagery of the Abyss in the late Victorian and Edwardian periods. We find the imagery, in its broad variety of meaning, in books by Dickens, Wells, Masterman, London, Gissing, Forster and Lawrence.

Not only the Abyss, but also the surface collision that sent the *Titanic* plummeting into it, was a powerful cultural notion with which English writers had already engaged. Hardy, Moore and Forster all depicted unhappy coincidences and the fatal collision of incompatibles in human life. The fate of the *Titanic* was a terminal object lesson in—almost caricature of—what concerned Moore and other writers of the time. The novels of these writers are but the tips of the iceberg: late Victorian culture was preoccupied with a universe of chance, from which a jealous God seemed to be withdrawing; with a society in which the classes collided more frequently; with a world of maladaptation that was, as it were, the everyday reality of evolution; and with an epoch coming to an end, not with a whimper but a bang.

The *Titanic*, in short, sailed and sank at the very centre of contemporary cultural preoccupations.

III

A more positive and, in the event, ironic imagery of the *Titanic* before its loss was generated by the Anglo-American White Star Line Company of Liverpool, owned by J. Pierpont Morgan (who came to Belfast for the launch) and managed by Ismay: in 1987, the Ulster Folk and Transport Museum issued a facsimile of the lively promotional booklet put out by White Star in 1911. The presence on board during the maiden voyage of Astors, Guggenheims, Strauses and Wideners associates the ship with the heyday of American plutocracy and the supersession of European power by American.

The promotion and marketing before the maiden voyage found their counterpart in the international memorabilia industry after the sinking: postcards, posters, booklets, coffee-table books, exhibits (with recent or current ones in Los Angeles, Vancouver and Belfast). The search for the wreck boosted the industry and placed the ship at the junction of popular culture and commercial enterprise. Michael McCaughan's booklet, *Titanic* (Ulster Folk and Transport Museum [1982]), deliberately imitates the White Star booklet and, thereby, effects the passage from hard-sell commodification to the cult of nostalgia, from modernity to postmodernity.

The *Titanic* has generated a copious iconography. Michael McCaughan drew my attention to memorial postcards from 1912 inspired by religious art, yet shown by the stylised postures of the depicted maidens to have been influenced by the Edwardian stage and early motion pictures. The sincere outpourings of grief were increasingly manufactured, yet the sentimental religiosity in which the event swam welled up from deep and disturbing notions, including that of the waiting Abyss, which was not just a secular literary image of crisis in English society, but one that derived from the Bible and ancient pictures of hell and purgatory. The ship lay, as it were, in the Christian abyss (with the 'souls' all ships carried), in Milton's darkness visible. The technical and social hubris contemporary commentators identified accorded with the Christian idea of retribution: this was God in the guise of Nature putting Man in his place. That more poor people were put in their place than rich would not have fazed the fundamentally religious. "God Himself could not sink this ship", a woman passenger recalled a crewman telling her. Nowadays, one can buy packets of commercial-religious reaction of the time marketed as *kitsch*, another example of the postmodern world self-consciously, even cynically, flourishing upon the modern.

Interestingly, the aura of piety (in another before-and-after parallel) was revived after 1985, since some people, including Ballard, have seen removal of items from the wreck not just as vandalism, but as grave-robbing and even blasphemy. Stephen Low offers his version of this in *Titanica*, which encourages us to see the wreck as a mausoleum, and its *débris* field as a submarine cemetery, holy Judaeo-Christian ground. Inside this aura, of course, are contested hard-nosed legalities, rivalries, and ethics of salvage. To the extent that genuine piety has been drowned by vested interests, one might almost imagine the ship as a symbol of sunken popular Christianity after it had shored up the Victorian, imperial states of the west, particularly England and the United States.

At the time, the aura of piety was enhanced by the story (that became a kind of folk belief) that, as the ship went down, the band played 'Nearer My God to Thee'. By reliable account, it was in fact the even more appropriate hymn, 'Autumn', which contains the lines "Hold me up in mighty waters,/Keep my eyes on things above". But the events of April 14th-15th, 1912, quickly became legendary in any case. According to Stephen Low, it was rumoured at the time that a worker was lost during the building and his body entombed in the ship's structure. When I heard this, I couldn't but recall the Welch photograph in which a workman has been crudely erased, leaving a ghostly, plasmic presence; perhaps Welch removed the figure himself, wishing to show more of the starboard tail shaft, but it gives one a queer feeling nonetheless.

The legendry enveloping the ship has not abated. Even if the stories behind the recent American tabloid's claim that "the spectre of a huge ocean liner has been sighted at least a dozen times during the past three years and hundreds of times since it sank", is full of elementary errors, the *fact* of the story is evidence of the saleable legendry of the ship. The captain of the Norwegian trawler whose crew, three summers ago, saw the ship—on the surface of the ocean *but in its present sunken condition*—is named and quoted, with that semi-corroboration we find in folklore of this kind, and in which ghost ships recur as actors. In this particular sighting, the *Titanic* appears as the folkloric Ship of Death, or the spectral ship of 'The Ancient Mariner' translated into the age of steam.

Intriguing in a way that might have caught the attention of J.W. Dunne or Jorge Luis Borges (with their experiments in time), or indeed Oscar Wilde with his claim that life imitates art (there was a Chief Officer Wilde on board), is the fact that there were a curious number of imaginative anticipations of the ship and its fate. In *A Night to Remember,* Lord exhumed Morgan Robertson's 1898 novel about a fabulous Atlantic liner that, while filled with rich and complacent people, hits an iceberg one April night and sinks. The specifications of the real *Titanic* were identical to those of Robertson's fictional liner which was, incredibly, called the *Titan.*

Wade has salvaged other anticipations, including a short story by Mayn Clew Garnett that was being printed as the *Titanic* prepared for her maiden voyage. Then there was Celia Thaxter's 1887 poem entitled 'A Tryst', that anticipates both the fate of the liner and Hardy's verse response to it. But any suspicion that Hardy had borrowed from Thaxter is allayed by the fact that 'the convergence of the twain' is a major motif in Hardy's work from the beginning: Hardy, like the others, had before 1912 already imagined the *Titanic.*

The impact of the sinking was as great in the United States as in Britain and Ireland—if anything, greater. Curiously, it was significant among black Americans, for whom the ship was a symbol of white racialist society: its building was a monument to white hubris and its foundering retribution for the mistreatment of black people. In one introduction to his song, 'Titanic', the famous bluesman Leadbelly said there were no coloured folks on the ship, that Jack Johnson, the world heavyweight champion, tried to board but was told by Captain Smith, "I ain't haulin' no coal". In the song, Johnson is safe on dry land and bitterly bids the *Titanic* fare thee well.

The sinking of the ship stimulated a figure already active in black urban folklore: Shine (presumably from Shoeshine), who was reborn as a mythical black stoker aboard the *Titanic.* He's a kind of Trickster, and hero of a species of long narrative poem called the 'Toast' (not unrelated to rap, the talking blues, and the dozens). In it, Shine is the only passenger or crewman capable of swimming from the sinking vessel and, in belated revenge, he refuses to help the white folks, even in return for the promise of all things white people thought black people coveted (including "all the pussy eyes ever did see"). In Leadbelly's song, when the white folks go under, Jack Johnson is on shore doing the Eagle Rock. In one version of the *Titanic* Toast:

... when all them white folks went to heaven,
Shine was in Sugar Ray's bar drinking Seagram's Seven.

The ship has figured in white lore, too. For example, there were innumerable jokes (Lady Astor: 'I asked for ice in my drink, but this is ridiculous'); jokes lie behind the satirical use to which political cartoonists have frequently put the disaster. According to McCaughan, the American folklorist D.K. Wilgus worked on an intensive study of the *Titanic* traditional ballad complex and considered that the *Titanic* disaster "contributed to what seems to be the largest number of songs concerning any disaster, perhaps any event in American history".

The internationalism of the *Titanic* complex is further evidenced by the number of flourishing Titanic Historical Societies in various countries, the chief society being in Indian Orchard, Massachusetts. These are normally serious conclaves, similar to local history societies, devoted to a narrow subject, but across disciplines and national borders. They belong to the history of clubs, enthusiasms and past-times. They are also custodians of the ship's legends and are often loose enough to accommodate the buffs and freaks who inhabit the no-man's-land between technological enthusiasm and devotional fanaticism. Lastly, there are those bars and hostelries displaying relics and replicas as decoration. In the cases of both private collections and public display, there is a gesture in one direction towards post-modernist trivialism, a secular parody of reliquary mentality and practice; and, in the other direction, towards the real thing, with history by the way of legendry sustaining something that begins to resemble a cult.

IV

The western cultural complex that the *Titanic* composes has its local version in Ulster, as in many other towns and neighbourhoods; but since the ship was built there, in some respects the complex takes its rise in the province, more particularly in the industrial city of Belfast.

With the two cataclysmic (if unequal) historical events, World War I and the foundering of the *Titanic*, Ulster people have identified intimately; both have supplied much of the sunken furniture of the collective Ulster mind. It would be untrue to say that it has been exclusively a unionist identification, but it has been largely the case. What is interesting is that, whereas the modern unionist consciousness was forged in the 1880s (in the defining opposition to English Liberal and Irish Nationalist plans for home rule), only 30 years later those doughty opponents identified with astounding losses and disasters (the *Titanic* and the Somme and World War I reversals), seeming to keep home rule at bay, as it were, largely by historical default.

It may be that there are certain setbacks of such magnitude and heroism (in this case, the vicarious heroism of many of the passengers and crew) that they serve to sustain and temper a people, instead of weakening them; or else, perhaps, the setbacks come to have an energising emblematic power. But it may also be that, like the Somme, the loss of the *Titanic* has come to symbolise unconsciously the thwarted nationhood of Ulster Protestants, that at the level of community dreamwork the foundering of the ship and the founding of Northern Ireland were intertwined, that the ship *became* Northern Ireland, a statelet that invited the pride in which it was fashioned, but was always in danger of being sunk by the chilling impersonal 'iceberg dynamics' of Irish nationalism.

Certainly, there have been nationalists who rejected the emotional appeal of the *Titanic* story for ideological reasons. I doubt if they did so because of the 113 third-class passengers the ship picked up on its last stop, at Queenstown (now Cobh), most of them Irish emigrants on their way to America, two-thirds of whom perished. The quarrel was with Ulster Protestants—of whom the Harland & Wolff shipyard workforce was predominantly made up—rather than English policy-makers in Ireland. Nationalists saw Orange hubris where American blacks saw white hubris; behind both were alleged injustice and mistreatment; and, in the sinking, blacks and nationalists saw Nemesis at work. Yet my hunch is that Ulster nationalist (or Catholic) reaction against the appeal of the *Titanic* disaster was strongest after the creation of Northern Ireland in 1921.

In any case, a friend tells me that at his National School in Tipperary, the loss of the *Titanic* was explained to him by a teacher as retribution for loyalist bigotry. This would have been the sectarian counterpart of overweening loyalist pride in the ships that Belfast built: 'If Britain rules the waves, Belfast builds the ships.' And the inequality of British society found its equivalent, perhaps, in the inequality of post-partition Ulster society. My friend also tells me that the same teacher explained how the registration number of the

Titanic, if held up to a mirror, revealed the slogan 'No Pope'!

But Ulster's fundamentalist Protestants (whose faith far outweighs their national identity) also saw the retributive hand of God in the sinking, and they continue to do so: a short time ago a knowledgeable little tract by Robert E. Surgenor, an evangelist, was delivered to my home in Belfast entitled 'The Titanic'. In it, the life and death of the ship illustrates biblical warnings and lessons (specifically from Proverbs 27:1, Job 33:14, Job 9:26, James 4:14, Matthew 7:14, Luke 19:10 and Acts 16:31): "unlike the Titanic, God has a Lifeboat for all, and that Lifeboat is Christ!" The tract originated in Lurgan, Co. Armagh.

The *Titanic* sinking dramatically reactivated the Christian Lifeboat metaphor, which we meet in General William Booth's 1890 *exposé* of London poverty, *In Darkest England*, wherein he devotes a chapter to those 'On the Verge of the Abyss' and refers to the answer to these social problems—the 'Salvation Ship'—of which the *Titanic* could be seen as a travesty. Yet the hymn-singing aboard the sinking vessel connects the tragedy with Protestant hymnody and salvationism and thereby returns the ship to its origin, one of the more evangelical corners of the world.

Northern Ireland has also produced its share of art inspired by the *Titanic*. Two notable paintings, Charles Dixon's 'Titanic Fitting Out at Belfast' (1912) and William Conor's 'Men of Iron' (1922), are on display at the *Titanic* exhibit at the Ulster Folk and Transport Museum. *The Iceberg*, a radio play by the late Stewart Parker, was broadcast in 1974. It uses contemporary reports of men killed during the ship's construction by having as its central figures two dead workers; Parker also uses the 'descent into hell' (i.e. into the boiler and engine rooms) motif. Perhaps, though, the two workmen are too reminiscent of Beckett's Vladimir and Estragon, and Stoppard's Rosencrantz and Guildenstern, to let this early Parker play truly succeed. The play might have done for one archetypal event in loyalist psycho-history what Frank McGuinness did for the other in his play, *Observe the Sons of Ulster Marching Towards the Somme* (1986), but is not densely textured enough to do so.

Ulster poets have not been drawn to the disaster as we might have expected. Samuel K. Cowan published a heartfelt, but artistically indifferent loyalist ode, 'De Profundis', in *From Ulster's Hills* (1913). John Hewitt in his sonnet 'Late Spring, 1912' (*Kites in Spring* [1980]) has some poignant lines on his memory of reading, as a five-year-old, the news of the sinking on the newsboy's bill (I can't but think of the newsboy in Welch's photograph!); but it was only a part of a season of bad news (Scott likewise foundered amidst ice). In 'Death of an Old Lady' (1956), Louis MacNeice combined the elderly woman's memory of seeing the ship in girlhood with the iceberg as a metaphor for her own sinking. The best local poem I know is 'Bruce Ismay's Soliloquy', in which Derek Mahon is characteristically attracted to the lost (and, in this case, reviled) figure amidst the crowd, and who strikingly recalls (in a Mahonesque blend of the homely detail, the punning metaphor, and the hollow existence), that

> As I sat shivering on the dark water
> I turned to ice to hear my costly
> Life go thundering down in a pandemonium of
> Prams, pianos, sideboards, winches,
> Boilers bursting and shredded ragtime.

Robert Johnstone essays the same event in his impressive suite of poems, 'Titanic', in *Eden to Edenderry* (1989): "all the innards slid forward and down:/the boilers and the turbine came adrift./Its organs loose, the ship gutted itself." Johnstone uses as epigraph for his suite lines from Enzensberger's celebrated long poem on the ship, neatly connecting for us the local with the international. For Johnstone, the wreck and its discovery excite nightmares, misshapen extrusions of a troubled psyche. The personal 'soul voyage' in 'Not an Explosion but a Crash' ("size had magnetised the ship to troubles") becomes, in 'Undertaker', the collective, feverish soul voyage of a society like Northern Ireland's.

While nothing comparable to the folklore of Shine developed in Belfast, the *Titanic* spread from historical fact into the general and potent folklore of a shipyard which has been a source of serious pride, deflationary humour, and even urban identity for the inhabitants of industrial (and now largely post-industrialist) east Belfast. Belfast citizens are not above a joke at their own expense: 'Did you know Belfast built the world's largest submarine?' 'No jokin'?' 'Aye, it was called the *Titanic*!'

Beyond Belfast, the folklore of the ship took the form of traditional ballad (McCaughan quotes one from County Fermanagh), nine of which were known to Wilgus, who found that the Irish songs tend to praise the ship and its crew, while American songs belabour them.

Another local version of response abroad has been the launch recently of the Ulster Titanic Historical Society, with its journal *CQD Titanic*, a reference to the distress call then in use before, in its difficulty, the *Titanic* switched signals and sent one of the first SOS calls in history. Finally, if, courtesy of Simon & Schuster Young Books, children can now make a model *Titanic*, then in Northern Ireland they can be the beneficiaries of an impressive educational pack available from the Ulster Folk and Transport Museum, and assembled by Elizabeth McMinn, Head of History, Strathearn School, Belfast; one hopes it is widely taught.

In order to stimulate pupil curiosity, the educational pack rightly addresses the kinds of questions posed by the American and British official inquiries, as well as the mystery of the *Californian*, which heightened both the dramatic and otherworldly dimensions of the tragedy. What it does not address, understandably, is the social, sectarian, and political surround of the building of the *Titanic*. The historian Jonathan Bardon writes that:

> On the very day people in Belfast were reading the terrible details of the loss of the *Titanic*, the first important vote on the Third Home Rule Bill had been taken amidst angry scenes in the House of Commons. It was a moment long awaited by the Nationalists of the Irish Party and long feared by the Unionists.

It was in 1912, five months after the loss of the *Titanic*, that tens of thousands of loyalists signed a covenant pledging opposition to home rule for Ireland.

This is an important and obvious local context for the making of the *Titanic*, and one colloquially much rehearsed, but I want to introduce a different and less familiar set of local meanings and try to weld them to the ship's cultural internationalism. For if there is a pattern to all that has gone before, it is the way the ship began as a triumph of modernity and, after its foundering, became a testament to postmodernity: of recycled and even mocked modernity, of caricature, cynicism, greed, bad taste, artistic promiscuity. Yet a core of serious meaning has survived, be it human bewilderment and sense of loss, or human pride in leading-edge achievement that calamity did not nullify but, instead, turned into nobility in the way of tragedy. In postmodernity is entailed modernity, after all, and we ought, in order to set the historical record straight, return that modernity to the city in which our particular example was created.

V

The basic specifications of the *Titanic* are startling. She was the height of an 11-storey building, her rudder was the height of a house, her length a sixth of a mile. She housed the largest steam-engines ever built, before or since; three million rivets went into her hull. There are photographs by Welch of the ship under construction which show her scale by alarmingly dwarfing human figures. Combining the statistical superlatives of her dimensions with her innovations in technology and fittings, we see clearly that the *Titanic* was a remarkable product of modernity. Not only was the ship, as Stephen Low claims, "the space shuttle of the early 20th century", and, as Wade asserts, "a wonder of 20th century technology", but because of the cultural meanings I've indicated, she was a symbol, and not just a product of, modernity. Even should we wish to 'interrogate' modernity, as Terry Smith does in his recent book, *Making the Modern: Industry, Art, and Design in America* (1993), we must first acknowledge it, as he does and I think we can do so in the case of turn-of-the-century Belfast; not just (and most easily) in terms of machinery and technology, not even just in terms of culture, but in terms of the aesthetic as well.

If we were to speak of the 'machine aesthetic', as Smith does, then the *Titanic* and other Harland & Wolff ships would be good examples of what we might call the 'marine aesthetic'. Early ships of theirs, built in the 1860s, were known as 'ocean greyhounds', and the *Oceanic* of 1899 was probably, in the words of Bardon, "the most elegant vessel ever launched by Harland & Wolff". Wade remarks on the "sheer aesthetic satisfaction" of the *Titanic*. We could speak also of the sensory impact of parts of the ship (boilers, rudder, propeller, funnels) that we can register even in photographs. We can register it in reality as well, for example outside the Ulster Folk Museum (Transport section) where there is a Harland & Wolff propeller screw on display. In this case, reality is recontextualised by the Museum in order to make a work of art: the screw is reminiscent of a Henry Moore sculpture; it is both machine part and work of art. But it is surely the case that yardworkers were not unimpressed aesthetically by the objects and the material they were fashioning or manoeuvring and that, in being so impressed, they were living a daily life of intensified sensibility. The visual imagery of modernity presented by photographs of the *Titanic*, particularly those of the ship under construction, is also striking. The still photography most closely associated with the *Titanic* is that of Ulsterman R.J. Welch. Welch is thought of as a chiefly rural photographer, and his photographs as chiefly social documentation, aids to the social anthropology of the Irish countryside. But some of his photographs of the Harland & Wolff shipyard, and of the *Titanic* in particular, bear comparison with those of Ford automobile plants taken by Charles Sheeler in the 20s and reproduced by Smith (who calls Sheeler "the Raphael of the Fords").

According to Smith, a certain iconography seems fundamental to the imagery of modernity: industry and workers; cities and crowds; products and consumers. Many of Welch's pictures of Belfast and Harland & Wolff's offers such imagery with an iconographic gravity. His photograph of the crowds of workers leaving the yard, with the growing *Titanic* and *Olympic* receding into the distance behind them, has always put me in mind of the image in *The Waste Land* by T.S. Eliot (a literary modernist) of the crowd flowing over London Bridge and the line from Dante that Eliot incorporates in to his poem, "I had not thought death had undone so many".

We seem to have erased from our awareness the powerful images of modernity originating in Belfast, by superimposing other images of the working and middle classes that created or inspired them. To their enemies, the Ulster working and artisan class is merely bigoted, the managerial class merely philistine. Here is Seán Ó Faoláin's critique of Belfast offered to the world in 1940 in *An Irish Journey*, one that goes beyond the moribund Ulster Sunday I recall only too well:

> One felt that nothing could indeed have possibly come of that 19th-century Sunday sleep, and the red factories and the grey buildings, and the ruthlessness with which the whole general rash of this stinking city was permitted to spread along the waters of the Lough but the bark of rifles and the hurtle of paving stones and the screams of opposing hates ... All the hates that blot the name of Ulster are germinated here. And what else could be germinated here but the revenges of the heart against its own brutalisation ... There is no aristocracy—no culture—no grace—no leisure worthy of the name. It all boils down to mixed grills, double whiskies, dividends, movies, and these strolling, homeless, hate driven poor.

(In 1940, Belfast was helping directly to confront Nazism; Ó Faoláin came from a country that called that war 'the Emergency' and stayed snug in its neutral bed.) In O Faoláin's fevered outburst—how dare he say what Belfast or any other place 'boils down to'?—there is betrayed as narrow an idea of what constitutes culture as that which he imputes to Belfast and an incapacity to look with curiosity at the work that filled the other days of the city's week.

But even if modernity were happening in Harland & Wolff's, and in other cutting-edge factories and foundries in Belfast, were not the working class disjunct from it in their essential lives? When they were not victimising Catholic fellow citizens (and Henry Patterson has analysed the anti-Catholic shipyard activism of 1920 in his book, *Class Conflict and Sectarianism* [1980]), were they not simply exploited by capital, not co-creators but lackeys and flunkeys?

Even sympathetic commentators have sometimes inadvertently encouraged this view by presenting workers as merely colourful, and the yard as a folk arena peopled by quaint characters; which is only a fraction of the whole story and a distortion when allowed to dominate our perception of what was going on in industrial Belfast in Victorian and Edwardian times. It may also be an unwitting translation by folklorists of urban workers into the familiar and conservative (however raggedly Romantic) idiom of rural Ireland that, since the time of the Irish cultural revival (1880-1920), has too often dominated our understanding of thought and action in the island.

But were the workers, as representative, modern, machine-driven as well as machine-driving man, not estranged and alienated from the modernity they were unwittingly advancing—perhaps even resembling Wells' Morlocks who mechanically maintain the indolent Eloi? Certainly, they were physically dwarfed by their own collective end-product, and it may be that the humour and urban folklore for which the yard is locally famous were generated to counter the estranging vastness of their successive productions with a sense of community that made metal and machine more human. Here is a passage from Wade, a quotation from an observer at the site of the *Titanic* construction; it is rather overblown, but may be no more than a verbal equivalent of the Welch photographs that capture the dismaying immensity of the ship:

> For months and months in that monstrous iron enclosure there was nothing that had the faintest likeness to a ship; only something that might have been the iron scaffolding for the naves of half-a-dozen cathedrals laid end to end ... at last the skeleton within the scaffolding began to take shape, at the sight of which men held their breaths. It was the shape of a ship, a ship so monstrous and unthinkable that it towered there over the buildings and dwarfed the very mountains by the water ... A rudder as big as a giant elm tree, bosses and bearings of propellers the size of windmills—everything was on a nightmare scale; and underneath the iron foundations of the cathedral floor men were laying, on concrete beds, pavements of oak and great cradles of timber and iron and sliding ways of pitch pine to support

the bulk of the monster when she was moved, every square inch of the pavement surface bearing a weight of more than two tons. Twenty tons of tallow were spread upon the ways, and hydraulic rams and triggers built and fixed against the bulk of the ship so that, when the moment came, the waters she was to conquer should thrust her finally from the earth.

If it is diminishing to regard industrial workers as urban peasants, it would be equally diminishing to see life in the Victorian and Edwardian Belfast shipyards as resembling that in the Ford automobile plants of the 20s and 30s that Terry Smith discusses—pure modernity without history, assembly-line production, a 'régime' of modernity—with its Sociological Department seeking to create the ideal Ford Man. Even though both kinds of plant were created by the massive shift from entrepreneurial to monopoly capitalism, I think David Harvey in *The Condition of Postmodernity* is relevant here:

> It is important to keep in mind that the modernism that emerged before the First World War was more of a reaction to the new conditions of production (the machine, the factory, urbanisation), circulation (the new systems of transport and communication), and consumption (the rise of the mass markets, advertising, mass fashion), than it was a pioneer in the production of such changes.

If the *Titanic* was a cultural complex—even during construction—then its modernism was pre-war modernism, just as its modernity was not Fordist.

So I think that Sheeler's imagery of Fordism on one side, and O Faoláin's lazy stereotypology of Belfast on the other, can be shouldered aside as extremes, while we leave the modernity of industrial Belfast (certainly in the productive environments of engineering and shipbuilding) intact. It is possible that the appalling phenomenon of anti-Catholic sectarianism associated with Harland & Wolff has prevented us from properly appreciating the modernism being enacted there. On the other hand, it might be investigated how far the modernisation of Ulster can be used to confirm locally Weber's famous 'Protestant ethic' thesis, linking modern capitalism to Calvinism, a thesis popularised by Tawney and re-examined by divers hands in *The Protestant Ethic and Modernization*, edited by S.N. Eisenstadt in 1968. There is an 1885 Welch photograph that might be a footnote to this: it is of a Trades Arch erected in the city centre by the citizens of Belfast to honour the visit of the Prince of Wales; models of a steam engine, loom, and ship adorn it, and around it appears as motto the biblical observation, 'Man Goeth Forth Unto His Work and to His Labour Until the Evening' (Psalm 104).

However, Habermas traced modernity to the Enlightenment and the scientific domination of nature (the *Titanic* project was popularly regarded as trying to do just that), while Adorno argued that the logic of Enlightenment rationally is domination and oppression: this seems too highly charged a scenario for turn-of-the-century, anti-Catholic Belfast, but the city and its industrial and modernising achievements are hardly beneath some sophisticated cultural analysis of the kind Smith devotes to Fordism.

VI

In the meantime, I was struck by Low's observation in *Titanica* that the sunken ship, lying on a flat, surprisingly fine-ribbed sea-bed (like exposed intertidal sand), has created a compact new ecosystem of fish and primitive animals; for it made me think, incongruously, of the shipyard that made her as the centre of a cultural ecosystem, for which the Great Gantry around the growing ship might serve as metaphor.

It is true that the hierarchy of the British class system, reflected to some extent in the crew hierarchy, was also reflected to some extent in the workforce of the huge shipbuilding company that built the ship, a hierarchy running from management through draughtsmen and foremen to workmen and apprentices, with journeymen a kind of floating lower middle class. But social class and division of labour are not one and the same, and satisfaction of workmanship is a potent cement in co-operative enterprises.

Moreover, the pride in shipbuilding of Harland & Wolff's magnitude was not just a pride shared by fellow workers in the great industrial triangle formed by the ports, basins and drydocks of Liverpool, Belfast and Glasgow that dominated marine engineering for decades. It was not even just Protestant pride or unionist pride. It was local pride, east Belfast pride. There was a network of family and kin within and across factories; the yard was a way of life, a subculture, as David Hammond's documentary film and book (*Steelchest, Nail in the Boot & the Barking Dog* [1986]) make clear. According to several historians, there was a working-class *élite* in Belfast, 'an aristocracy of labour', composed of highly-skilled workers whose activities derived from day-time training and night-time education—all complicating a picture of an exploited, exploiting, benighted, bigoted working class.

Also, the *Titanic* was built at the sharp point of a tradition of Belfast shipbuilding (it marginally improved on its own, fractionally-elder twin, the *Olympic*), in a seaport with its own lengthy history, itself a conduit for a vigorous mercantile community. And feeding into that community were the advanced educational establishments of the city, themselves the product of progressive thought. As William Gray tells us in *Science and Art in Belfast* (1904):

> ... the material prosperity of Belfast was the direct outcome of that intellectual activity that characterised the early years of the 19th century, when our chief educational institutions were founded, which were in advance of similar institutions of many of the chief cities of the United Kingdom. There is an obvious and direct connection between the educational results of the Royal Academical Institution and our chief shipbuilding yards and other important manufacturing establishments.

Modernity was not a ruthless rupture with the past ("History is more or less bunk"—Henry Ford), but was pushed forward by innovation from an existing reality and absorbed past, not merely imposed from without and above by Pierpont Morgan, Ismay, or Lord Pirrie. In this as in other cultural manifestations of modernism, punctuated equilibrium is a more accurate description of progress than the usual 'radical disjunction' idea favoured by cultural theorists.

This modernism had, save in one lamentable respect—sectarianism—a human face. Was Welch a paid promoter of capitalist industry, like Sheeler, as well as a loving visual chronicler of country ways? We need a serious biography of him before being able to answer this question. But both were artists, recorders of modernity, and Welch tempers the artistic and industrial hard edge of his shipyard representations with a humanity borrowed from his rural images.

Even the middle-class designers and builders cannot be dismissed as uncultured Bounderbys. The career of Thomas Andrews, the Comber-born chief designer at Harland & Wolff during the era of the *Titanic*, the master-builder of the ship, and who went down with her, is an apparently challenging case in point. The novelist Shan Bullock's 1912 biography is "a labour of love", as Walter Lord remarks, and Bullock is unapologetic in describing Andrews matter-of-factly as a good unionist, capitalist and imperialist. Yet this "wonderful man", as Lord calls him, was by all accounts an engineering genius and administrator *par excellence* (who moved frequently and at his ease among yardworkers), working his way up the hierarchy though all the chief shops and offices in Harland & Wolff, if not from working-class scratch like Pirrie (who rose from boilermaker to baronet). If anyone embodied the continuity between the two realities depicted in the Welch photograph with which I began this essay, it was Andrews.

By Matthew Arnold's standards, this captain of industry was a bit of a philistine, but if so then we need to expand our idea of culture to accommodate him. On his Christmas card for 1910, he printed a sentence from Ruskin: "What we think, or what we know, or what we believe, is in the end of little consequence. The only thing of consequence is what we do." I was pleased to read this in Bullock, for I had been simultaneously reading Ruskin on iron in art and policy (in *The Two Paths: Being Lectures on Art and its Application to Decoration and Manufacture* [1958-9]) and thinking of my own engineering forebears.

I see Andrews standing at the junction of Victorian industriousness and 20th-century modernity, and it is a pity that this man was lost at the age of 39. Recalling a visit to Andrews in Harland & Wolff, the Irish nationalist, Erskine Childers, wrote of him:

> His mind seemed to revel in its mastery, both of the details and of the *ensemble*, both of the technical and the human side of a great science, while restlessly seeking to enlarge its outlook, conquer new problems, and achieve an ever fresh perfection. Whether it was about the pitch of a propeller or the higher problems of design, speed, and mercantile competition, one felt the same grip and enthusiasm and above all perhaps, the same delight in frank self-revelation.

The description makes a nonsense of the Two Cultures, both inside and outside Ireland. It is also, I believe, an image of an ideal modernity, unmatched elsewhere in Ireland before or after.

Irish Unionist Imagery, 1850-1920

Alvin Jackson

This paper seeks to explore some of the ways in which sympathetic images of Britishness and positive images of the British empire were made commonly available in Ireland in the 19th and early 20th centuries. I want to lay some stress on the permeation of leisure time with these anglo-centric and imperial images, and I want to deal with (or, at any rate, begin to deal with) both pictorial and verbal imagery. Organised unionism undoubtedly drew upon these images, and was able to appeal to a public excited by imperial fervour and conditioned by a pervasive British sentiment.

Of course, I do not intend to suggest that unionism was simply a by-product of the anglicisation of Ireland in the 19th century—that Victorian unionists were unionist merely because they were pathetic victims of a crude but successful public relations campaign celebrating Britain and Britishness. Unionist organisation in the 19th century built upon a newly-coherent sense of Protestant identity—a more evangelical Protestantism; unionist organisation built upon the regional economy of eastern Ulster, as it built upon divisions within the Belfast workplace. The workplace was important for the evolution and promotion of unionism, because it supplied an economic justification for this creed, and also because it represented an organised arena within which conservative and paternalist values might be propagated.

But unionism was more than an industrial by-product—a creation of the factory or of the urban economy. Informal unionism, unionist imagery, permeated the leisure and recreation of many Irish people long before the hardening of this sentiment into a formal electoral organisation. Unionism sprang not simply from evangelical Protestantism or from a popular perception of Protestant economic advantage, but from the autonomous development of a loyalist popular culture in the 19th century. What I propose to do is to look at two changing aspects of this culture and its related imagery: first the various ways in which the image of Britishness filtered into Ireland; and second (and related), the images generated by unionism in the home rule era. Historians in the past have tended to explore the origins of unionism in relation to the industrial development of eastern Ulster, but I wish to shift the focus of this search towards leisure activity, and the imagery propagated by and through leisure activity.[1]

In urban Ireland, and particularly in Belfast, leisure opportunities developed after the brutalities of early Victorian capitalist expansion. By the end of the 19th century, the weekend had been invented as a leisure space, and with it a much more diverse recreational culture. As leisure developed, so too did the commercial, religious and political opportunities which it afforded. Entrepreneurs sold organised entertainment to those whose leisure activity had once been freer and more informal.[2] Churchmen saw in popular leisure time space for the spread of moralising or missionary work; political activists saw the opportunity to purvey propagandist images. Leisure opportunities therefore grew, leisure pursuits became more institutionalised and regimented; and leisure time, attacked and occupied by the churches and parties, helped to promote religious and political polarisation. Leisure, quite simply, grew in importance: it involved the health of business and the health of the soul and, as such, was intimately bound with evolving unionism.

As leisure opportunities increased in the north-east, so the religious segregation of leisure activity grew, and as leisure opportunities grew, so they became more commercially based, and more British in inspiration. In Belfast, the Easter Fair on the Cave Hill, informal and drawing support from each confessional tradition, gave way in the middle of the century to the more formal pleasure grounds at, first, the Queen's Island, and, by the 1870s, at the Botanic Gardens. Boozy and bawdy singing saloons—glorified inns—popular at the beginning of the century, similarly gave way to variety theatres and music halls.[3]

Informality yielded to institutionalisation. Local, homespun entertainment had given way to a commercial and often imported variety. In England, the music hall was a bastion of popular imperialism and British chauvinism, and its export version was scarcely less jingoistic. Like television in the 1960s, the theatre of varieties represented, in its diversity, a window on the outside world. And, given the origins of the entertainment form, and the origins of many of the entertainers themselves, this was unquestionably a window which looked out over the Irish Sea to England.[4]

The commercialisation of Belfast's entertainment meant, in many cases, its anglicisation. This was reflected not simply in the content of songs, in the material of the comedians, but in the very names of the principal theatres—the Empire Theatre of Varieties, the Royal Theatre.[5] Frank Matcham's Grand Opera House evokes the splendours of the Indian empire.[6] Penny Summerfield, in her essay on the late 19th-century music hall, refers to the "manipulative Conservatism" of this form of popular entertainment.[7] It was the popular songs of the 1870s, above all else, which won the music halls their reputation as vehicles for British patriotism and British imagery. The most famous of these was a song called 'By Jingo', written in 1877 by G.W. Hunt, and exported to the Belfast music halls:

> We don't want to fight, but by jingo if we do
> We've got the ships, we've got the men, we've got the money too,
> We've fought the bear before, and while we're Britons true,
> The Russians shall not have Constantinople.[8]

'By Jingo' was, as I say, the most famous of these British patriotic lyrics, but it was by no means unique or a new departure: it reflected, instead, other songs and melodrama which emphasised the morality of British supremacy. It reflected, as well, a celebration of British military and naval predominance—a celebration of the essential virtues of the British soldier (sympathetically caricatured as Tommy Atkins) and the British sailor (the archetypal Jolly Jack Tar).[9] Melodrama has been described by John MacKenzie as "a strongly non-intellectual tradition in which characterisation, subtle emotional nuance, or philosophical problems ... had no place. Plot, physical sensations and stereotype were all". Melodrama occupied an important position in the popular theatre of late Victorian Belfast and other industrial cities, with its uncomplicated representations of British morality and glorification of imperial and xenophobic themes.[10] Patriotic, imperial images remained essential features of the music halls and other forms of popular entertainment until the outbreak of the Great War in August 1914.

With the introduction of the cinema, a new vehicle for the propagation of British national imagery had been located. Films were, by definition, imported films. The first reels were shown to Belfast audiences in 1896, and among the first images projected were those of the Diamond Jubilee of Queen Victoria (in 1897).[11] Further royal and loyal images followed in 1902, with the coronation of Edward VII and the conclusion of the Boer War; and in 1911, with the coronation of George V.[12] By the time of the third Home Rule Bill, in 1912, unionist leaders like James Craig had been made fully aware of the importance of the cinema as a means of manipulating public opinion both within Ireland and beyond. Unionist festivals such as Ulster Covenant Day, 28th September, 1912, were filmed for the benefit of the Irish public outside Belfast, and for the benefit of British voters. Mr. Copeland Trimble, commander of the Enniskillen Horse (an outpost of the Ulster Volunteer movement) demanded a full turn-out of his men, in May 1913, "because of the presence of cinematographic operators".[13]

Other visual images flourished, and urged a British nationalism. Advertising grew more obtrusive with the development of cheap mass-produced posters and—after the 1880s—luscious enamel signs: these last, as John MacKenzie argues, were particularly favoured by the major imperial enterprises (tea, soap, cocoa and tobacco companies) and broadcast exotic imperial images.[14] The packaging of household goods—biscuit boxes, tea caddies, tin cigarette boxes—increasingly brought imperial and royal imagery into Irish households. Cigarette cards, cards in tea packets, depicted British military and imperial themes. Postcards carried similar subjects after the 1890s.[15]

Like advertisers and entertainers, the Irish Protestant clergy were active and subtle as colonisers of leisure time and of the mind. Clergy supplied the leadership and Protestant evangelicalism the emotional drive to a wide variety of recreational and proselytising organisations. The Girls' Friendly Society, the Young Women's Christian Association and the Women's Temperance Association were created in England to address the perceived social and spiritual needs of late Victorian women, and they spread quickly into Belfast and the north of Ireland generally.[16] In a town like Armagh, at the end of the 19th century, the Daughters of Empire movement provided imperial and unionist imagery for young women. Even the Girls' Friendly Society, an off-shoot of the Church of Ireland, discreetly propagated the unionist sympathies of women by offering British patriotic entertainments.[17]

There were male equivalents in the form of numerous local and national recreational bodies. These institutions (the Presbyterian Young Men's Guilds, the Church of Ireland Mutual Improvement Societies) were promoting, by the 1870s and 1880s, a strong sense of Protestant identity through the propagation of the history of the reformation, the works of Foxe and Bunyan and other Protestant classics. In Armagh, in 1883, the Protestant Mutual Improvement Society celebrated the 400th anniversary of the birth of Martin Luther by purchasing an enormous lithograph of 'Luther at the Diet of Worms' and displaying it at their subsequent gatherings. Such bodies were also promoting a sense of imperial mission through their evangelical and recreational passions. They frequently bought popular jingoistic literature (the works of G.A. Henty, for example, or the *Boy's Own Paper*) as a resource for their members.[18] Indeed, in Britain in the 1870s there was an explosion of juvenile literature—a literature which emphasised an "adventurous and militaristic patriotism"; and this explosion resonated within the north of Ireland.[19]

Both men's and women's voluntary and recreational associations built upon the evangelical and anglophile creed which the Sunday schools, with their stress on the missionary and imperial ideal, were drumming into Protestant children. With the foundation of the Hibernian Sunday School Society, in 1809, the youngest elements of Protestant society learned the basic features of their evangelical faith.[20] A paternalistic and conservative conception of society was hammered home virtually from the cradle. As the 19th century developed, it became increasingly likely that a child could spend its early years in an exclusively Protestant and often anglo-centric environment. Sunday schools propagated the images of union and empire. Sunday school lessons celebrated Protestant missionary work within the British empire, and the christianising—and therefore improving—aspects of empire. More tangibly, Sunday school prizes often included books celebrating British pluck or morality, or the dignity of the British royal family. At coronations, or jubilees, (1887, 1897, 1902, 1911, 1935) Sunday school children might receive cheap pottery mugs bearing the royal image—or sometimes brass or aluminium medallions. In Armagh, in June 1911, when George V was crowned, the Unionist MP for the constituency presented coronation medals to hundreds of bedraggled Sunday-school children.[21]

One of the clearest institutional and religious beneficiaries of the development and politicisation of leisure time was the Orange Order. The Order had emerged in 1795 from the sectarian rivalries of north Armagh: it was originally little more than a veterans' association for the victors of one of the numerous party clashes in the county (the Battle of the Diamond, Loughgall). Late 19th-century Orangeism differed in origin, in form, and in content from its predecessor at the beginning of the century.[22] It drew inspiration from a much more coherent Protestantism, and from a much more coherent threat, in the shape of a resurgent Catholicism and a developing home rule movement. It was, therefore, a more extensive movement, and much less localised: by the second half of the century, Orangeism was motivated less by local communal animosities than by a sense of universal threat. It had, by the 1870s and 1880s, established for the first time an extensive Belfast base, and was developing for the first time in over-whelmingly Protestant, as opposed to denominationally-mixed areas. It now had a much stronger social and recreational dimension and a greater than ever respectability within Protestantism, playing for the first time a very considerable role in popular Protestant culture.

How may these developments in Orangeism be explained? Partly, as I've hinted, Orangeism developed because Irish Protestantism developed, and because Protestants perceived a more direct and comprehensive threat to their existence. But the spread of Orangeism was related, not simply to changing motives, but also to changing opportunities, and the changing form of the movement as it responded to the increased leisure time of the Belfast artisan and lower middle classes. The opportunity for Orange growth arose because of the development of a popular loyalist culture, to which I shall return, and because the propertied elements inside Protestantism began, from the late 1860s, to patronise the Order. Propertied patronage lent respectability. Moreover, the Order was developing away from vigilante origins and into a more diverse institution, catering for women, and providing politically-loaded entertainment and recreation. Orangeism grew, by the last quarter of the 19th century, not simply because it reflected Protestant anxieties; it developed because it supplied recreational needs, and satisfied social aspirations.

The growth of the Order was aided by the rapid spread of material imagery and the diffusion of loyalist sentiment through songs and music. The widespread application of the techniques of mass production, in the early 19th century, made for more plentiful and cheaper books, sheet-music, and decorative ware for the unionist (and nationalist) household. Cheap chromolithography from the 1840s on meant that Orange songs began to appear in colourful, illustrated wrappers, and that cheap prints were available for the walls of the unionist home.[23] The ending of all direct forms of newspaper taxation by 1860 opened the way for mass journalism. The development of transport, in particular rail transport, permitted the swift distribution of goods and ideas.

Orangeism, and ultimately unionism, developed partly in the way that nationalism developed—this is, because technical and educational innovation permitted the more effective politicisation and mobilisation of the communities in Ireland. A national education structure after 1831 made for a more receptive public.[24] Cheap mass-production and improved distribution meant that both nationalists and unionists could be supplied more effectively with images and goods appropriate to their faith and their politics. These images and goods did not in themselves create a nationalist or loyalist commitment—but they did help to consolidate and enliven political and religious creeds.

From the mid-19th century, Irish Protestants could buy household objects representing their political and religious faiths. The Staffordshire potteries supplied portraits of Garibaldi, Louis Napoleon and Prince Albert to English homes—while supplying the familiar image of King William III on his white horse for Irish Protestants. Local and Scots pottery manufacturers provided cheap, transfer-printed cups and plates with William III and his horse and the Orange 'No Surrender!' motto.

The most pervasive loyalist image was that of William III—but, as Belinda Loftus has revealed, the nature of this image, and the medium in which it was represented, changed decisively between the 18th and 20th centuries.[25] The vision of William which held sway in Ireland until the early 19th century was that supplied by the sculptor Grinling Gibbons through his equestrian statue of the king, created in 1701. This was, as befitted the age, a classical vision, with William represented as a Roman *Imperator*—stiff, formal and elegant. And it was a vision which was reproduced on glassware and crockery and banners until the 1820s, and (less commonly) later in the century. But Gibbons' classical portrayal fell victim to the Romanticisation of European tastes, and was superseded by an image supplied by the painter Benjamin West in a canvas exhibited in 1780, 'The Battle of the Boyne'. West's portrayal of William leading his armies—his portrait of an active and heroic monarch—proved more accessible to 19th-and 20th-century tastes, and it is this painting which has monopolised the artistic imagery of modern unionism.[26] West's image, not Gibbons', has formed the basis for the 20th-century tradition of loyalist mural art—a tradition which originated around 1910, and which has been maintained sporadically until the present day. A pervasive feature of the industrial terraces of Protestant north and east Belfast is the wall-painting of William at the Boyne. And, almost without exception, the ultimate inspiration for these murals is Benjamin West's image of 1780.

King William predominated among the crockery images in Irish households, though he held no monopoly. Royal commemorative ware, though produced in the 17th and 18th centuries, started to penetrate Irish loyalist homes with the coronation of Victoria in 1837, and the marriage of the Prince of Wales in 1863; the peak of this loyalist imagery came with Victoria's Diamond Jubilee of 1897, when commemorative prints, crockery—even commemorative jewellery (little silver brooches embossed with '1837-1897') were produced in enormous quantities. Contemporary Orange heroes, such as William Johnston of Ballykilbeg, were celebrated through the transfer-printed portraits on cheaply-produced local glazed ware. Johnston's imprisonment in 1868, and his election to parliament later in that year, inspired a rash of commemorative pieces which found places of reverence in the homes of Belfast artisans and Orangemen.[27]

Improved printing and literacy meant better quality pictorial representation and the enhanced significance of the printed word for all Irish people. Orange prints, elaborate certificates of membership and office, and, above all, Orange song-books, were distributed with increasing frequency through the 19th and early 20th centuries. These prints and certificates, proudly displayed in front parlours, were an essential part of the way in which Orange iconography became firmly entrenched in Irish Protestant homes. Orange song-books, printed in Belfast and Glasgow, offered a wider audience for Orange ballads and choruses than the earlier spread of these songs by simple word of mouth. Concentrating on party clashes and disputes, from the Siege of Derry, in 1689, through to the Battle of Garvagh, 1813, and Dolly's Brae, 1849, such song-books both fed off and contributed to the developing sectarian polarisation of Ireland. As one of the most popular forms of historical conditioning, these song-books helped decisively to shape Protestant identity; and they are at the heart of the cultural heritage of modern unionism.

But books of all kinds had an increasing significance. As literacy increased and the cost of printing declined, so the Irish book market developed both in diversity and capacity. Books ceased to be quite the luxury objects that they had been, even at the end of the 18th century (when the most popular form of literature, the chap-book, might well cost 6d.). By the end of the 19th century, books had become part of the furniture of the socially-ambitious working-man's home. Libraries had ceased, in this time, to be the preserve of the gentry and professional classes and had become educational resources, or resources for self-improvement, rather than social institutions. Two measures—the Irish Public Libraries Acts of 1855 and 1894—created and consolidated the library as a truly popular educational and recreational resource.[28]

Orangeism and unionism ultimately benefited from these developments in a number of ways. The commercialisation and popularisation of the Irish book market meant that it was, to a considerable extent, anglicised. Some Irish publishers prospered, but—by the second half of the century—English book publishers and English authors dominated the sales and lending figures. Belfast publishers were eclipsed by London rivals. The Belfast-based popular publishing house, Simms and M'Intyre, sold out in 1853 to their London agents.[29] Popular publishing in the north of Ireland in the second half of the century came to be dominated by cheap book series published in London: Routledge's Railway Library of 1849, Milner's Cottage Library Series of 1853, and Cassell's National Library Series of 1856.[30] London publishers and English authors, especially nationally— or religiously—chauvinistic authors, dominated Belfast library loans (Dickens, Marryat, Rider Haggard, Mrs. Henry Wood).[31] The book trade was, quite simply, one of the chief vehicles for the propagation of English culture in the north of Ireland. The popularisation of the book had meant its relative anglicisation; English books implied British images and ideas; and this propagation and these perspectives contributed materially to the formation of Irish unionist attitudes.

Organised unionism built upon, perhaps even depended upon, these sympathetic images of Britishness which were becoming more common; but organised unionism also generated its own imagery, and to some extent reversed the pattern of cultural influence, exporting images to Britain. The most careful and successful image-building came in 1912-14, but there is evidence of stage-management and marketing in 1886, at the time of the first Home Rule Bill, and in 1893, at the time of the second Home Rule Bill. The unionist political organisations which flourished in the 1880s, especially the Dublin-based Irish Loyal and Patriotic Union, were chiefly important as producers of propaganda: each year the ILPU published tens of thousands of posters, pamphlets, cartoons, all designed to propagate a sympathetic image of Irish unionism and a harsh image of Irish nationalism within Britain. Familiar unionist images from this source included distressed Irish women confronting brutal agrarian agitation, or idealised portraits of unionist heroes like Arthur Balfour. Organisations such as the ILPU also propagated their imagery through the magic lantern—through slide shows designed to underline nationalist illegality and unionist morality.[32]

The unionist imagery generated in 1892-93 was much more diverse and much more self-conscious than at the time of the first Home Rule Bill: in particular the focal point of unionist opposition to home rule, the Ulster Convention of June 1892, stimulated a complex range of souvenir and propaganda materials. This convention was held in Botanic Gardens, Belfast, and is well-documented through the photographs of Lawrence and through intricate press reports.[33] The convention was designed to act both as a boost to Ulster unionist morale and as a proof to the British electorate of the undiminished opposition to home rule. There was, therefore, much riding on the success of this event, and considerable attention was paid by the organising committee and by other unionist businessmen to advance publicity, and to the commemoration of the achievements of the convention.[34] The imagery generated by the convention often combined Celtic revivalism with the iconography of British patriotism. Harps, shamrocks, motifs culled from the Book of Kells, and Irish language mottos rested alongside the royal coat of arms, the crown, idealistic representations of Ulster and Britannia. In 1892, unionist propagandists were plugging into two distinctive and powerful sources of imagery: Celtic romanticism and British jingoism. This was done without any sense of incongruity, because the propagandists were anxious to demonstrate that Irish unionism was simultaneously Irish and unionist: they were keen to underline that the Irish Parliamentary Party had no monopoly over (as they saw it) Irish patriotism, and that (again, as they saw it) a true Irish patriotism was compatible with the imperial connection. Just as the Church of Ireland and the Catholic hierarchy have periodically disputed the legacy of St. Patrick and of the Celtic church, so late 19th-century unionism was concerned in some of its visual imagery to lay claim to a Celtic legacy.

The images produced in 1892 filtered into many homes. Commemorative medals were produced by the Belfast jeweller, Sharman Neill, and sold in thousands; they were manufactured in gold, silver, bronze gilt and bronze, with the latter two categories priced for popular demand. Souvenir booklets, lavishly illustrated and decorated, were sold. Special editions of the Belfast newspapers were brought out to commemorate the convention. Badges of all sorts were manufactured: a common type (which can be seen in the Ulster Museum) was a metal bar embossed with the motto 'Ulster Unionist Convention, 1892', with a royal crown, and carrying a rectangle of woven silk bearing the royal coat of arms.

The imagery of 1892-93 may perhaps be seen as a transitional stage in unionist self-assessment. Unionism drew upon the positive images of Britishness, which were increasingly important in Ireland, but it modified these images in ways particular to the needs of the unionist movement. Unionists spoke the language of Britishness, therefore, but with an increasingly peculiar vocabulary. And this reflected the increasingly local nature of unionism—its growing detachment from the parliamentary process, and its deepening reliance on local, as opposed to parliamentary or British, political resources. The localisation of unionism came to a head at the time of the third Home Rule Bill; and unionist imagery was, by this time, both more influential than at any time in the past, as well as being further removed from the British patriotic imagery which had been an early inspiration within the movement. Much more than in 1886 or in 1893, unionism in 1912 was promoted through a personality cult. King Billy had been at the heart of Orange Protestant celebration in the 19th century, but as a mono-dimensional, iconic figure; Sir Edward Carson emerged in 1912 as a multi-dimensional, though still idealised, figure.

In so far as unionism achieved its goals in 1912-14, success lay primarily in the area of salesmanship, of image-building.[35] Carson was marketed with much the same vigour as was applied to Sunlight Soap, or to Dunville's whiskey; and it was James Craig who acted as marketing manager. Carson's electoral experience had been gained within a none-too-testing forum—Trinity College, Dublin—where unionism was routinely triumphant, and a Unionist MP guaranteed a comfortable tenure. Electoral management did not come easily to Carson, for it had never been necessary. Craig's political schooling, on the other hand, had been more rigorous, for he had come to prominence in the context of a divided and threatened unionism. Craig, his brother Charles Curtis Craig, William Moore, and a handful of other, younger Conservative Unionists had, in the year before 1906, successfully warded off an electoral challenge from one of the most skilled politicians of the home rule era—Thomas Wallace Russell. Russell, an independent Protestant radical, had leached away unionist votes in key rural marginal constituencies, yet he had also in effect reinvigorated mainstream unionism in the north. He had compelled his Unionist opponents to reconsider their electoral strategies in Ulster, after years of an enervated reliance on sectarian and party polarity. Craig was one of a younger generation of loyalist activists who successfully and creatively replied to Russell's onslaught. He became a vigorous platform speaker, and he carefully exploited other media of communication— from Orange and masonic contacts, through to the gewgaws of Edwardian electioneering (badges, rosettes, crude woodcut portraits and cartoons, cyclostyled campaign messages).[36]

Craig's training in electoral management, and his flair for publicity, were of central importance to the marketing of unionism between 1912 and 1914. He and his colleagues on the standing committee of the Ulster Unionist Council formulated images of cohesion and determination within unionism through carefully marshalled displays: they cultivated an image of leadership and of the venerability of its purpose, choreographing Carson's movements and stage-managing his public appearances.[37] The skill with which Ulster unionism was marketed should not obscure the extent of the manipulation which was involved. The constant appeals to antiquity were of doubtful persuasiveness. Public displays of unity only temporarily bolstered a unionism which had been characterised by schism since its institutional foundation in the 1880s. Yet—crucially—these were the images which lasted. It was the skill of the image-builders, rather than the elusiveness of their subject, which shaped subsequent attitudes towards the events of 1912-14. The apparently sustained success of unionist negativism, chronicled admiringly by historians such as Ronald McNeill (*Ulster's Stand for Union* [1922]) or Henry Maxwell (*Ulster was Right* [c.1934]) supplied a paradigm for subsequent unionist behaviour. In so far as the ways in which Ulster 'said no' in 1912-14 have been echoed in the ways in which Ulster 'says no' in the 1980s, then contemporary unionist activists have shown themselves both to be historicist, and to have been directed by their reading of their own past.[38]

This should be less surprising if one examines the achievement of the image-builders of 1912-14. Craig, for his part, helped to transform the uncomfortably histrionic and highly-sensitive Carson into an object of popular loyalist devotion. Craig managed his visits to Ireland, the demonstrations at which he spoke, the photo-calls. It was evidently Craig who suggested that the signing of the Covenant by Carson and the other luminaries of the movement should be filmed for the benefit of country audiences and the education of the British. It was Craig who fabricated a political genealogy for Carson, and for Ulster unionism, by evoking comparisons with William III and with 17th-century Calvinist dissent. He was largely responsible for obtaining a banner which had been carried before William in 1690 and which was reused as Carson's standard in 1912.[39] The Covenant of 1912, again partly Craig's inspiration, and on which the first signature was Carson's, carried echoes of the Scots' covenants of 1638 and 1643. Indeed the evocation of God in the Ulster Covenant, and its pious language, suggested even more ancient, Judaic precedents for loyalist strategy.[40]

Yet what is most impressive about the marketing of unionism in 1912 is, perhaps, the comprehensive application of Edwardian technology to this task. Film was exploited to publicise unionist festivals and demonstrations. Motor vehicles and motor-cycles were deployed within the UVF, drivers proclaiming their unionism through brass fender badges.[41] The resources of the printing industry were exploited to the full. That central medium of communication in Edwardian Ireland, the half-penny postcard, was used to carry loyalist propaganda, from coy depictions of unionism in the form of pugnacious little boys, or vulnerable young women, through to images of Carson.[42] Carson's grimly ironic features appear everywhere: in dozens of poses on tens of thousands of cards, on mass-produced lapel badges, on charity stamps. German porcelain manufacturers supplied parian busts of Carson and the Tory leader, Andrew Bonar Law, to the china cabinets of suburban Belfast. If, as Ronan Fanning has pointed out, the homes of the Irish Republic were adorned with the triptych of Pope John XXIII, Robert and J.F. Kennedy in the early 1960s, then the unionist household gods were the king-emperor, King Billy and— above all—Carson.[43] The commercial classes of Belfast may occasionally, and discreetly, have questioned the latter's leadership, but their business sense out-ran their political equivocation. Carson's image was marketable, and these classes responded to the challenge of retailing their leader.

Through signing the Covenant, through wearing their badges or joining the UVF, unionist men and women were bound to their leadership in an unprecedented way. In a limited sense, to return to an earlier analogy, Carson and Craig reformulated O'Connell's political achievements, politicising their constituency as thoroughly as the Liberator had done with his people 90 years earlier. In mechanical terms, their task was easier in that they had the resources of the Edwardian advertising industry and the machinery of modern party organisation at their disposal; they also built upon the sympathetic images of Britain and the empire which had permeated into Ireland throughout the later 19th century. Like earlier populist nationalists, Carson and Craig conveyed a simplified political creed with considerable effect. On the other hand, the success of unionist salesmanship has tended to obscure the substance of unionist policies and strategies; and, in so far as this is true, then subsequent unionists, in looking back to 1912, are devoted to an ideal rather than pondering an actuality.

I have argued that organised unionism in the late 19th century drew on a more pronounced sense of Britishness, and that this was related to the spread of sympathetic British and unionist images in everyday life. These images alone are not sufficient to explain the origins of unionism, but they did help to consolidate British patriotism among Irish Protestants. The spread of these images was, in turn, related both to improvements in mass production and to the development of leisure time. British patriotism combined with Celtic revivalism to define the material imagery of unionism in the 1880s and 1890s; but, thereafter, much greater emphasis was laid upon specifically northern emblems (such as the Red Hand), or specifically northern personalities (especially Carson who—though a Dubliner—was the Ulster unionist *generalissimo*). The images propagated in 1912-14, the personality cult of Carson, and the imagery associated with the idea of a besieged and self-reliant northern loyalism have, by and large, survived as the distinguishing features of contemporary unionism.

Notes

[1] See for example John Walton and James Walvin, *Leisure in Britain, 1780-1939* (Manchester, 1983).
[2] John Gray, 'Popular Entertainment' in J.C. Beckett (ed.), *Belfast: The Making of the City* (Belfast, 1983), pp. 102-3.
[3] Ibid.
[4] Penny Summerfield, 'Patriotism and Empire: Music-Hall Entertainment, 1870-1914' in John MacKenzie (ed.), *Imperialism and Popular Culture* (Manchester, 1986), pp. 105, 107
[5] Gray, pp. 105, 107.
[6] Robert McKinstry, 'The Grand Opera House, Belfast: Restoring a Matcham Theatre for Today's Audiences and Actors', in Brian Walker (ed.), *Frank Matcham: Theatre Architect* (Belfast, 1980), pp. 95-118.
[7] Summerfield, p. 19.
[8] Ibid., p. 28.
[9] Ibid., p. 37.
[10] John MacKenzie, *Propaganda and Empire: The Manipulation of British Public Opinion, 1880-1960*, paperback edition (Manchester, 1985), p. 44.
[11] Gray, p. 110.
[12] See *Belfast News Letter*, 19th September, 1902, 3rd July, 1911, 14th July, 1911.
[13] Alvin Jackson, 'Unionist Myths, 1912-85', *Past & Present*, No. 136 (August 1992), p. 172.
[14] MacKenzie, p. 30.
[15] Ibid., pp. 24–7.
[16] Brian Harrison, 'For Church, Queen and Family: The Girls' Friendly

Society, 1874–1920', *Past & Present*, No. 66 (1973), pp. 107-38.

[17] Alvin Jackson, 'Unionist Politics and Protestant Society in Edwardian Ireland', *Historical Journal*, 33, 4 (1990), pp. 860-1.

[18] Ibid., p. 862.

[19] MacKenzie, pp. 199-226. J.S. Bratton, 'Of England, Home and Duty: The Image of England in Victorian and Edwardian Juvenile Fiction' in John MacKenzie (ed.), *Imperialism and Popular Culture* (Manchester, 1986), pp. 73-93.

[20] David Hempton and Myrtle Hill, *Evangelical Protestantism in Ulster Society, 1780–1900* (London, 1992), pp. 59-60.

[21] Jackson, 'Unionist Politics and Protestant Society', p. 859.

[22] Hereward Senior, *Orangeism in Ireland and Britain, 1795-1836* (London, 1966), pp. 274-84.

[23] Belinda Loftus, *Mirrors: William III and Mother Ireland* (Dundrum, 1990), p. 26.

[24] Mary Daly, 'The Development of the National School System, 1831-40' in Art Cosgrove and Donal McCartney (eds.), *Studies in Irish History Presented to R. Dudley Edwards* (Dublin, 1979), pp. 150-163. See also D.H. Akenson, *The Irish Education Experiment* (London, 1970).

[25] Loftus, p. 24.

[26] Ibid., p. 18.

[27] Aiken McClelland, *William Johnston of Ballykilbeg* (Lurgan, 1990), pp. 35-58.

[28] J.R.R. Adams, *The Printed Word and the Common Man: Popular Culture in Ulster, 1700–900* (Belfast, 1987), pp. 168-9.

[29] Ibid., p. 155.

[30] Ibid., pp. 162-4.

[31] Ibid., p. 169.

[32] Patrick Buckland, *Irish Unionism II: Ulster Unionism and the Origins of Northern Ireland, 1885-1922* (Dublin, 1972), p. 76.

[33] Peter Gibbon, *The Origins of Ulster Unionism: The Formation of Popular Protestant Politics and Ideology in Nineteenth Century Ireland* (Manchester, 1975), pp. 133-4.

[34] Gibbons, pp. 133-38.

[35] This section of the essay is taken from Jackson, 'Unionist Myths', pp. 169-72.

[36] For T.W. Russell see Alvin Jackson, 'Irish Unionism and the Russellite Threat, 1894-1906', *Irish Historical Studies*, xxv, 100 (November 1987), pp. 370-404

[37] St. John Ervine, *Craigavon: Ulsterman* (London, 1949), p.181. For comment of the importance of political pageantry see David Cannadine, 'Introduction: Divine Rites of Kings' in David Cannadine and Simon Price (eds), *Rituals of Loyalty: Power and Ceremonial in Traditional Societies* (Cambridge, 1987), p. 19.

[38] For comments on the parallels see Jim Allister, *Anglo-Irish Betrayal: What Choice for Loyal Ulster?* (Carrick, 1986), p. 12; *Shankill Bulletin*, 29th November, 1985; *Ulster* (December 1985-January 1986), pp. 24-5.

[39] Public Record Office of Northern Ireland, Lady Craigavon Papers, D.1415/B/38: Diary for 1st September, 1912.
[40] Ervine, *Craigavon*, p. 221.
[41] Philip Orr, *The Road to the Somme: Men of the Ulster Division tell their Story* (Belfast, 1987), p. 17, suggests a total of 827 cars in the UVF.
[42] John Killen, *John Bull's Famous Circus: Ulster History through the Postcard* (Dublin, 1985), pp. 55, 72.
[43] Ronan Fanning, *Independent Ireland* (Dublin, 1983), p. 203.

'Spiritual Beyond the Ways of Men'
Images of the Gael

Aodán Mac Póilin

A few classical writers were aware of an island perched on the northwest periphery of the known world called, in Latin, *Hibernia*—'winter'. The earliest description we have of the Irish is from the Greek geographer Strabo, who, in the first century AD described them as incestuous cannibals "who are complete savages and lead a miserable existence because of the cold".[1] Solinus, in his third century description of Ireland, was equally unenthusiastic:

> There are no snakes there; only few birds, and an inhospitable and bellicose race of people. Those who are victorious in battle paint their faces with the blood shed by their victims: custom and abberation amount to the same thing. When a mother gives birth to a male child, she puts its food first on her husband's sword, and gently feeds it into the little one's mouth on the swordtip; and does so with heathen prayers that it may not meet its death but in battle and in arms.[2]

Like most stereotypes of the Irish throughout the last couple of millenia, this picture of unrelieved barbarity and aggression was remarkably persistent.

One of the few things the experts seem to agree on is that the word 'Gael' is not Irish, but Welsh. Its early form is Goidel. Irish, like many other languages, has a tendency to swallow syllables. No consonant stranded between two vowels can regard the future with complacency; as mother, father and brother become mo'er, fa'er and bro'er in Belfast, Goidel became Gael. Goidel appears to derive from a Welsh term, gwydd, which can mean an untamed forest, as well as embracing nuances of 'wild' and 'uncultivated'.[3] If this etymology is correct, a

Gael to a fifth century Briton was a Gwyddel, a wild man of the woods. This negative perspective is quite understandable, for the Irish spent much of the fifth century plundering the Welsh coast.

It has been argued that the early Christian missionaries from Britain first used the uncomplimentary term 'Goidel' to mean an inhabitant of Ireland. Alternatively the Goidels are identified as a Continental Celtic tribe which settled in Ireland a century or so before Christ, ultimately dominated the island, imposing their language and customs on the previous inhabitants. This theory is complicated by the fact that they do not appear to have originally called themselves Goidels, and that the Goidelic language appears to have dominated the country before the Goidels did. When the Dál Riata from what is now north Antrim invaded Scotland in the fifth century, the language they brought with them to Scotland was Goidelic. However, neither they, nor the Dál nAraide of south Antrim, nor the Ulaidh, who were by that time restricted to what is now County Down, had been conquered by the Goidels.[4] One fact does appear to be indisputable: although the country was ethnically very heterogenous, it had achieved a remarkable linguistic and cultural unity by the early Christian era.

Linguistic unity was followed, possibly as early as the seventh century, by a conscious attempt to create a sense of racial unity among the Gaels. T.F. O'Rahilly has argued that this project was inspired by "a desire to unify the country by obliterating the memory of the different ethnic origins of the people",[5] through an attempt "to provide a fictitious antiquity for the Goidels".[6] An origin-myth was deliberately created which combined an inextricable mixture of genuine tradition and straightforward lies, underpinned by a mixum-gatherum of the entirety of current scholarship, which at that time involved the Bible and the classics. The ultimate result of this programme was the *Lebor Gabhála*, the *Book of the Takings of Ireland*, commonly known by the mistranslation 'The Book of Invasions'.

The compilers of the *Lebor Gabhála* were, however, handicapped by a reverence for the traditions they were trying to subvert. Although the basic ideological thrust of the construct was never in question, those involved had so much respect for the genuine material that they kept trying to incorporate it into an essentially hostile narrative. In attempting synthesis, they achieved chaos: different interest groups kept trying to incorporate different traditions, resulting in an editor's nightmare of at least fourteen separate versions.[7]

However, the basic plot remains the same, as does the basic intention of replacing the heterogenity of seventh century Ireland with a sense of unity. The account begins with Adam and Eve, and ends with the conquest of Ireland by the Goidel. We can look on the Book of Invasions as a sort of seventh century community relations project. Everyone in Ireland knew that the country was full of non-Goidels, pre-Goidels, and anti-Goidels, all of whom took a very dim view of the Goidels. The consensus-seekers, however, put their trust in the long view. They buried past differences by proving beyond reasonable doubt that all pre-Goidelic people in Ireland had either perished or been banished. The first two settlements were wiped out by plague and flood, and the people of Nemed were driven out by the Fomorians, a race of pirates who caused trouble to everyone. The next group was the Fir Bolg, nowadays usually identified with the Belgae, a Celtic tribe which gave its name to Belgium, but described in Irish literature as the Bagmen, who, in one version, made a living selling bags of Irish earth to the Greeks to spread around their cities as a protection against snakes.[8] These were defeated by the Tuatha Dé Danann and all killed: "except for a few. And those who survived fled from the Tuatha Dé to the islands and peninsulas of the sea, where they have lived ever since".[9] The Tuatha Dé were themselves defeated by the Gaels, who had come to Ireland from Israel by way of Spain in order to justify their other name as the Milesians, the children of Míl Espáne, itself a variant of the Latin 'miles Hispaniae'—the soldier from Spain. The Tuatha Dé Danann are represented in the *Book of Invasions* as a very powerful people with extraordinary magic powers. They were not totally destroyed by the Goidels, but driven underground, where they live in raths, hills, islands and under the sea, from whence they complicate the lives of people living above ground. O'Rahilly argues that the *Lebor Gabhála* version of the story of the Tuatha Dé Danann represents the destruction of pagan religion, and "owes it origin to a desire to reduce the deities of pagan Ireland to the level of mortal men".[10]

The Goidels themselves are traced to a certain Goidel Glas, a descendant of Shem's brother Japhet, by way of Magog. Goidel Glas is credited with fashioning Goidelic from the best of the 72 languages of Babel, which accounts for the perfection of the language. His mother was a daughter of the Phareo, and was called Scotta. Just before the escape from Egypt, Goidel Glas was bitten in the thigh by a snake. Moses cured him with his miraculous staff, but the spot where he was bitten remained green throughout his life. Hence the epithet 'glas', which means 'green'. Moses also prophesied that the descendants of Goidel Glas would live on an island in the north that would always be free from snakes, that no Gael would ever die from snake-bite, and that the Gaels would hold Ireland until the end of time.[11]

This useful Biblical justification proved to have a shelf-life of extraordinary length and tenacity. It surfaces as late as the 19th century in a sectarian song from the south Armagh/north Louth area. The song was, interestingly, written in English, although the area was bilingual at the time. This version of the origin of the Gael may have derived from the re-telling of the legend in Keating's 17th century *History of Ireland*. The ballad is particularly interesting in that its nationalism does not even make a tokenistic nod in the direction of the non-sectarianism of the republican tradition.

> Ye true sons of Granuaile, Milesians so pure,
> Who sprang from the stock of Cordelius [*recte*: Goidel Glas]
> That was bit by the snake, and by Moses was cured,
> And green was the spot he was healed on.
> Patriot David was chosen our King
> And Goliath the giant he slew with a sling
> And down from his race our Virgin did spring,
> Who bore the Messiah, who trampled the serpent
> That came to the garden where Adam was tempted,
> And he died on the cross for to have sin exempted
> While St. Peter's day was a-dawning.
>
> And now to conclude, my advice to you,
> Is to tear down all rotten foundations
> And banish this crew that our land did pollute
> And corrupted our true ordinations.
> We'll raise up a storm and chase them away
> All the informers from King Harry's day
> And all other tribes that with them would say;
> We'll send them a-sailing, all useless and carrion,
> To some other island that's fruitless and barren,
> For this one was promised to Moses and Aaron,
> While St. Peter's day was a-dawning.[12]

The fundamental message of the *Book of Invasions* was simple and straightforward. Everyone in Ireland, except for a few low-lifes on the western seaboard, was a Gael. For the next thousand years, the term Gael was synonymous with Irishman (or woman). Interestingly, this perception persisted in the face of a comprehensive counter-narrative, a version of which survives in Dubhaltach Mac Firbisigh's enormous manuscript *Book of Genealogies*, dated 1650: "the time of the religious war between the Catholics of Ireland, and the heretics of Ireland,

Scotland and England".[13] In this, he quotes an earlier acount of the characteristics of the various ethnic groups in Ireland, which Eoin MacNeill describes as "fine old ascendancy talk"[14]:

> Here are the distinctions which profound historians draw between the different races which are in Ireland, namely, between the descendants of the Firbolgs, Fir Domhnann and Gailiuns and the Tuath Dé Danann and the Milesian.
>
> All who are white of skin, brown of hair, bold, honourable, daring, prosperous, bountiful in the bestowal of wealth, property and jewels, and who are not afraid of battles or combats, they are descended from the Milesians in Ireland.
>
> All who are fair-haired, vengeful, large, every plunderer, all who are musical, professors of music and entertainment, those who are adepts in all druidical and magical arts, they are descended from the Tuath Dé Danann in Ireland.
>
> Every one who is black-haired, who is a tattler, guileful, tale-telling, noisy, contemptible, every wretched, mean, strolling, unsteady, harsh and inhospitable person, every slave, every mean thief, every churl, every one who loves not to listen to music and entertainment, the disturbers of every council and every assembly, and the promotors of discord among people, these are the descendants of the Firbolg, Gailiuns, Liogairne and Fir Domhnann in Ireland, but the Firbolg are the most numerous of these ...
>
> This is taken from an old book. And, indeed, that it is possible to identify a race by their personal appearance I do not take upon myself positively to say, for it may have been true in ancient times, until the race became repeatedly intermixed.[15]

While the Norman invasion barely dented the positive self-image of the Gael, it did set in train a series of events which eventually led to a division between Gaelic identity and Irish identity. For the first half-dozen centuries after the Norman invasion, however, the terms Gael and Irish remained indistinguishible. The continuity of both the self-image of the Gael and the picture painted of them by hostile outsiders in this period is also remarkable. Giraldus Cambrensis, a Welsh Norman priest who wrote two books describing Ireland in the late 12th century, justified the invasion, in terms which echo ominously through the centuries, as both a civilising mission and an ecclesiasiastical reform of the church in Ireland, a reform which was actually under way before the Normans came. His moral unease finds its expression through the most extravagant abuse. The only thing Giraldus praises about the Irish is their musical skill: "their external characteristics of beard and dress, and internal cultivation of the mind, are so barbarous that they cannot be said to have any culture".[16] As a Welshman himself, he may have understood the derivation of Gwyddel, the Welsh word for the Irish, for he describes them as: "forest-dwellers, and inhospitable; a people living off beasts and like beasts".[17] He also assumes that civilisation can only take root in the 'civis' or town, and, as the Irish did not have towns, they were automatically debarred from civilisation. They were also lazy: "For given only to leisure, and devoted only to sloth, they think that the greatest pleasure is not to work, and the greatest wealth is to enjoy liberty".[18] To a picture of laziness, barbarity and irreligion, Giraldus adds the vices of deceit and cunning: "above all other people they always practice treachery"[19], uncontrolled violence, and a predeliction for thievery, along with low standards of sexual morality—including incest and intercourse with cows: "a particular vice of that people".[20]

It can be instructive to compare this image of the Irish to the contemporary self-image of the Gael. Not only was there a high consciousness of the contribution Ireland had made to Christianity during the dark ages, but the Gaels had St. Patrick's word for it that Irish was the first official language of heaven. Ireland in the 12th century had a high degree of cultural autonomy, a standardised literary language, and the oldest and largest vernacular literary tradition in Europe, which included poetry of awesome metrical and self-referential complexity. There was also a profound sense of the antiquity of Irish society. A near contemporary of Giraldus Cambrensis, Muircheartach Mac Lochlainn, king of Tír Eóghain, could trace his pedigree accurately through 23 generations to Niall of the Nine Hostages, at the dawn of Christianity. With rather less accuracy, he could trace himself back through a further 53 generations to Érimón son of Míl, from which it was only 35 generations to Adam.[21] To members of this society, the Normans were the worst kind of parvenus, corner-boys and freebooters.

This uncomprehending mutual contempt of Norman and Gael set the pattern for the next half-millennium. The struggle for political domination ebbed and flowed, although the English interest gradually gained the upper hand. The struggle for cultural dominance had a rather different pattern, and London was frequently alarmed enough by the Gaelicisation of the Norman and English settlers to pass laws against it.

However, beginning in the 16th century, and coming to a head in the 17th, the pattern began to change under the influence of a new set of interlocking factors. During this period, the Gaelic aristocracy was defeated, the reformation began to make a serious impact, new waves of settlers undermined Gaelic society, and the English language made increasing and ultimately irreversible advances. One constant, however, is the continuing unremitting hostility of English-speaking writers to the Gaelic way of life. Richard Stanyhurst, for example, in a work published in 1577, says of the Gaelicising process: "... this cancer took such deepe roote, as the body that before was whole and sounde, was by little and little festered, and in maner wholly putrified".[22] Stanyhurst prayed that God would help those who governed Ireland to enlighten the natives:

> ... reduce them from rudeness to knowledge, from rebellion to obedience, from trechery to honesty, from savagenesse to civilitie, from idelnes to labour, from wickednesse to godlynesse, wherby they may sooner espy their blyndnesse, acknowledge their looseness, amende their lives, frame themselves plyable to the lawes and ordinaunces of hir majestie ...

It is interesting that the Anglophone Stanyhurst was an Irishman and a Catholic. From this point in history, the automatic equation of Irish identity with Gaelic identity becomes increasingly inaccurate. An overlapping and constantly shifting complex of new polarities affecting allegiance and identity began to develop in Irish society: Irish against English against Scottish, Catholic against Protestant, Gaelic-speaking against English-speaking, Native Irish against Old English against New English.

The Anglophone view of the Gael, however, remained largely locked in colonial mode. Of the many examples given by Joseph Leerssen in his superb study, *Mere Irish and Fíor-Ghael*, this synthesis by Baron Ronsele in 1692 represents almost a paradigm of the colonial view of the native Irish:

> Those that have described the humours of the natives would speak of the Irish in this manner. They are naturally strong, very nimble, haughty of spirit, silly in their discourse, careless of their lives, great admirers of their foolish and superstitious religion, which they neither understand nor follow, according to the canons of the Church of Rome: they are patient in cold and hunger, implacable in enmity, constant in love, light in belief, greedy of glory, great flatters and dissemblers, stubborn as mules, great cheats in their dealings, ready to take an oath on all occasions, commonly great thieves, very barbarous when they have the upper hand, of a bloody temper, very unjust to their neighbours, breakers of their trust, mortal enemies to all those that are not of the Romish religion, and ready to rebel

against the English on all occasions. A fine description indeed of a nation.[23]

The self-image of the Gaels also underwent a radical change in the 17th century. The 'flight of the earls' and the defeat of the Catholic Confederacy had, of course, destroyed the Gaelic aristocracy, which had until then been the lynch-pin of Gaelic culture. Gaelic society now moved into a new phase, that of a culture of dispossession. At the same time, the more perceptive among the Catholic clergy saw that the deep-rooted Gaelic sense of identity and anti-English sentiment could be used as very powerful weapons in the Counter-reformation. Just when the culture should have lost self-confidence, it found a new ideological justification based, not on the Gaelic aristocracy, but on Catholicism. As early as 1618, Aodh Mac Aingil, writing from Louvain, identified loyalty to the Catholic faith as a source of Irish pride and identity:

> It is certain ... that Ireland is a pure maiden in the faith, and kept her maidenhood for Christ since the time she accepted the faith through the preaching of our noble apostle, nor ever yielded to any kind of error or heresy. And this is her greatest privilege in the eyes of God and the world, for no other region in the world received this privilege, i.e. to be free from all heresy.[24]

This last formulation, Ireland free from all heresy, implicitly excludes Protestants from membership of the Irish people. Over a hundred years later, Tadhg Ó Neachtáin took Mac Aingil's arguments several steps further:

> And although the Jewish race were God's own family and people ... they were given such a blow as never befell any other people but the Gaels. From this it is easy to understand that there is no people in Europe more dear to God than the Gaels, and that he loves them the more because they never allowed their faith to be extinguished as did the Jewish race. For they lost their faith and their heritage, and although the Gaels lost their heritage, their faith still lives. This proves that they are being helped and protected by the love of God more than other races. From this it can be said that they are God's chosen people.[25]

This redefining of Irish identity in terms of religion also had a secular aspect, which involved a defence of Gaelic civilisation. As in the majority of redefinitions of this kind, the most creative minds were among those whose own identity was problematic. The leading propagandist in this programme was one of the Gaelicised descendants of the Normans, the historian Geoffrey Keating.

It is a remarkable testament to either the self-confidence or the short-sightedness of the Gaelic tradition that hardly anyone before Keating had bothered to answer Giraldus Cambrensis, not to mention Spenser, Stanyhurst, Hammer, Camden, Barclay, Morrison, Davis, Campion or any of the other detractors of the Irish he names in the foreword to his history. Keating, although himself descended from the very Normans Giraldus represented, set himself to refute their slurs on Gaelic civilisation by demonstrating its antiquity and outlining its achievements; by proving, in other words, that Gaelic society was genuinely civilised. The fundamental thrust of his programme can be seen in the unlikely etymology he developed for the origin of the name 'Gael', gaoith-dhil which he himself glosses as 'grádhuightheoir na heagna'[26]—'lover of intellect and learning'. This seemingly secular programme was as essential to the Counter-reformation in Ireland as the devotional literature.

In his foreword, Keating cleverly adopts the tone of a neutral, objective observer:

> I deemed it not fitting that a country so honourable as Ireland, and races so noble as those who have inhabited it, should go into oblivion without mention or narration being made of them ... if any man deem that I give [the Gaels] too much credit, let him not imagine that I do so through partiality, for I belong, according to my own extraction, to the Old Galls, [the Anglo-Normans]. I have seen, however, that the natives of Ireland are much maligned by every New Gall [New English] who speaks of the country.[27]

Later in the same passage, Keating unites the Gaels and the Old Galls under the common name of 'Éireannaigh'—Irishmen, claiming that they are comparable with any other people in Europe in three things: "... in valour, in learning, and in being steadfast to the Catholic faith".

At one stage, while gathering material for his history, Keating was refused access to a number of important sources by some northern Gaelic families because he was of Norman descent. Equally blinkered was the approach taken by the Established Church to the question of converting the natives to Protestantism. Attempts made since the time of Elizabeth I had been hampered by the fact that the colonial elite could never decide whether it was their language or their religion which contributed most to the barbarity of the natives. The Act of Supremacy of 1560 itself undermined one of the principal foundations of Protestantism, the use of the vernacular, by ordering that clergy who could not read the Book of Common Prayer in English should conduct the service in Latin.[28] Throughout the 17th and 18th centuries, the leaders of the Church of Ireland showed great reluctance to do anything which might increase the status of Irish, even at the cost of depriving monoglot Irish-speakers of the word of God, and undermined nearly all attempts to use Irish for prosyletising purposes. The policy of the Anglican Church involved Anglicisation in language as well as religion. William Bedell, who as an Englishman had no such hang-ups, was savaged by his fellow Anglo-Irish bishops for producing an Irish language version of the Old Testament in the 1640s. Ussher, the primate, rebuked him severely:

> The course which you took with the Papists was generally cried out against, neither do I remember in all my life that anything was done here by any of us, at which the professors of the gospel did take more offense, or by which the adversaries were more confirmed in their superstitions and idolatry, wheras I wish you had advised with your bretheren before you would aventure to pull down that which they had been so long a building.[29]

This letter of Jonathan Swift, in spite of his characteristic self-subversion, illustrates the extent to which the language issue was entangled with the questions of religion, class and politics in his time:

> It would be a noble achievement to abolish the Irish language in this kingdom, so far at least as to oblige the natives to speak only English on every occasion of business, in shops, markets, fairs, and other places of dealing ... This would, in a great measure, civilise the most barbarous among them, reconcile them to our customs, and reduce great numbers to the national religion, whatever kind may then be established ... I could heartily wish some public thoughts were employed to reduce this uncultivated people from that idle, savage, beastly, thievish manner of life, in which they confine sunk to a degree, that it is almost impossible for a country gentleman to find a servant of human capacity, or the least tincture of natural honesty; or who does not live among his own tenants in continual fear of having his plantations destroyed, his cattle stolen, and his goods pilfered.[30]

The attitude of the Established Church essentially left the field to the Counter-reformation activists. As a result, the labours of such as Keating, Peter Lombard and Theobold Stapleton, as well as scions of old Gaelic learned families such as the O'Husseys, O'Clerys, Wards and O'Mulconroys developed a body of religious and secular literature in Irish which resulted in an extension of the meaning of the word 'Gael'. By the end of the 17th century, it is not always easy to know whether the term 'Gael' means an descendant of the Goidel, or an Irish-speaker, or a Catholic. Its opposite, 'Gall', except in a historic context, invariably meant both 'English' and 'Protestant'. This development parallelled a shift in the English language, by which 'Irish' was interchangeable with 'Catholic', and the Established Church was known as the English Church.

In most of the sources in Irish from the 17th and 18th centuries, the twin themes of dispossession and religion are the most prominent in all references to the Gaels, parallelling the decline of their social, political and economic status, and the increasing unlikelihood that Gaelic civilisation could survive. The convention of bemoaning the fate of the Gael for every misfortune to hit Ireland was so strong that even such an extravagant burlesque as 'The Midnight Court' justifies its theme in terms of Ireland's oppression:

> Old stock uprooted on every hand
> Without claim to rent or law or land;
> Nothing to see in a land defiled
> Where the flowers were plucked but the weeds ran wild;
> The best of your breed in foreign places,
> And upstart rogues with impudent faces,
> Planning with all their guile and spleen
> To pick the bones of the Irish clean.[31]

Another extraordinary shift in consciousness took place. Although Gaelic society had been aristocratic in the extreme in its social mores, the more depressed that society became, the more the rural poor began to identify themselves with their dispossessed aristocratic masters of long-ago. This perception appears to have transferred easily with the language shift from Irish to English.

As they became less and less of a threat, the English image of the Gaelic Irish as dangerous and warlike barbarians gradually became replaced by that of the Irish as buffoons in any language. The picture of the foolish, unreliable, childlike, basically loveable but essentially inferior Irish which developed in English literature and in the English consciousness did not particularly distinguish between the Irish in general and the Gaelic Irish in particular. It also failed to make that distinction between Protestants and Catholics on which Irish Protestant self-esteem rested. In Ireland, however, the English-speakers consoled themselves for their low status in English eyes by despising their Irish-speaking fellow-countrymen. To some extent, this became internalised even among Irish-speakers: 'Gael' developed a further nuance through the adjective, 'gaelach', which has a secondary meaning of 'unsophisticated', 'simple', 'commonplace'; "Nach Gaedhealach na ruidíní iad—What common folk they are".[32] Mozart's friend Michael Kelly (b. 1764), during an audience with the Emperor of Germany, was addressed in Irish by the aristocratic General Kavanagh of Borris-in-Offaly. When he was unable to reply, the Emperor asked him why he did not know his own language, and he explained, to the amusement of the Emperor, and in the face of the evidence, that "none but the lower orders of the Irish people speak Irish".[33]

Kelly's remark reflects the perceived reality of his own class, and within a couple of generations it actually became the reality. However, in spite of the fact that they had no leadership, and were despised by most of the English-speaking population, in some parts of the country Irish-speakers retained a strong sense of identity and loyalty to their culture that lasted through until the first half of the 19th century. Monck Mason, who led one of the most intensive drives to use Irish for prosyletising purposes, wrote in 1829, at a time when more than a third of the population spoke Irish:[34]

> The peasant is assiduously instructed to consider the Protestant Bible an heretical book, but nothing will persuade him that heresy can be uttered in his native tongue, and he imagines that Satan is dumb in it.[35]

In his history of the Irish Society, published in 1846, Mason noted that:

> In the North of Ireland, where it is generally supposed that the use of the Irish language has died away, there are places among the mountains and even hills where it has lingered and where its extinction is prevented by the circumstances of peculiar affection; the old inhabitants appear to anticipate its departure with great regret, and to be jealous of every approach to it. No wonder, therefore, that they are anxious to have it taught, in the fond hope that this will contribute to restore it. This feeling is quite general in the Glens of Antrim.[36]

In fact, more Gaelic manuscripts survive from the early 19th century than from any other period. The difference between this and all other periods of Gaelic literary activity is that the late scribes were, like the rhyming weavers in the same period, overwhelmingly of the artisan class; small farmers, stonemasons, hedge-schoolmasters. This surge in scribal activity in part grew from a conscious attempt to rescue what could be saved of the tradition from annihilation, a pattern which is repeated in all periods of Gaelic culture as far back to the legend of Seanchán Torpéist's quest for the lost *Táin Bó Cuailnge*. However, the number of Irish-speakers dropped markedly in this period, and political and religious leaders of Irish society threw their weight and esteem behind the Anglicisation process. O'Connell famously recommended the abandonment of Irish. In some areas, the Catholic church, alarmed at the success of the proselytisers in using Irish to convert the natives, saw English as a bulwark of the faith. They launched a campaign against literacy in Irish, destroyed manuscripts, and encouraged the use of English in bilingual communities. Rising emigration made knowledge of English essential, and the spread of the national schools, in which the teaching, or even use, of Irish was forbidden, played a major part. The Famine accelerated the Anglicisation process: after it, the flood of manuscripts reduced to a trickle, and any remaining pride in the language seems to have left the common people. In the 50 years between 1841 and 1891, the number of Irish speakers in Ireland declined from close to three million to three-quarters of a million. A society which has a secure sense of identity and self-esteem does not commit this sort of cultural suicide. In the rush to learn English the loss of Irish was deemed both inevitable and desirable, and almost the entire population appears to have been keen to throw out the bathwater, the baby, and ultimately the bath. Mícheál Ó Raghallaigh of Ennistymon in Co. Clare captures something of this loss of heart in the foreword to a manuscript collection of poetry he completed in 1853:

> Dear reader, do not blame or condemn me for the badness of the writing in this book, for I am a tradesman and it was in my spare time I made this collection. For this reason it cannot be as neat as a manuscript written by a proper copyist. But for all that, when it appeared to me that none of my contemporaries was collecting any of the works of our poets I thought I would not let them all be lost. But there is not much use in saving them, for our young people are ashamed to learn the language of our ancestors. For this reason, there will not be a word of Irish in the kingdom one hundred years from now if they continue in the manner they are following in my own time.[37]

Before we go ahead to the time of the Gaelic League and the language revival, It may be well to trace the gradual growth in tolerance towards the Gaelic tradition among some elements among the English-speaking population since the 17th century. This increased tolerance developed first into sympathy, and ultimately to identification, and eventually affected the sense of identity of English-speaking Ireland.

From the 17th to the 19th centuries, the linguistic situation has never been simply Catholic/Gaelic versus Protestant/English, in spite of the best efforts of ideologues on both sides. Some Irish-speakers, sometimes from aristocratic or learned Gaelic families, converted to Protestantism. Douglas Hyde records evidence that some of the children of Cromwellian settlers could not speak a word of English.[38] Pádraig Ó Snodaigh has shown that large numbers of Gaelic-speakers from Scotland settled in Ulster[39], and we have evidence of Presbyterian communities which were Irish-speaking by descent or social absorption until the late 18th century. Landlords often needed to know Irish to deal with their tenants, and prosyletisers who learned Irish to convert native-speakers, often became interested in the language for its own sake. The situation, in short, was both complex and fluid.

Another factor which increased understanding of Gaelic Ireland, and one which should not be underestimated, is that of scholarly curiosity. This process began as early as the 17th century when Archbishop Ussher, although deeply hostile to Gaelic Ireland, as we have seen, began investigating pre-Norman ecclesiastical history, and his pupil Sir James Ware wrote a history of Ireland which drew on the work of Dubhaltach Mac Firbisigh. Later histories of Ireland, particularly by Irishmen, began to draw Gaelic civilisation in a more sympathetic light as more historic material became available.

Several other factors accelerated this process throughout the 18th century. That the country did not rise with Scotland during 1715 and 1745 seemed to prove that Ireland had been entirely pacified. Sympathy with the natives could now be safely indulged, and even a recognition of the noble past of a defeated people could add an extra frisson of empathy for their condition. Ironically, Protestantism, with its emphasis on the vernacular Bible, had created the new science of comparative linguistics, improving the status of Irish in scholarly circles, so that it became fashionable for a time to trace Gaelic back to its supposed Scythian and Hebrew roots. The sublime as an aesthetic standard became stylish, and, towards the end of the century, wild untamed scenery was sought by converts to the new sensibility. Irish-speakers were, of course, particularly thick on the ground where the scenery was at its most sublime, and at its least useful in terms of agriculture. McPherson's Ossian put Scottish Gaelic on the cultural map, and Irish antiquaries rushed into print to prove that Ossian was originally an Irishman, a project that soon expanded into one to prove that Ireland had once had a great and ancient Gaelic civilisation. The quality of Irish music was the one aspect of Irish life which had never been dispraised, and Irish music reached new heights of fashion through the adoption of such as Carolan by the 18th Century landed gentry. It is notable that the image of the 'real' Irish in their remote mountain fastnesses is not, in its essential elements, all that different to the hostile caricatures of earlier ages. Joseph Leerssen has pointed out that the individual ingredients composing the image of Ireland were simply adapted to the new fashions.

The final, and possibly critical factor in the change in attitude towards Gaelic Ireland developed in the interval between the religious wars and the rise of democracy. Now that Catholic Ireland was no longer seen as a threat, Protestant Ireland could afford to indulge its resentment against England, and did so by developing a consciousness of its own Irishness. Among a minority of the Ascendancy, the attraction of the Gaelic past as the essence of Irishness, and its ancient wrongs as a metaphor for present disaffection, proved irresistible. Lawrence Parsons, a prominent member of the patriot party, in an uncanny echo of Keating, defended the study of older Gaelic manuscripts on the grounds that such study would: "... relieve this country from its most unjust charges of ignorance and barbarism, at a time when it was far more enlightened and civilised than any of the adjacent neighbours".[40] Charlotte Brooke, in her *Reliques of Ancient Irish Poetry*, wrote of her "endeavour to rescue from oblivion a few of the valuable reliques of [Ireland's] ancient genius" as well as informing the British muse "that she has an elder sister in this isle". She went on to claim that "the portion of her [Britain's] blood which flows in our veins is rather enobled than disgraced by the mingling tides that descended from our heroic ancestors".[41]

It was equally in the interests of English-speaking Catholics to extol the virtues of their Gaelic heritage. While most 17th century apologists for Gaelic civilisation wrote in Irish or Latin, 18th century scholars like Charles O'Connor wrote in English. Their attitudes percolated the drawing rooms of the English-speaking Catholic *bourgeois* in the 19th century through the songs of Thomas Moore, long after they had gone out of fashion in England, and were reinforced by the work of scholars and literary men such as Ferguson, Mangan, O'Donovan, O'Curry, and Petrie, and the publications of the various learned societies. Eventually the Gaelic legacy was incorporated into political nationalism through the work of Thomas Davis and the Young Irelanders. Together, all these influences created a vague consciousness of former greatness which was subscribed to by members of all sections of society.

It should be pointed out that, with the notable exception of late 18th and early 19th century Belfast, which was then as far ahead of its time as it is now behind it, most of these developments tended either towards antiquarianism or towards the depiction of a romanticised remote past. Few of them embraced the living language of the Gaelic-speaking poor, who continued to be regarded with the kind of disdain evident in George Moore's memory of the tenants on his father's estate:

> ... the ratlike faces with the long upper lip that used to come from the mountains to Moore Hall, with banknotes in their tall hats, a little decaying race in knee-breeches, worsted stockings and heavy shoon, whom we used to despise because they could not speak English.[42]

The great achievement of the Gaelic League, founded in 1893, was convincing the likes of George Moore that the language of this decaying race with its ratlike faces was worth reviving. Moore became—temporarily—so enthusiastic about reviving Irish, in fact, that he set about creating a modern literature in Irish—which he did not speak, although he tried to master it by proxy by threatening to disinherit his nephews if *they* didn't learn it. The process behind that shift in consciousness is worth investigating.

It developed, first of all, as a function of the English language. It is a cliche worth repeating that the ideology of the Gaelic League never caught on in the Gaeltacht. It was originally formulated by middle-class English-speaking intellectuals who were *au fait* with the current thinking of their time. It had its most potent influence on upwardly mobile, lower middle-class, urban, English-speaking Catholics. Its leadership cadre included a spectacular proportion of priests educated at English-speaking Maynooth.

One of the League's first aims was, obviously, to counteract the perception of the Irish-speaker as the epitome of backwardness and ignorance, a perception which was deeply embedded in the Irish psyche. Professor Mary Hayden, on an expedition to find Irish-speakers in the Dublin Mountains asked an old man if he could speak the language: "Do I speak Irish, is it?" he replied, "I may be ignorant, Ma'am, but I'm not as ignorant as that".[43] Inevitably, and understandably, the counter-image of the Irish-speaker was expressed in over-emphatic terms. It was idealised, and idealisations distort as much as do caricatures. However, it should not be thought that the pre-Gaelic League attitudes towards the native speaker died out instantly because some crowd of Dublin counter-jumpers decreed that the Irish speaker embodied the essence of all that was best in the Irish character. Indeed, such attitudes are alive and well a hundred years later.

The unfortunate people of the Gaeltacht thus found themselves the subject of two contradictory versions of themselves. On the one hand, their nearest neighbours, who had just lost Irish, even if they still had not acquired English, were conscious that Irish-speakers were the most benighted and backward people on earth. This contempt was compounded by resentment and jealousy. English-speakers on the edges of the Gaeltacht saw distinguished foreign scholars and other paying guests distaining their own area, which had just, painfully, acquired civility, and flocking to the houses of unlearned bogtrotters who still spoke Irish. On the other hand, a new species of Irish-speaker, the Gaeilgeoirí, east-coast enthusiasts who had learned Irish, created an ideal which endowed Gaeltacht people with every virtue known to Gaelic civilisation, and a few which had been specially invented for the occasion: "the patient white-souled Ireland of the Irish-speaking districts" as Pearse put it.[44]

A further complication was that the revivalists themselves often held deeply ambivalent views of native speakers. Many of them were urbanised middle or lower-middle class, who secretly despised all culchies, munchies and teuchters, of which Gaeltacht people were the ultimate example. Those who genuinely fell in love with the Gaeltacht, and there was, and is, much to fall in love with, wanted it to remain in an undeveloped, pre-industrial timeless state, complete with thatched cottages, turf-stacks, donkeys, curraghs and chimney corners, and deeply resented the modernisation which the people who lived there all the year round wanted most. Gaeltacht people have still not recovered from this multiplicity of role-models.

The process of idealising the Irish-speaking people of the most remote parts of the west of Ireland stemmed, in part, from the fact that these scattered communities were the only places in Ireland where Irish was alive as a community language, and the only ones which embodied, in no matter how attenuated a form, this 2,000 year-old civilisation. It was also rooted in the most modern form of political ideology.

There is obviously no space here to investigate complexities of nationalism in any depth, but it should be made clear from the outset that nationalism was central to the ideology of the Gaelic League, although Douglas Hyde, in one of the greatest creative fudges of modern Irish history, created an ethos in the early days which attracted a number of unionists into its ranks. This was made possible by one of Hyde's formulations—the argument for cultural continuity—which was essentially apolitical: "I believe that it is our Gaelic past which, though the Irish race does not recognise it just at present, is really at the bottom of the Irish heart."[45] "... do what it may, the race of today cannot wholly divest itself from the mantle of its own past".[46] "The Gaelic League is the only body in Ireland which realised that Ireland had a past, had a history, had a literature, and the only body in Ireland which sought to render the present a rational continuation of the past".[47] His other main contribution to the revivalist ideology was to make an appeal for cultural nationalism as a logical extension of political nationalism. This turned out to be the most potent argument of the two:

> I wish to show you that in Anglicising ourselves wholesale we have thrown away with a light heart the best claim we have upon the world's recognition of us as a separate nationality. What did Mazzini say? What is Goldwin Smith never tired of declaiming? What do the *Spectator* and *Saturday Review* harp on? That we ought to be content as an integral part of the United Kingdom because we have lost the robes of nationality, our language and customs.
>
> It has always been very curious to me how Irish sentiment sticks in this half-way house—how it continues to apparently hate the English, and the same time continues to imitate them; how it continues to clamour for recognition as a distinct nationality, and at the same time throws away with both hands what would make it so. If Irishmen only went a little further they would become good Englishmen in sentiment also ... It is a fact, and we must face it as a fact, that although they adopt English habits and copy England in every way, the great bulk of Irishmen and Irishwomen over the whole world are known to be filled with a dull, ever-abiding animosity against her, and right or wrong, to grieve when she prospers, and joy when she is hurt ... It is just because there appears no earthly chance of their becoming good members of the Empire that I urge that they should not remain in the anomalous position they are in, but since they absolutely refuse to become one thing, that they become the other: cultivate what they have rejected, and build up an Irish nation on Irish lines.[48]

This aspect of the language revival movement found its ideological roots in that thread of modern European romantic and cultural nationalism which derives partly from Rousseau, but mostly from the

German historian Herder. Herder was a Lutheran minister who had been profoundly influenced by a sect in his native Germany, the Pietists, which believed in the innate wisdom of the common, unlettered people. He postulated the nation as the product of a complex of influences; climate, environment and the accidents of history, which through a long, slow process of development, produce the language which is both the reflection of the experiences of the nation and the tool by which its consciousness is formed. For Herder, organic nations were manifestations of the divine plan, each nation reflecting an aspect of God's multiplicity, and making a unique contribution to civilisation. He saw the language of the common people as the essence of the nation. Herder influenced Goethe, inspired the folklore and linguistic work of the Grimm brothers, and changed the focus of the study of history from that of the leaders of society to that of the community.

His enormously sophisticated theories sometimes came through in the propaganda of the Gaelic League in a rather simplified form. In 1898 R. Mac Searraigh Gordon wrote:

[God] wished us to be by ourselves out in the ocean, with our own particular language, music, religion, customs and other things. In addition, he made the ancient Romans afraid to come near us, so that we are not like any other nation in Europe.[49]

The Gaelic League sems to have been genuinely free from undue political or sectarian influence between, say, 1893 and 1899. In the next ten years, however, it came under the influence of two groups of ideologues; radical nationalists—the IRB in particular—and the Catholic Church. It should also be said that these years were also those in which the League made its greatest impact on Irish society, and it can be argued that, without the support of these two groups, the Irish language movement would never have had even the limited success it has had. I intend to concentrate here on the influence of the Church, as the more complex and interesting of the two.

In the ideology of Herder, as filtered through the League, the native speaker of Irish embodies the soul and consciousness of Ireland. It need not surprise us if the Catholic Church, another body with a stake in the welfare of the soul of Ireland was attracted to the work of the League. This issue is extremely complex: the Church and the League clashed on a number of issues, and many of the Catholic clergy were influenced by the burgeoning nationalism of the time, and sincerely involved in the ideals of the revival. There is also some evidence to indicate that the Church itself did not initiate its involvement, but was targeted by the League as the organisation which could best deliver the ideals of the revival to a broad public. What is not in doubt, however, is that the Catholic Church was involved in a conscious attempt to influence the League's ideology. There were two prongs to the campaign. One involved defining the immutable essence of the Gaelic mind—the mentality and world-view which is moulded by the language. The other involved resisting the corrupting influence of English civilisation, and, in particular, English literature. Both these themes were addressed by Cardinal Logue in 1899, just six years after the founding of the League:

> Now anyone that knows, as I know, to my sorrow, and as many heads of families know that we never had in Irish that broad and fetid stream of corruption which is flooding the country at the present day through English literature. Wherever the Irish language is spoken, the people are pure and innocent, and it is only where this flood comes in, which is not merely a flood now but a torrent, that if there is not care taken by the priests and clergymen of every denomination, and by the heads of families, the flood will corrupt the innocence of the youth of holy Ireland.[50]

Father John O'Reilly, in a Gaelic League pamphlet published the following year, with the dramatic title, *The Threatening Metempsychosis of a Nation*, argued that because the Gaelic mind was essentially Catholic, it was incapable of expressing such anti-Catholic thoughts as 'No priest in politics'. "That phrase", he said, "could not be rendered into the Irish idiom. The Genius of the Gaelic tongue could no more assimilate it than the human system could assimilate a dagger in the stomach".[51]

He was also in the privileged position of being able to define the Gaelic mind:

> The Irish mind, away back in its most pagan days, was emphatically and eminently a mind inclining to religion. It was chaste, idealistic, mystical. It was spiritual beyond the ways of men; and it could not rest, or live, without contact with the other world; without the conviction of some ideal hereafter. It was clean of heart, and saw God, darkly and from afar, if you will, but with the invincible conviction of the clean heart's instinct. It was passionately loyal to the chief, whether earthly lord or spiritual shepherd ... The Irish mind was the most kind and towardly soil ever known under the sun for the seed of the gospel to fall upon. That seed fell at last and it grew; and it

endured, and it remains, and we are here today on the strength of it, and our country is still a trumpeting witness for Christ in the wilderness of an almost re-paganised world ... The Irish mind was loyalty itself to spiritual authority. It knew no envy of the influence of its pastors, and it never dreamt of invidious malicious distinctions between the man and his office, between the doctrine and the preacher; and this is a great part of the secret of the sound and splendid endurance of our faith to this day.[52]

This was to be contrasted with its opposite, the English mind, in which O'Reilly neatly fuses nationalist, anti-English sentiment with an attack on the corrupting influence of the English language on the thought-processes of those who speak it. It did not appear to strike either himself or his readers that the pamphlet itself was written in English:

> It is a fleshly spirit, bent towards earth; a mind unmannerly, vulgar, insolent, bigoted; a mind whose belly is its God, yet which cannot endure the word belly; a mind to which pride and lust, and mammon are the matter-of-course aims of life, the only objects conceivably worthy of pursuit; a mind to which real Christian virtue is incredible, and sure to be set down as clever hypocrisy, or stark imbecility; a mind where every absurd device, from grossest Darwinism to most preposterous spiritualism, is resorted to and hoped in ... a mind to which the virtue, or the idea of humility is unknown; contrition or self-condemnation an absurdity.[53]

This claptrap, of course, had nothing to do with the people of the Gaeltacht. It was created as an role-model for the unfortunate idealistic revivalists, who henceforth spent their time and energy in the pursuit of purity rather than prepositions. It was also a spectacularly dramatic example of internalised colonialism. The ideals offered were not those of the Gaelic way of life of any period, as anyone with any knowledge of the sources will know. The ideals were, in fact, those of Victorian England, filtered through French Jansenism, with a touch of theocracy, and embodied in an extreme form the convergence of Victoria's England with ultra-montaine Ireland.

This campaign was remarkably successful. There is still a current perception of Gaeltacht people as being spiritually superior to those of the rest of the country, and a common picture of the revivalist Gaeilgeoir which is still remarkably similar to that in Behan's 'The Hostage', the gun-toting, fáinne-wearing, joyless, puritanical non-smoker non-drinker with the cold eyes. There are other images of the 20th century Gael: neolithic Blasketman, earth-mother, the pedant, the set-dancer wearily seeking the crack, the boyo, the activists of whom Seosamh Mac Grianna said: "It must be the unending dry pleasureless work which dries the sap from them and leaves them without joy", the ones who blame it all on the government, and those who have been so offended by the received caricature that they have dedicated their lives to the equally self-defeating task of publicly embodying its diametric opposite.

All current images of Irish-speakers diminish us. Attempts to define a civilisation may pass a few pleasant hours in a pub, but a civilisation, a tradition, is far too complex to be captured by any definition. The process of defining has itself an inbuilt weakness, in that a definition is always in danger of turning into a self-sustaining prescription, which is in danger of being turned into an orthodoxy, and an orthodoxy, if it is not careful, can finish up as a slogan—the ultimate simplification. This tendency towards prescriptiveness is of course a permanent temptation to ideologues, and we have seen ideologues with agendas of their own moulding the image of the Gael from the earliest times. The thousands who have found that the language enriches their lives have benefited very little from any of these creations. A new understanding of Irish-speakers, a more generous one which accepts the wide diversity of a group of people whose only common characteristic is that they speak Irish would be a welcome development. What is not needed is a new image, with all the implications of prescriptiveness involved in the process of image-making. The issue is far too important for that.

Notes

[1] Joseph Leerssen, *Mere Irish and Fíor-Ghael, Studies in the idea of Irish Nationality: Its Development and Literary Expression prior to the 19th century* (Amsterdam, 1986), p. 33.
[2] Leerssen, p. 34.
[3] David Greene, *The Irish Language* (Dublin, 1966), p. 11. Myles Dillon & Nora Chadwick, *The Celtic Realms* (London, 1967), p. 56. I am grateful to Rhian Andrews for investigating the earliest Welsh forms of the word.
[4] M.A. O'Brien, 'Irish Origin Legends', in Miles Dillon (ed), *Early Irish Society* (Dublin, 1954), pp. 50-51.
[5] T.F. O'Rahilly, *Early Irish History and Mythology* (Dublin, 1946), p. 194.
[6] O'Rahilly, p. 267.
[7] R.A.S. McAlister (ed), *Lebar Gabála Erenn*, London, 1938-56, Introduction.
[8] Eoin MacNeill, *Phases of Irish History*, (1919) (Dublin, 1968), p. 77.
[9] R.A.S. McAlister & Eoin MacNeill, *Leabhar Gabhála* (Mícheál Ó Cléirigh's version) (Dublin, 1916), p. 151.

[10]O'Rahilly, p. 264.
[11]McAlister, Vol. II, 1939, pp. 184-5.
[12]Sung by Paddy Tunney on the record *The Irish Edge*, Topic, London.
[13]Colm Ó Lochlainn, *Tobar Fíorghlan Gaeilge, 1450-1850* (Dublin, 1939), pp. 159-60.
[14]MacNeill, p. 79.
[15]Douglas Hyde, *A Literary History of Ireland*, (1899), (London, 1967), pp. 159-60. Quoted from: Eugene O'Curry, *Manuscript Materials for the Study of Irish History*.
[16]Gerald of Wales, *The History and Topography of Ireland*, translated and edited by J.J. O'Meara (1951), (London, 1982), p. 101.
[17]Leerssen, p. 37.
[18]O'Meara, p. 102.
[19]O'Meara, p. 106.
[20]O'Meara, p. 74.
[21]M.A. O'Brien, p. 39.
[22]Leerssen, p. 46.
[23]Leerssen, p. 66.
[24]Aodh Mac Aingil, *Scáthán Shacramuinte na hAithridhe* [The Mirror of the Sacrament of Penance], Louvain, 1618. C Ó Maonaigh (ed.) (Dublin 1952), p. 190.
[25]Tadhg Ó Neachtáin, *Eolas ar an Domhan* [Geography of the World], 1729, Méabh Ní Chléirigh (ed.) (Dublin, 1944), p. 13.
[26]*Contributions to a Dictionary of the Irish Language*, G., Mary E Byrne (ed.) (Dublin, 1966).
[27]Hyde, 1899, p. 556; Leerssen, p. 318; Keating, *Forus Feasa ar Eirinn*, D. Comyn & P.S. Dinneen, (eds.) London 1902-04, Vol. I, p. 77.
[28]Alan Ford, 'The Protestant Reformation in Ireland', Ciaran Brady, Raymond Gillespie (eds), *Natives and Newcomers* (Dublin, 1986), p. 51.
[29]Hyde, 1899, p. 619.
[30]Leerssen, p. 371.
[31]Brian Merriman, 'The Midnight Court', translated by Frank O'Connor, *Kings, Lords and Commons* (1959), London, 1962, p. 138.
[32]P.S. Dineen, *Foclóir Gaedhilge agus Béarla* (Dublin, 1927), p. 507.
[33]Hyde, 1899, p. 622.
[34]45.87 per cent of the population of Ireland born between 1791 and 1801, and 39.9 per cent of those born between 1811 and 1821, were recorded as Irish-speakers in the 1881 Census. The percentage for earlier years should obviously be higher. M. Ní Mhurchadha, 'Pleanáil Teanga i Leith na Gaeilge, 1800-1922'. Unpublished thesis, quoted in M. Ó Murchú, 'An cúlú ón Ghaeilge, an ainilís staitistiúil agus gnéithe eile', in: James Dooge (ed), *Ireland in the Contemporary World, Essays in honour of Garret FitzGerald* (Dublin, 1986), p. 124.
[35]H.J.M. Mason, *Reasons, Authorities and Facts* (Dublin, 1829), p. 15.
[36]H.J.M. Mason, *History of the Origin and Progress of the Irish Society* (Dublin, 1846), p. 98.

[37] Ó Lochlainn, p. 221.
[38] Hyde, 1899, p. 621.
[39] Pádraig Ó Snodaigh, *Hidden Ulster*, (1973) Revised and expanded version (Dublin, 1977).
[40] Leerssen, p. 421.
[41] Leerssen, p. 423.
[42] George Moore, *Hail & Farewell, Salve* (1911), London, 1919, p. 67.
[43] Recorded by Don Piatt, *Feasta* 1952, in: Seán Ó Laighin (ed), *Ó Cadhain i bhFeasta*, Clódhanna Teoranta, 1990, 3p. 95.
[44] *An Claidheamh Soluis*, 21st December, 1907.
[45] Douglas Hyde, 'The Necessity for De-Anglicising Ireland', (1892) in C.G. Duffy (ed.), *The Revival of Irish Literature* (London, 1894), p. 121.
[46] Hyde, 1894, p. 124.
[47] Tomás Ó hAilín 'Irish Revival Movements', in B Ó Cúiv (ed.), *A View of the Irish Language* (Dublin, 1969), p. 96.
[48] Hyde, 1894, pp. 116-7.
[49] R Mac Searraigh Gordon, 'Náisiúntacht', *Fáinne an Lae*, 24th September, 1898, p. 20.
[50] *An Claidheamh Soluis*, 17th June, 1899, p. 216.
[51] Reverend John M. O'Reilly, *The Threatening Metempsychosis of a Nation*, Gaelic League Pamphlets No. 24, p. 5, n.d. (This was delivered to the Maynooth Union, June 1900.)
[52] O'Reilly, pp. 1-2.
[53] O'Reilly, p. 2.

Tomorrow with His Notes
Editing the Collected Poems of John Hewitt

Frank Ormsby

Dissertation I

Tomorrow with his notes a man will come
enquiring when I wrote that verse or this,
where such and such an image sprouted from,
if I concur with his analysis,
the day, the hour, what infantile event
and in what order should these carry weight;
so, explicating what I must have meant,
I'll flick my notebooks through to check the date.

I'll give what help I can. But humbly, pleased
that anyone should show the least concern
for words I named that secret springs released
out of the shadowy culverts of my mind,
eager for what I've sought so long to learn,
and anxious too for what we both may find.

John Hewitt wrote that poem in 1973 on the eve of a visit by an American research student, Bruce Bidwell. Not surprisingly, perhaps, it was one of the poems in my head, some ten years later, when I found myself flicking through those same notebooks, along with 'Dissertation II', in which Hewitt records his "anxiety" as the student in the next room reads his letters and manuscripts, and finds the experience more nerve-wracking than a visit to the dentist, and the sonnet 'On the Preservation of Work-Sheets':

It should not matter how I shaped my lines;

hit on a cadence; shuffled adjectives,
replaced a showy word with one that gives
a truer texture or, precise, defines
a signal smudged by clumsy countersigns,
or altered phrase to mark a change of gear
when word proposing word at once combines
to make some level of intention clear.

So it was with a certain sense of impertinence and trespass that I entered that room in the University of Ulster at Coleraine which houses Hewitt's library, his manuscript poetry notebooks, the typescript of his unpublished autobiography *A North Light*, his scrapbook of early published poems, his folders of clippings and so much else. Or sat down in the Public Record Office to read diaries and letters and the great range of material gathered there. The sense of trespass gave way quickly to other feelings: excitement (and horror!) at the prospect of trying to do justice to some 60 years' work, a deepening awareness of Hewitt himself, of how he thought, how he felt, how he functioned as a poet, a growing respect for the stubborn integrity of his enterprise. There is a particular intimacy involved in working on the papers of someone you knew personally, someone just a few years dead, and I hope it doesn't sound sentimental if I say that, for much of the time, Hewitt seemed not far away. It was still possible in the published poems and the thousands of unpublished notebook verses, to hear the living voice—still possible sitting among Hewitt's books or in the Public Record Office in Balmoral Avenue to have immediate visual memories of visiting Hewitt in Stockman's Lane, of talking to him among the same books and papers. And it was impossible not to be aware, on the numerous drives to and from Coleraine, of the landscape immediately to the east which left such an indelible mark on Hewitt's life and work.

I've given a broad, general account of Hewitt's poetic development in my introduction to the *Collected Poems*, and the textual procedures involved in editing the poems—ordering, dating, standardisation of spelling and so forth—are, I suspect, of limited interest, so I thought I would try to convey something of the pleasure and stimulation of 'discovering' Hewitt, so to speak, among his papers. In some ways, of course, he gave researchers like myself a running start. The poetry notebooks are numbered and dated, the unpublished autobiography, *A North Light*, is neatly typed and bound, the early socialist verses have been meticulously preserved in a scrapbook of cuttings from the long-defunct journals in which they were published. All this material is instantly accessible and affords fascinating pictures of Hewitt at every phase of his life from boyhood, through his years as "an Art Gallery man" and traveller, to the final period. In addition, however, the Hewitt archive contains a wealth of unsorted material. I was able to locate a miscellany of manuscript worksheets, manuscript drafts of chapters for *A North Light* and Hewitt's other exercise in autobiography, *Planter's Gothic*, jottings, lists, manuscripts and typescripts of radio talks, as well as notes for articles and lectures. Every day among these papers—sorted and dated—a window would open suddenly, a revealing detail to catch the eye.

There are many glimpses, for example, of the poet at work. Few writers have been so tirelessly industrious, so dauntingly prolific in both poetry and prose. In addition to the 700-odd published poems, Hewitt's poetry notebooks contain, by my calculation, about 3,500 unpublished poems and there is evidence that these were selected for inclusion in the notebooks from an even larger body of work. In an unpublished poem of 1936, entitled 'Desk', Hewitt recorded:

> I have written on shining tables beside flowers
> I have torn out a cigarette packet
> and written on the plain side of the carton
> I have written on the backs of envelopes and
> election addresses.
>
> But as against this seeming carelessness
> I have always copied the verses out
> in a neat and regular series of exercise books
> like this
> frequently revising in the process
>
> I remember the summer mornings when I was
> first a poet
> wakening with delight
> and writing on my raised knee in the slant sun
>
> Most of all
> I have written with my leg flung over the arm
> of a comfortable chair
> resting the titled paper on my thigh

In the same piece, he assures us that he does "not make poems on the spot" and that he does "not sprint home breathless to spill the clenched words on a white page" and that it has taken some of his poems up to 25 years to germinate. Nevertheless, it is difficult not to have a sense of Hewitt as an incorrigible versifier. Every walk seems to have produced at least one poem—and he did a lot of walking. Indeed, he took pride in his prolixity. It was partly the pride of the apprentice craftsman learning his trade, trying his hand at every verse form man to man, but also a kind of Protestant work-ethic pride in sheer productiveness and quantity. Many of the earlier notebooks end with an inventory of lines written during the period covered. Notebook 21, for example, which covers the last four months of 1936, records solemnly:

Best Year 1928 396 poems
Worst Year 1935 35 poems
Best Month Ever May 1928 65 poems

Of course, Hewitt was capable of poking fun at this aspect of himself and does so in a number of interviews. He seems also to have recognised the ephemeral nature of most of this material; very few of the occasional pieces, loose extempore effusions, nondescript topographical verse, and so on, survive into his books and when he began to salvage earlier work for books such as *Time Enough*, *The Rain Dance* and *Loose Ends*, he subjected much of this work to rigorous revision. In relation to Hewitt's prolixity, it is interesting that at the end of Notebook 46, among 20 pages of (mainly) prose quotations about the nature and function of poetry, drawn from writers as diverse as Pound, Rilke, Hopkins, Randall Jarrell, Jeffers, George Meredith, Thoreau, Frost, Synge, Baudelaire, he should include the following from Herbert Read's *Annals of Innocence*: "The very act of writing and rhyming is a call boy to the unconscious". Like many writers, Hewitt is working his new material in the hope that it will prompt or yield something more profound.

Much of Hewitt's poetry is, of course, directly autobiographical. His autobiographical writings are an interesting study in themselves, not only for the light they shed on the sources of the poetry, but for what they add to our knowledge of his family background, his formative experiences and beliefs. *A North Light*—subtitled *Twenty-Five Years in a Municipal Gallery*— is particularly rich in this respect. Here we catch sight of the young Hewitt, in July 1927, visiting the art galleries of Ghent, Bruges, Brussels and Ostend in the company of his father and stopping on the way home though London to watch cricketing heroes such as Holmes and Sutcliffe play at Lords. Hewitt returning from

Paris with a copy of *Ulysses* secreted in his trousers. Hewitt at work as Art Assistant in the Belfast Museum and Art Gallery. Hewitt being asked to show two visitors around the Rodin exhibition in the Museum in the autumn of 1932 and recognising one of them as Roberta Black—"the youngest of three daughters of a genial little widow who had been very friendly with my parents for many years"—returned home on holiday from Canada. Hewitt and Roberta at the Summer School of the Independent Labour Party at Welwyn Garden City where he has his "first acquaintance with the tame and orderly English countryside" and meets the Chinese poet Shelley Wang who visits the Hewitts in Belfast and some of whose poems Hewitt translates. The Hewitts at Middleton Murry's Adelphi Centre near Langham in 1936, where they meet George Orwell.

I think also of the chapters on the politics of the 30s, on regionalism, on the war years in Ulster, and the portraits of friends such as John Luke, Brendan Behan and Colin Middleton, of the accounts of trips to cities such as Venice, Vienna and Amsterdam.

Perhaps a few quotations will convey the flavour. At the beginning of his account of the war years, Hewitt describes some of his attempts to join up:

> A few days after war had been declared, Harold and I went down to the recruiting office. We found a crowd before us, mostly, by their appearance, young unemployed men. But, although there was no conscription in Northern Ireland—the Catholic population would have resisted it as they did all over Ireland over twenty years before—and of the rest, not even the hyper-loyal Orange Order suggested it—we were told that as we were both Local Government Officers we were in a reserved occupation, and could not be taken unless we resigned and became unemployed, which seemed a silly sort of thing to do, since we had assumed that our salaries would have been made up by the Local Authority for the maintenance of our dependants. Our patriotism was rather more provisional than headlong. This ruling seemed, later, somewhat anomalous when Douglas Deane, our colleague, not many years younger, joined the RAF as a photographer. Later, a press notice asked for graduates to be considered for commissions; but when it was understood that I had no OTC experience I was sent home.
>
> Maybe 18 months later, feeling rather guilty at my earlier status, with Patrick Maybin in the RAMC, Cecil Cree in the RAF and George MacCann somewhere in Burma with the Enniskillen Fusiliers, I started negotiations to join the camouflage people, went to the Northern Ireland HQ at Lisburn for interview, and, after a couple of drinks, it was agreed that I should have to wait till a Colonel Beddington, then in Malta, arrived, for a final decision.

I still have the note on my files but I never heard from the Colonel. And so, though I tried, admittedly not hard enough to hurt, I was not able to take any part in what I realised must have been the greatest imaginative experience of my generation; and maybe in that loss I have suffered a serious deprivation which has left me perhaps less adult than my years require.

As it turned out, the army's loss was Ulster's gain and both the Hewitts had an enviably energetic and constructive war. They moved to 18 Mountcharles which became a meeting point for local *literati* and artists and soldier-writers stationed in the north; they joined the local Civil Defence organisation; Roberta was helping to pioneer nursery school education. Hewitt lectured on art and, after Germany's attack on the Soviet Union, Marxism to troops stationed all over the region, getting to know the north more extensively than ever before. At the same time, he was reading the books which helped to deepen and extend his regionalist ideas, acting as a founder member for the Committee for the Encouragement of Music and the Arts, writing new poems such as 'Freehold', 'Conacre', 'Once Alien Here', 'The Glens' and 'Because I Paced My Thought'. The account given in *A North Light* of the war years and the development of Hewitt's regionalist ideas conveys, in a briskly factual way, the practical, intellectual and creative energies of these years; the poetry he wrote at this time, much of it unpublished, is more troubled and tension-ridden, more aware of the need to counters the destructive forces loose in Europe with action at a local level, more aware of the vulnerability of such action. So the quietness and peace of Glendun is set against the threat of war. Or Hewitt exhorts his WEA students to embrace "the high purpose of the human heart" as embodied in the work of the great artists as consolation and sustenance in days of crisis—a time when, to quote an unpublished poem, art became "an aimless scribble in the dirt". Or Hewitt celebrates his friendship with various Europeans in Belfast, such as the Austrian Karl Frankl, the German Siegfried Alexander and others, with poignant awareness of them as victims and refugees. Something of these tensions is conveyed by Hewitt's use, in Notebook 46 (April 1940-November 1943), of an epigraph from Ó Faoláin's *King of the Beggars*:

> You can always smell disaster when a poet begins to transcribe; he is garnering in the past; he smells the darkness. Once before, in Ireland, the poets did that in a body–in the 12th century, the age of the great manuscript collections, the leatherbound books, the vellum epitaphs, the last will and testament of the men who were waiting for the Norman knocking at the door.

On a lighter note, among those who served with the Hewitts in Civil Defence was the English writer F.L. Green, then living in Belfast, author of the novel *Odd Man Out*. Green was one of those critical of Hewitt's regionalist enthusiasms on the grounds that it led him to overestimate provincial mediocrity and the two clashed in a fairly cheerful, knockabout way in the letter columns of the local press. The character Griffin in *Odd Man Out* is Green's caricature of Hewitt as Belfast's cultural one-man-band and there is a short chapter in *A North Light* entitled 'Griffin' in which Hewitt good-humouredly—so far as I can tell—quotes the following passage:

> Griffin was man of Lukey's [an artist and one of the novel's main characters] age. He was employed as a seminar assistant in a local firm of antique dealers. Tall, thin, and of an incisive temperament, humorous, kindly, he was an established authority not only on painting but on literature, the drama, religion, politics, and many other diversions by which the public sought an outlet for energies which were hemmed in by the sea which divides them from England, and by their temperament, which separates them from the outer world. There was hardly a platform which he could prevent himself from talking, and from which he theorised in a robust, crisp fashion. There was scarcely a stranger to the city whom, coming to the North for information regarding its history, literature, drama, painting, politics, commerce, hopes, was not swiftly and adroitly contacted by Griffin and as swiftly loaded with facts. And, similarly, when a new artist or novelist, poet, politician, playwright, appeared from amongst the population, Griffin was there to study him from some vantage point and thereafter applaud him or dismiss him in a few theorising remarks ... It did not occur to Griffin that, in the past, he has sometimes exalted fools or made little mistakes regarding men of talent. What mattered to him was the fact that he had to safeguard certain principles and defend the gateway of art from charlatans.

Hewitt had appropriate revenge for this later when he won a competition in the *New Statesman* with a parody of Green's prose style.

There was also, as I have said, among Hewitt's papers, numerous handwritten drafts and scraps of autobiographical writing—some of it semi-legible but worth, I think, salvaging. Much of it complements the essays published under the title 'Planter's Gothic', giving more detailed information about, for example, the Clifton Park Avenue area where Hewitt grew up, his family, his schooling and other matters, the kind of material that is invaluable to a biographer. To take just one endearing example, Hewitt refers several times to one of his English teachers at Methodist College, Belfast: Mary—knowns as Mamie—Logan. In one jotting he confesses that he was secretly in love with her and records that in order to counteract what she considered "sparse and undernourished" in his prose style, she lent him "Kenneth Graham and Walter Pater". Is it any wonder he was in love? In another he tells an interesting anecdote from the same period, when Hewitt was 15 or 16:

> When I was in the 4th form at Methodist College, I had an English teacher with whom I was in love, Mary Logan, a bright-eyed, pretty girl with a husky Scots accent. Once, noting the references in my essays, she asked me, for interest's sake, to jot down the titles of any books I had been reading in the last few months. So I set down, as I remember them now (?), Wells' *Mankind in the Making*, Morris' *Dream of John Ball*, Holyoakes' *Sixty Years of an Agitator's Life*, Tolstoy, Shaw ... About a week later, in the first post one morning, my father received a letter from the headmaster, enquiring if he was aware that I was reading *Socialist* literature, and setting down (?) the offensive titles. My father replied simply (?) by saying that he had secured most of the books for me himself and that I had his full permission. What had happened, I think, was that Mamie Logan had been surprised at the range of items (?) I was reading and showed my list to the head as a remarkable phenomenon.
>
> This did little to bind me fast in loyalty to the School.

A couple of familiar elements there—Hewitt the precocious, eclectic reader and the beloved supportive father facing up with dignity to reactionary authority. The head, by the way, was James Watson Henderson, also the subject of Hewitt's virulent sonnet 'A Great Headmaster' in *Mosaic*.

In the introduction to the *Collected Poems*, I have quoted other revealing snippets about Hewitt's reading in the late 20s and early 30s, particularly in the fields of comparative religion, popular archeology, folklore and mythology—all material retrieved from one big cardboard box or another.

Shortly before I started work on the Hewitt papers, I had re-read the special Hewitt issue of the magazine *Threshold* and a few matters raised there were on my mind. John Kilfeather, in his article 'Remembering John Hewitt', remarks:

> He had ingrained prejudices not dissimilar from bigotry through he said that in his case it was hatred of the Roman Catholic clergy that motivated it and not any special attitude he adopted towards Catholics.

And John Montague, in his piece, 'Spiritual Maverick', writes that he found Hewitt's poetry more to his taste than the then fashionable poetry of W.R. Rodgers:

> ... even the bigoted bits, like "the Romish pit" in 'The Glittering Sod'. To offset that there was his shy visit to a Catholic church in 'The Lonely Heart':
>
>> The years since then have proved I should have stayed
>> and mercy might have touched me till I prayed.

"It reminded me [says Montague] of my Protestant neighbours, dour but friendly, coming to contribute a coin at the end of the Funeral Offerings, a dreadful Romish practice of the period."

I won't attempt to summarise here Hewitt's fluctuating attitudes to Catholicism as expressed or scrutinised in prose pieces such as 'The Family Next Door' and in poems such as 'Freehold', 'The Glens', 'The Green Shoot', 'May Altar', 'The Hill Farm' and 'The Priest goes through the Motions of the Play'. It is well known that he altered some lines in his poem 'The Glens' because they were what he called "arrogant" and because they might give "offence to kindly and gentle Catholics". So the image of "the lifted hand between the mind and truth" became "the lifted hand against unfettered thought", a rather hasty emendation in which Hewitt falls back on a phrase he had used before. Oddly enough, this did not extend to Hewitt's revision of 'Freehold', a few years later, and the line about those who "drop gurgling down into the Romish pit" which Montague objects to and which does indeed sound like one of Amanda McKittrick Ros' worst nightmares, is allowed to stand. Very similar fluctuations are to be found in the unpublished material on this subject. There are moments when Hewitt is at his most receptive and tolerant and others when the stink of burning flesh is in his nostrils. There is, for example, an unpublished poem from 1969 which begins "I have no liking for the Catholic Church" finished on the same day Hewitt wrote 'A Mobile Mollusc' which originally began "I early took a Protestant to be" but became, in its final version:

> He learned, as a dissenter, he must be
> a man who'd never fail to speak his mind

An admirably judicious piece of revision. And some 26 years earlier, Hewitt wrote a poem called 'Contra Roma' which I will quote in full:

> Your flame-lick'd victims are a stubborn crew:

> in Spain you struck your thousands merciless.
> Your feeble father hobbled out to bless
> the shining bombers sallow braggarts flew
> against the tribesmen's spears.
>   This is not new
> and other creeds have match'd your sharp excess
> but none has dared to claim what you profess
> or held unaltered usage long as you.
>
> I claim no virtue. There were other men
>   who spoke the true word when to speak was death
> and others will when your sick power again
>   unleashes the rank venom of its breath.
> I have but written this that some recall
>   the firing squad and terror at the wall.

On the other hand, there is the poet who can salute the "faith and haven" of the Glens people. Among Hewitt's papers is a long autobiographical typescript entitled 'Meeting Houses' from which he quarried sections afterwards published in 'Planter's Gothic' and 'The Family Next Door'. 'The Family Next Door' is partly about his friend Willie Morrissey, hero, so to speak, of the poem 'The Irish Dimension' and the following unpublished paragraphs from 'Meeting Houses' arose from Willie Morrissey's confirmation:

> Yet Willie's confirmation must have in a subtle way impressed me, for, years later, when, one by one, the McDonnell girls of Cloughglass put on the white dress or veil and were photographed when their turn came, I found myself unaccountably moved, moved enough to write a little poem I am still fond of; and when I was in Poland in 1962 and saw, coming out of a village church the procession of little girls each in white and with coronets of twined flowers, carrying on a white silk cushion an angel figurine, the taller lasses shouldering a shafted platform bearing a large plaster Blessed Virgin, I felt the impact of a rich and comely tradition from which I was forever excluded.
>   And among my most memorable experiences which, for want of a more exact description I must call religious, three are associated with the Catholic Church, though it is significant that none of these occurred in Ireland. The first was when a young man with a fine bushy red beard played the organ and in the absence of a choir sang out the responses like a mellifluous archangel in the Sacre-Coeur; afterwards I buttressed my protestantism by walking round the outside of that mosque-like edifice to glimpse again the statue of the chevalier martyred by the Inquisition, now

practically and symbolically masked by tall thick shrubs. The second was when in San Moise, that delightful example of Venetian Baroque, my first love in that genre, Roberta and I suddenly observed across the dusty, shabby interior, a little brown-skinned, bare-legged boy lean forward on his bench to whisper to his hidden confessor in the tall box draped with grubby red curtains. I shall never forget the rapture of his expression or the innocence of his attitude. The third occasion was in another village church on Whit Monday in the poor country somewhere between Warsaw and Cracow, as the thronged peasant congregation was singing a hymn unknown to me, an old woman with a weathered face under a bright headscarf held the melodic line with a strong, harsh, unwavering voice, the suffering and endurance and triumph, as of life itself, finding utterance, giving the moment a timeless significance. No High Mass with the Patriarch of Venice in St. Mark's in a glory of vestments and a glitter of liturgical vessels, not even the kindly old Pontiff himself at his window blessing the Sunday multitude, approaches any of these in penetrative and expansive effect, the particular becoming the transcendent, the trascendent the absolute.

There's a passionate openness about that and a humorous self-awareness which is endearing. I think Hewitt's attitudes to Catholicism and the way he reflects upon and examines these attitudes have a particular interest and significance for Northern Irish readers. No doubt there are particular lines and phrases likely to offend gentle and kindly Catholics, not to mention the bristling and militant ones, but they should not be given more weight than they actually possess. They should not be allowed to obscure the generosity of spirt and intellectual tenacity which characterises Hewitt's work as a whole, its positive, constructive, affirmative impulses.

The editing of John Hewitt's work—poetry and prose—is unfinished business. So much remains to be done. It seems to me that the typescript which Hewitt left of *A North Light* ought to be published with an appendix incorporating as much of his other autobiographical writings as possible, published and unpublished. It is time also for a full-scale critical study of Hewitt's poetry drawing on the thousands of unpublished poems in the notebooks. It would be interesting to have papers on Hewitt's correspondence, for example, with W.R. Rodgers, Michael J. Murphy and Patrick Maybin, on his writing about art and artists and on Roberta Hewitt's journal which is in the possession of his literary executor, Keith Miller. Most urgently of all, perhaps, it is time someone with five or six years to spare made a start on a biography of the poet. In a radio talk shortly after his 70th birthday, Hewitt notes that the Methodist church he attended as a boy is no longer a church, that the school he attended is closed and that the house where he was born and grew up has been demolished:

> It seems now that I am an elderly man, these changes have conspired to eliminate, to abolish, the emotional landmarks of my early life. I sometimes feel like a non-person, the signs of my passage through the years, through this city, wiped out—like some dissident victim of a Communist state, all record of whom has been expunged from the books. The instances pile up. My late wife and I were married at the Registrar's office in Great Victoria Street. Only the husk of a building remains. For a while we lived in a flat in the large house belonging to my brother-in-law; that whole terrace has gone; the site is a splay of tarmacadam. There is now so little physical evidence for me to point to, indicating the exact places of my childhood and youth, where I could say: 'Here and here I was born, attended church, went to school, was married and lived ...' So I have sadly learned the uses of change and mortality.

A year or so later, Hewitt himself started the process of rebuilding and recovery in *Kites in Spring: A Belfast Boyhood*. It is time now, while contemporaries are still alive, to extend that work in a full biographical account. Only then will we have an adequate, comprehensive perspective on the person described by Louis Gilbert in a letter to the press at the time of Hewitt's death as, not just a good poet, but a "tremendous man".

Notes on Contributors

MICHAEL ALLEN lectures in English at Queen's University, Belfast, and writes on modern Irish and American poetry. His article appears courtesy of *The Southern Review*.

NEAL ASCHERSON is a columnist for the *Independent on Sunday*.

TOM CLYDE is the editor of the *Honest Ulsterman* magazine. He has edited *Ancestral Voices: The Selected Prose of John Hewitt* (1987).

PATRICIA CRAIG is a freelance reviewer and editor. She has edited an anthology of Northern Irish prose, *The Rattle of the North*.

PATRICK CROTTY is senior lecturer in Welsh Studies and English at Trinity College, Carmarthen.

C.L. DALLAT is a musician and writer who works as a computer consultant. A selection of his poetry appeared in *Trio 7* (1992).

RICHARD ENGLISH lectures in the Department of Politics, Queen's University, Belfast. His books include *Radicals and the Republic: Socialist Republicans in the Irish Free State* (1992).

JOHN WILSON FOSTER is professor of English at the University of British Columbia. His publications include *Fictions of the Irish Literary Revival* (1987) and *Colonial Consequences* (1991).

COLIN GRAHAM teaches in the School of English at the University of Huddersfield.

PATRICIA HORTON is a post-graduate student at the Department of English, Queen's University, Belfast.

EAMONN HUGHES lectures in the School of English, Queen's University, Belfast. He is the editor of *Culture and Politics in Northern Ireland 1960-1990* (1991).

ALVIN JACKSON lectures in History at the Queen's University, Belfast. He is the author of *The Ulster Party: Irish Unionists in the House of Commons 1884-1911* (1989) and *Colonel Saunderson: Land and Loyalty in Victorian Ireland* (1995).

JERZY JARNIEWICZ is one of Poland's leading poets and cultural commentators.

FRANK KINAHAN, who died in 1993, lectured in English at the University of Chicago.

KARLIN J. LILLINGTON teaches at Trinity College, Dublin.

EDNA LONGLEY is professor of English at Queen's University, Belfast. Her most recent book is *The Living Stream: Literature and Revisionism in Ireland* (1994).

KATHLEEN McCRACKEN lectures in English at the University of Ulster.

PETER McDONALD is senior lecturer in English at the University of Bristol. He is also a poet and critic. His collections of poetry are *Biting the Wax* (1989) and *Adam's Dream* (1995). He has published *Louis MacNeice: The Poet in his Contexts* (1991), and co-edited MacNeice's *Selected Plays* (1993).

MARTIN McLOONE lectures in Media Studies at the University of Ulster. He has edited *Culture, Identity and Broadcasting* (1991) and is co-editor of *Border Crossing: Film in Ireland, Britain and Europe* (1994).

AODÁN MAC PÓILIN is director of ULTACH Trust, an Irish language funding body. He is the editor of *Styles of Belonging: The Cultural Identities of Ulster* (with Jean Lundy, 1992), *Krino 11* (Irish language edition) and *Ruined Pages: New Selected Poems of Pádraig Fiacc* (with Gerald Dawe, 1994).

GEORGE O'BRIEN is associate professor of English at Georgestown University, Washington D.C. His volumes of autobiography are *Village of Longing* (1993), *Dancehall Days* (1994), and *Out of Our Minds* (1995).

FERGUS O'FERRALL is the author of *Catholic Emancipation: Daniel O'Connell and the Birth of Irish Democracy 1820-30*.

FRANK ORMSBY is a poet and editor. His volumes include *A Store of Candles* (1977) and *A Northern Spring* (1986). He has edited *Poets from the North of Ireland* (1991) and the *Collected Poems of John Hewitt* (1991).

HENRY PATTERSON is a reader in politics at the University of Ulster. His books include *The Politics of Illusion: Socialists and Republicans in Modern Ireland* (1990).

BOB PURDIE is a tutor at Ruskin College, Oxford. He has written *Politics in the Streets: The Origins of the Civil Rights Movement in Northern Ireland* (1990).

MARY THOMPSON is a post-graduate student at St. Patrick's College, Maynooth.

NORMAN VANCE is a reader in English at the University of Sussex. He is the author of *Irish Literature: A Social History* (1990).

JAMES D. YOUNG has was a reader in History at the University of Stirling until his recent retirement. His books include *Socialism and the English Working Class* (1989).

DATE DUE

NOV 2 0 1996	
MAY 2 8 2003	

DEMCO, INC. 38-2971